Whiskey River Ranger

West Texas, Alone by Donald M. Yena. USED BY PERMISSION.

Whiskey River Ranger

The Old West Life of Baz Outlaw

Bob Alexander

Number 16 in the Francis B. Vick Series

UNT Press
University of North Texas Press
Denton, Texas

10 9 8 7 6 5 4 3 2 1

Permissions:
University of North Texas Press
1155 Union Circle #311336
Denton, TX 76203-5017

The paper used in this book meets the minimum requirements of the American National Standard for Permanence of Paper for Printed Library Materials, z39.48.1984. Binding materials have been chosen for durability.

Library of Congress Cataloging-in-Publication Data

Names: Alexander, Bob, 1943– author.
Title: Whiskey River Ranger : the Old West life of Baz Outlaw / Bob Alexander.
Other titles: Frances B. Vick series ; no. 16.
Description: Denton, Texas : University of North Texas Press, [2016] | Series: Number 16 in the Frances B. Vick series
Identifiers: LCCN 2016000552| ISBN 9781574416312 (cloth : alk. paper) | ISBN 9781574416398 (ebook)
Subjects: LCSH: Outlaw, Baz, 1854–1894. | Texas Rangers—Biography. | Peace officers—Texas—Biography. | Law enforcement—Texas—History—19th century. | Frontier and pioneer life—Texas. | Frontier and pioneer life—West (U.S.)
Classification: LCC F391 .A295 2016 | DDC 363.2092--dc23
LC record available at http://lccn.loc.gov/2016000552

Whiskey River Ranger: The Old West Life of Baz Outlaw
is Number 16 in the Frances B. Vick Series

The electronic edition of this book was made possible by the support of the Vick Family Foundation.

Cover painting is *West Texas, Alone* by Donald M. Yena. Used by permission.
Cover and text design by Rose Design

Contents

Preface

RANGER BAZ OUTLAW IS AN ENIGMA. Academicians and aficionados focusing on the merits and/or misdeeds of nineteenth-century Texas Rangers are quite likely familiar with the name and may believe they know the man. And, perhaps, they do. On the other hand, casually dismissing the quick chance to sharpen the lens examining his life's story could well be a wrongheaded methodology within the historical Old West framework. In the context of a broad overview Baz was no Ranger policy maker: He was a problem solver and in not just a few cases *the* problem. During the exhilarating time-period Baz Outlaw lived and worked—carrying a badge for the Lone Star State and/or as a Deputy U.S. Marshal—frontier-era lawmen had dangerous enemies and haranguing detractors. On occasion the chosen career path was littered with dead or dying desperadoes subsequent to dodging bullets. Sometimes the ill-fated lawman came in second during a gunplay—pushing up daisies. At other times it actually seemed as if cigar-smoking penny-pinching politicos walking legislative hallways were more troublesome than any coldhearted terrorists from Bitter Creek. Then as now, fickleness of the general public vis-à-vis its attitude regarding many law enforcing matters is predictably unpredictable. And, yes, on occasion indiscriminate enforcement actions of a commissioned peace officer were anything but professional or peaceful or practical. Baz Outlaw fit the Wild West profile perfectly: He could be a fearless and crackerjack lawman, as well as an unmanageable manic. Proffering that from time to time Baz Outlaw was his own worst enemy will withstand any challenge—from any quarter. Hard truths are unbendable, even if disconcerting. However, living a wholly worthy life is not the sole precursor for leaving behind a worthwhile story.

Oversimplification in writing of the past is common but in most instances proves to be less than a prudent device in the quest for forging historical accuracy. Baz Outlaw's life is paradigm. Asserting that he was judged by the egregious upshot as consequence of several very real gunshots is correct. In fact, it's right on target, dead center. Typically that's the beginning—and that's the end of his story. There were, however, many days creditably spent and many days senselessly wasted between the womb and the tomb. Lawman Baz Outlaw's life was—for lack of better terminology—complicated. There were—now and again—weird spiders in his mind. While he lived, somewhat surprisingly in light of where and why and how he died, Baz had many personal friends and supporters—enough so that Texas Ranger history came ever so close to being rewritten. Scoring Baz Outlaw's tough battles with desperadoes and demons is doable. And, revealing!

The intrinsic value of peeking in on the life and adventures and misadventures of Baz Outlaw is threefold. First and perhaps most importantly that scrutiny—if conducted carefully and impartially—provides insight into the realities and sociological imposition of a criminal justice system always in flux. Watching those transitions is fascinating. Witnessing the so-called frontier era in its naked and rawest and untamed nomenclature gradually—sometimes grudgingly—give way to progressivity, morphing into arenas of civility, enlightenment, and modernization is crucial for incorporating an understanding of societal acceptance or rejection of particular behaviors. Those evolving and ever readjusting ideas of what was tolerable and what was not drums a darn good story within itself. Testing communities' temperature—and it varied from place to place—with regards to just what was prohibited and who was chosen to police those prohibitions is worthy of notice.

Secondly, since the majority of Baz Outlaw's allotted time as an Old West lawman was spent employed with the Texas Rangers, his biography raises the window for an improved knowledge of that outfit, as an institutional arm of the state's law-enforcing mechanisms. If one were to suggest from an ivory tower that at this late date, the twenty-first century, there are already enough books and biographies and autobiographies illuminating the Texas Ranger organization and/or spotlighting specific Rangers and/or dissecting an incident starring Rangers, that the bookshelf is full, the library closed, such an idea is and would be ill conceived. With celebration of a Texas Ranger bicentennial on the horizon it should not come as any great grand revelation that compressing so much legitimate history into one- or two-volume treatments, though they may be unarguably laudable contributions, would be inadequate—almost by definition. There is yet room for exploring new material, watchfully reviewing old and previously published data, and/or offering fresh analytical appraisals. Aside from a generalized worthiness or updating and expanding the biographical look at Baz Outlaw, there are no books about him per se. His actual life's story brings forth its exclusive uniqueness: By any man's measure Baz Outlaw was a puzzle—an asset one day, trouble the next.

The Frontier Battalion's managerial staff assigned to Texas Ranger headquarters at Austin, all the way down the line to company level in-the-field commanders, were responsible for tackling disciplinary difficulties for the outfit's overall good. In the troubled case of Baz Outlaw, sometimes his law-enforcing deportment was simply outstanding. Occasionally he was decidedly irresponsible—sometimes not good and sometimes real bad—but at all times poisonous as a Diamondback. Irrevocable disaster lurks in that tetchy space between itchy trigger-fingers and hot tempers. Observing exactly how Frontier Battalion hierarchy chose to deal with a Ranger commendably virtuous one day and condemnably vicious the next serves as discerning backdrop for the handling of vexing personnel matters within a workforce where everyone—everyone—is carrying one or two six-shooters, a Winchester nearby.

Sensibly probing primary source paperwork pertaining to Baz Outlaw's Texas Ranger tenure is helpful with putting him under the spotlight of fair-mindedness. Too often the offhand mentions of Baz Outlaw have been quick treatments, primarily focused on generalization and sensationalism. Preprogrammed and agenda driven armchair critics of Texas Rangers—and there are not just a few in this modern age of revisionism and inane political correctness—will be able to and have been allowed to cherry-pick parts of Baz Outlaw's tale in their writings, typically ignoring inconvenient truths while trying to bridge readers into dreamscape adaptations where villainy is absolute.

Sadly, others, apparently thinking their trickery is invisible, inappropriately tweak truths until there is rigid conformity to their dogmatic levels of religious sensibilities—plainly a nonfiction no-no. There will be no deceptive effort herein to hoodwink readers. Such transparent missionary work—zealotry—may issue elsewhere in contemporary Ranger biography, but for Baz Outlaw's story that slant will be deemed tasteless, tactless, and censurable.

Likewise, in the same vein, loosely labeling certain frontier period personalities "gunfighters" is not unusual, and seems to suggest such persons were technical masters at handling six-shooters, drawing and shooting with expertise. Hardly ever did they miss hitting the second button on their mean adversary's boiled and starched lily-white shirt. From the practical angle of down-to-earth logic and taking a wide, but realistic overview, such tagging is melodramatically misleading. Sure-shot six-shooter heroes decked out in fastidiously pressed trousers and wearing dazzlingly polished high-top boots while donning pristine white Stetsons, fast-drawing their Colt's .45s with lightning speed is a fanciful make-believe characterization. Even now, the twenty-first century, particular naïve chroniclers of the Old West era are loath to bed down with hardcore truths. Albeit there may be universal acknowledgment that Hoppy and Matt Dillon were fine folks, but fictional nonetheless, such truths seem to escape certain scribes' proclivity to inflict on readers their interpretation as to how the Old West should have been, not how it really was. Drama and mythos is their scandalously cancerous addictive drug of literary choice. Thankfully, most judicious nonfiction writers and historians of the era are not near so gullible. Regrettably, sometimes the genre is forced to now and again acknowledge—not necessarily adopt—the findings of a less than fully credentialed scholar, or a wannabe lawman, or a pseudo intellectual. Truth hurts sometimes.

Raconteurs writing of days past do own assets not readily available to folks living and making decisions in real time. Hindsight is real handy, but its usefulness is an after-the-fact experience. The wicked desperadoes and good citizens and dutiful coworkers Baz Outlaw was interplaying with—and Baz Outlaw—were not advantaged with a crystal ball or a fortuneteller's foresight. How the Texas Ranger management team actually dealt with their sometimes faultless and sometimes debauched but always gutsy gun-carrying subordinate is insightful. The state's law enforcers' hard road to professionalism was swamped with pitfalls and problems: That journey is interesting and informative from a looking-back perspective.

Lastly, promoting the preservation of Baz Outlaw's story is fun. Such simple logic is upfront and straightforward. Recapping escapades of players on the real Wild West stage, apart from offering worthwhile historical value or thoughtful conclusions that may be drawn, has thus far indisputably served as an entertaining platform for furthering both breathtaking fictionalized and tamer nonfiction narratives. Writers and/or researchers and/or scholars advantaging themselves of the popular appeal derived from exploiting—in the best sense of the word—the Old West genre has long been appreciated. Entertainment and education are not necessarily at cross-purposes, not mutually exclusive. Professional educators, grass-roots historians, eager page-turners, mesmerized movie goers, and enthralled television audiences, as well as period-dressed amateur actors, have voted with their work products and pocketbooks. Blood and thunder has not lost its allure.

As the drama surrounding Baz Outlaw unfolds, taking their places on center stage is a near unbelievable cast of cutting-edge characters, many having by now had banked—for the most part posthumously—their very own Old West tales of thrills, tensions, and temptations. Baz Outlaw's true-life story is jam-packed with fellows owning well-known names. Some were fêted Texas Rangers, ex-Rangers, city marshals and/or policemen, popularly elected sheriffs, federal law-enforcing officers and a cadre of admiring townsfolk, while others were steely-eyed mean-spirited miscreants of the deepest dye. A few, depending on space and expediency, wore both hats: dingy gray sometimes, sinisterly black at other times. For now there will be no tease, no hints blueprinted to entice potential readers by reeling off a roster of legendary Wild West personalities—their identities will surface in due time when chronologically fitting.

So, while following Baz Outlaw's trail there are cerebral profits to be had, his biography in every sense of the word is a full-fledged Western. Readers will not be shortchanged. In reliving Baz Outlaw's tale there isn't a deficit of wearisome horseback chases, explosive train robberies, supposed buried treasure, vigilante justice (or injustice), nighttime ambushes and bushwhacking, running-iron brand-blotching artwork, and scary episodes of scorching six-shooter finality. Unfortunately but truthfully Baz's sad tale is one of travel: Paddling hard upstream against the amber current of a raging whiskey river. This then is his story, no apologies for Baz Outlaw, just truth unvarnished.

Acknowledgments

BAZ OUTLAW, HIS MIND SOMETIMES NUMBED by tarantula juice, fought hard to keep from going under—drowning—in that remorseless whiskey river of despair, hopelessness, and craziness. However, not everyone connected with living his story or telling his story sinks. There is a drift allowing for lazily floating downstream with pleasurable thoughts surfacing in the forefront of a nonfiction writer's mind. Respectfully passing along a word or two of thanks, paying homage if you will, to the several considerate folks lending a helping hand with literally making Baz Outlaw's story round is obligatory but no heavy lift: It's an unmitigated delight to honor their hard work and stellar contributions.

First and foremost appreciation must be extended to Donaly E. Brice, Texas State Library & Archives Commission, Austin, TX. As a thoroughly dedicated and affable archivist Donaly has no peer. Thankfully nineteenth-century state bureaucrats, including Texas Ranger officialdom, possessed a mania for record keeping. Voluminous paperwork documenting both the moving and mundane activities of early day Rangers is extant. Reports concerning rations and supplies and manpower and payroll and, yes, imposition of disciplinary penalties, are all there, as well as the detailed accounts of gunplay and the bookkeeping tally of misdemeanor and felony arrests made by Rangers throughout the Lone Star State. Knowing where to find what is the daunting work: Except for the dependably dutiful Donaly E. Brice. His expertise is legendary! That said, his archival proficiency is exceeded by his genuine desire to expand the use of those papers for the enrichment of researchers, writers, and historians of all stripes—professional and neophyte alike. Looking forward to a well deserved retirement, he will, perhaps, have more time for his personal and sundry writing projects. It's a safe bet—a surefire bet—he'll never be too busy to lend a helping hand to those in need of navigating the amass of historic treasures warehoused at the Texas State Library & Archives. A casual tip of the hat is absolutely insufficient reward, but thank you Donaly E. Brice, my friend.

Not unexpectedly and, appreciatively so, a warm vote of thanks must also be extended to Deputy Director Christina Stopka, Head of the Armstrong Ranger Research Center, Texas Ranger Hall of Fame & Museum, Waco, TX. As designated by the state legislature, TRHF&M is the official Repository for the Texas Rangers. And, correspondingly, by formal resolution of the Commission for the Texas Department of Public Safety, the superlative facility at Waco was named the official steward for the upcoming Texas Ranger Bicentennial, a distinction of honor and relevance. Apart from the artifacts and archived documents, TRHF&M is a wellspring for old-time and contemporary photographs detailing Texas Ranger activities, both investigative and ceremonial. Christina and Research Librarian Raymond "Rusty" Bloxom indeed went the extra mile in making Baz Outlaw's story whole, as did the remarkably knowledgeable Shelly Crittendon, Collections Manager, and her genial assistant Kate McCarthy. Thankfully the ever affable and proficient Casey R. Eichhorn, Education Coordinator, supplemented this text through the lens of his photographic talents, a cameraman extraordinaire. The TRHF&M's Marketing, Promotions, and Development Coordinator, Christine W. Rothenbush, as always, provided sidebar data helping make Baz Outlaw's story round. Aside from being first-rate professionals, they, too, are all good friends, as is the institution's erudite Byron Johnson, Executive Director.

Another *bueno amigo* is Robert W. Stephens, formerly of Dallas but now residing at Dunwoody, GA. For near fifty years he has been researching and writing nonfiction books about the Old West, primarily focused on Texas lawmen and their adversaries. The catalogue of his work is splendid. Adding to the treasure of Robert Stephens' published works are the manuscripts and memoirs he storehouses—and considerately shares. Early on, before the old-timer's twilight years faded to eternal darkness, Robert Stephens was astute in comprehending the historic worth of conducting interviews and visiting with their straight-line descendants and surviving spouses. The gems he unearthed are remarkable. Much of the foundation work herein may be laid at the doorstep of Robert Stephens' due diligence and his devotion to preserving Texas history.

Also riding to the rescue with his considerable wealth of knowledge was award-winning author Rick Miller, the preeminent authority on many Old West personalities and happenings, such as outlaws Sam Bass or Rube Burrow or Bloody Bill Longley, bounty hunter Jack Duncan, or the workaholic headman of the Frontier Battalion's early years, Major John B. Jones, not only a warrior but a farseeing administrator transitioning the Texas Rangers from Indian fighters into a meritorious institutional law enforcing outfit. Rick Miller's persistence and patience in writing Major Jones' biography earned warranted accolades, one of which was WWHA's Best Book of the Year, as well as other handoffs of appreciation and, more importantly, was a noteworthy contribution to the writings focused on accurately documenting and preserving the rich—and sometimes controversial—history of the Texas Rangers. Courteously setting aside his own research and writing projects—which are many and meticulous—Rick Miller was never, never, too busy or uninterested to forgo putting his work on hold, graciously sharing his sage comments and advice.

Additionally two more good friends, both published and respected nonfiction Western writers, made significant donations to making *Whiskey River Ranger* round and Baz Outlaw's thrilling narrative whole, Dave Johnson and Doug Dukes. Frequently they were pressed into service and tapped for their expertise not only on matters of storytelling relevance, but technical questions dealing with computers and scanning and pixels and such. Not one time did Doug or Dave sidestep or shy away from the intricacies of problem solving. And, as with pal Rick Miller, these two were fountainheads of wise counsel and thoughtful analysis. Dave, now the consummate authority on nineteenth-century feuds of the American Southwest, is widely revered for his thorough research and skilled breakdowns, separating fact from legend, truth from hokum. Doug's overall knowledge vis-à-vis frontier era outlaws and lawmen is exceptional, however, more specifically he is the go to gentleman regarding questions about development, distribution, and how firearms were put into play by both good guys and bad men—and especially, over the years, how ever evolving technology impacted Rangers and their transitional law enforcing roles. Certainly limiting their acknowledgment to but a few sentences is inadequate, but Dave and Doug know—hopefully—their keenness for preserving the Old West genre and helping a behind-the-times friend is never unappreciated or undervalued.

Assuredly it would be remiss not to mention the sterling contributions of Bill O'Neal, the distinguished Texas State Historian. Bill is favorably known statewide for his near innumerable string of books and articles, and for his valued and highly sought after talent as a public speaker. Whether writing or talking, Bill's enthusiasm for safeguarding and promoting Texas history is noticeable—a tornado of passion and a hurricane of dedication. Thankfully, and somewhat fortuitously for *Whiskey River Ranger*, many years ago Bill was in receipt of correspondence from an Outlaw family member. Not surprisingly, our congenial State Historian shared those letters and readers are now beneficiaries of Bill's unbridled commitment to fulfilling his professional responsibility as a first-rate educator and historian.

From his base at San Antonio, Western artist extraordinaire Donald M. Yena has contributed his matchless expertise to *Whiskey River Ranger*. Although his personal cattle brand may be fastidiously registered at a historic county courthouse and known to but a few local cowmen, his artwork is favorably known and recognized worldwide by spellbound museum patrons and/or avid collectors of Old West excellence. Don's signature style is simple to read—authenticity. The dazzling painting gracing the cover of this volume, *West Texas, Alone*, not only captures the scenic grandeur of the lonesome Big Bend Country where Baz Outlaw roamed, but also epitomizes an underlying theme of the biography in hand: Our protagonist was in many ways a Lone Wolf, a man unto himself in spirit, mind, and reality. An awestruck spectator standing before *West Texas, Alone* is openly drawn into a very real and intriguing quandary. Is that solitary rider—armed with a Colt's six-shooter and Winchester—and leading the pack horse, Texas Ranger Baz Outlaw hunting for an outlaw? Or would it be a West Texas outlaw in quest of an enemy, a Ranger named Outlaw? Could it be Baz Outlaw in the Far Wild Country searching for truths about rumors and gossip of buried treasure taken during a train robbery? ¿Quién *sabe?* Such guesswork or speculation aside, there is a bona fide hard and fast bottom line: Donald M. Yena's canvas masterpieces are legit—in every sense of the word.

Other folks have made their mark and they, too, are worthy of mention: John Anderson, Texas State Library and Archives, Austin, TX; James Baird, San Francisco, CA; Melletta R. Bell, Archives of the Big Bend, Sul Ross University, Alpine, TX; Elizabeth Blodgett, The Early West, College Station, TX; Jim Bradshaw, Ret., Nita Stewart Haley Memorial Library and J. Evetts Haley History Center (HML&HC), Midland, TX; the late Jeffrey Burton of England, a beloved friend and dearly missed colleague; Clifford R. Caldwell, Kerrville, TX; Derek Carlon, Merced, CA; Christa Clavria, San Antonio Public Library, San Antonio, TX; Bob Cox, Flint, TX; Jackie Culpepper, Allen Statenville Library, Statenville, GA; Ronald G. DeLord, Georgetown, TX; Jan Devereaux, Maypearl, TX; Zachery Distel, The Frazier History Museum, Louisville, KY; Candice DuCoin, Round Rock, TX; Jim Earle, College Station, TX; Robert Ernst, Perkins, OK; Jerri Garza, Archives of the Big Bend, Sul Ross University, Alpine, TX; Suzanne Giffin-Garcia, Alameda, CA; Lt. West Gilbreath, UNT Police Department, Denton, TX; Roberta Durbin Gutierrez, San Jose, CA; Charles H. Harris III, Las Cruces, NM; Kurt House, San Antonio, TX; Ron Hyatt, Tombstone, AZ; Frank Jardim, Vintage Ordnance Company LLC, Elizabethtown, KY; Kathy Johnson, Fergus Falls, MN; Harold E. Jobes, Cedar Park, TX; Josh Lehew, Waxahachie, TX; Robert W. Lull, Waco, TX; Frank

Malinak, Asst. Chief, Texas Rangers, Austin, TX; Patty Martin, Valdosta/Lowndes County Chamber of Commerce, Valdosta, GA; Joe and Patsy Mathews, Dilley, TX; LeRoy Merz, Merz Antique Firearms, Fergus Falls, MN; Deana Mills, Director, Rector Library, Rector, AR; Lupe Nielsen, Nielsen Magic, Las Vegas, NV; Ted and Ruth J. Outlaw, Moore, TX; Jeri and Gary Radder, Alamo, CA; Shirley Aten Roberts, Amarillo, TX; Chris Robinson, Corpus Christi, TX; Louis R. Sadler, Las Cruces, NM; Cathy Smith, HML&HC, Midland, TX; an especially dear personal friend, the late John D. Tanner, Fallbrook, CA; Michael L. Toon, Associate Professor and Librarian, Ret., The Texas Collection, Baylor University, Waco, TX; John R. Troubaugh, Thurmont, MD; Joseph H. Troubaugh II, Carlisle, PA; David S. Turk, Historian, U.S. Marshals Service, Washington, DC: Deen Underwood, El Paso, TX; Bobbie Walker, Shallowater, TX; Larry J. Walker, La Pine, OR; the late Sally Walker, Cal Aten's granddaughter, Hereford, TX; Harold J. Weiss, Jr., Leander, TX; Jim Willett, Director, Texas Prison Museum, Huntsville, TX; Charles L. Wright, U.S. Customs and Border Enforcement, Las Cruces, NM; James Wright, Whitney, TX; and Louise Yena, San Antonio, TX.

Again, accolades are in order for the University of North Texas Press at Denton. Were a casual reader picking up *Whiskey River Ranger*, thumbing pages and perusing photographs, he/she might not give much thought to just who published the book. On the other hand, those people seemingly obsessed or unexplainably compelled to read and broaden their understanding of the Wild West era definitely know about UNT Press, today's preeminent publisher for the genre. Long has the outfit's headman, Director Ron Chrisman, recognized the worth of delving into rich tales of the Old West as paradigm for expanding an appreciation of sociological and criminal justice issues. Texas history cannot be examined adequately unless at times played out against the backdrop of her troubled and violent past. Solidly grounded grassroots historians and gifted scholars alike have contributions to make, a fact well established at UNT Press. History doesn't have to be boring to be good history. Assistant Director/Managing Editor Karen J. DeVinney adds her masterful touch at insuring the transition from manuscript to book does not lose the author's voice, nor distract from its overall readability. Persnickety she is not—but as a conscientious editor—near perfect she is. Crates of books stacked in warehouses are valueless. Overseeing that UNT Press creations are effectively and ultimately placed in readers' hands falls under purview of the capable and energetic Bonnie Stufflebeam, Marketing Manager, a most talented distribution and public relations tactician. *Whiskey River Ranger* also owes much to an interminably cordial whirlwind of productivity, Amy Pierce, Administrative Assistant.

CHAPTER 1

A Magnetic Lone Star

LEE COUNTY, DUE NORTH OF ALBANY, GEORGIA, was pleasantly sited in the southeastern section of what in due time would be nicknamed the Peach State. It was a part of the Old Plantation South. There the Alabama-born Meshack Napoleon Bonaparte Outlaw, subsequent to his 1847 graduation from the Medical College of New York City, upheld his medical practice as a country physician.[1] And although now it might seem insignificant in the overall story, such will not prove to be true: Meshack's older brother by four years, Young Pinckney "Y.P." Outlaw, a veteran of the Florida Indian Wars and former Dooly County deputy sheriff, chose to forego his position as an industrious and heavy-hitter Georgia cotton broker in Bibb County, near Macon. The ever adventurous Y.P. had opted to try his hand at something new. Migrating to the Lone Star State, settling at pretty Seguin, Guadalupe County, just a touch northeast of the Alamo City, Y.P. Outlaw took up the cattleman's life, becoming a "stock raiser."[2]

Meanwhile, in Lee County, by his wife Mourning Temperance "Mona" (Smith) Outlaw, the twenty-eight-year old physician had fathered his first child, Young M. Outlaw, named after his uncle now with a Texas address. Doctor Outlaw was then, and could now be, journalistically characterized as a member of that stereotypical social and economic cultural class, an aristocrat.[3] Quite naturally that portrayal, assuredly historically accurate, would also suggest at least a reasonable degree of economic affluence, an assertion somewhat borne out by the fact that the good Dr. M.N.B. Outlaw was a slave owner and at the bare minimum, a gentleman farmer.[4]

Whether Dr. Outlaw personally handled a hands-on delivery is not now known and really is somewhat irrelevant; perhaps practiced midwives welcomed the new baby into the world that late summer or early fall of 1854. At any rate it may be spoken with reasonably accurate clarity, Bazzell Lamar Outlaw was born.[5]

Though it's historically somewhat foggy, the best guess is that while Young M. Outlaw was yet a toddler in diapers and infant Baz was whining for breast milk, their loving mother Mona passed to the other side, dying on the twenty-second day of October 1854, probably due to natural causes—an undisclosed or unidentified malady. There certainly—as of now—is no sound reason for any idle speculation regarding a suicide, homicide, buggy wreck, or divorce, or whether she died as a result of the childbirth.[6] What may be spoken with confidence is that Dr. M.N.B. Outlaw remarried, this time taking a teenaged wife eighteen years his junior, Mary Ann Elizabeth (Smith) Outlaw. The new blushing bride was Mona's niece, the daughter of her brother Britton Gainer Smith and his wife Sarah (Livingston) Smith. Not surprisingly Doctor Outlaw's young second wife would love her two stepsons as her own, and they due to tender ages when Mona had passed, would only know one mother, Mary Ann.[7]

Of course, as an infant, little could he have had knowledge of 1854's agenda of current events, but tough happenings and harbingers for forthcoming episodes of Texas history would in due course significantly impact Baz's life and place in the wild and woolly Old West. Settlers and speculators hunting prosperity both before and during the Republic of Texas era had long contended with raiding Indians. One such industrious foray during 1840 had been a humdinger. Comanche traveling from the Texas interior, raiding and killing and plundering near the village of Victoria, had moved twenty-odd miles south to the Gulf Coast. There a few frightened folks had speedily hopped into rowboats, seeking safety in the over-your-head waters of Lavaca Bay.[8] Even subsequent to Texas statehood, during the year of Baz Outlaw's birth, Texans, Rangers, the U.S. Army, and Indians were yet vigorously and violently making war.

On the ninth day of May in what is now southern Jim Wells County, but then Nueces County almost due west of Corpus Christi by thirty miles, Lieutenant George B. Cosby and eleven troopers of Companies F and I, U.S. Mounted Rifles, and a band of forty Lipan Apaches tried their darnedest to kill one another. Although designated as Mounted Rifles, for as yet an elusive explanation, the tall-in-the-saddle soldiers were armed only with handguns. The Lipan Apaches were plentifully supplied with arrows, and exceptionally skilled at unleashing them with near unerring accuracy. Lieutenant Cosby caught one arrow to the chest, a second to the arm. Sergeant John Byrne's head was creased by an arrow, his horse a runaway straight into the lair of Indians. He was killed outright. Two other troopers became separated from their comrades and paid the ultimate sacrifice for service on the terrible Texas frontier. Maybe Lieutenant Cosby, who survived, was close in tallying the Lipan Apaches' loss at three dead, two wounded—or perhaps not.[9]

Shortly, west of the above-mentioned battleground, Captain Michael E. Van Buren with a sixteen-man detail from Companies A and H, U.S. Mounted Rifles, fought a hard engagement with Comanche Indians wherein the warriors suffered the heaviest loss, five killed, but the troopers' commander was a mortal casualty.[10] Sixty days after Captain Van Buren's succumbing to a Comanche's handiwork, Captain John G. Walker sallied forth from Fort Inge in surveyed but yet to be organized Uvalde County, territory Baz Outlaw would come to know quite well. Guided by a whiz at following marauding Indians' trails, Policarpo "Polly" Rodriguez, Captain Walker and his combined forty-man detachment from Companies D and K, Mounted Rifles, were intent on overhauling a band of Lipan Apaches and recovering their purloined livestock, as well as issuing punishment for such audacity as crossing the Rio Grande and raiding into the Lone Star State. On Texas soil not too terribly far removed north from the Mexican village of Piedras Negras the soldiers found their quarry, but earned more than they bargained for: 300 Indians. Nevertheless Captain Walker ordered the bugler to sound the "Charge" and the fight commenced in earnest. Seven Lipan Apaches died. Several federal troopers were wounded, including Polly Rodriguez and Lieutenant Eugene A. Carr, but none were killed. Wisely Captain Walker called time-out, opting to retire from the battlefield and transport his injured men back to Fort Inge where medical attention was available.[11]

Seemingly there was no letup. Near what would become Batesville, Texas, in Zavala County, Captain Benjamin H. Arthur commanded a small squadron that killed two Lipan Apaches. And before the year 1854 was extinguished, way out in West Texas, near Fort Davis, Lieutenant Theodore Fink at the front of Company G, 8th Infantry, fought Mescalero Apaches, who after killing three enlisted men vanished.[12] Texas was a bleeding mess. Texans, especially those staking their financial futures on the frontier, were more-or-less fed up with the U.S. Army's supposed impotency.

Although trying to particularize the reasons Doctor Outlaw moved about in Georgia would be tricky, nevertheless such would be the case. By the time Baz Outlaw was six years old the family was living near what would become Valdosta, Lowndes County. What Baz and his older brother by four years, Young M. Outlaw, thought about relocating goes unrecorded. Their baby sister Mary Elizabeth—four years old at the time—and Morgan, measuring his earthly existence at but three years when the family moved, would have had no option or opinion, nor could have had the baby, Emma, not yet twenty-four months. At age twenty-one, the seemingly ever expecting and fertile Mary Ann had been a regular—figurative—baby-factory.[13] Clearly, the M.N.B. Outlaw family may not have been wealthy but they were, for the time and place, pretty well fixed. Doctor Meshack Outlaw's personal property appraised at $25,820 and his real estate holding added another $4,900.[14]

About the time Baz and his family moved to Lowndes County, ironically, was the same timeframe that folks at the county seat, Troupville, learned that a new railway line was proposed by the Gulf & Atlantic Railroad's powerbrokers. The new steel ribbon of tracks would connect Savannah, Georgia, to Mobile, Alabama. As townsmen soon discovered, the railroad right-of-way missed Troupville by a paltry four miles to the southeast. Unsuccessful with efforts to change railroad executives' minds or effect new surveys readjusting the route, Troupville's movers and shakers opted to pick up and relocate the town. Troupville died. Valdosta was born, formally incorporated on December 7, 1860.[15]

With no shortage of bountiful black dirt in places and near virgin sandy loam soils in others, fertile Lowndes County was a fine growing country for cotton—Sea Island Cotton—pecans, peanuts, and tobacco as would be the towering timber industry in later years when pine and oak forests were commercially harvested. Life for near anyone in pre-Civil War Lowndes County, after a few fits and starts, was on the upswing. During the tragically futile war, however, growth and greatness sidestepped Valdosta. Harrowing bloody engagements would not be elements of Valdosta's rich history, but refugees fast flocking to southern Georgia, Lowndes County included, would make their marks of squalor, overpopulation, and a wretched depletion of commodities sometimes taken for granted.

The same could not be said regarding Y.P. Outlaw—that part about the war passing him by. When the Guadalupe Rangers Cavalry Company, CSA, was being recruited by Captain John P. White at Seguin, Y.P. put his name on the dotted line, with the guarantee that he and his fellow enlistees would serve "wherever needed in the State."[16] Leading a rugged life on the bloody Texas Frontier had toughened the transplanted Georgian. For his second go-round Y.P. signed on as a farrier in the Texas Mounted Rifles, Company D, then captained by William L. Foster, under the overall command of Colonel P. C. Wood. For this tour of duty Y.P. had committed for a period of "three years" or duration of the war.[17]

While kinfolks at Valdosta would not see blood and guts and savor the metallic taste of fear on the battlefronts, Y.P. would: Particularly during the battle at Blair's Landing, the engagement wherein in General Tom Green was killed. In fact, Y.P. Outlaw was so close to the general when grapeshot tore off the top of his head—"exposing the brain, but without breaking the membrane that inclosed [*sic*] it"—he too was splattered with Tom Green's blood. Though they dutifully tried under the rain of an intense bombardment to remove the general's body from the crimson-stained battleground, Y.P. was forced to jump up behind Nathan Busby, who had caught Tom Green's horse, and ride hell-for-leather for shelter and cover in "the brush and cane further back." Y.P. Outlaw was wounded twice—not severely—and two bullets tore through his campaign hat before that day ended. With a macabre twist of honoring the slain general, Y.P. refused to wash Tom Green's blood from his clothing, just allowing for time and weather to accomplish that end. Y.P. saw other harrowing frontline service during the battles of Yellow Bayou and Marksville, but kept his body parts intact enough to honorably take leave of the war, returning to Seguin where he would ultimately take a wife.[18]

A promising future was to be had, especially at Valdosta. Well, most people there had a reasonably expectant bright future. One, John Henry "Doc" Holliday, who had been born at Griffin, Georgia, between Atlanta and Macon three years ahead of Baz's birthday, seemed intently bent on self-destruction, whatever the underlying psychological reasons.[19]

Though armed clashes between Union and Confederate forces in and around Lowndes County were noticeably absent, resentment through the prickly era of Reconstruction was omnipresent at Valdosta.[20] With freedmen holding public office and city streets patrolled by black policemen, bitterness ran high. The lid would soon blow off, literally. Richard Force, ex-Confederate and wounded veteran of Gettysburg, was alleged to have assaulted a black man. Nineteen-year-old Force was arrested and detained for awhile—a little while. Richard's escape from incarceration had been perfectly executed—walking out the lockup's backdoor. Escapee Force was, of course, a fugitive from occupying military forces, but had the undying support of most Valdosta townsmen—especially the younger crowd, of which fourteen-year-old Baz Outlaw was one. Elated that their likeminded confederate had daringly gained his freedom—though lying low—a celebratory party was kicked off at Richard Force's home. Frustrated Union soldiers getting wind of the possibility of Richard Force in attendance, advanced with sharpened bayonets and plenty of bullets. During a heated dustup Richard Force was shot—critically wounded—and in time would forever succumb to the injury. Lady Luck had overseen Richard Force's nondescript survival at Gettysburg, but had only saved him for martyrdom at Valdosta: Richard Force's death was *cause célèbre*. The Old South was yet alive! Those disgraceful Yankees, well, they could just go straight to Hell.

Subsequent to an intransigence regarding change on the part of dyed-in-the-wool Southerners, Radical Republicans now the powerbrokers, initiated Phase II of Reconstruction. The U.S. Army had taken control of the South, now divided on paper and in fact into military districts. General John Pope assumed command of the Third Military District, to later be replaced by General George F. Meade. Heated political machinations and shenanigans were at a fever pitch; white Georgians tried mightily to "keep the state from falling into the hands of carpetbaggers, scalawags, and blacks." Dr. Outlaw was on call as a state guardsman.[21]

On the fourth day of April 1868 a Republican candidate for the U.S. Congress, J.W. Clift, made his campaigning appearance at Valdosta. Forgoing strictures that he must first attain a permit for any rallies, Clift forged ahead with his politicking, championing an assembly set to take place during late afternoon or early evening on the courthouse lawn. Though some of Valdosta's prominent local politicos were there, as well as other curious whites, the predominant crowd were freedmen. Candidate Clift harangued from front courthouse steps, while a fast burning fuse was shortening behind the building. The thunderous ovation from Clift's supporters was near deafening, but not near as loud as the explosion.[22]

Thankfully the keg of powder—loosely packed—and the apparent absence of metal shrapnel caused more scare than injury to spectators or significant destruction to Lowndes County's gemstone courthouse. Pride was the victim. The terroristic act was condemned. Local lawmen made arrests and local lawbreakers made bond. A forgiving newspaper correspondent writing for the *South Georgia Times* extolled: "It is idle to suppose there was any intention on the part of the boys, if they did it, to blow up their friends and relatives."[23]

Federal authorities were not inclined to such benevolence. Soldiers rearrested A.H. Darnell, Ben Smith, John Rambo, John Calhoun, and Iverson Griffin. Needless to say their quite prominent fathers were not happy. Their displeasure was ratcheted up a notch after learning that their "prank" playing sons had been hustled off to Savannah in chains.[24] Somewhat later others were implicated, several being quite young. By most accounts, during the latter roundup, the then teenage John Henry Holliday—along with others unidentified—were criminally charged.[25] Certainly any assertion that Baz Outlaw, at age fourteen, was in some way involved would measure as but wild guesswork, on the other hand it is fascinating conjecture—and possible, taking into account his family's presence at or near Valdosta and Baz's appetite for aggression. Nonetheless, elders at Valdosta thought the participating boys were heroes. In the end, no penalties were forthcoming in state or federal courts or by any military commissions, criminal charges having fallen into the abyss of indifference.[26]

Detailing the day by day childhood activities for the subjects of most biographical profiles is normally weighted with an abundance of speculation, a shortage of sustainable hardcore facts. The early life of Baz Outlaw does not qualify as an exception. There are, though, reasoned inferences that may be fairly drawn. That he was literate is true—and from examples of his penmanship and literary construction—quite articulate, too. Whether formally schooled or simply homeschooled—at this point in time—is immaterial, though later there is confirmation of classroom attendance. In the traditional sense of Old South hospitality and congeniality young

Baz Outlaw was cultured and courteous, almost to a fault.[27] He was conversant and a good dancer, self-assured and accomplished at mingling within the upper-echelon social and economic strata. He was by birthright imbued with another doctrine of Old South legacy—the Code of the Duello. The debts of certain wrongs or perceived wrongs could be settled in but one way—with blood. Sometimes it was the "only recourse left" to diehard Southern gentlemen.[28] Stepping on Baz's sense of honor—purposefully or inadvertently—was risky.

There were, well, just certain things a boy of the Old South was forced to endure while shedding his adolescence: Experiences such as fighting, wagering on horse races, playing cards for money, smoking hand-tailored cigarettes, cursing blue-streaks, consuming copious quantities of hard liquor and suffering through but surviving inevitable hangovers with blistering headaches and cramping bellies and, of course, profitably dallying with the ladies—or wenches—were all behaviors winked at and slyly expected.[29] Proselytizing preachers had their rightful place—the pulpit. But they were selling salvation, an ideology young folks—hot blooded and hormonally charged males—didn't usually buy into, not devotedly if it meant forgoing fun. Eternal forgiveness—if it was real—could come later.

Somewhere along the road moving Baz Outlaw from boyish mischief to manful maturity he acquired the knack for handling firearms. For a boy of the Old South it was, among other things, a plainly understood rite of passage. Little girls had tea parties, cuddled doll babies and over time were schooled in politeness and proper manners. Little boys fished, ran trotlines and pulled catfish from the abundant rivers and deep running creeks. At first they hunted rabbits and squirrels then graduated to the fine art attendant to bagging turkey and deer and feral hogs—or even an occasional bear roaming the thickets. Breathlessly chasing after baying hounds in the middle of the night, at least for the first few times, was exciting, but there was little sport in knocking raccoons out of forked tree limbs—once the new wore off. As they grew older most adolescents were lovingly acquainted with single-shot target pistols paired in polished wooden or elaborate leather-bound cases—and for Baz's youthful place in time, ultimately introduced to big revolvers and little derringers, too. Fitting history will rightfully record, Baz Outlaw, in due time, would be particularly adept with employing Colt's six-shooters. Secondary characterizations that Baz Outlaw "could pull his Colt like a flash of lightning and his aim was deadly," or that he owned "an uncanny proficiency with his Colt .45" no doubt at least in part will ring true—even after allowing for the journalistic hoopla.[30]

Pinpointing when the upright Dr. Outlaw chose to relocate to Statenville, Echols County, Georgia, is up for grabs. The township was located just across the Lowndes County line southeast of Valdosta by about twenty miles. Further east, another fifty miles or so, was what would in later years bear an official designation, the Okefenokee Swamp. At the time the Outlaw family relocated to the Statenville township, Baz Outlaw could—and maybe did—boast that he was a four-year senior to Echols County's creation, which was officially given birth by the Georgia Legislature on December 13, 1858, and named in honor of Colonel Robert M. Echols, a veteran commander of the Georgia Regiment during the 1840s war with Mexico.[31]

The Outlaw family, as previously noted, was not a hardscrabble lot wondering where their next meal would come from or how to put shoes on the children—and that brood kept growing. Though the oldest of Doctor Outlaw's girls had passed away due to an unknown cause, the Outlaw clan at Statenville had multiplied. In addition to the aforementioned kiddos, there were now, 1870, a few more: eight-year-old Edwin B., Perlisane about six, Sallie, age four, and a toddling two-year old, Ella. Still yet a baby in arms was Tallula, nicknamed "Little Tussie."[32] Doctor Outlaw was invested in land, owning a good number of "improved acres" and had under cultivation 160 acres of corn. During a roundup he could tally for the tax man approximately 175 head of free-ranging cattle, at least according to one interpretation of the county's agricultural census.[33] Unquestionably as but speculation at this point in his upbringing, the fact Baz's family was associated with the livestock business would permeate its tradecraft tentacles into his future plans and psyche.

For the meantime, at age sixteen (1870) Baz was attending school at Statenville, that was the good news. There was, however, bad news. Baz Outlaw's beloved younger sister Emma, barely a teenager, passed away on October 31, 1872, and precious "Little Tussie" died the following year "while in her 2nd year." Both little girls were lovingly and peacefully laid to rest on the eastern banks of the Alapaha River in Statenville's city cemetery.[34]

At this juncture determining the emotional devastation resulting from burying his innocent daughters would be but tentative, as would be whether or not Dr. Outlaw temporarily gave up his medical practice or simply supplemented his income as a mercantile owner. At any rate, by 1873, both nineteen-year-old Baz and his older brother Young M. had jobs at their daddy's dry goods store at Statenville. Young M. managed the enterprise whereas Baz clerked and tended to menial chores.[35] Storekeeping was monotonous.

Meanwhile, and it's more than relevant—extraordinarily relevant—for Baz Outlaw's bio: Post-Civil War Texas was anything but dull. Mentally picturing the historical and cultural stage Baz Outlaw would soon walk onto is crucial for incorporating his life's story into the unfolding Wild West drama at hand. Industrious hostile Indians were continually raiding, taking hostages and killing unlucky settlers caught unawares on their warpath of devastation, destruction—and death. The same year of his sister Emma's premature passing, very real newsmakers shocked even frontier hardened Texans.

During April of 1872 Kiowa and a few Comanche warriors led by Big Bow and White Horse rode as headmen for raiders numbering near 100. Deep in Texas, near the Rio Grande, they killed hapless Texans and Mexicans without discrimination, stealing horses.[36] Moving back north, on the twentieth day of April they attacked a wagon-train captained by Anastacio Gonzales bound from the Devils River country to Pecos County and the U.S. Army's Fort Stockton and the liked-named civilian settlement. At isolated Howard's Well, some twenty-odd miles southwest of Fort Lancaster in what is now Crockett County (Ozona), the Kiowa and Comanche assaulted Anastacio's ten-wagon train. Aside from what goods were hauled in the lumbering wagons, the caravan was an inviting target for another reason: First-rate mules harnessed for each wagon's team numbered ten. White Horse and Big Bow couldn't resist converting ownership of material goods and valued livestock. Murdering and mutilating amidst the madness and chaos, well, that was okay too—a fringe benefit. Killing most of the teamsters, emboldened Indians then lashed the male survivors to wagon wheels, callously doused them with kerosene and set them ablaze. Their bloodlust yet sated, Indians killed tearful Marcela Sera's one-year-old baby "by dashing its head against a wagon wheel."[37] Not unexpectedly they then made prisoners of Marcela—and her mother—also traveling with the doomed caravan.[38]

Later, much to Marcela's relief, the Indians were overhauled by Buffalo Soldiers of Colonel Wesley Merritt's 9th U.S. Cavalry. Much to Marcela's disbelief and disgust, however, the warriors before taking flight cold-bloodedly executed her mother, lancing and scalping her.[39] Then the broncos—Indians off the Reservation—"dumped" the pitiably grieving and terrified Marcela Sera in a thicket, where good fortune finally prevailed: Buffalo Soldiers rescued her. The horror story was far from over, though.

During the foregoing clash with cavalrymen, White Horse and Tau-ankia, the son of Lone Wolf, had been wounded. Working their way north toward Fort Sill, White Horse opted for more action. Near Fort Belknap on the Brazos River he left behind a younger brother, Kom-pai-te, and other young and less than fully matured warriors, apprentices tasked not with fighting but guarding horses and mules. Impatience won out over White Horse's orders. The boys, eyeing opportunity, attacked L.H. Luckett's surveying party east of Round Timber, near present-day Megargel in the southwestern corner of then surveyed but yet to be organized Archer County. Although the young aspiring scalp hunters were successful in killing a surveyor, the rod and chain boys' unerring aim unhorsed three circling Indians. Kom-pai-te and another Kiowa were killed, and Pohocsucut, the natural brother of Tabananica, a Comanche chieftain, was wounded. Upon returning to the supposedly secreted stolen herd and learning that his brother Kom-pai-te had been killed, White Horse angrily and vociferously vowed vengeance. He would not leave the Lone Star State and return to the Fort Sill Reservation and Indian Territory lest he extract blood. A white man must die.[40]

During June 1872, White Horse, with five warriors and a woman, hunted for a helpless victim. Near the Clear Fork of the Brazos and its confluence with Kings Creek in what is now northern Stephens County the raiders closed in on the isolated homestead of Able Lee, nicknamed the "Professor" due to his Sunday School singing and sermonizing. A Kiowa bullet emptied the Professor's front porch rocking chair, dethroning Able into lifelessness atop pooling blood, his. Hearing the sound of gunfire and registering the immediacy of saving themselves, Lee's family raced through the cabin's backdoor seeking safety and salvation. Their desperate prayers, if they were praying as they ran for dear life, went unanswered. Fate ruled the day, not Jesus and mercy. Mrs. Lee was downed with an arrow in her back, then savagely mutilated as one Indian scalped her and cut off her ears, another chopping off both of her arms. Frances, age fourteen, fell mortally wounded from the arrow plowing into her back. Nine-year-old Mille and her brother John, six, were forthrightly taken prisoners, as was the oldest of the Lee children, seventeen-year-old Susanna. Subsequent to pillaging the house, filling a milk cow full of arrows and slaying the family's pet dog, the marauders raced for sanctuary at their Rainy Mountain camp in Indian Territory. There, after receiving a hero's welcome, the captured children were "parceled out to tribe members as slaves."[41]

On the fifteenth day of June 1872, but six days after the killing at Lee's place near the Clear Fork, other Indians attacked a small detachment of soldiers at Johnston's Station, some twenty-odd miles west of historic Fort Concho near what is now Mertzon (Irion County). Corporal Hickey, Company H, 11th Infantry commanded the small detail of soldiers responsible for guarding the mail station. During the hostile engagement he apparently remained self-assured and creditably directed his men's field-of-fire, killing two Indians.[42] The very alive warriors, perhaps a few nursing bullet wounds, successfully orchestrated disengagement and sought to fight another day. Texans, again, were openly and irritably questioning why the U.S. Military couldn't or wouldn't control Indians. "Truly, as, Texans charged, Fort Sill became a city of refuge, where warriors received government supplies and protection while resting between raids."[43]

Texans, during this same timeframe, in general, were miffed regarding another matter of martial mismanagement: The Texas State Police. Due to post-Civil War lawlessness, which was not necessarily exaggerated, Republican Governor Edmund J. Davis, directing Reconstruction policy, had conceived and acted as midwife for birth of the Texas State Police—surely a bastard child in the minds of most Texans.

Beyond doubt the governor's state-paid policemen did some fine work; they, too, were plagued by problems, perceptual and bona fide. The practice of filling rank and file positions with freedmen—although forward thinking—was ahead of the times for most Lone Star State folks. The very thought of former slaves being given big Colt's six-shooters and badges coupled with the legal authority to actually make arrests and search their homes and barns and corrals was not popular outside a shrinking circle of statehouse Republicans—Radical Republicans. Defensibly there were good men on the outfit's roster—black and white—but there, too, was a downside of weight. With the good came the bad and some members of the divisive Texas State Police were bad, real bad. A few were stone-cold killers, executing prisoners under the guise of "escaping" before they were delivered to county jails to await their day in court. For citizens of several counties—justly or not—Martial Law was declared, impositions that did not bode well for the Texas State Police's long-term viability.[44] Adding to the curdling menu of complaints was the unscheduled and untimely hiatus of Adjutant General James Davidson, Chief of the Texas State Police and $37,434.67 of state funds. Metaphorically speaking the dough had soured, the bread had burned.[45]

By and large policing is reflective of society's wants. Texans didn't want the State Police. There was a changing of the guard inside the state capitol and those newly elected lawmakers had change on their agenda. The trouble-plagued and incessantly controversial Texas State Police would be no more:

> The people of Texas are today delivered from an infernal engine of oppression as ever crushed any people beneath the heel of God's sunlight. The damnable police bill is ground beneath the heel of an indignant legislature.[46]

From political perspectives the much maligned and damned State Police would be but a memory. Common sense dealt its reality. Though the discordant institution had been politically destroyed, the overriding reason for its existence had not dehydrated: Texas was saturated with lawlessness. Aftermath of the Civil War in Texas was decidedly more violent than elsewhere, and certainly in southern Georgia where Baz Outlaw was clerking behind the counter, chained to a humdrum job. Although predicated with a "perhaps" it was about this timeframe that the young man's ears perked at the mention of Texas—and its gripping lure.

The newly inaugurated governor of Texas was Richard Coke, a Democrat. A veteran of the Civil War and a lawyer by education and profession, Governor Coke was passionate with efforts calculated to bring a semblance of law and order to Texas, and extinguishing hard-hitting Indians' mania for raiding and robbing therein. Ruthless bandits based inside Mexico but crossing the Rio Grande for piracy were also worrisome for the governor. Thankfully for Texans, now, Richard Coke would be backed at the statehouse by a Democrat-controlled legislature. There were big doings astir on Congress Avenue.

For forwarding Baz Outlaw's story it is not necessary to highlight with specificity details creating various militia units blueprinted to be called upon for emergencies, an extreme emergency—a Texas State Guard of sorts. There was another plan in the works.

For forcefully dealing with desperadoes and warriors and banditos, Governor Coke had a proposal:

> An Act to provide for the protection of the Frontier of the State of Texas against the invasion of hostile Indians, Mexicans, or other marauding or thieving parties.[47]

The Fourteenth Legislative Session for the State of Texas put into play what Coke had touted. On paper and in fact the Frontier Battalion had been birthed. History and the world and Texans would proudly know men and some beardless boys of the Frontier Battalion as Texas Rangers. To suggest there had not been Rangers before—in Texas—would be ludicrous, not funny, but preposterous in the eyes, hearts, and minds of most Lone Star folks. In the main, previously volunteering Texans answering demands of immediacy—even though colloquially called Texas Rangers—were put into the field provisionally. Find and fight the enemy. Once pressing needs had been disposed of, officers, as well as the rank and file, returned to plowing or chasing wild cattle or picking up paychecks wherever. Founding of the Frontier Battalion ushered a new era, the Texas Rangers had been institutionalized. It was now a job.

The organizational structure—on paper—was that of six, seventy-five-man companies, designated A through F, each commanded by a captain answering to the Frontier Battalion's major, who in turn reported to the adjutant general. Deployed along a north/south line on the Texas frontier, built on a military model, the men were to act as highly mobile and hard-charging cavalry troops.

The term of enlistment was for four years in the enabling legislation but administratively cut to one year due to budgetary constraints. For trading their time to the State of Texas recruits were to be remunerated at the rate of $40 per month, paid quarterly. Enlistees were to supply their own horse, while the state would furnish arms under a strictly adhered to payroll deduction plan. The state would stand for the cost of bullets, beans, bacon, and other commissary needs as well as house the men in tents—when and where available. Otherwise the nighttime canopy overhead was one of moon and stars—or dangerously illuminating thunderstorms. Whiners need not apply.

It was outside work—twenty-four and seven.

Recruiting standards were loose. There were, however, three big disqualifiers for applicants. Fellows atop horses that wouldn't pass muster had no place as Rangers and would be rejected. Too, "Persons under indictment or of Known bad character or habitual drunkards," would not be allowed a spot on the Ranger roster. And, lastly, since the work would be arduous and dangerous, coupled with the fact that the force was to be "Kept actively employed," which translated to mean they would be near constantly in the saddle, married men need not apply. Paleface warriors were to be thoroughly committed to chasing, catching, and crushing the enemy. Rangers with a wife and kids—quite naturally—would want a furlough from time to time. From management's perspective family life would create a nightmare of administrative headaches and lessen unit cohesion and effectiveness. Predictably though, such a prohibitive stricture was only applicable to privates and noncommissioned officers. Lieutenants, captains, and the major could be married. Such policy, while seeming sensible on paper, was inherently flawed and propagated unintended consequences. For several years into the future the Frontier Battalion's turnover rate was atrocious, a fact that will in due time play into Baz Outlaw's colorful Wild West story.

At the Frontier Battalion's inception the job description for Rangers was straightforward. They were to hunt for and kill Indians raiding the settlements. At this juncture there was no need to debate policy decisions in the field. Politicians and the statehouse crowd could argue about how best to handle that untidiness. At this point in time Texas Rangers were quasi soldiers, and soldiers took orders.

Though but conjecture, at Statenville a daydreaming Baz Outlaw, head down, nose to the grindstone, was taking orders too: the doctor's orders. There's room for but little doubt that Baz envisioned more for his future than growing into a gray-headed old man, tottering around selling persnickety ladies high-buttoned shoes and canned goods and calico, all the while making sure sneaky kids' sticky fingers didn't pilfer too many peppermint and licorice sticks. Whether he pictured himself a Wild West lawman, at this time, is fuzzy. More likely—and it's somewhat documentable—he visualized himself a drover herding Longhorns from somewhere in Texas to the raucous and lively end-of-the-trial cattle towns of Kansas, like Abilene or Dodge City, or maybe Ogallala, Nebraska, and, from there, maybe to the snow-capped Rocky Mountain Country. On the other hand, it would seem Young M. Outlaw was more entrepreneurial and more solidly grounded, wanting to engage in some type of commercial enterprise. Lazy he was not. Though somewhat short on specifics it may be reported that Young M. Outlaw—probably while managing the store—had also contracted with the U.S. Post Office to handle mail. Whether he did or did not cut Baz in on the annual $150 draw from the federal government he was pocketing goes unrecorded.[48]

At some point, about this timeframe and exactness is more than elusive, Baz Outlaw's musings and/or fantasies about tasting the sinful and exciting flavors of a life in the wild and woolly west—like Texas—came to fruition. By 1876 Baz's brother Young M. Outlaw had opted for the other direction, back east, obtaining an advanced education in New York at the Eastman National Business College and was so conclusively enumerated in the Directory of Eastman College Graduates: "Outlaw, Y.M., Statenville, GA. At College. Student."[49]

What isn't conjecture is that Doctor Outlaw, now sixty, again was itching to relocate—the wanderlust overpowering. This time the family moved west, settling at Mifflin, Henderson County, Tennessee, just southeast of Jackson. Making the migration into Tennessee during 1877 it seems the whole clan followed daddy Outlaw's lead, even the youngest child as of that time, Robert L, age nine. The last of M.N.B. and Mary Ann Outlaw's children would not be a Georgian by birth. James C. would be a Tennessean. Understandably now, as young men neither Young M. or Baz Outlaw would be a part of the patriarch's jam-packed and bushy household.

And though it uncomfortably cultivates a chronological/genealogical jump, now seems an appropriate time for weaving into Baz's story another item or two of pedigree. Standing alone, the facts speak well of Dr. M.N.B and Mary Outlaw's offspring, but also is illustrative of the economic and social strata swirling about Baz's upbringing and his ripening into adulthood. Later, 1894, the family would again relocate, this time across the Mississippi River into Arkansas, settling at Rector, Clay County. There, the elder Dr. Outlaw would practice medicine, as would two of Baz's younger brothers: Morgan having earned his physician's credentials from the Barnes Medical College at St. Louis and Edwin B. from the Memphis Hospital Medical College. At Rector the Outlaw clan was highly regarded and, in fact, Morgan Outlaw served two laudatory terms as the city's mayor and E.B. Outlaw was considerately commissioned a captain in the Arkansas State National Guard. The Outlaw family tree could rightly claim hardwood. Bazzell Lamar Outlaw's roots ran rich and deep.[50]

Baz—regardless the dearth of early life's facts—would not and never submitted to boredom. And therein is the underpinning for a genuine thriller, a mystery—one as yet to be satisfactorily explored—much less solved. By more than one account—allegedly drawn from Baz Outlaw's very own words—during some type of terrible dustup or accident or self-defense at or near Statenville or in an Old South locality, he killed someone—supposedly a relative.[51] ¿Quién *sabe?* Rather than face the legal music—*if* being played—Baz Outlaw danced out of Georgia.

Subsequent to marauding and murdering and taking captives near Victoria and then Linnville on Texas' Gulf Coast, the Comanches suffered a stinging defeat at Plum Creek in Caldwell County, near present-day Lockhart. Although the 1840 episode took place prior to Baz Outlaw's birth, and was a backbreaker for Indians' further *en masse* raids into the Lone Star State's interior, the aftermath and repercussions would obliquely affect his life story. *From, Indian Depredations in Texas by J.W. Wilbarger.*

Strategically reduced to conducting raids in smaller war-parties than those of earlier days, unsmiling Indian warriors were yet issuing heartache and headstones in the frontier Texas era, the timeframe while Baz Outlaw was but a youngster in southern Georgia. *Courtesy Tobin and Anne Armstrong Ranger Research Center, Texas Ranger Hall of Fame & Museum.*

Of Baz Outlaw's several residences in Georgia, Statenville, Echols County, was the last. Pictured herein is the county courthouse. *Courtesy Allen Statenville Public Library.*

Even in the southeastern United States, the place of Baz Outlaw's origin, these Echols County, Georgia, lawmen demonstrate law enforcement work was yet horseback work. *Photographic contribution of Stephen B. Thompson, courtesy the Allen Statenville Public Library.*

Sadly, two of Baz Outlaw's little sisters, Emma and Tussie, passed to the other side while at Statenville. Pictured here is their shared headstone at the local cemetery. The poetic inscription reads: "So fades the lovely Blooming Flower—Frail Smiling Solace of an hour—So soon our transient comforts fly—And pleasure only blooms to die." *COURTESY JACKIE AND WAYNE CULPEPPER, STATENVILLE, GEORGIA.*

Prior to Texas Rangers becoming institutionalized as a permanent outfit, many Texans served in provisional companies, i.e., the Frontier Force, actively pursuing raiding Indians as the occasion arose. Here is a delightful period photograph of three such Medina County Rangers: Standing, Joseph Beck; Seated from L to R, Jacob Haby and Joseph Burrell. *COURTESY DONALD M. AND LOUISE YENA COLLECTION.*

Baz's uncle, Young Pinckney "Y.P." Outlaw had migrated from Georgia, settling near Seguin, Guadalupe County, Texas. A Civil War veteran, Y.P. was alongside Tom Green when the celebrated colonel was killed during the Civil War at Blair's Landing. Collectively the surviving members of Green's Brigade and the United Daughters of the Confederacy erected this monument in the Oakwood Cemetery at Austin, memorializing Green's service to Texas. Baz, too, would take up residence at Seguin, conceivably with or in near proximity to his resilient fighting and farming uncle Y.P. Outlaw. *COURTESY DOUG DUKES.*

Lonesome travelers and undermanned caravans were—for a time period in Texas—subject to relentless warfare and an absence of mercy. *FROM WILBARGER, INDIAN DEPREDATIONS IN TEXAS.*

Not wholly satisfied with the federal government's Indian-fighting U.S. Army, the political powerbrokers of Texas opted to breathe breaths of permanency to the Texas Rangers, institutionalizing the fabled Frontier Battalion during May 1874, legislation that would amend Baz Outlaw's life forevermore. *Courtesy Nita Stewart Haley Memorial Library and J. Evetts Haley History Center.*

Heading up the Frontier Battalion was Major John B. Jones. *Courtesy Tobin and Anne Armstrong Ranger Research Center, Texas Ranger Hall of Fame & Museum.*

Although Baz would never reside there, the Outlaw family home at Rector, Arkansas, quite literally suggests the prominence and affluence of his kith and kin. Two of Baz's brothers and his father were practicing physicians. *Courtesy Rector Public Library.*

CHAPTER 2

Great Prudence and Good Judgment

CANDIDLY THE PHRASE "GONE TO TEXAS" was applicable to an earlier time, but Baz Outlaw went: Straight to Guadalupe County.[1] Honestly it may be reported there is—as of yet—no particular document placing Baz as a temporary resident in or near his uncle Y.P. Outlaw's home, but the supposition is buttressed by a primary source. Baz Outlaw would a short time later declare that he hailed from Seguin, the county seat of Guadalupe County.[2] Whether Baz was running from the law or simply relocated in order to scratch that burning itch for adventure will likely never be authenticated. Supposing that Dr. Meshack Outlaw instructed Baz to make contact with his older brother in the Lone Star State is not hollow foolishness—not after factoring in common sense and logic.

There are not any grounds to suspect that Y.P. Outlaw would, whatever the reason, turn his back and a blind eye on his Georgia-born nephew—even though they may have never even met until Baz made his show in Texas. At any rate, Y.P. Outlaw was a standup guy, hard-working and loyal to family and friends. He, too, was a warrior when need be and as previously mentioned a veteran of the Seminole Indian campaign in Florida as well as the Civil War, and that's discounting that timeframe he served as a local deputy sheriff in Georgia's Dooly County. Yes, Y.P. Outlaw was a fighting man. When the tough nut cracked open, he could eat the meat. For a youthful dreamer like Baz Outlaw, one breaking the shackles of tedium and prospects of a life-long lackluster future, having a mentoring man to look up to like uncle Y.P. was good—and as would be probable, somewhat fulfilling for a young man on the make.

Mindreading is not within the realm of nonfiction storytelling. However, it's not unreasonable to suggest that during the late 1870s Baz Outlaw found Guadalupe County, with her rich history and mesmerizing vistas overlooking the Guadalupe River, appealing: Even for a guy with girls, guns, and good times at the forefront of his cerebral workouts. The county, only two years old when Y.P. had settled there during 1848, could historically trace human footprints backwards in time to when Alonso De León traipsed through the countryside in 1689.[3] Purportedly, and of even more interest for Baz in light of his forthcoming career, were the methods and manners of dealing with miscreants at or passing through Guadalupe County. By the time Baz had arrived on the scene the public "whipping post" was a thing of the past. County prisoners were confined in the jail, a wooden two-story edifice built of live oak blocks during 1854, the year of his birth. Enlightened penal reforms were decades into the future. In the interim between barbarism and progressiveness a rather ingenious method of transporting prisoners from Seguin to Gonzales on the east or San Antonio to the west was staked into place, quite literally. Driven deep into the roadways connecting the three cities were a series of "iron holding posts" where prisoners marching afoot could be chained for rest periods or overnight stops, while fatigued deputies caught an afternoon nap or forty winks beneath moonlit skies. "Families who lived along the way were also known to provide food and security for the weary lawmen."[4] At this point, picking up with precision just what and just how much Baz Outlaw was learning about convicts or cows is indefinite. There was, though, something real and reportable.

Besides his agricultural interest, Mr. Young Pinckney Outlaw also had a wife, Celestina E. (Little) Outlaw, a native Texan twenty years his junior. In addition to giving her heart to her husband, she had also given Y.P. not just a few kiddos, one of the boys named Meshack in honor of her physician brother-in-law.[5] Predictably, as Y.P.'s family and fatherly responsibilities increased, the time he spent chasing and corralling wild cattle as a "stock raiser" lessened and keeping closer to the homeplace he "successfully farmed and raised fruit. . . ."[6] Selling canned peaches at his father's Statenville dry goods store or picking peaches from Y.P.'s orchard was not Baz Outlaw's cup of tea—well, cup of nectar. He'd already dabbled with the catch-rope and screwed down tight in the saddle as his fresh horse crow-hopped working out the morning kinks. Cowboy life was exhilarating. Plodding behind stinky mules' behinds and/or gathering bushel baskets of ripe produce was not fun, but tiresome, tedious, and less than stimulating. Wannabe fulltime cowboy Baz Outlaw stepped into the stirrup, bid his uncle and Guadalupe County adieu, heading west, Junction City on the horizon and in his plans.

Situated west of Austin, past Fredericksburg, Kimble County had been carved from Gillespie County when Baz Outlaw was but a live-wire four-year-old, 1858. Prettily sited with striking uplifts some folks call mountains and a fair share of more-or-less gently rolling plains with creeks and tributaries draining to clear and sparkling waters of the Llano River's forks, Kimble County was then and is now an inviting piece of Texas real-estate.[7] Problematically, then, Kimble County too had been inviting ground for a near unbelievable and dodgy conglomeration of miscreants, misfits, and murderers—many one jump ahead of the law. But a few years prior to Baz Outlaw's arriving in outlaw country, an undercover Texas Ranger had classed Kimble County as "a thiafs stronghold, the two Llanos and all tributaries are lined with them. . . ." and the lawbreakers were of such ferocious disposition that they would most likely "kill every stranger that comes into the neighborhood fearing that he is a detective."[8]

By that time, 1877, after a rather poor showing during the Mason County "Hoo Doo" War, Texas Rangers under the Frontier Battalion's Major John B. Jones were transitioning from Indian fighters—when they could catch them—into crime fighters.[9] Many, perhaps most, of the fellows enlisting in the Frontier Battalion didn't know or had paid but scant attention to wording of the facilitating legislation, which said, in part:

> Each officer of the battalion and of the companies herein provided for shall have all the powers of a peace officer. . . ."[10]

Legalese, at Frontier Battalion headquarters and by field commanders was interpreted—literally. Texas Rangers could make arrests and apprehend fugitives without regard to that exasperating hindrance for the sheriffs and their deputies—the county line. Rangers could go anywhere within the state. Even though a number of "Buckskin officials" had been operating in "full blast" and with impunity in Kimble County, their days of outlawry and corruption were now numbered.[11] The ensuing roundup—raid—under the strategic management of Major John B. Jones would be, truly, a watershed moment in action and time for the Texas Rangers.

Secretly moving into Kimble County under the screening cover of darkness, Ranger tactics were based on surprise and superiority and six-shooter supremacy. There would be no worthless palavering, no excuses. Those with outstanding warrants were to be arrested. Those that should have had outstanding warrants were to be arrested. And, furthermore, those without a damn good reason for being in Kimble County were to be arrested. Bothersome impediments to the Texas Ranger roundup such as that guarantee promised by the U.S. Constitution's contract regarding Probable Cause, well, that little niggling inconvenience could be suspended—temporarily.[12] Kimble County was literally overrun with lawless *mal hombres* and the courts could deal with legalities—or the lack thereof—later.[13]

All told, according to Major Jones' official report to headquarters, he and his Rangers had arrested forty-one fellows, thirty-seven in Kimble County.[14] And it was here and during this enforcement action, that Texas Rangers, for the most part, begin seeing themselves as civilian peace officers rather than soldiers. Particularly Major Jones commended his Rangers on their newfound criminal work: "Each man seems to take a personal interest and pride in catching every one he is ordered to arrest."[15] Texans were now taking notice of Rangers acting as lawmen. And in truth, that favorable and deserved publicity had spread well past those borderline rivers, the Red and Sabine, into the Congressional hearing room of the Committee on Military Affairs at Washington, D.C. During their rather wide-ranging investigation of "Texas Border Troubles" an excerpt from the *San Antonio Express* praising the Rangers was entered into evidence.[16]

> If there is any one thing more than another the people of western Texas have to congratulate themselves upon in connection with the progress of the year 1877, it is the breaking up and almost entire eradication of the bands of cut-throat desperadoes that infested our section a year ago. Strong in numbers and the self-interest that banded them together, they had defied the officers of the law, and laughed at the idea of arrest and punishment for the serious crimes almost daily committed. But the rangers entered in among them, and their presence gave encouragement to the officers of the law and now the penitentiary and jails are almost crowded with the scoundrels; most of the ringleaders have been arrested, and the others have become demoralized; they are being hunted down and driven from the country. . . .[17]

In a nutshell, the workload of Texas Rangers had undergone a dramatic shift. No longer was their primary focus on hounding after marauding Comanche or Kiowa or Apache and killing them. The transition into a statewide civilian policing agency had not taken place overnight but, relatively speaking, in the larger scheme of time, the changeover to peace keepers and crime busters and fugitive hunters had come rather quickly. As an outfit within the broader system of criminal justice, the Frontier Battalion—the Texas Rangers—would sink or swim dependent on adaptability; that was the institutional challenge.

Exactly following Baz Outlaw's every footprint or horseshoe tracks from a distance of time so far removed is, for the most part, guesswork. Clearly he was in Kimble County by the summer of

1880.[18] And just as clearly, so it seems, any assertions that he had killed his older brother—as sometimes is written—is somewhat belied by the fact that Young M. Outlaw was enumerated in that same 1880 federal census at Dyer County, Tennessee, northwest of his physician father's household at Mifflin, Henderson County.[19] Was it wholly impossible for Baz Outlaw to have returned—at some time and at some place killed a relative? No. Was that unlikely? Yes.[20] Snapping the hammer on chambers stuffed with speculation strikes wide of the mark. Pulling the trigger on truth is what keeps Baz Outlaw's story on target.

Later, when asked what he did for a living, with a fulsome voice and probably pride Baz declared that he was a "Cow Boy."[21] Were Baz actually dodging the law—which yet lacks substantiation—the comings and goings and no-questions-asked environment of the cowboy life was ideal. In the cow camps and around the corrals and brush catch-pens personal matters were just that—personal. A man's past was his business. What mattered was adherence to cow camp etiquette, stuff not taught in a classroom, but nonetheless critical. Inattention to the accepted conventions could prove disastrous—deadly.

Though somewhat overblown—and certainly overly romanticized by clueless and naïve writers—there was, and to some extent still is, an unwritten rulebook of what's okay and what's not with regards to men and boys playing together in the cowboy game. "Had God wanted men to fight like cats and dogs, He'd givin' 'em claws and paws," was an overworked adage in the Texas frontier cow camps, but a saw not necessarily outdated in Baz Outlaw's day. Translation was plain. Pulling a trigger was a much easier and preferred course when settling disputes than any bare-knuckle pounding of an enemy's skull. Knots on one's forehead and black eyes weren't worn with pride. Six-shooter settlements were sanctioned. Everybody carried a gun—or two. Many still do. Vocally tagging some guy a son-of-a-bitch was best said with an unconditionally sociable and full-size smile: Otherwise there might be hell to pay. Differentiating between slurred and drunken utterances spoken in jest—harmless fun—and words spit with sinister barbs was not taught in the stuffy classroom, but in the school of hard-knocks and no nonsense. Sanctimonious preachers protectively ensconced in pulpits churning out fanciful biblical notions were in short supply around cow country campfires. That congregation, so to speak, was made up of gristly men and plucky boys with the bark still on—real dangerous creatures when riled. Baz Outlaw was keeping hard company.

By temperament and the harshness of Mother Nature, cowmen and cowboys are a tough lot. Blizzards, blisters, and bulls that would hook you—or Old Dan—were, well, just part of the fun. There was/is no room for crybabies. No, not in a world of green-broke horses, mad mama cows, and catch-ropes that can saw off a finger or thumb during that split-second of carelessness. Playing in the game of roping, tripping, branding, and doctoring wild cattle or topping off cold-backed horses when a morning sun starts begrudgingly squinting her first sliver of light is taxing. Baz Outlaw, like all legit cowboys, whetted his cow savvy on the grindstone of hazard and work. Pitching loops and dragging bawling calves toward the white-hot embers and red-hot irons is a sweaty and strenuous job. It's even harder afoot, manhandling, legging those snotty and slobbery calves to the ground. Ear-notching and castrating and branding amid the stench of scorched hair, burnt hide, and cow shit is tiresome and dirty duty just to make a day's pay—a dollar. It wasn't an overnight process to be sure, but there's not any substantive doubt that Baz Outlaw grew fairly tired of the cowboy life, wearisomely working from can to can't—that is from the time you *can* see first light until darkness finally overhauls another day and you *can't* see nothing. Though no doubt said in jest, when one cowboy questioned a friend about what he thought about working on a new ranch for a new boss, the reply was short and snappy—and pointed: "Pretty damn good place. The biscuit roller feeds twice a day—and it's dark both times!" Night was short, real short. Did Rangers have it better?

The whys and wherefores of the relocation are missing, but Baz Outlaw by late summer of 1885 was in the Pecos River Country at

Toyah, the oldest townsite in Reeves County.[22] The county was but two years old by survey and, when Baz Outlaw can be provably placed there, had officially organized only the year before with Pecos City as county seat. Like Valdosta back in Baz's home state, and as with so many towns in far West Texas, Reeves County could concede her creation to the coming of a railroad, the Texas & Pacific, industriously inching its way across the vast Lone Star State. Baz Outlaw, for whatever reason, was such an early arrival he found that the first Reeves County sheriff didn't yet have a jailhouse.[23] Toyah, some twenty-odd miles southwest of Pecos City, was small but bustling. There were railroad shops and roundhouses, a hotel, and at least one café as well as a drinking emporium—or two, or seven.[24]

Toyah's six-shooter history, even prior to birthing of Reeves County, was rich—with blood. During July 1883 eight wild-eyed ring-tailed tootin' cowboys rode into Toyah intent on "treeing" the town. Discharging their Colt's revolvers and Winchesters the yahoos frightened the wits out of honest and hardworking folks scampering for cover. Toyah's population was small but scared. Texas Rangers from Company A—then commanded by George Wythe Baylor—strongly urged the cowboys to cease and desist, an order flatly and loudly refused. Rather than surrendering weapons or submitting to arrests, the revelers took refuge in a nearby caboose and commenced making war. The battle waxed hot. Shortly thereafter, Captain Baylor who was not actually on the scene, by telegram updated the adjutant general—posting the score:

> Cow boys tried to take town at Toyah one killed three wounded & five prisoners none of rangers hurt am on my way down[25]

The Rangers had been thoroughly unimpressed with the cowboys' supposed badness. The dead man, a harebrained loser named Kelly, "had threatened to clean up the town several times and wanted to 'Kill three or four Ss of b___ there.' He had on his last trip there Shot through a caboose & came near Killing a man Sleeping in there." Two Ranger bullets through Kelly's midsection put him to bed—eternally. Three of his cohorts had been wounded, two seriously, and one superficially before Toyah's mothers began singing lullabies that evening.[26]

Several months later, before she became Reeves County's shiretown, it turned "Western" at Pecos City. Once more idiotic cowboys were the culprits. While a Texas & Pacific locomotive was taking on water, they tanked up on fiery fluids. A detachment of Company A Rangers riding under the leadership of a genuinely salty noncom, Sergeant Lycurgus S. "Kirk" Turnbo, dampened down waddies' keenness for shooting into boxcars and popping caps at telegraph-line insulators and shattering windowpanes. In all of West Texas, according to Captain George W. Baylor's judgment, Pecos City and its scattered area railroad town neighbors up and down the line were one of the "worst populations" anywhere in that far-flung part of the Lone Star State.[27] Toyah was tough ground to cover.

On the eleventh day of August 1885 the lean and mean five-foot ten-inch Baz Outlaw, falsely asserting he was only twenty-six, but truthfully declaring he was a cowboy, enlisted in Captain James T. Gillespie's Company E, Frontier Battalion.[28] Company A—on paper—temporarily disbanded earlier that year. Payroll records would not indicate the greenhorn lawman would have his pay docked for the issue of a Colt's .45 six-shooter, pistol-belt and holster, or an 1873 Winchester .44-40 repeater and saddle scabbard—Bazzell Lamar Outlaw was already "fixed." The boy from Lee County Georgia by way of Guadalupe and Kimble Counties was now a man, a Texas Ranger.

As would be expected there was a learning curve, so in the initial stage of his apprenticeship as a lawman he no doubt was paired with other Rangers for this or that assignment and most likely—as a rookie—tasked with performing some of the routine and less than glamorous chores: policing the camp, peeling potatoes, scrubbing pots and pans, and tending to Company E's seven pack mules, etc. Maybe, for that end-of-the-month report, the Monthly Return, Baz had been charged with sitting down and tallying the number of cartridges on hand: 2,068 for the revolvers, and 2,411 for the carbines. Luckily, if it rained—which wasn't too likely—the Rangers at the Company E camp could stay somewhat dry playing cards and shooting-the-bull inside one of the seven wall tents. Baz Outlaw's life had changed forevermore.[29]

Three of his fellow Rangers returned from a scout some eighteen miles south of Toyah in the ranch country west of Saragosa, Reeves County. They had in tow three downtrodden prisoners, fellows to be formally charged the next day with cutting the fence of cattleman Clayton Cooksey, though the detainees were "citizens of good standing" and were vigorously professing their innocence.[30] A fellow not in good standing with many Reeves County folks was their sheriff, J.T. Morris. Sheriff Morris, a New Yorker by birth, had migrated to Texas, eventually pinning on a deputy sheriff's tin-star in Erath County (Stephenville) during 1880 where he "established a reputation by killing two men," prior to his moving farther west.[31] Sheriff J.T. Morris was wrapped tight. Were Baz Outlaw not to have known the hardness and hazards of what would be expected of him as a greenhorn Texas Ranger, within a week an eye-opener happened at Toyah. And it would be something to write home about.

Sheriff Morris was on a tear, drunk, mad, and mean. On the evening of August 18, 1885, after stepping off the 6:40 westbound train coming in from Pecos City, Sheriff Morris, according to Captain Gillespie, insolently demanded the Rangers furnish him a pair of mules and a buggy. Reluctantly, Captain Gillespie demurred, readily noting that the sheriff was in his cups, telling Morris that it was "out of my power" to equip him with state-owned property. Morris ratcheted up his ranting, making very insulting and abusive remarks about Captain Gillespie in particular, and the Rangers of Company E in general. Rather than add fuel to the fire, Captain Gillespie brushed aside the scorching tirade, returning to the Rangers' tent-camp on the outskirts of Toyah. Perhaps Sheriff Morris misinterpreted Gillespie's good sense, thinking he had the Rangers and their captain cowed.

Most folks believed—and there may be some truth in it—that Sheriff Morris had come to Toyah to kill Jep Clayton and because the local Texas Rangers were now keeping a close eye on him his anger spiraled. According to an official bureaucratic report the sour-mouthed sheriff was vociferously declaring that "I Run Pecos and d—d if I don't run Toyah." Stupidly, the smashed sheriff continued the hot rhetoric and escalated his unbridled foolishness by irresponsibly whipping out his six-gun and "carried it in his hand and insulting any one That chanced to meet him."[32] On more than one occasion Sheriff Morris "did cock his pistol [and] throw down on people. . . . calling them ugly names without any provocation."[33] Six-shooters and sour mash are a volatile mix. Several citizens, scared to death, rushed to the Company E Ranger camp, advising Captain Gillespie the fuse was burning and the looming explosion would not be a pretty sight.[34] Company Commander Gillespie saw the light:

> At this point it seemed that things had gone as far as possible and I saw it was necessary to arrest Morris or he would either be Killed or Kill some body. At this I give Sergt. Cartwright instructions to arrest and disarm Morris and do so without hurting him if possible.[35]

Under orders from Captain Gillespie, Sergeant L.F. Cartwright, in the company of Rangers William S. Hughes, Frank W. DeJarnette, and Thomas P. Nigh, moseyed into Toyah for the purpose of putting the quietus on Sheriff Morris' belligerence. The Texas Rangers found the sheriff just outside Sam Lane's saloon, the Favorite. Sergeant Cartwright forthrightly told the thoroughly drunken sheriff "to surrender & give up his pistol." Yet with his six-shooter in hand, never having replaced it once removed from its scabbard earlier in the evening, Morris balked, pointed the six-shooter and touched the trigger. The Colt's hammer fell, as did Ranger Nigh, the sheriff's bullet zipping into his chest and gushing his blood while dispensing an instant death. Then, as would certainly be anticipated, "the firing became general among the Rangers until Morris fell," five bullets plowed into the sheriff's upper torso.[36] Which Ranger's bullet—or Rangers' bullets—did the trick absent any ballistic technology and expert testimony is indefinite. The wording of Captain James T. Gillespie's telegram to Adjutant

General Wilburn Hill King at Ranger headquarters in Austin is definite though, repeated herein unedited:

> Morris, sheriff of Reeves Co. Came here drunk abusing rangers Sargent Cartwright with three men went to arrest him a fight ensued private Nigh and Sheriff Killed full particulars by mail[37]

Part of those "particulars" then not spoken was that immediately after the shooting Sheriff Morris was taken to Toyah's Field Hotel, operated by Charles M. Fields, where he lasted but five minutes before passing to the other side. Purportedly Ranger Tom Nigh had a wife and two young children—the stricture about married men being sometimes winked at—and was buried in the local city cemetery at Toyah, the State of Texas picking up the tab. Concerned citizens passed the hat, collecting money for the fatherless kids' and widow's well-being. Also unsaid, perhaps purposefully in official reports, is that someone—an innocent bystander—suffered a bullet wound to both legs during the blistering exchange of gunfire.[38]

Though generally downplayed, by this time the Texas Rangers were actually doing their damndest to maintain forward momentum regarding professionalizing their ranks, a reality underscored with AG King's remarks to Captain Gillespie regarding the shooting of a bellicose and bullying sheriff: "desire that you get the written statements of reliable eyewitnesses of the actual occurrences at the fight and statements to Morris' previous conduct. These occurrences always create more or less prejudice against the ranger service, and I wish to have the rangers side well fortified by proof showing that the provocation was such that the Killing of Morris could not well be avoided."[39]

Another matter required immediate attention. There was not now a sheriff, the deceased Morris serving but seven months before stupidity had overhauled good sense. Reeves County Commissioners were quick to act. On the twentieth day of August 1885, just two days after the shooting, they appointed former Texas Ranger Kirk Turnbo to hold down the job until the next regularly scheduled election or as Captain Gillespie advised his Austin-based headquarters: "Turnbo was appointed before the office hardly got cold."[40]

Clearly public sentiment was in support of the Texas Rangers. Captain Gillespie plainly valued that, making sure headquarters did too: "every one says Rangers did only their Duty & a benefit to the county in ridding it of a man whom they were the most of them afraid of as he was both dangerous & quarrelsome when Drinking."[41] Saloon owner Sam Lane, speaking on behalf of the community, backed the Rangers in a letter to the adjutant general: "we certify that the Killing of Morris was unavoidable under these circumstances."[42] The Reeves County Grand Jury after reviewing testimony concurred, no-billing the Rangers involved in killing the sheriff who'd slipped the track and run amok.[43]

What Baz Outlaw had to say about a fellow Ranger—a friend of but a few days—being killed is not a matter of record. Did Baz Outlaw know that another Company E Ranger, Benjamin Goodin "Ben" Warren had been fatally bushwhacked at Sweetwater in Nolan County by a trio of alleged fence cutters earlier in the year? And, did he realize that in the Texas/Mexico borderlands only a few months later—prior to his enlistment—Ranger Private Frank Sieker, Company D, had been mortally gunned down during a stop-and-identify enforcement action gone terribly awry?[44] If Private Baz Outlaw had forsaken long days spent in the saddle hunting and herding wild cattle with high-hopes of an adrenalin intoxicating thrill, becoming a Ranger had been a smart move. The wait, relatively speaking, would be short.

During the interim Captain Gillespie was in a quandary. The Company E lieutenant, thirty-year-old James Martin "Jim" Sedberry, had assuredly stepped out of character and bizarrely misbehaved. On the night of September 25, 1885, he "met several old friends and indulged a little too freely in drink and it being an uncommon thing for him to drink. When he did become intoxicated He was reckless and discharged His pistol." Captain Gillespie being nearby rushed to investigate, disarmed his normally well behaved lieutenant without incident, and "put him to bed" to sober up, rather than shoot up the town. With a well-known order that Rangers forego carrying firearms while visiting saloons and when using intoxicants the Company

E captain had—through no fault of his own—been backed into an uncomfortable supervisory corner. Lieutenant Sedberry—discarding this anomaly—had a splendid record as a first-rate Ranger and according to the captain had "a Brilliant record for sobriety (seldom ever drinking at all) and as to His record for work & courage, I don't think any will surpass Him."[45] Jim Sedberry, if the situation turned Western, could be and had proved to be "a regular bear in a fight."[46] Four years earlier, at Colorado City in Mitchell County, Rangers Jim Sedberry, Jeff Davis Milton, and new-hire Private L.B. Wells, were compelled into resorting to deadly force during a gunplay with W.P. Patterson, a pretty decent fellow but regrettably the notable cowman "got drunk often and stayed drunk long."[47] Outside Colorado City's creatively named Nip and Tuck Saloon, Patterson jumped tacky pulling his revolver and at but spitting distance unleashed a hot round at Sedberry. Certainly the idiocy may not have been intended to be "suicide by cop" but it was, as the Texas Ranger trio turned loose their barking six-shooters on Patterson. He died whimpering in the dusty street, whiskey and blood leaking into the dirt. Though the Rangers would have to clear prosecutorial hurdles regarding the killing near the Nip and Tuck, in the end they came free of suffering legal penalties.

What was not free, however, was a *carte blanche* license for Frontier Battalion peace officers to act on the street without regard to what the front office at Austin had to contend with regarding their men's exposure to legal jeopardy—or any accumulation of negative publicity for perceived overreaction or supposed indifference. The killing of Patterson at Colorado City had sparked an in-house review into whether or not these three Texas Rangers' solution had been reasonable—a "good" shooting. Admittedly in its infancy, this examination by a somewhat disinterested and neutral commissioned officer, an Internal Affairs investigation, demonstrated the practicality of taking the road leading toward professionalism—notwithstanding potholes and pitfalls and politics. Too, and it must not go unnoticed, the rank and file were standing together—showing solidarity—clearly exhibiting *esprit de corps* by collecting funds battalion-wide dedicated to paying defense lawyers' legal fees—which could prove steep for folks drawing but $30 per month, their salaries having been pared down from $40 a month paid earlier Rangers of the Frontier Battalion.[48]

Unmistakably such complexities would in due course play into Baz Outlaw's narrative, but in the near term Captain Gillespie's conundrum was real: How much weight to grant an act of bad behavior on the scales of otherwise good—sometimes even great—behavior. Was there leeway? For supervisors, finding an apt balance is never easy—nor was it then.[49]

Lieutenant Sedberry tendered his resignation to take effect on October 5, 1885, ten days after his foolhardy wild night of sour mash and six-shooter merriment, misbehavior, and morning-after misery.[50] Lieutenant Sedberry had opportunely—sheer luck—advantaged himself of an administrative escape valve. During its annual readjustments and realignment of personnel, trying to intertwine battalion staffing levels with appropriated fiscal resources, the Texas Ranger front office issued General Order No. 27. Pursuant to a cost-cutting move the commissioned officer's rank of lieutenant was chopped—eliminated. There wasn't any namby-pamby mush-mouthing, no evading reality: "Lieutenants of Cos B, C, D, & E are requested to resign to take effect from same date [October 5, 1885]."[51] About prospects of any punitive action for Sedberry, AG King notified Captain Gillespie that the General Oder "precludes any further action in this matter."[52] For the short-go, Company E's Captain Gillespie had providentially dodged the bullet of having to delicately weigh discipline against dedication, punishment against past performance.

Short too would be Baz L. Outlaw's first-round tenure as a Texas Ranger. Due to those parsimonious politicos at the statehouse, funding for the Frontier Battalion—as noted—was in a perennial state of flux. Administratively complying with those impositions and the continual manpower and staffing reorganizations and budgetary shortfalls were nightmarish troubles for in-the-field Ranger commanders. Misinterpretation and innocent confusion was commonplace. For Lieutenant Sedberry the repositioning and tinkering with staffing models had worked to his good fortune—an honorable way out, ahead of a possible dishonorable discharge. Unfortunately for Private Baz Outlaw, and several other stunned Company E Rangers, Captain Gillespie had misread front-office intention with regards to manpower levels and attendant distribution of supervisory positions within the unit. Gillespie had mistakenly discharged several Rangers. Somewhat along the lines of last hired, first fired—Private Baz Outlaw and four other enlisted men were discharged on October 5, 1885.[53] The civilian ex-cowboy could now measure his time as a hard-charging frontier lawman at fifty-five days. Captain Gillespie manfully owned up to the error, writing to Captain/Quartermaster Lamartine Pemberton "Lam" Sieker at headquarters who had just been promoted to replace Captain John O. Johnson who had in turn resigned to accept a lucrative federal patronage position: "and when the time for reduction came myself & Sergt. were both under the impression that the order allowed 1 Cpt. 1 Sgt. 1 Corpl. 1 Teamster & 7 Prvts. Thus the reduction was made and upon the Recpt of your letter the order referred to read. I see my very careless mistake. . . . the same will be corrected."[54] And it was.

Private Baz Outlaw was back on Captain Gillespie's books as of December 14, 1885, but by this time the Company E headquarters had shifted to Murphyville, a delightful West Texas town now known as Alpine.[55] And scarcely a month later Private Baz Outlaw was mentioned in Company E's January Monthly Return as the lead Texas Ranger for a scout after an alleged horse thief.[56] For whatever reason Baz Outlaw—even as a neophyte lawman—had gained or was gaining favorable notice from the company's management team.

Someone else who had caught more than favorable notice at headquarters and in the field was Isaac N. "Ike" Lee, a former but experienced Ranger noncommissioned officer, but as of May 1, 1886 a Special Ranger carried on the Muster & Pay Roll of Company E.[57] The designation Special Ranger was a connotation of importance on the one hand, meaningless on the other. Politicians sanctioning formation of the Frontier Battalion in 1874 had been liberal, excessively so, with authorization to place on the six companies' Muster & Pay Rolls an aggregate of 450 men, rank and file, officers and non-coms. From the get-go such a staffing model had been too ambitious. The State of Texas may have had a bona fide need for 450 fighting men at the time, but assuredly not the financial wherewithal for such expenditures. And, as mentioned, the battalion's expenses and manpower levels were ever the target for penny-pinching lawmakers and their dizzyingly obsessive tinkering. The Frontier Battalion had, truthfully, been drastically downsized. AG King had rather astutely interpreted the legislation, however. On paper he was still permitted 450 men; there simply was not money to guarantee paychecks. His solution was straightforward and simple. He would, not exceeding the 450 man allotment, commission Special Rangers with all the authority of a Texas peace officer with regards to enforcing the law, making arrests, and carrying arms. Those Special Rangers would and could earn their pay as employees of railroads or mining firms or cattlemen's associations or whomever. Or, they could simply carry a peace officer's commission and a six-shooter gratis, a political or personal favor.[58] Soon enough, the process and particulars—Ike Lee included—will play into Baz Outlaw's fascinating and sometime spellbinding Wild West narrative.

Though as a Texas Ranger, to this point, Baz Outlaw's law-enforcing work had not obliged him to shoot anybody—or at anyone: As much cannot be said of several Company E comrades. On the ninth day of May 1886, a very intoxicated Tom Patterson was acting stupid at Murphyville. Not only was he drunk and disorderly, he was "flourishing his six shooter" at Company E Ranger Sam Patton, and was "keeping him in a dangerous position. . . ." Much to Patton's relief and much to Patterson's abhorrence, Ranger Sergeant L.F. Cartwright along with Privates J.W. Baxter and W.L. Cartwright, had literally ridden to the rescue. Pluckily Sergeant Cartwright "advanced and demanded the surrender of Patterson." Whiskey does not automatically make one bullet-proof, a fact sometimes overlooked by mindless overindulging imbibers. Rather than submissively give up his weapon, Tom Patterson "turned and snapped his pistol at W.L. Cartwright." The crescendo of gunfire most probably was deafening, but how much Patterson heard before he crumpled to the floor is indeterminate. He was dead. Rangers Cartwright and Cartwright and Baxter, all three, in unison, holstered their still-smoking Colt's .45 six-shooters.[59] Private Sam Patton's lucky stars had been shining brightly during this hullabaloo, but the Grim Reaper is capricious. The following month Captain Gillespie sadly reported that Patton's number was up, he having died at Murphyville on June 15, unable to whip a debilitating case of smallpox.[60] Disease and desperadoes and dynamite-minded saddle horses—ever ready to explode—pitching to the high-heavens, were but few of the misfortunes stalking Rangers.

Private Baz Outlaw would not get a free pass. He, too, would have to stand tall during a cow country dustup. On the night of August 6, 1886, cattleman and sometimes justice of the peace E.M. Hereford on a ranch at or near Peña Colorado south of Marathon, Texas, was fatally gunned down by Jim Davenport. The *Fort Worth Daily Gazette* characterized the event as an assassination. Hard revenge for being fired the previous day was the mad cowhand's motive.[61] Heartlessly, Jim Davenport had pumped five .45 bullets into E.M. Hereford before making for parts unknown—at least so he hoped. Captain Gillespie, though the murder occurred some fifty miles south of his headquarters camp and Davenport had the jump by "21 or 22 hours," put two scouts into the field and onto the manhunt.[62] One of those scouts was comprised of Ranger Privates Baz Outlaw and a guy with little more than a month's service, Joseph M. "Joe" Mize.[63] The two Rangers, slyly picking up bits of intelligence as they scouted toward the Rio Grande in the lower Big Bend Country, eventually meandered into the G4 cow camp. The foreman, former Texas Ranger Jim Gillett, was at El Paso, but he had left Pink Taylor as the cowhand in command of the headquarters camp. Baz Outlaw, at least by virtue of seniority, was in charge and chose to concoct a plausible cover story—that they were in pursuit of damnable horse thieves, probably Mexicans. The deception was sharp, after taking into account that the suspected murderer's brother, Jeff Davenport, was a G4 cowboy and was in camp and might prematurely spill the beans if he knew too much, too quick. Therefore, only Pink Taylor was cut in on the truth, the suspect's brother, along with cowboys H.J. Bowles, Rozell (also spelled Roselle) Pulliam, John A. Ward, Henry Reynolds, and future suspect in a humdinger of a newsmaker, a quadruple homicide, Richard "Dick" Duncan, were for the short go kept in the dark.[64]

Thinking Jim Davenport might make a show to contact his brother Jeff, the two Rangers opted to recruit their jaded horses by staying overnight at the G4.[65] Albeit somewhat a ruse, both lawdogs and horses could use a brief rest. Who could know when or where a killer would show? Baz Outlaw's guesswork paid its dividend—in bullets.

About midnight Jim Davenport rode into the G4 camp, he and his horse tired and thirsty. His nosily asking for a water-bucket had awakened near everybody, and certainly the catnapping Baz Outlaw—who silently nudged his partner.[66] Though it would not always be in sync with Ranger shootings, this time Baz Outlaw's terse command to "Halt and throw up your hands" came first. Jim Davenport submitted to the stop, but while he was supposed to be reaching for the sky the moonlight shone on his Winchester's barrel—pointed straight at Rangers Outlaw and Mize. Hesitating for not even one split-second, not wishing to earn a second-place finish in a gunfight, the Texas Rangers fired.[67] The close range battle waxed hot, with shifty Jim Davenport squatting and shooting, while Outlaw and Mize sought what little cover "an old camp wagon" could provide. Cowboy H.J. Bowles, who was there, graded Davenport pretty handy with the Winchester, proffering his suppositional rundown: "He would have killed the Rangers had it not been for the old wagon."[68] Maybe not toe to toe, but damn close, the combatants kept feverishly shooting until their weapons ran dry—then Davenport opted to disappear into the night—scooting for the nearby hills. Baz Outlaw and Joe Mize were glad—at least for a minute—to be rid of him. Rustling through their bedrolls the two Rangers did retrieve more cartridges but—and it's but reasoned speculation—Outlaw could no longer count on Mize to back any play in the dark. Baz Outlaw was irked.

There was, of sorts, a scorecard. Jim Davenport had caught one of Outlaw's bullets, the second one, "a flesh wound in [his] side low down." Both Texas Rangers had received bullet wounds—superficial injuries—when lead from Davenport's peppering shattered into bits of shrapnel while striking "iron on the wagon." Ranger Baz Outlaw was "slightly wounded over one eye and in hip" and Private Joe Mize was "slightly wounded in shoulder."[69]

With morning light cresting the hills, something dawned on the wounded Texas Rangers: They were in outlaw country, Jim Davenport was an outlaw, and the cat was now out of the bag. They were hunting and had been shooting at cowboy Jeff Davenport's brother, and at the G4's out-of-the-way cow camp Jim Davenport had good friends—bad men—but damn good friends, hard friends. There was no need for any false pride or phony mush-mouthing: "Owing to Davenports brother and other friends being at place of fight and odds being against Outlaw and Mize they deemed it prudent to return to camp and get help so they started and was met at Nevills Ranch by Sgt. Cartwright and two men."[70]

From an isolated and naturally fortified spot overlooking the G4 cow camp, Jim Davenport watched Rangers Outlaw and Mize strike for the road heading north. Convinced that the Rangers would not return, at least for awhile, Davenport rode back into the G4 amid the reassuring welcome from cowboys. There he was fed and furnished with a fresh horse to make flight across the Rio Grande. Unfortunately he had to go through not over the river—and it was up—raging. On the first try at migrating to Mexico, Davenport's borrowed horse drowned and he lost his six-shooter in the swirling current. Atop another horse with witnesses wishing him farewell the fugitive from Texas justice finally made it across. Though it's but another story, Davenport's sojourn in Mexico was but temporary and ultimately he was taken into custody, tried and convicted in Texas. He caught the nickel—one buying him five years in prison.[71]

Upon learning of his Rangers' near brush with death, Captain Gillespie raced to intercept Privates Outlaw and Mize, determined to "procure them medical assistance" and learn what had taken place. At Peña Colorado he was updated as to details, but quickly ascertained that their wounds were but slight and "medical aid was unnecessary."[72] Seemingly, Captain Gillespie learned a bit more, too.

Dissecting exactly what happened is understandably problematic, but thc best guess is that Baz Outlaw had not been overly impressed with the standup deportment—or lack thereof—of Ranger Joe Mize during the shoot-out with Jim Davenport. Reasoned deduction is that Captain Gillespie obtained his information straight from the horse's mouth, Private Outlaw, and he wasn't any too happy either. Subsequent to the borderland gunfight Captain Gillespie had traveled to headquarters conferring with Captain Lam Sieker on a wide-ranging array of Texas Ranger related topics. That they discussed Private Joe Mize is perfectly clear from Captain Gillespie's follow-up letter after returning from his Austin visit.

> Mize "the man of whom I was talking to you about in Austin of discharging upon my return," He skiped [*sic*] the country some Days past to save being fired for cowardice.[73]

Whatever the reason for Joe Mize skipping, he ostensibly thought it well worth forfeiting $12. The Muster & Pay Roll was marked: "Pay forfeited on account of desertion." And a like notation placed on the Company E Monthly Return for September 1886: "Prvt. J.M. Mize Deserted on September 12' 86 from Camp Johnson Co. 'E' Hd quarters."[74] Clearly from Captain Gillespie's words to Captain Sieker the missing Joe Mize was not made of the right material to be a Ranger. On the other hand, Ranger Private Baz Outlaw, the young man from Georgia, had demonstrated that his grit was true, he had sand, and could stay hitched when the world turned upside down. Baz was fearless. Captain Gillespie—as others would be—was more than impressed with the overall work ethic, courage, and levelheadedness of Baz Outlaw. He staked his name on it.

Adjutant General King was apprehensive about a possible outbreak of violence during the upcoming 1886 November elections. He was particularly concerned regarding the village of Presidio on Texas' side of the Rio Grande opposite Ojinaga, State of Chihuahua, Mexico. Taking pen in hand AG King voiced those concerns to Captain Gillespie and promulgated special orders, herein excerpted in part:

> For the purpose of preventing illegal voting & to Keep the peace during the election on the 2nd of Nov. next, you will detail about four (4) men, of your Command to proceed to Presidio, Presidio County, Texas. It may not be amiss to remind you that the men detailed for this duty should be instructed that under no circumstances must they become involved in the controversies of the different political parties or the local questions agitating Presidio County. . . . Let the man in charge of this detail be of the best material you have & be cautioned to exercise great prudence & good judgment.[75]

Despite certain proselytizing preacher-type writers' cunning omissions—purposefully it seems—there is a hardcore truth: Ranger Baz Outlaw got the call. Captain Gillespie handpicked him for the delicate assignment, where diplomacy was paramount. Baz Outlaw was placed in charge of the detail sent to the border, leaving Company E headquarters, Camp Johnson, on the last day of October 1886 with the stated purpose of going "to Presidio Del Norte to attend election day and to assist civil authorities Keeping the peace & prevent illegal voting and arrest violators of the law."[76] Exactly how much influence his detachment had or did not have with keeping the peace would be suppositional, though it may be reported: "Everything having passed off Quietly." Private Outlaw and members of the Ranger detachment returned to Company E's headquarters camp on November 5, 1886.[77] Private Outlaw's good work was noted. At this point in his chosen law enforcing career Baz was doing okay—earning a dollar a day—but doing okay.

As reflected in the letter from Captain Gillespie to Captain Sieker there was a respite from the rude belches of six-shooters and the impolite coughs of Winchesters—all was quiet, for awhile. Well, Gillespie did notice the relative silence was broken by "the roar of defeated candidates" which he guessed would soon "be a thing of the past."[78]

The lull in West Texas gunfire was short-lived at tough Toyah. On December 28, 1886, "there was a chinaman [*sic*] shot through the hip and calf of the leg Without any provocation."[79] Because of his thorough knowledge of the area, his past experience as a Ranger captain, and influential standing with Texas politicos, George Wythe Baylor was updated about the incident: "We have been having the Devil's own time here. Jepp Clayton has been shooting up the town for the last month and we have no officers to arrest him. Kirk [Sheriff Turnbo] is either afraid of him or stands in with him. I do not know which. . . . People have actually been afraid to go on the Street and business men would have to close up. . . . Clayton Shot a Chinaman the other day without any provocation what ever. The Chinaman went into a Saloon where C. was drunk and he ordered him out. . . . the party probably not knowing what he Said, he commenced Shooting at his feet, the Chinaman then ran and he still kept shooting at him and Struck him twice. . . . I write to you to get you to use your influence with Genl. King or the Governor to have a detachment Stationed here. . . . We cannot get a deputy Sheriff here that will Stay. . . ."[80]

Moreover, in hotel owner and Justice of the Peace C.M. Fields' missive to Texas & Pacific Railroad executives, he bewailed his personal observations regarding the local and overwhelmed Reeves County deputy sheriff stationed at Toyah: "our deputy Sheriff Stationed here, when there is trouble brewing or any Shooting going on he goes and hides himself in a cellar until it is over, then he Shows up brave as a lion. . . ." Noting that the "R.R. [railroad] mens lives are in danger" too, the distraught Fields implored L.L. Keller of the Texas & Pacific to use his influence with the governor or the adjutant general to have a detachment of Texas Rangers deployed to Toyah.[81]

From his Dallas office John C. Brown, Receiver, Texas & Pacific Railroad, dictated a snappy but not snippy letter to AG King. The railway line's powerhouse player simply said, in a two-sentence typewritten epistle: "I beg to say that there has been more or less trouble in the region of Toyah for some time past. There is a rough, bad element there; and if the state could spare a small detachment of Rangers for duty there, it would afford a great protection to our line."[82]

It should come as no surprise. Three days after receiving the correspondence, AG King took pen in hand, writing two letters on January 7, 1887. The first was to Captain Gillespie, ordering him to look into the conditions at Toyah and station a detachment at that point, making arrangements for their provisions and subsistence until "matters quiet down." Paying particular attention to the political delicacy of a request for Texas Ranger presence at Toyah, AG King also notified John C. Brown of his instructions to Captain Gillespie.[83] Again, it should not be a shocker, because there was every likelihood that there really would be more gunplay at Toyah, Private Baz Outlaw was chosen to accompany Company E's new 1st Sergeant, W.F. Sheffield, who had replaced L.F. Cartwright subsequent to his discharge from the unit, and the abject desertion of his brother, Private W.L Cartwright.[84]

Though latter-day historians and/or writers would be deprived of any thrilling episodes regarding Baz's short-lived deployment to Toyah during that first part of 1887, there is little doubt that he and Sergeant Sheffield were pleased and relieved—not having to have killed anyone—or thumped a head with their Colt's barrels. Baz Outlaw was building a reputation, a hard reputation, and at this point a good reputation. From a lawman's preventive perspective, that was a good thing. Testing his mettle was foolhardy—and that helped keep peace and quiet at Toyah.

Another Company E Ranger had not been doing well. Private J.H. Burney, a veteran Ranger, had been overcome with Pneumonia.[85] Sergeant Sheffield and Private Outlaw, returning to

Camp Johnson on February 3 were given the disheartening news. Just the day before, Private Burney had died. Knowing that one of Private Burney's last requests was not to be buried in faraway West Texas, Captain Gillespie with good intentions made arrangements and had the body shipped back home—in a metallic "case which cost $183. . . ."[86] Perhaps due to the ensuing firestorm about finances and protocols, Sergeant Sheffield and Private Outlaw, had they the chance, would have willingly scooted back to Toyah. Adjutant General King was not happy, and the two-page letter he wrote Captain Gillespie made that perfectly clear. To his way of thinking Private Burney "should have been buried where he died," in a traditional and less costly coffin. Then, if relatives and/or friends wanted to stand the expense, it would be their liability financially and sensitively to honor Private Burney's deathbed wishes—not the State of Texas. AG King closed his remarks to Captain Gillespie: "These extraordinary expenditures are not warranted by law, and must not be incurred."[87]

Ironically it seems, the very same day Private Burney died, another happening unfolded, one having momentous and meaningful impact on the everyday life of Texas Ranger Baz L. Outlaw. On the second day of February 1887, Brewster County was birthed, chopped from lands of gigantic Presidio County, and later supplemented with real-estate from Buchel and Foley Counties which had never organized and would be abolished. Brewster County in due time would become the largest county in Texas, an area encompassing 6,169 square miles of rolling plains, gorgeous mountains, breathtaking winding canyons, a huge chunk of the Chihuahuan Desert, and a southern boundary defined by the ever snaking and shifting Rio Grande.[88]

Brewster County was in need of an organized local government and Captain Gillespie had his eye on the position of sheriff, gingerly toying with the idea of resigning from the Texas Rangers. More-or-less covertly he messaged Captain Sieker regarding same.[89] Captain Gillespie again updated Captain Sieker—this time asking him to "keep this to Yourself." The confidentiality pertained to Captain Gillespie pushing hard—since he would be sheriff of Brewster County—to name his replacement on the Company E roster. Gillespie favored Sergeant Sheffield, but others were vying for the job, too. The competition was escalating into quite a bitter inter-battalion squabble.[90] Company E's former 1st Sergeant L.F Cartwright was campaigning fiercely for Gillespie's old job. In a letter dated February 10, 1887, the aggressively aspiring L.F. Cartwright made his case for promotion to the adjutant general, enclosing a petition of support from rank and file, including Private Baz Outlaw and Sergeant W.F Sheffield.[91] Then, seemingly from out of nowhere, the tide turned. Sergeant Sheffield, but four days after Cartwright's plea for promotion, had apparently been coached from behind the table to make his pitch and present his petition. There's no ironclad proof—but little doubt—that Captain Gillespie had counseled Sheffield to gather signatures from Company E Rangers in support of his candidacy to become the new company captain. Once Sergeant Sheffield's name was in the hat, several Rangers who had signed Cartwright's petition jumped ship and sided with Company E's top noncom, including but not limited to Captain Gillespie and Baz Outlaw.[92] Saddling the right horse is sometimes shrewd. Baz Outlaw was smart.

Adjutant General King was of no mind to become entangled in an interagency imbroglio where even the winners would carry taint across the finish line. No, AG King had a solution, a simple solution for this unpleasant brouhaha. He issued Special Order No. 106: Company E was no more, the personnel to be mustered out of service on or before April 6, 1887.[93]

And herein, not hidden, is a salient truth about Baz Outlaw's narrative: He was exempted from losing his law enforcing job. For the time at Frontier Battalion headquarters Private Outlaw was favorably known as a standup Texas Ranger, a lawman not acquainted with fear or shackled by duplicity or any issues challenging his honesty. Rather than boot him out of the service, the battalion quartermaster, Lam Sieker, traveling to Murphyville to oversee the disbandment of Company E, stepped to the forefront in

Private Baz Outlaw's and Sergeant W.F. Sheffield's behalf. His recap is plainspoken:

> I succeeded in disposing of the supplies by peddling them out to the citizens of Murphyville without loss to the State. I transferred Sheffield & Outlaw to Co. "D." I secured a car to Uvalde at 45$ and just sent the mules, and horses belonging to Sheffield & Outlaw to that place. I will take the passenger train tonight for Uvalde and may go to Capt Jones camp before I return to Austin.[94]

Somewhat emblematic of the everyday grueling work of legit cowboys is reflected in this realistic image, *Cattle Dust and Long Hard Day*, by renowned Western painter Donald M. Yena. Baz Outlaw opted to forego the catch-ropes and branding irons, replacing them with handcuffs and six-shooters. *Courtesy the artist, Don Yena.*

George Wythe Baylor, Ranger Captain, Indian fighter, newspaperman and Texas political powerhouse. He captained a Ranger company and his administrative and geographical jurisdiction was tasked with keeping the peace, among other places, at Toyah and Pecos City, Reeves County. Captain Baylor noted the section was home and haunt for some of the "worst population" in West Texas. Tough ground to cover for rookie Baz Outlaw, cowboy turned Ranger. *Courtesy Kurt House Enterprises, Inc.*

Texas Ranger Sergeant Lycurgus S. "Kirk" Turnbo and, later, sheriff of Reeves County. *Courtesy Tobin and Anne Armstrong Ranger Research Center, Texas Ranger Hall of Fame & Museum.*

Bazzell Lamar "B.L." Outlaw—standing tall and raring to go—subsequent to enlistment with the now legendary Texas Rangers during the Frontier Battalion era. *Courtesy Tobin and Anne Armstrong Ranger Research Center, Texas Ranger Hall of Fame & Museum.*

Texas Ranger Captain James T. Gillespie, Commander of the Frontier Battalion's Company E, the Ranger unit Baz Outlaw was first attached to as a novice lawman in far West Texas. *Courtesy Archives of the Big Bend, Bryan Wildenthal Memorial Library, Sul Ross University.*

Captain Gillespie's Company E headquarters camp in West Texas. Ranger Baz Outlaw was first assigned to this unit and worked on a daily basis with some of these Rangers. Standing, L to R: "Boggs" Davis, Nick Brown, George W. Simons, Jeff D. Milton, James Martin "Jim" Sedberry, W.H.C. Caruthers, unidentified, Isaac M. "Ike" Lee and William F. "Bill" Sheffield. Seated, L to R. (??) Haskell, L.B. Mills, Captain J.T. Gillespie, D.W. "Doc" Gourley, Edward G. "Ed" Sheffield, John Brockman, and Bob Neville. *Courtesy Nita Stewart Haley Memorial Library and J. Evetts Haley History Center.*

Jeff Davis Milton, celebrated Southwestern lawman. As a no-nonsense Texas Ranger, he and two other Rangers, James Martin "Jim" Sedberry and L.B. Wells, would undergo nightmarish legal headaches subsequent to their on-duty shooting and killing at Colorado City of W.P. Patterson, normally a good natured fellow, but one who also "Got drunk often, and stayed drunk long." Photo an extract from the 1908 edition of *Camp-Fires on Desert and Lava* by William T. Hornaday, *Courtesy Nita Stewart Haley Memorial Library and J. Evetts Haley History Center.*

James Martin "Jim" Sedberry was the Company E Lieutenant. Though he had a brilliant record for bravery and sobriety, on at least one occasion he lost a bout with the bottle, causing supervisory heartburn for the perplexed company captain, something Ranger Baz Outlaw—in due time—would accomplish with escalating regularity. *From Texas Ranger Sketches, courtesy the author, Robert W. Stephens.*

Texas Ranger L. F. Cartwright and wife Mollie. As the 1st Sergeant of Company E, Cartwright was the immediate supervisor of rookie Ranger Private Baz Outlaw. He also personally participated in more than one law enforcing West Texas gunplay. *Courtesy Tobin and Anne Armstrong Ranger Research Center, Texas Ranger Hall of Fame & Museum.*

James Buchanan Gillett, an ex-Ranger and author of *Six Years With the Texas Rangers, 1875 to 1881*. At the time Baz Outlaw first knew Gillett, Jim was foreman of the Big Bend's G4 Ranch, and later sheriff of Brewster County, the largest county in Texas. *Courtesy Archives of the Big Bend, Bryan Wildenthal Memorial Library, Sul Ross University.*

West Texas cowboy and celebrated cowman Pink Taylor knew Baz Outlaw—favorably or otherwise? *Courtesy Tobin and Anne Armstrong Ranger Research Center, Texas Ranger Hall of Fame & Museum.*

Senior Captain Lamartine Pemberton "Lam" Sieker, seated at left, recognized the worth of Baz Outlaw as an utterly fearless Texas Ranger, transferring him into Captain Frank Jones' Company D, rather than dropping him from the Muster Rolls when Company E was temporarily disbanded. *Courtesy Tobin and Anne Armstrong Ranger Research Center, Texas Ranger Hall of Fame & Museum.*

CHAPTER 3

A Fighting Business— Robbing a Train

PROBABLY LITTLE DID HE KNOW IT THEN, but Private Baz Outlaw had been transferred into one of the more celebrated and active Frontier Battalion units, Company D. At the time he transitioned into his new headquarters the company was commanded by Captain Frank Jones, an utterly fearless Ranger who had come from the bottom tier, through the ranks from private, climbing steps on the noncom's ladder, to junior commissioned officer, and finally promoted to company captain. Frank Jones was, now, a career lawman wholly committed to service and looking after the well-being of his subordinate Rangers. Likewise, Company D Texas Rangers, rank and file, adored him.[1] Frank Jones was a man's man, a Ranger's Ranger. He was legit.

Exactly when Private Outlaw managed his initial appearance and gained an audience with Captain Jones is not precise, the Monthly Return for April 1887 in that regard simply reflecting: "B.L. Outlaw transferred from Co. 'E' by Capt. L.P. Sieker, QM."[2] Where he reported to is not indistinct, Camp Ross, Barksdale, Edwards County, on the Nueces River northwest of Uvalde. Though in due time Rocksprings would gain status as the county seat, when Private Outlaw made his show that honor went to Leakey, a spot now—after madcap political tinkering—in southeastern Real County. There's little doubt, a few of Company D Rangers' unhappy prisoners were turned over to Edwards County Sheriff W.J. "Jeff" Sansom, who in turn ensconced them in "an iron cage in the center of a wooden building."[3]

It might be iffy as to whether or not Baz Outlaw had to lollygag around Camp Ross a day or two before meeting Captain Jones, but it would be a surefire bet he and the other Company D Rangers made note of the big catch. Captain Jones and Private Austin Ira Aten had returned from a scout to the upper end of Edwards County, hunting hard for some notorious horse thieves; the brothers Odle, John, Will, and Alvin. The fugitive Odle boys were tough customers, dangerous, and likely to seriously resist arrest, hoping at all cost not to see the inside of Sheriff John W. Wolf's two-story limestone jail at Burnet, the county seat of Burnet County. Captain Jones and Private Aten had a story to tell, and Ira told it:

> . . . and located their kinfolks where they would likely be. There was a number of horses there. We got there after night. We judged from the saddles and horses that they were in the house. Captain Jones wanted to make a raid on the house that night. I said, "Cap, let's don't do that. They are very dangerous, you have got a telegram that they are very dangerous men, and have killed a man." I said, "Let's wait until daylight and go in just as they get up. They are off their guard then and the house is unlocked." The Captain said, "Well, maybe you are right. We will just stay here." We were at a spring about 100 yards from the house, where they carried their water from. The next morning about daylight here come a boy down to the spring after a bucket of water. Of course we held him. We got ready and ran around the house and I went in the back door. I said, "Capt, I will go in the back door." I went in the back door, in the kitchen and the Captain was at the front door. Had one of these strings that pulled. Odle was just waking up. There were two of them. I covered them with my six-shooter and arrested them, opened the door, pulled the string, and the Captain came in. . . .[4]

Absent any blustery trumpeting Captain Jones—always ready to lead from the front—and Private Aten had simply done what was expected of them—they were lawmen, Texas Rangers. Prisoners Will and Alvin Odle, along with Henry Cavius aka Henry Wilson, had been taken off guard, not a shot fired or a head thumped. It had been a clean arrest, competently executed. Shortly the prisoners—in chains—were escorted to Uvalde. There they were to be given over to the elated and appreciative sheriff from Burnet County.[5] In due time, Texas Ranger Outlaw would meet the mean-spirited Odle boys, face to face.

Private Baz Outlaw's first mention by name in the Company D paperwork came quickly, a surprisingly specific notation in light of his recent arrival that very same month. At any rate, he and Private John Woodard "Wood" Saunders, two years Baz's junior and an audacious lawman "devoid of fear," a gritty Ranger adept at both frolicking or fighting, teamed up to find and arrest T.M. Willmore, wanted for Assault & Battery. It took but one day for them to locate and arrest the target of their quest, turning him over to the "proper authorities."[6]

The big news registering for the Company D Rangers was not necessarily searching for and snaring desperadoes, but internal workplace politics. The company's 1st Sergeant, Benjamin Dennis "B.D." Lindsey, a real fire-breather, voluntarily resigned so that he and another former Ranger, W.W. Collier, could become businessmen, financial partners, and proprietors of the Tariff Saloons, with locations at Eagle Pass (Maverick County) and Uvalde (Uvalde County). The vacancy created by the top-sergeant's sabbatical—and that's what it proved to be—was quickly filled. On the second day of May 1887 the aforementioned Austin Ira Aten, a genuine gunfighting Texas Ranger with more than his fair-share of grit was promoted to 1st Sergeant, Company D.[7]

Ira Aten was no counterfeit cop. By the time Baz Outlaw transferred into Company D, Aten had earned a solid reputation as a proficient Ranger on manhunts and as an undercover operative. He had survived a somewhat questionable shootout along the Texas borderlands, coming through unscathed during an exchange of gunfire wherein a Ranger was killed and another seriously wounded. Though in this instance the Rangers were forced to undergo a twenty-six-day layover in Webb County Sheriff Dario Gonzales' hoosegow at Laredo, the lawmen were eventually cut loose, the criminal indictments quashed. Due to fear of Rangers harboring and acting on grudges, Company D was transferred away from the border—temporarily.[8]

Ira Aten had also been actively involved in a hunt for the cold-hearted murderers of an exceptionally well-liked Johann Wolfgang Braeutigam at Fredericksburg in Gillespie County, ultimately dueling with one of the homicide suspects twice. During the first trading of gunshots the merciless guy had made good his getaway for a awhile—a little while. Shortly, during the second go-round, Ranger Ira Aten boldly rushed through the backdoor of Nichols Dayton's place at Liberty Hill (Williamson County), while civilian helpmate John Reynolds Hughes had been ordered to guard the front door, preventing an escape attempt. Inside the residence Ranger Aten killed Wesley "Wes" Collier while the unwise owlhoot was hurriedly reaching for one of his two .45 caliber six-shooters and/or a .38 caliber five-shooter. That same year, 1886, Ranger Ira Aten had also managed to stay alive during a scorching nighttime skirmish in Brown County (Brownwood), an episode where two fence-cutters gave up the ghost after being commanded to quit snipping wire. Sergeant Ira Aten was forged from tempered steel.[9]

Sergeant Ira Aten was also, besides being a salaried Texas Ranger, a Deputy U.S. Marshal, officially commissioned by the politically chosen U.S. Marshal for the Western District of Texas, John T. Rankin.[10] Cross-deputations of this type, a customary practice for the time, will in due course play—quite significantly—with regards to properly narrating Baz Outlaw's intriguing life's story. Dissimilar to the Special Rangers, who were officially commissioned out of the adjutant general's office at Austin and were not drawing any pay from the State of Texas, but could be compensated from the coffers of private enterprise, the federal deputyship turned that law enforcing model upside-down. There were full-time Deputy U.S. Marshals to be sure. On the other hand, certain persons could be handpicked and were deputized by the politically appointed U.S. Marshals, rendering their service on a part-time basis, pocketing a few federal dollars here and there through the government's fee system for services provided: Such as serving subpoenas on witnesses, grand jurors and petit jurors. Or seizing property by authority of the U.S. District Court's decree and/or transporting prisoners under a fixed mileage and per diem schedule. They, too, had all of the necessary legally sanctioned authority to carry firearms and make custodial arrests for federal violations, such as smuggling or counterfeiting or interfering with the mail, etc. They were paid by the job, piecemeal work if you will.[11] By any man's measure Ira Aten as a Texas Ranger or as a Deputy U.S. Marshal was the Real McCoy.

Some other fellows were genuine too—genuine gangsters. Brackston E. "Brack" Cornett aka Captain Dick and William Henry "Bill" Whitley captained a hard-riding gang of terror dispensing train robbers. These boys were cool customers. Cornett had a bad history but a good escape from prison in his résumé. It was penned by one who knew him—a crony in crime—that Captain Dick was mean and "as quick and strong in his movements as a panther. . . . a phenomenal hand with a six-shooter and rifle." Bill Whitley, as the fellow hooligan noted, seemingly had ice water in his veins, and could "look into the muzzle of a double-barreled shotgun in the hands of an enemy and never flinch."[12]

Some train robbers "enjoyed a special place at the top of the criminal pecking order" but not these darling felonious fellows. "In the public mind, there was a little bit more derring-do involved in overpowering a huge locomotive and its cars, trains then being a symbol of the growth and commerce of the United States." Had Cornett and Whitley simply settled for highjacking a train, they might have cleaved unto themselves a smidgen of somewhat perverted status, due to the fact "railroad corporations served as a symbol of the capitalism that led to exploitation of farmers and ranchers forced to cede valuable right-of-way, leading to some popular admiration for the train robbers."[13] Hardly ever content to merely take their plunder and ride into the shadows, these thugs particularly prided themselves on dishing out brutality by shooting folks, pistol-whippings others, and even—on occasion—slitting an ear or two with their pocket knives.[14] While these yahoos were making plans to fill their purses and saddle pockets with other folks' hard-earned money, Private Baz Outlaw was on the move.

He and four other Rangers under the nominal leadership of Private Henry Piper had been deployed to Del Rio, Val Verde County, on the Rio Grande opposite Ciudad Acuna in the Mexican State of Coahuila, arriving and setting up camp on May 7, 1887. The command decision to establish a Company D detachment along this section of the border was in response to inquiry from Texas Ranger headquarters, and clearly Captain Jones was satisfied that they—the five men—could "do as much good there as the whole Company."[15] Captain Frank Jones, with reference to Val Verde County, was in the know. His brother, a lawyer and former Ranger, William Kenner Jones, was one of the original movers and shakers concerned with carving the newly established county from lands once surveyed and a part of Crockett, Kinney, and Pecos Counties.[16] Soon after Val Verde County's boundaries were a matter of record, Del Rio had been awarded the county seat honors on May 2, 1885.[17] Subsequent to harnessing the then flowing and still flowing waters of San Felipe Springs which were collectively the wet components of San Felipe Creek, the little settlement at the crossing of the ancient road connecting Chihuahua, State of Chihuahua, Mexico, and the Texas Gulf Coast port of Indianola, Calhoun County, blossomed into a desert oasis. Although charted before formation of the county, The San Felipe, Agricultural, and Manufacturing Company and its thousands of acres of ditches and spider-webs of canals, did in fantasy and fact "stimulate the growth of Del Rio, since the irrigation canals provided water to the city as well."[18]

Del Rio may have been undergoing a righteous population boom, eager speculators and upstanding citizens vying for opportunities to lay foundations for productive livelihoods, it was really a pretty nifty place. On the other hand it was a border town, and with the good came the bad. The Rio Grande marked sovereignty's line, which was necessary, but proximity to the river—then as now—presented unscrupulous folks, border-jumping ne'er-do-wells, and hardened criminals with easy jack-in-the-box access for sidestepping jurisdictional penalties. Then as now, Rangers were and would be an integral part of the law enforcing landscape.

At the time Company D's detachment took up residence in their tent camp on the outskirts of town, the first Val Verde County sheriff, W.H. Jones, surely could boast of precious water as a part of Del Rio's landscape, but he had no jailhouse. The nearest lockups were at Uvalde some seventy-odd miles to the southeast or downriver half-a-hundred miles at Eagle Pass.[19]

Hardly had Private Baz Outlaw and his workmates been deployed to Del Rio, introducing themselves to citizens and instilling a touch of fear in would-be troublemakers, when news broke from tiny McNeil Junction, some fourteen miles north of Austin: Robbers had made their own brand of acquaintances, introducing themselves to frightened passengers and a powerless train's crew on the night of May 17, 1887, assaulting the northbound Missouri Pacific while parked at the depot. The nastily disposed Cornett/Whitley gang was at work, doing what train robbers do. During a senseless spate of six-shooter fireworks two innocent passengers were wounded, thankfully not mortally. Following the gunplay and gathering up $4000 in spoils, the brigands thundered into the night, merrily daydreaming—though it was dark—about divvying the loot. Knowing that if they, individually, drew standard cowboy wages—or Ranger pay for that matter—that it would take a million days to earn a $1,000,000 salved their consciences and skewed their scruples.[20] The posse following behind—far behind—was predictably ineffective. The contemptible cry from an outraged newspaperman was somewhat foreseeable though, penning his great displeasure that—in this modern age—horseback marauders could "within a few miles of the capital of the State" strike with such viciousness and audaciousness. An act like that was, well, "it was intolerable even to think of such a thing happening so close to Austin! Nevertheless, it did happen."[21]

Roughly thirty days later, the larcenous Cornett/Whitley gang struck again, this time robbing the Galveston, Harrisburg & San Antonio Railroad's No. 19 at Flatonia in Fayette County, about the midpoint between Houston and the Alamo City. During these June 18 wrongdoings the gang's systemic sadism was once again flaunted: "When Messenger Frank Folger threw away the keys to his safe, the bandits pistol whipped him and tortured him by slitting his ears with pocket knives until they received the keys. The masked men attacked sleeping travelers in their bunks and beat up a Mexican Army lieutenant and a woman passenger. . . ."[22] The outlaws' haul this time was a whopper, approximately $15,000 plus a wide assortment of rings and watches—some quite valuable—stripped from frightened passengers.[23] Needless to say, Texas Governor Ross was not a happy camper—he was real mad, damn mad, and he upped the ante, publicly declaring that in the near future the crime of train robbery would "be a fighting business and attended with almost certainty of failure and destruction. There will be five to ten well-armed fighting men on each train."[24] The governor's bombast was rich. Practically speaking the state's coffers were short—Texas was strapped for cash.

Two of the Odle brothers were short of something else—a reasonable chance of escaping hard time at Huntsville, site of the Texas State Penitentiary. Will and Alvin languished on the second floor of the Burnet County jailhouse at the corner of Washington and Pierce Streets in Burnet. Though mindreading from up close or from afar is inappropriate, there is little doubt the two desperadoes were gauging the bleakness of their future. The actual strength of the prosecutor's evidence was relatively insignificant, especially for Will, as surely he would catch time for at least one of the four cases of "horse-theft" or one of the two charges for "house breaking." Though formally charged and being held at this time in Burnet County for but one case of stealing horses, Alvin had legal problems elsewhere, and was almost guaranteed his spot hoeing cotton under the watchful eye of a tobacco-spitting horseback prison guard with a Winchester across the pommel of his saddle.[25]

Meanwhile, from Company D headquarters at Barksdale, on June 28, 1887, Sergeant Aten departed for a trip to Austin. On that same day Private Baz Outlaw, in the company of Private C.C. Wood, a Ranger of but two months but already having ineffectively popped caps at an escaping fugitive, Louis Paderas, also initiated a journey. They were dispatched back to the Company D headquarters camp at Barksdale, greeting their campmates on June 30, 1887.[26] Captain Frank Jones had a big play on tap, updating AG King that he had "ordered two of the Del Rio detachment [Outlaw and Wood]," to return to camp, and that "he was going to begin work on the West Nueces after cattle that have had the brands burnt out. . . . The West Nueces is the head center of most of the cattle and horse stealing in this section."[27] Perhaps a bit more comfortable with making a prediction to his mentor, Captain Lam Sieker, Captain Jones puffed: "I think I will strike the burners a blow that they will feel for a long time."[28]

Ranger Baz Outlaw's adventures along the Texas/Mexico border for his recent deployment, if there were any, went unnoticed—or unrecorded. At any rate, Baz Outlaw's trip had been of short duration, returning to camp without mention of any huge successes or dismal failures, scary firefights or undisciplined foolishness.[29] At this point in Baz's work history, it's germane to note that based on his past Ranger service—good service—with Company E and a perceptible streak of independence, the captain was not adverse to sending him on scouts absent supervision. Private Baz Outlaw could think and act on his own.

On the eighth day of July 1887 Private Outlaw "and one man" scouted into the West Nueces Country and arrested Hank Sylvia and Sam McKee, wanted for cow stealing in Edwards County. They promptly turned their prisoner over to the justice of the peace. A week later Private Outlaw "and one man" temporarily latched onto Jess Bass and Jess Parker, suspected horse thieves. Unable to actually—and legally—put the two in possession of stolen livestock, Baz turned the boys out—no doubt with a stern warning.[30]

How much secrecy revolved around Sergeant Aten's visit at Frontier Battalion headquarters is somewhat fuzzy, the upshot of the meeting is not. The governor and the adjutant general were demanding a full-court press in regards to running to ground or into the cemetery that damn pesky gang of train robbers. Sergeant Ira Aten, owing to past manhunts and shootouts, was specifically tasked—commanded—to make that his number one priority, an order straight out of the front office. Factoring in Ira's next move and request, somewhat augments the esteem he was carrying as a first-rate Ranger, a lawman worth tying to in a pinch. Due to the amicable working relationship budding from his killing of alleged murderer Wesley Collier, Sergeant Aten asked that he be allowed to recruit civilian John R. Hughes into the Rangers, at least for the job at hand. That he was, in a manner of speaking, holding an Ace is underscored in the adjutant general's unequivocal order to Captain Jones, no room for misinterpretation:

> For Special reasons connected with our efforts to Capture the Train robbers I have enlisted John R. Hughes and assigned him to your Company, and you will therefore enter his name on Your next Muster and pay roll as a regular ranger on pay from August 10th 1887. As you are Carrying more men than is prudent under our Small appropriation, it will be well for you take advantage of your reorganization Sept. 1st, and get rid of Such as are least valuable.[31]

Smartly, Adjutant General King had assigned Hughes to Company D, where he would be under the direct supervision of Sergeant Aten, a proven commodity, and up the chain-of-command to Captain Frank Jones, a talented manager of men. Despite some twentieth-century (and later) hoopla, at this time Private John R. Hughes was not a legendary lawman with an impeccable record of law enforcing deeds under his belt. John Hughes was in truth and fact a Ranger rookie. Good lawmen are not born with badges of proficiency pinned to their diapers. Time, tutors, and experience move the neophyte to professionalism. For good or bad or somewhere between, Hughes owed his appointment to Sergeant Aten, an unmistakable fact, with emphasis added, particularized in AG King's follow-up letter to Captain Jones:

> Yours of the 21st instant at hand, and your reorganization may be carried out on the basis therein Suggested. Hughes, however is not intended to be a permanent Member of your Company unless he desires so to be and favors himself a Suitable man: as the object of his present enlistment is to enable him to *aid* Aten in his efforts to

> Catch some of the train robbers. You must carry him on your rolls however until further notice from this office as I *promised* Aten his assistance for Such Time as might enable him to fairly test the probabilities of catching some of the train robbers."[32]

While the big plans to catch train robbers was being blueprinted in the minds of Sergeant Aten and AG King—and maybe Governor Ross—Ranger Private Baz Outlaw, in the saddle, too, was busily engaged in the hunt. Riding in the leadership role for a four man scout, Baz had sallied forth from the Company D camp on the first day of August 1887. How much actual geographical familiarity he owned regarding the ground he was to cover is somewhat indistinct, but he had earlier lived and worked in Kimble County, that "thiafs stronghold," and that territory was on his list, as was Edwards County. The bad boys were nowhere to be found and after nine grueling days searching nooks and crannies, canyons and streambeds, rabbit trails and following false leads, Baz Outlaw and his scouting party woefully returned to camp atop jaded horses—weary and frustrated.[33]

Consequent to resting his worn-out horse a few days and filling his belly with cathead biscuits sopped in deliciously greasy gravy, chased by swirling mouthfuls of super-heated Arbuckles coffee, Baz Outlaw was in the saddle, ready to go again. This time Captain Jones had instructed him to take one man and catch a cow thief, a particular cow thief. They found their man in the country above Bullhead Mountain in Edwards County—a site Baz Outlaw would come to know quite well. The arrest of William Connell came off absent a hitch or mishap, and the two happy Texas Rangers turned their prisoner over to the local justice of the peace—to do with as he deemed appropriate.[34]

During the following month, September 1887, Private Baz Outlaw was placed in charge of two other Texas Rangers and they were dispatched to the West Nueces where he established a Company D subcamp. From there, for the next umpteen days Baz Outlaw was plainly a breezy whirlwind of law enforcing activity, scouting hither and yon, hunting hard for livestock thieves and fugitives dodging apprehension and their guaranteed return to Texas counties or extradition to states and/or territories where warrants had issued.

One of the most notable fugitives was William "Bill" Mitchell aka Baldy Russell, wanted for killing a fellow southwest of Fort Worth near Granbury in Hood County. Fortunately for Mitchell, it might be presumed, he had already skipped out for New Mexico Territory, as the proficient sleuthing of Ranger Outlaw revealed. Five days later, on the twelfth of the month, Baz and an unnamed teammate tried to determine the validity of reports indicating two horses had been stolen from a nearby ranch. The report apparently was unfounded as there were no arrests and no trailing and tracking to be registered. Three days later Baz and another—or maybe the same Ranger—were hunting for suspected murderers near Silver Lake, but soon learned that the fellows had already been arrested. He had better luck on September 19, 1887, by once again arresting Sam McKee, ultimately turning the prisoner over to Private W.W. Jones, who escorted him in handcuffs back to civilization. Toward the end of the month, Baz and his detachment scouted to the Devils River Country and the headwaters of the Llano searching for reported stolen cattle, but struck a dry hole and returned to camp after eight days and meandering about for some 300 miles.[35]

During the first week in October, Private Outlaw and his three-man detachment returned to Company D headquarters, quickly internalizing three items of particular interest. Sergeant Aten and his friend and trainee John R. Hughes had not been successful with their efforts to catch the train robbers, even after staking out the house in Lampasas County—day and night—where one of the crooks' wives was staying with her brother.[36] It had been a sound strategy, from the shadows or bushes watching the residences of wives or mistresses or sweethearts. Usually, sooner or later, the scoundrel would appear, but this time it proved futile. Private Hughes, who Baz may or may not have known at the time, would report for the first time to Company D's headquarters.[37] Secondly, and it would prove meaningful for Private Baz Outlaw, Will Odle and Ep McCarty, a convicted cow thief awaiting transfer to prison, had broken out of jail at Burnet and were on the run. Texas Rangers were on the hunt.[38] Lastly, the whole of Company D had been transferred to the Texas/Mexico border, the move to take place at the end of the month.[39] Yep, October '87 was newsy for Bazzell Lamar Outlaw.

Assuredly the political maneuvering and policy making were above the rank and file Rangers' pay grade, but shifting companies around throughout the state—normally in response to someone officially bitching to Austin about too many Texas Rangers or too few Texas Rangers was but routine. For Company D this proved not to be an exception. Adjutant General King—and presumably the governor—were responding to noise being generated by the Honorable James Livingston, County Judge of Starr County. Livingston's complaints about general lawlessness and bandits breaching the border for piracy were not unfounded. The adjutant general right fast notified the county judge: "In reply to your letter of the 22nd instant, I am glad to be able to say your wishes have been anticipated by an order made yesterday in directing rangers to proceed as promptly as possible to the help of your people. Your letter is the first official information I have had of the situation of affairs in your section, but acting upon private and published accounts of your conditions, I had already directed Capt. Jones to proceed to your county. . . . Jones is intended to be kept down there for awhile, though it will take sometime for his Company to reach your County."[40] The orders from headquarters to Captain Jones were explicit:

> On receipt of this you will call in the Several detachments of your Company on Scout or on detached Service & with your whole command proceed by way of Laredo to make a thorough Scout down the Rio Grande, and through the Counties of Zapata and Starr, reporting by letter to this office now & then as to the Condition of the Country in way of lawlessness, and its necessities in way of protection of citizens against criminals & You will particularly inform your Self as to threatened or actual of part invasion of Texas by Mexican bands of robbers, assassins & cattle & horse thieves.[41]

Anticipating some moaning coming from the upright and honest citizens of Uvalde County upon suffering the loss of protection of a whole Ranger company—and its economic interaction with local businessmen and contractors—Captain William Scott was ordered to move his command, Company F, from Ballinger in Runnels County east of San Angelo, and backfill behind Captain Frank Jones and Company D.[42]

Although it would necessitate considerable travel time, Captain Jones and company marched south from Uvalde County, passing through Carrizo Springs in Dimmit County, Laredo in Webb County, and Carrizo, now Zapata, Zapata County, finally reaching their ultimate destination in Starr County, Rio Grande City on November 20, 1887.[43] Establishing his headquarters' camp three miles from town, Captain Jones notified Ranger officialdom at Austin, where he was situated and that he was at least moderately supplied with good grass, firewood, and sufficient water for men and livestock.[44] Relatively speaking, permanency of the camp in Starr County, as the Company D headquarters was short-lived.

Also on its figurative deathbed was the Frontier Battalion's Company C then commanded by Bavarian-born Captain George H. Schmitt, a crusty workaholic, somewhat effective and always stubborn as the proverbial cross-eyed mule. His domineering pigheaded persona earned him collective disdain. Most Ranger commanders and enlisted personnel loathed him, grading him wholly insufferable. Captain Schmitt's immediate family liked him—maybe? While George Schmitt merits a biography, this is Baz Outlaw's story. Suffice to say, the Rangers' top-brass at Austin grew weary of the arguing, backbiting, and rebuffing of consequential orders. Pursuant to Adjutant General King's Special Order No. 119, as of November 30, 1887, Company C would be no more, formally disbanded.[45]

Knowing the writing was on the wall, Captain Frank Jones made specific requests to Austin: He wanted—felt compelled—to be allowed to enlist a person who could speak "Mexican."[46] Frank Jones, too, with his typical forward-thinking approach to sound administrative practices, asked for the "privilege of appointing a Corporal" as he was thoroughly convinced for "the need of a noncommissioned officer in Camp to look after the men. A private put in charge is [was] not near as efficient as a regularly appointed officer."[47] Captain

Jones had another matter on his mind regarding the shutting down of Company C, telling Captain/Quartermaster Sieker: "If you can have Durbin transferred to Co. D. I would be glad to have him."[48] Captain Frank Jones had—colloquially speaking—pulled off a coup. On December 1, 1887, he enlisted former Company C Ranger Joseph Walter Durbin, a veteran Frontier Battalion lawman and a standup *amigo* when from time to time it turned Western in South Texas.[49] For Baz Outlaw, Durbin's coming over to Company D would be meaningful—on several fronts.

Subsequent to receiving a message from Captain Sieker, and after conducting a personal inspection, Captain Jones implemented another move. Leaving a four-man detachment behind at Rio Grande City, the Company D headquarters was shifted to Duval County. By the tenth day of December the Company D nerve-center was located in a pasture owned by Bob Savage, five miles from tiny Realitos, southeast of San Diego the county seat. Quite expectedly—and politely—the spot was christened Camp Savage.[50] This section of South Texas was teeming with wild game—Whitetail were generally seen in groups numbering ten to twenty-five, and before very long the cracks of Rangers' Winchesters echoed across the wind-swept and brushy country and eight deer were field-dressed and hanging in camp.[51]

Although Duval County, per se, was not actually a border county with a boundary adjacent to the Rio Grande, for enforcing the law in the several counties of South Texas it was a near perfect spot. Aside from the fact Duval County had already banked its fair share of lawlessness and banditry it was geographically staked as a commercial junction of relevance. Travelers and treasure moving on the north/south line between busy San Antonio and the Lower Rio Grande Valley at the state's southern Gulf Coast tip traversed Duval County, going and coming. The piece of real-estate became even more significant once locomotives of the Mexican National Railway—Texas Division began regularly scheduled runs between seaport Corpus Christi and Laredo, a gateway into Mexico's rich commercial and mineral interior. Progressively and socioeconomically Duval County was pinned at an international crossroads. Captain Jones's choice was practical.[52]

As Father Time relinquished his hold on 1887, Frontier Battalion bigwigs at Austin and Company D Rangers in the field were of the same mind: Their captain, Frank Jones, was a prince of a fellow, through and through dedicated to their well-being. In fact, the adjutant general, pen in hand, shared his personal assessment of the captain with Sheriff A.J. Lewis of Milam County at Cameron, grading Frank Jones as being "active and fearless."[53] Demonstrating that Adjutant General King's evaluation of Frank Jones wasn't a hasty spur of the moment remark is also revealed by his later writing that the Company D captain was "An excellent man, and a most efficient, energetic, and fearless officer and Ranger. . . ."[54]

Assuredly living with and functioning on a daily basis, as well as skillfully supervising a workforce where men were carrying Colt's .45 six-shooters and Winchesters, was no easy task. Admiration and respect in that setting—guaranteed—is not capriciously awarded—it's earned. Frank Jones was the type of manager who could and would settle disciplinary disputes and award penalties, warranting compliance of battalion orders, with finesse and faithfulness: But always face to face, man to man. Captain Frank Jones was just as proud of his men, as they were of him, writing to Captain Lam Sieker that "I have the best and most honest lot of men that I have ever known. Not one of them owes a cent that I am not authorized to settle."[55] There was not in Captain Frank Jones' eyes any room for deadbeats or drunks or disobedience in Company D. Subsequent to Sergeant Aten's reporting to Camp Savage after an absence from Company D headquarters—wherever it might have been at the time—on detached special assignments and court appearances since the twenty-eighth day of June the preceding year—and after registering some 5,000 miles of railroad and horseback and stagecoach travel, he and the men of Company D, including Baz Outlaw, sat for a photographer.[56]

Aside from Texas Rangers' proclivity for lining up before enthusiastic cameramen, there was for this instance a special occasion in South Texas to be celebrated. After on the sly contributing to a passing of the hat, the Company D Rangers had collected sufficient funds to purchase their captain a token of their heartfelt and genuine esteem: An A.W. Waltham & Co. pocket watch and chain with a jeweler's engraving on the exquisite timepiece: "For Captain Frank Jones From the Men of Co. 'D' Rangers, Realitos/March 12, 1888."[57]

While Captain Jones was ogling his surprise gift, and while Sergeant Aten was reacquainting himself with familiar Company D faces and introducing himself to more recent enlistees, had Private Baz Outlaw supposed he would have been chasing crooks and battling bandits along the twists and tangles of the Rio Grande and its adjacent South Texas counties the awakening would be rude and right fast. Trouble was brewing elsewhere.

As a come from the bottom ranks Texas Ranger, Captain Frank Jones well knew the law enforcing ropes. Perhaps even more importantly, however, was his talent at managing men, earning him accolades both from the top tier echelon, as well as the working Ranger privates and the company's select noncoms. Texas Ranger Baz Outlaw would make him proud—and test every ounce of his supervisory patience. *COURTESY CANDICE DUCOIN.*

Benjamin Dennis "B.D." Lindsey, a genuine tough cookie: A Texas Ranger sergeant, borderland saloon owner, U.S. Mounted Customs Inspector and Bexar County (county seat San Antonio) Sheriff. *FROM TEXAS RANGER SKETCHES COURTESY THE AUTHOR, ROBERT W. STEPHENS.*

Sergeant Austin Ira Aten was probably the most widely known noncommissioned Texas Ranger during the Frontier Battalion era. Though he had two brothers with Texas Ranger service—both veterans of gunplay—Ira Aten didn't rely on siblings rushing to his aid when push came to shove. He had sand, and could and would stay hitched—participating in gunfights by himself on more than one occasion. Aten, in addition to service as a Texas Ranger was also the sheriff of two separate counties, Fort Bend County (Richmond) and Castro County (Dimmitt). *Courtesy Tobin and Anne Armstrong Ranger Research Center, Texas Ranger Hall of Fame & Museum.*

Although Captain Frank Jones was elsewhere when this image was snapped, these Company D Rangers were dutifully saddling up to chase after desperadoes—or send a colorful photo to friends and relatives. At any rate, Private Baz Outlaw is standing far left by his horse, Winchester in saddle-scabbard. *Courtesy Tobin and Anne Armstrong Ranger Research Center, Texas Ranger Hall of Fame & Museum.*

Philip Cuney "P.C." Baird, like many Company D Rangers, maintained—and legitimately so—Texans' prideful perception that Frontier Battalion lawmen knew no fear. Baird would later become the much respected sheriff of Mason County—through multiple election cycles. *Courtesy James Baird.*

William Wallace "W.W." Collier would tender his resignation to the Texas Rangers, opting to go into business with former Sergeant B.D. Lindsey, operating the Tariff Saloons, with imbibing locations at Eagle Pass, Maverick County, and Uvalde, Uvalde County. *Courtesy Tobin and Anne Armstrong Ranger Research Center, Texas Ranger Hall of Fame & Museum.*

John Reynolds Hughes would in due time become a fêted Texas Ranger Captain. But, like most Rangers, while a rookie he was tasked with menial and mundane duties—no glamour but essential nevertheless. *Courtesy Jeri and Gary Boyce Radder.*

Texas Rangers were issued—through a payroll deduction plan—the Colt's .45 New Model Army Metallic Cartridge Revolving Pistol, more commonly known as a six-shooter, thumb-buster, or Peacemaker. *Courtesy Tobin and Anne Armstrong Ranger Researcher Center, Texas Ranger Hall of Fame & Museum.*

Rangers in camp—Realitos, Duval County, Texas. From L to R: Joseph Walter Durbin, Ernest Rogers, John Reynolds Hughes, Gerry "Dood" Jones, James William "Tink" Durbin, Charles Henry Vanvalkenburg "Charley" Fusselman, John Woodard Saunders, Bazzell Lamar Outlaw, Sergeant Austin Ira Aten, Captain Frank Jones, and an unidentified teamster. *Courtesy Nita Stewart Haley Memorial Library and J. Evetts Haley History Center.*

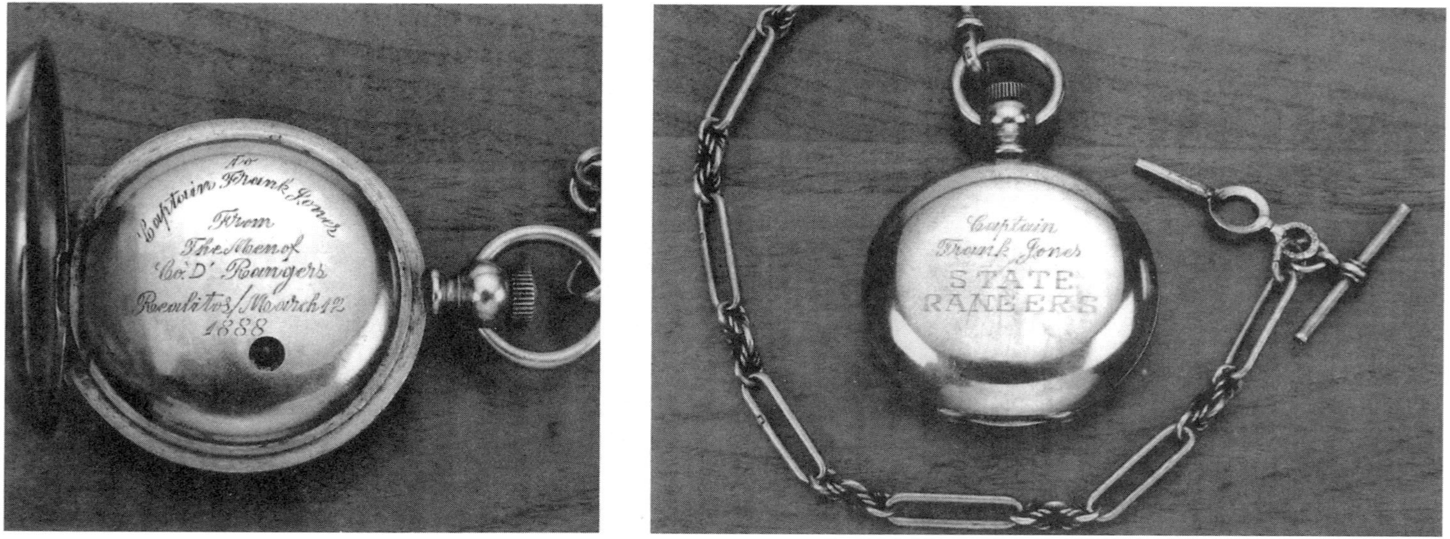

This especially engraved A.W. Waltham & Company pocket-watch was presented as a token of esteem and admiration to Captain Frank Jones from the rank and file Company D Rangers on March 12, 1888, while camped at Realitos. *Courtesy Kurt House Collection ©Paul Goodwin Creative Services.*

CHAPTER 4

Making the Shoe Pinch Too Close

THE WHEELS HAD COME OFF in Wharton County. Situated not too far southwest of Houston, Wharton County was/is perfectly suited for its deserved agribusiness productivity and heritage. Bisected by the Colorado River, bestowed with a lengthy growing season, blessed with abundant rainfall, and positioned but one county removed from the Texas Gulf Coast, Matagorda, Wharton County was rich with rice production and the rewards from cotton, sorghum, soybeans, and multicolored fruit orchards were bountiful. Insect-resistant cattle with upturned pointed horns and humps on their backs grazed the lush grasslands not otherwise given over to crop production. Dating its founding to pre-Civil War days of 1846, the county and its like-named county seat, somewhat shared a bond with its immediate neighbor to the east, Fort Bend County. They were irrefutable economic holdouts of the Old South—Plantation Country. At the time, and undeniably so, this section of near seaside Texas real-estate shared a Code of the Duello legacy with her former Confederate States' neighbors to the east, say like Georgia the birthplace of Texas Ranger Baz Outlaw. For this geographical stretch, as elsewhere, not everyone during the days of Reconstruction had been reconstructed.

Events took a nasty turn. Depending on the version chosen, either a smattering of haughty and overbearing black farmhands or half a dozen or so diligently hard-working and pleasantly disposed black sharecroppers were the opinionated focus of white men's ire near Spanish Camp, eight miles west of Wharton.[1] Regardless, what happened is reprehensible. In one insightful recounting it was reported that "oil had been poured on the house rented by the Negroes, who were shot as they ran from the fire that followed."[2] Not at all unpredictably the public's outrage was igniting its own conflagration. Hot written—and presumed oral—complaints were engulfing Austin's statehouse. The demand for redress was loud—real loud! Those coldblooded murders on one day, at the same place, what upright and dignified community could stand for that? From the judicial bench and from the district attorney's office of Texas' 23rd Judicial District came pleas for state military aid to ride to the rescue and "assist the overwhelmed civil authorities." The governor was taking the matter seriously, as was the adjutant general, and Company D's Captain Frank Jones was expected to, also:

> You are directed to Send a detachment of four picked men to report to The Sheriff of Wharton county; and this being a Matter of importance, you are authorized to appoint a Corporal and send him in charge of this detachment. . . . As soon as your supplies reach you, send this detachment as here in directed, and have them to carry their rations to supply them for at least two weeks. . . . This detachment will proceed by rail & the most practical route I guess will be from Laredo or Corpus Christi to San Antonio and thence by Sunset route to Rosenburg Junction & from there on horseback to Wharton. . . . A pack mule will be necessary, I suppose, and one boxcar will easily accommodate the entire outfit—Men and horses—unless you find it better to send one man in charge of the Stock & Supplies, and let the Corporal and the other two men go in advance by regular train. The details of the trip will be left to your judgment and to be determined according to circumstances. The important point being to send the detachment to Wharton County as soon as practicable and in such Condition as to enable the men to be effective at the earliest moment. . . .[3]

Dutifully the good Captain Frank Jones didn't dither, for a second. The company commander forthwith appointed J. Walter Durbin to the noncommissioned rank of corporal. Within five days of receiving orders to dispatch a detachment to Wharton the captain had also hurriedly cut through railroad bureaucracy's spools of red tape and secured a boxcar for transporting four horses, a pack-mule, and necessary provisions from Realitos by way of Corpus Christi—and points beyond.[4]

Corporal Durbin, as Captain Jones had noted, was "an old Ranger and has been an officer before and is a good man."[5] Captain Jones' selection of Baz Outlaw as a member of the detachment destined for Wharton County suggests—at least at this time—that the tried and true Ranger, a veteran of the gunfight with Davenport in the Big Bend Country, was playing well with others and had the moxie necessary for making tough arrests and trailing saddle-hardened criminals.[6] The second private picked for the detail was Dennis Edwin "Ed" Lindsey, a cousin of Company D's ex-sergeant, a top-notch borderlander and future U.S. Mounted Customs Inspector.[7] Rounding out the Wharton-bound detachment was Private John R. Hughes, a man yet in the down and dirty law enforcing trenches learning the protocols and policing practices of being a Ranger—a good Ranger.[8]

Captain Frank Jones, ensuring the detachment got off on the right foot, accompanied them to Corpus Christi by rail on the March 15, 1888.[9] From that point, Corporal Durbin and Privates Outlaw and Lindsey would sit back in the comfort of a fast passenger train. Private John R. Hughes, figuratively drawing the short straw by virtue of his notch on seniority's totem pole, was relegated to follow behind in a freight train's fragrant livestock car, dutifully assuring the detachment's supplies, saddle horses, and pack animal got to where they were supposed to be: Mundane duty, but necessary.[10]

With the stops, layovers, and jockeying of schedules, and after conferring with the sheriff of Wharton County, J. Wade Jones, Corporal Durbin finally caught a minute to catch his breath and pen a note to Captain Sieker. Assuredly the Texas Rangers had been busy since their arrival at Wharton on the nineteenth day of March.

Already they had executed three arrests "for a shooting scrape that taken place a few nights since up the [Colorado] river. . . ."[11] Though it cannot be confirmed with irrevocable certainty it's more than likely that Private Baz Outlaw was one of the "2 men" that accompanied Corporal J. Walter Durbin and participated in the arrests of Tom Pruitt, Hilliard Williams, and Tom Handy for Assault to Murder, thereafter jailing them in Sheriff Jones' two-story lockup on Wharton's Residence Street, where the inmates assuredly were reluctant residents.[12]

Corporal Durbin was pretty well of the mind, that given but a little more time "the prospect was good to get some of the Spanish Camp Murderers." He did candidly acknowledge, however, that "A few of the negroes [*sic*] know more than they will tell" but thought as court dates drew nearer everything would "come out."[13] During the Rangers' poking around at the crime scene, Corporal Durbin noted the disturbing reality: "I saw some of the remains of the negros burnt Bones and some cooked flesh on them [that] had never been taken up[.] Also the burnt Guns and out a way some twenty steps was at 4 or 5 paces I found from 2 to 6 empty Winchester shells and at corner of fence I picked up 4 10 gage shot Gun Shells[.] Could not find aney one who would tell a thing of this affair." At long last, after a number of gradually productive interviews with the "old negro" Corporal Durbin, employing interrogative skills and inspiring confidence, was successful in eliciting part of the tragic (and unedited) story:

> he taken me to a big old Log seed House that was nearly full of cotton seed a bout 100 yards from the burnt House told me he was sleeping there the night of the Killing and could see it all and give the names of nine very prominent men and property oweners. . . . I taken the old negro in to Wharton and he swore out affidate for arrest of entire bunch and Sheriff Jones and his Deputy a man by name of Coffey went out with me and my men and wee arrested and brought the entire bunch in and placed in Jail the examining trail lasted several days the old darky stuck to his story all the way through. . . .[14]

Analogous to most police actions—as legit lawman learn—is that the congratulatory praise is many times offset by the niggling denigration. Company D's detachment at Wharton was dishing it out, but taking the incoming barbs, too! Corporal Durbin—in his unique and colorful manner of speaking and writing—updated headquarters: "the Sheriff and a few officials are highly pleased with us, while others are doing all they can to get us away as they think we are likely to make the shoe pinch too close."[15]

With little more than a full week under their law-enforcing belts in Wharton County, Rangers J. Walter Durbin, Baz Outlaw, Ed Lindsey, and John Hughes—the whole detachment in tandem—working together, as cited above had pulled the metaphorical shoestrings real tight, arresting homicide suspects Jim Baty, J.H. Hughes, Lee Andres, and J.A. Stratton, charging them all with Murder and transporting them to the calaboose on the twenty-seventh day of March.[16]

On April Fools' Day while Sergeant Ira Aten's nineteen-year-old-brother Calvin Grant "Cal" Aten was holding up his right hand at Realitos, swearing to his oath of office as a spanking new Company D Texas Ranger, Private Baz Outlaw and either Hughes or Lindsey, were on the hunt for another alleged man-killer, Ben Barker. The wanted fellow was, that first day of April, 1888, arrested without incident and added to the jailhouse population peering outside, from inside Wharton County's downtown steel-barred hotel.[17] Shortly Privates Outlaw and Aten, at another place and time would share an adventure, a six-shooting nightmare.[18] On that very same day Corporal J. Walter Durbin—inside Wharton's city limits—took into custody one George Dorman, charged with Murder. The Ranger boys at Wharton were racking up an impressive string of arrests, most of them felonies.[19]

They, too, were racking up a few unpaid invoices for everyday necessities furnished by the Wharton business house of C.H. Waterhouse & Co. Though the mercantile was advertised as a dealer in general merchandise, the firm's letterhead stationery, at least for hardcore Rangers must have inspired a smile—a touch of humor for the tough men doing a tough job—part of the printed sales banner touted—among other things—that the enterprise dealt quite extensively in guns and cartridges—and coffins.[20]

Clearly it seems there had been a brisk business at Wharton regarding funerals and caskets, Corporal Durbin, after tallying the numbers, advised Texas Ranger headquarters of his findings: "I have secured a list of the murders in this Co. since the middle of nov [*sic*] 87 which is 14 in number."[21] The Rangers at Wharton were no doubt having an impact, but Sheriff Jones was predicting trouble at the looming term of district court set to meet during the latter half of April. Corporal Durbin, cognizant of the quality of fighting men at his command, had a differing take: "I hardly think any of them be so boaled [*sic*] as to try any thing of the Kind."[22] Through exceptionally astute and adept investigative work the Rangers had developed—either collectively or individually—sufficient Probable Cause to prompt more arrests and re-arrest subsequent to the return of indictments for the killings at Spanish Camp, in large part due to information obtained on the QT from that " aged Negro." As so often is the case of real world crime fighting, in the field and/or the courtroom, the alleged badmen—assassins in this instance—skated smooth across the Blind Mistress of Justice's scales.[23]

Company D Ranger John Hughes—presumably through no fault of his own—was removed from Corporal Durbin's detachment, orders from headquarters. Whether or not Captain Frank Jones, Sergeant Ira Aten, or Corporal J. Walter Durbin—Company D's command staff—were consulted beforehand or not is and, most likely, will forevermore remain a mystery. Clearly someone with the big stick thought Hughes would be of more—and by correlation—better service to the Texas Rangers somewhere else. Distasteful as the assignment might have been, on May 14, 1888, Private John R. Hughes bid Durbin, Outlaw, and Lindsey adieu, and as ordered straight out of the adjutant general's office left for Navarro County to work undercover. There was a spate of fence-cutting breaking out, and Private Hughes was supposed to snare some Knights of Knippers, a casual but common euphemism for nighttime destroyers of other folks' fences.[24] The work for Corporal J. Walter Durbin's detachment was far from finished, and by any man's reckoning at this time Private Baz Outlaw was—must have been—too valuable to send elsewhere.

There was trouble brewing at Hempstead, Waller County, north of Wharton and adjacent to Harris County where Houston held honors as the county seat. An ongoing feud was underway at Hempstead, popularly known to area residents and Texans statewide as Six-Shooter Junction.[25] Purportedly, and it would have made the Rangers chuckle, when the conductor asked a drunk who had boarded the train in Houston without paying where he was headed absent a ticket, the nitwit spit out: "Well, I guess I'm going to Hell!" The unruffled conductor obliged, told him that they were already there, and let him off at Hempstead.[26] For the redeployment at hand, Corporal Durbin and Private Lindsey started the trip to Hempstead horseback, while Private Baz Outlaw suffering some type of leg infection, traveled by train and upon arrival in town checked into a local hotel and waited for the May 27 appearance of his cohorts.[27]

Once in place the Rangers got an earful. The Waller County sheriff, Thomas S. McDade, and local newspaper editor Steven Alchen were at war—with words and weapons. An edition of the paper alleging that the sheriff was too soft on relatives—not pressing for conviction in a murder case—was more than a tad unappetizing for McDade's son-in-law, a Waller County deputy sheriff. The young fellow was smart enough to know who buttered his bread, and who starched and ironed his shirts, and how blind loyalty to father and daughter was expected if there were to really be peace at work and harmony at home—or in the bedroom. At a downtown Hempstead business house the dutiful deputy quite literally attempted to force-feed pages of the caustic broadsheet to the startled newspaperman—absent salt and pepper or pride. During the irrational madness—and that's what it proved to be—the deputy lived up to the town's nickname, wounding the newshound with his six-shooter prior to accessing a junction with safety outside the store's front door. He was too slow and too late. Wounded, but with Winchester in hand, the newsman set his lead type—into the deputy's back—killing him on the spot and in time for the evening edition.[28]

Corporal Durbin, reporting after-the-fact, knew that the sheriff had been "badly humiliated" and had purportedly started conspiring to guarantee the demise of his son-in-law's slayer. According to Corporal Durbin, one of the sheriff's nephews, Jack McDade, and another relative, Dick Springfield, were drafted to do what the deputy had failed to do, make dead meat out of that damn busybody newspaperman. These two, according to an unedited J. Walter Durbin, well,

> they taken a fine Hammerless double Barrell shot Gun each and consealed them down town in a Butcher shop and lay around waiteing for Alchen to come in he come in shortly afterward and Stopped at the store where he had Killed the Deputy had his Winchester and as soon as through in the Store went out and got on his Horse to leave in the mean time McDade and Springfield had him located and taken the shot Guns & run through Alley back way and come round corner Just as he starting off on Horse and he rec four loads of Buck Shot in side and Back he fell to the ground and Springfield run up and shot him in head severl times with a pistol[.][29]

After the bushwhacking, Jack McDade and Dick Springfield, knowing they had the sheriff's backing, threatened anyone wanting to taste the fare of their death-dealing dishes. Most, and smartly so, Hempstead citizens weren't inclined to sample that menu and had hollered for help. Thus Corporal J. Walter Durbin, and Privates Baz Outlaw, who was limping along, and Ed Lindsey were on the scene. Captain Samuel A. "Sam" McMurry and his Company B Rangers, having been rushed from their station in the Texas Panhandle by train, soon joined the Company D detachment at Hempstead. As yet there was no riot, but there was definite need for more than one Ranger.

Subsequent to their handiwork with hammerless scatterguns, McDade and Springfield and several of their faction, aided by Sheriff Tom McDade, all heavily armed, had commandeered Waller County's courthouse as a place of refuge and re-thinking. As the head Ranger in town, Captain Sam McMurry stepped to the mark. Though the courthouse was cordoned by Durbin, Outlaw, Lindsey, and the others from Company B, as the ranking Ranger onsite Captain McMurry acted alone, entering the courthouse for a confab with the sheriff. Generally known for his soft spoken manner and easygoing style—averse to ever playing to the press for self-aggrandizement like some better known Ranger captains would do, Captain Sam McMurry was also known for his no nonsense demeanor and controlled courage: He'd not bulldoze anyone, but no man would run over him.[30] The Texas Ranger captain's demand was plainspoken: He would and was going to have his prisoners. Sheriff McDade needed time to think. Captain McMurry thought until morning would be right. In the meantime, outside, Captain McMurry ordered the eighteen Rangers to "get their Guns in good order that he was going to take McDade and Springfield the next morning."[31]

No doubt fidgeting throughout the long night, trying to make up their minds whether to shoot or surrender, when the sun shone down on Six-Shooter Junction that next day at the crack of dawn, Jack McDade and Dick Springfield, counseled by the sheriff, capitulated to common sense. They were arrested and stood their Preliminary Hearing. Before climbing the stairway to watch the legal show in the second floor courtroom, two steely-eyed Texas Rangers disarmed the McDade faction, temporarily seizing seventeen guns and "a great many more pistols."[32]

Complying with the letter of the law and affording defense lawyers the opportunity to fairly represent their clients the hearing dragged on; calling witnesses and taking testimony and not an inordinate amount of time devoted to security issues. When, at the end of nearly two weeks, the lower court bound the defendants over for trial, bail was denied. Though Captain McMurry and his full complement of manpower were no longer needed at Hempstead, he detailed Company B Rangers George R. Adamson and James Magruder "Grude" Britton to remain in Waller County, temporarily assigned to J. Walter Durbin's detachment, then consisting of but the corporal and Private Outlaw, Private Ed Lindsey having voluntarily opted out of Ranger service to secure more lucrative prospects, later becoming a federal officer.[33]

Initially defendants McDade and Springfield were—under Texas Ranger guard—transferred to Brenham, Washington County and into the jail of County Sheriff N.E. Dever, it having been deemed foolhardy to have Sheriff McDade looking after these prisoners at his partisan facility.[34] All too soon—within a week—word was picked up regarding a plot to put the boys out of jail. Corporal Durbin in a surprise move took custody of the prisoners scooting them off to Austin, where he thought he could count on the faithful cooperation of Sheriff Malcom M. Hornsby. Alas, the Travis County Jail was undergoing renovation, new cells were being installed and the sheriff could not accept any new prisoners. Absent a jail to hold the prisoners, until they could obtain a proper court order, Corporal Durbin and, as will be seen most likely Privates Outlaw and Britton, simply remained in town for a day or two with prisoners confined by their watchful eyes. Not soon enough the prisoners were escorted to balmy and breezy Galveston where the sheriff, the multi-termed and well regarded Patrick Tiernan was overseeing an impressive brick and barred edifice, and was instructed to hold the prisoners for trial under District Court Judge William H. Burkhart's authority.[35]

When it came time for trial, rather than release prisoners McDade and Springfield to Sheriff McDade, Corporal Durbin was specifically ordered by Judge Burkhart to escort the defendants to Hempstead for their courtroom appearance.[36] That Baz Outlaw was involved in this transfer is fixed by Durbin: "I taken 2 men Outlaw and Britton and returned with Prisoners next day."[37] Although the McDade faction felt betrayed, it should come as no shocker the trial—on a motion for a change of venue—was moved to Houston.[38] The Rangers escorted the prisoners to that point, where the accused murderers eventually earned prison time; McDade eight years and Springfield caught the quarter—a quarter of a century.

The brouhaha was not over at Hempstead. Six-Shooter Junction had a reputation to fertilize. Two young warriors from the McDade tribe put on their figurative war-paint, fueled their idiocy with fire-water, and began whooping and shooting on Hempstead's hardly ever peaceful main thoroughfare—right downtown. Rushing to the scene were an irate and inexperienced but armed gang of citizens intent on converting chaos to calm. Perhaps the saloon man was wobbly due to twisting the cork, maybe not, but his trigger-finger was itchy and he carelessly let loose a round from his Winchester. The would-be lawmen gasped. A surprised shooter screamed in agony, having "shot off his big toe." Rather dryly Corporal Durbin noted: "that broke up the citizens Gun club for that night." Real Rangers put the bad boys in jail.[39]

Another fellow should have paid attention to the fact Rangers were put in Waller County not for monkey-business but to enforce the law—regardless. A black man rode into town, stopped at a Hempstead barroom and bought a bottle of whiskey. Outside, while stepping into the stirrup the six-shooter he was wearing under his blouse was momentarily exposed. Notified of the illegality, Corporal Durbin mounted a horse, caught up with and confronted the fellow—it turned Western. When the "negro" was asked about the concealed six-shooter, the fellow reached for his hip pocket and then, according to the corporal, "Jumped the Horse from me and pulled the pistol[.] I fired Killing him instantly[.] He fell from the Horse and never Spoke a word," J. Walter Durbin's .45-caliber bullet "had gone clear through his body near the Hart."[40]

A very similar situation had taken place that spring for another Company D Ranger—Captain Frank Jones. While home at Boerne visiting an ailing daughter, a Kendall County deputy sheriff asked the captain to lend a hand with the capture of "a man who was wanted in several Counties for felonies." Captain Jones was never known to shirk duty or hide from responsibility, though his report could have been spiked with more detail. He simply advised Ranger headquarters at Austin: "We found the party about 3 miles from here and when we demanded his surrender he Caught for a pistol he had in his pants and wheeled the horse and ran. We killed the horse and it is thought fatally wounded the man. He is now in jail."[41]

Fellows not in jail were those Navarro County fence-cutters. Whatever were the reasons or reason John R. Hughes' undercover investigation was a bust. Safely removing himself from Navarro County, Private Hughes took time during a stopover at Waco to update Captain Sieker:

> I was getting along very well with the fence cutters until some one made a confident of the rong [*sic*] man and gave the whole thing away. . . . they are the best organized band that I ever worked after. They keep spies out all the time. . . .[42]

The who, why, and wherefores of spilling the beans—purposefully or unintentionally—about Private Hughes' role as an undercover operative falls into and cannot rise above conjecture's deep well of murkiness. At any rate, after leaving Navarro County the ineffective Texas Ranger returned to Company D headquarters in South Texas, apparently to a not overawed and thoroughly unimpressed captain: "June 18—Prvt. Hughes returned to Camp from Navarro County having been sent there from Wharton County to try and work up some fence-cutting cases, failed to accomplish anything. . . . out 34 Days, mched 1000 miles."[43]

Notably less than thrilled with the outcome in Navarro County thus far, yet passionate with desire for Rangers to put a mark on the scorecard, the adjutant general tasked Sergeant Ira Aten with doing what Private John Hughes had not done—infiltrate the haunts and hangouts of the Navarro County fence-cutters, gather admissible evidence, make apprehensions, jail said felons if they peacefully submitted to lawful arrests—kill 'em if they didn't! Taking Ranger Private Jim King with him and using the pseudonym Ira Wheeler, Company D's sergeant struck the road for Navarro County that sweltering July of 1888.[44]

Interestingly and it makes for its own story, Sergeant Aten, on the one hand, met with no more real success in Navarro County catching fence-cutters in the act than had Private Hughes. Principally due to the fact Navarro County ranchmen, suffering financial devastation, were not continually rebuilding fences only to have them destroyed shortly thereafter. Realistically, there was no wire to cut. On the other hand, figuratively dying of boredom Sergeant Aten either came up with an idea on his own merit or plagiarized the plan.[45] He would, and so he advised Ranger headquarters, ingeniously build some "booms." The destructive devices would be jerry-rigged with a charge of dynamite and a double-barreled 12 gauge, both buried underground, affixed to a hardly noticeable section of smooth wire linking the shotgun's trigger to the fence to be cut. Subsequent to cutting, inertia of the once taught strand of whipsawing barbed-wire would in turn discharge the interred shotgun's blast—a booster charge—into the slyly secreted explosives. To what end, what outcome? The damn fence-cutter would be blown to smithereens—no sympathy, no prisoners, no substantial expense, and no courtroom drama.[46]

Needless to say that when the Ranger front office and the governor learned that their Ace undercover operative in Navarro County was concocting a plan to indiscriminately vaporize unsuspecting fence-cutters they were the ones detonating with displeasure and panic. What would happen if ten-year-old Sally and her six-year-old brother John, playing Hide & Seek, inadvertently and unconsciously brushed against a booby-trapped fence? Sergeant Ira Aten was ordered out of Navarro County—right fast! There is no evidence or substantive reason to believe that Sergeant Aten ever constructed a "boom" and surreptitiously placed it along a fence line. There is good reason to postulate that once the possibility of such a device being planted leaked to the public, it served as a deterrent to folks mulling over the wisdom of snipping wire and taking a chance on being launched into eternity. So, in the short go Aten's strategy was sound, it removed him from Navarro County: Long term, the unintended consequences were measurable—a decline in fence-cutting.[47]

Back at Hempstead the Company D detachment could not have been caught off guard with the move underfoot—Sheriff Tom McDade's fiscal books were undergoing some eagle-eye scrutiny. It was perfectly clear to the Texas Rangers and honest citizens that, despite their not wanting it to be true, the sheriff had been "getting from bad to worse." Too, subsequent to that meticulous accounting and numbers crunching it soon became perfectly clear that those financial shortages of Waller County's scarce monies were not due to some inadvertent clerical errors. The sheriff was removed from office.[48]

That Baz Outlaw was yet part of the Company D detachment stationed at Hempstead is plain: Authenticated by official Texas Ranger correspondence. In fact, he was "still on duty here" even though having been "sick" a short time during the month of August.[49] Private Baz Outlaw, ever feisty, was rip-roaring and ready to go by mid-September 1888. John Culey could attest to that. On September 14 he opted to forego a gunplay or fight and go peacefully with Private Outlaw. Baz had arrested him for Theft of Cattle and delivered him into the hands of Waller County Sheriff R.M. Thornton, who had been appointed to replace the ousted Tom McDade.[50]

Toward month's end, the twenty-fifth of September, Corporal Durbin and his little detachment, including Private Baz Outlaw, were on the move again. Via a stopover at Austin, then offloading their horses, pack mule, and provisions at Laredo, on orders straight out of the adjutant general's office the detachment was to report at Rio Grande City.[51] At widely scattered points throughout South Texas other Company D Rangers had received like instructions: Private Hughes and four men scouting through counties along the Lower Rio Grande Valley; Private Jim Robinson and one man abruptly turned around in Nueces County near Banquete, the jumping off place for folks heading south across the Wild Horse Desert, and were now making tracks for rendezvousing with their fellow Rangers. Captain Jones and three Texas Rangers, likewise, were on the march with Rio Grande City as their destination.[52] On horseback and rail they came. By the thirtieth day of September all was good. The broadly disbursed Rangers had obediently complied with orders: All was not so good in Starr County though.

With telegraph wires humming, official communiqués crisscrossing in the hurried mail, and newspapers carrying hard truths liberally peppered with unverified gossip and specious rumors, there's little doubt that Private Outlaw—smart as a whip—took in the news about where he had been and where he was going. Behind him in Waller County the quarrel was yet alive and well. Private Baz Outlaw and his fellow Texas Rangers learned that ex Sheriff Tom McDade had been bushwhacked: fatally gunned down by a fellow that would become the son-in-law of the slain newsman whose article had ignited and fueled the feud in the first place.[53]

In front of Baz Outlaw lay uncertainty. Much like the sometimes restless and sometimes docile river marking Starr County's southern boundary and laying its claim to America's sovereignty, the bona fide state of affairs at Rio Grande City were roiling with ambiguity. As a ground-level trooper Ranger Private Baz Outlaw had been—as would be expected of all good lawmen—commissioned to obey orders, certainly not at liberty to pick and choose based on his personal interpretative spin. Thus, whether or not borderland newspaperman Catarino Erasmo Garza Rodriquez was a firebrand or fool or patriot was—or should have been—irrelevant. Laying aside the rights or wrongs, the jingoistic justifications or the lame excuses there is a hard and readily definable bottom line. Suspected kidnapper Abraham Recéndez, a prisoner, had been mortally gunned down during an abortive try at jumping out of custody and making for the river. So lawmen held. Garza said and editorialized it was murder. U.S. Customs Inspector and former Texas Ranger Victor Sebree felt the stinging accusations, grading them as insolently defaming and criminally libelous. Then or now in Texas, publicly and indelibly labeling someone an "assassin" and a "coward" in newsprint was/is a dicey proposition.

Who pulled for pistols first—there are competing versions—at Rio Grande City is vague. Second place in a gunfight is never reserved—by choice. On that twenty-first day of September 1888, exhibiting he was pretty handy with a six-shooter, Victor Sebree reached for the premium—the blue ribbon—but he did it on the run. While Catarino Garza and Federico López were leaking blood and nursing nonfatal bullet wounds and hunting for lost pride, their friends and supporters were hunting too—for Victor Sebree's head on a platter. The embattled U.S. Customs Inspector expeditiously sought and was granted refuge behind the fearsome-looking Gatling Gun at nearby Fort Ringgold, under command of the no-nonsense Colonel David R. Clendenin. Drawing up short of actually storming the fort, the fuming and furious lynch mob made demands for Sebree. Though the good colonel's words are lost for an exacting quotation, their essence is quite clear: The infuriated mob could pound sand or go to hell or lock and load. Making war on a warrior is chancy at best, perhaps even suicidal.[54]

Figuratively the run amok crowd shot themselves in the foot, a self-inflicted wound of idiocy. Someone among the armed swarm snipped the telegraph wire connecting Fort Ringgold with the outside world. It was a momentous blunder. To register as an effectual tactical move the lines of communication should have been cut prior to any outgoing messages. In this instance, the cutting was behind not before a telegrapher had sounded the alarm. The U.S. Army's command staff at the nation's capitol, the governor of Texas, and the state's adjutant general, were all in the loop and, in turn, plain orders had trickled down expeditiously triggering the deployment of Rangers and county sheriffs riding as the headmen of resolute posses, all hurrying to Rio Grande City. For anyone of sound mind to think civil—much less military—authorities would have not reacted quickly and decisively subsequent to irately disposed and armed folks flexing their muscles in the face of a colonel commanding an army garrison would be puerile. Texas Rangers from both Company D and Company F, as well as Sheriff Santigo Brito and eighty men from Cameron County (county seat Brownsville) and thirty tough men riding under the leadership of Sheriff James M. McGloin of San Patricio County (seat Sinton) and a few more from Hidalgo County (Edinburg), were dispatched by the state's chief executive. Were a throng of irascible hotheads from Rio Grande City really desirous of wetting their oars in troubled waters? If so, then, Texas officialdom at Austin would chart the course with its six-shooter surrogates, the Texas Rangers. Private Baz Outlaw was but one of the several.

And one of those several, though a good man most of the time, was causing the captain heartburn. It was the perennial problem facing the Texas Rangers' management team, the workforce were but human beings, a dynamic ruinous to mythical notions of around-the-clock perfection and flawless discipline. Private Wood Saunders had stepped in it—again.[55] This time, before Captain Frank Jones could devote his efforts and attention to the righteous mess from a near riotous mob and the upcoming November elections in Starr County—a hotbed of volatile local politics—the whiskey bottle, well, what was once inside the bottle had refocused his mind. What was he to do? Exactly how long he mulled it over is understandably obscure, but the verdict he reached is clear-cut and plainspoken. From Rio Grande City the captain advised the adjutant general: "I discharged Private J.W. Saunders yesterday on account of drunkenness and gave him pay certificate. . . ."[56]

Though the number is approximate, some three dozen Starr County denizen also owned certificates with their names affixed—arrest warrants charging them with Conspiracy to Murder and Assault to Murder, allegations stemming from the so-called race riot, which in truth had been somewhat overblown and sensationalized, there having been no firefights, funerals, or financial destruction worthy of note—but for the telegraph wire. Truths by and large backed up by Colonel Clendenin's detached and neutral appraisal.[57] Nevertheless, Starr County's grand jury heard testimony, making its formalized returns, while a local justice of the peace accepted signed and sworn Complaints, automatically issuing additional arrest warrants.

Joined by Lieutenant James Abijah Brooks commanding Company F and his 1st Sergeant John Harris Rogers and their rank and file Rangers, Company D's Captain Frank Jones began blueprinting his plans and outfitting his legions for an unshakable enforcement action.[58] The ensuing roundup of individuals at Rio Grande City and downriver at the village of Roma was executed absent a serious glitch, perhaps at least in part to Corporal Durbin's straightforward and unsmiling pledge: "the Rangers will attend to all the killing to be done in this county for a while."[59] Private Baz

Outlaw's participation in these arrests is by inference, rather than by specific mention: He was, provably, at the time working that section of the Rio Grande borderlands. The Monthly Return summarizing this string of arrests is understandably concise, the arrests being conducted by "Companies 'D' and 'F'" with no Rangers identified by name.[60]

During the following month, November 1888, Private Outlaw is particularly mentioned as the lead officer, along with a Company F Ranger, on a six-day scout into Hidalgo County where they were looking to arrest a fellow named Ybarro wanted in connection with a homicide there and theft of livestock in DeWitt County (Cuero). Rather efficiently it seems the suspect was scooped up and the two Rangers physically delivered their prisoner to Hidalgo County's two-story brick jailhouse on Esperanza Street near the Rio Grande, where the arrestee was confined.[61] At this point in time, the Frontier Battalion's Baz Outlaw—at least evinced by the official reports and correspondence—was making a good name for himself as a Texas Ranger.

Having more-or-less accomplished his mission in Starr County—though the cases against the supposed rioters would eventually be dismissed—Captain Jones was instructed to reposition Company D once more, this time in Uvalde County or thereabouts.[62] Taking advantage of the company's downtime Captain Jones left transportation details to Corporal Durbin's discretion, other than the specific order not to layover at Laredo. Captain Jones would visit home at Boerne for a brief furlough.

The old adage, "While the cat's away the mice will play," seems but appropriate at this juncture in Ranger Private Baz Outlaw's narrative. Corporal J. Walter Durbin unerringly recalls, "He [Captain Jones] gave me orders not to stop over night in Laredo."[63] A guarded suspicion that Rangers of Company D might venture across the Rio Grande and bend to a good time in Nuevo Laredo's neighborhood now euphemistically known as "Boys' Town" was but shrewd. Captain Jones knew—had to have known—that his hormonally charged warriors might fervently embrace an overnight indulgence of fiery mescal, enjoying the company and pleasures of flashily attired and hot-blooded *senoritas*. Durbin rationalized the unauthorized layover, laying it off on having to obtain needed provisions. And for the story at hand, there may be a clue to Baz Outlaw's future, for it is at this place in J. Walter Durbin's memoirs he pointedly reflects: "I had 15 men Some of them was fussy and dangerous when drinking."[64] Baz qualified on both counts.

J. Walter Durbin, standing at left, had been specifically asked for by Captain Frank Jones, Commander of Company D. Upon transferring into his new company Durbin was promoted to corporal and placed in charge of the four-man Texas Ranger detail dispatched to Wharton to investigate several vicious—and racially motivated—murders. *Courtesy Suzanne Giffin-Garcia.*

Ranger Private Dennis Edward "Ed" Lindsey, B.D. Lindsey's cousin, along with Privates Baz Outlaw and John Hughes were suitably chosen for the extremely hazardous investigative assignment at Wharton. *From Texas Ranger Sketches courtesy the author Robert W. Stephens.*

Samuel Alexander "Sam" McMurry, the soft-spoken Captain of Company B, a Ranger guaranteed to tackle assignments with pluck and grit—but more importantly—with common sense and coolness. *Courtesy Tobin and Anne Armstrong Ranger Research Center, Texas Ranger Hall of Fame & Museum.*

James Magruder "Grude" Britton, one of Sam McMurry's fire-breathing Company B Rangers, worked closely with Rangers J. Walter Durbin and Baz Outlaw during the aftermath of the violent Waller County brouhaha at Hempstead, aka, Six-Shooter Junction. *From Texas Ranger Sketches courtesy the author, Robert W. Stephens.*

Sheriff John Hornsby's Travis County Jail at Austin. Texas Rangers Durbin, Outlaw, and Britton tried to ensconce prisoners here, but alas, the hoosegow was undergoing renovation and Rangers had to take prisoners to the county lockup at breezy seaside beaches of Galveston. Disagreeable duty—it's presumed! *Courtesy Doug Dukes.*

John Woodard "Wood" Saunders, certainly a gutsy and capable Ranger. Like his plucky comrade in arms Baz Outlaw, Saunders would sometimes bend to a liquor bottle's amber current of foolishness, launching his canoe on the metaphorical Whiskey River. *COURTESY NITA STEWART HALEY MEMORIAL LIBRARY AND J. EVETTS HALEY HISTORY CENTER.*

Nearly forgotten today, the introduction of newfangled barbed-wire throughout the Lone Star State was rife with controversy and bloodshed, forcing Governor John Ireland to call a Special Session of the Texas Legislature to make fence cutting a felony. Donald M. Yena with his chilling *Fence Cutter's Hot Lead and Tempers* brings awestruck spectators into the deadly affray. COURTESY THE ARTIST, DON YENA.

Elijah Robert "E.R." Ashcraft was a Brown County fellow with active membership in the Farmers Alliance, a group more-or-less sympathetic to and in league with those fellows not scared by a midnight wire snipping venture. Family lore—by some folks—is not shy with implications that occasionally the bearded E.R. Ashcraft would handily grab his shotgun and nippers, disappearing into the night. *Courtesy Jan Devereaux.*

Though a replica, pictured here is the "boom" contraption undercover Ranger Ira Aten thought would put an end to folks' fence cutting careers. Thus far there is no evidence such a device was ever placed along a fence-line, but such was not known to the Knights of Knippers. The mere chance of being blown to smithereens served as a deterrent. Not surprisingly acts of illegally cutting someone else's barbed-wire appreciably waned after word of this tactic leaked—no doubt as intended and anticipated. *Courtesy Tobin and Anne Armstrong Ranger Research Center, Texas Ranger Hall of Fame & Museum.*

James Abijah Brooks, famed Ranger captain. Although the jury of absoluteness has yet rendered the final verdict, several knowledgeable Old West photograph collectors credit this image as a heretofore unpublished image of Captain Brooks and his company of ready for action and readily armed Rangers. *Courtesy Donald M. and Louise Yena Collection.*

Pictured here as a Texas Ranger Captain, John Harris Rogers, seated on the chair second from left, at an earlier time during the Frontier Battalion era, was 1st Sergeant of Company F while his valued contemporary Baz Outlaw maintained an equal noncommissioned officer's position with Company D. *Courtesy Tobin and Anne Armstrong Ranger Research Center, Texas Ranger Hall of Fame & Museum.*

Chapter 5

One of the Worst and Most Dangerous

BY CHRISTMAS OF 1888 THE COMPANY D CAMP alongside the Leona River, six miles from alluring Uvalde, had been reactivated.[1] Private Baz Outlaw wasn't allowed an overabundance of time for sitting around at Camp Leona stuffing himself with scrumptiously roasted wild turkey or wandering into Uvalde to sample any other delicious pleasures or whiffs of perfume the town might afford young men. Three days after the holiday Private Outlaw and two others, riding under command of Corporal Durbin, were in the saddle headed for the broken and rocky Devils River Country west of Uvalde, hunting hard for a herd of stolen cattle and the yahoos pushing them for the border.[2] The search—although unproductive—would consume eleven grueling horseback days, covering an estimated 400 miles."[3] Of this slice of Texas geography and of the jaunt back toward Company D's camp, Corporal Durbin remarked: "wee filled canteens and set out east across the devide for neauces which wee struch next Day and started down by Kickepooh Springs & aney one who read this that has come down the Neauces will Say no other Place in Tex with so much Rock as this Route."[4] Despite melodrama masquerading as truth, sometimes the Mounties don't always get their man—and neither do legendary Texas Rangers. Due to inclement weather most of the remaining month of January was spent gathering wood, huddling around the campfires, and trying to stay warm and dry in deteriorating wall tents that often leaked like sieves.[5] Real camp life isn't always idyllic. Biting cold winds can blow romanticism to the next county in a jiffy.

As the weather began to break in the Rangers' favor, Private Baz Outlaw, apparently working alone, was sent to Eagle Pass. His task was to locate and arrest George Holmes, a fugitive from Uvalde County wanted for Theft of Cattle. Although the wanted man had skipped for parts unknown—probably just across the Rio Grande—Frank Jones' selecting and sending Private Outlaw on this mission seems to suggest the captain had every confidence that this Ranger could act independent of supervision and close oversight.[6]

Later that same month, March 1889, subsequent to bodies of three women and a man being found floating in the Rio Grande upriver from Eagle Pass the previous month, a befuddled private citizen took pen in hand. Former Ranger B.D. Lindesy, then operating the Tariff Saloon, wrote to Captain Frank Jones suggesting that someone should "have the country in this neighborhood thoroughly examined for some clue to this horrible murder. . . . and some effort Should be made to ferret out this murderer. . . ."[7] Herein will not be the place to scrutinize the step by step investigation conducted by the Texas Rangers regarding this dreadful crime—at the time a genuine whodunit. Eventually, subsequent to some super sleuthing and the application of rudimentary forensics—comparing known dental work to the deceased—Sergeant Ira Aten and his protégé Private Hughes closed the case with an identifiable and chargeable defendant, Richard H. "Dick" Duncan, a "red-headed, dancing, idling, singing cowboy, who'd as soon go to a fight as a frolic."[8] In due time, after arrest, courtroom conviction, and more than one unsuccessful motion before the appellate courts, an unrepentant Duncan, clinging to an avowal of innocence, was hanged behind the tall fence at Maverick County's jail-yard. The high-profile investigation was a legit public relations coup for the Texas Rangers as institutional crime fighters and a feather in Sergeant Aten's hat in particular.[9]

Spring of 1889 would also exhibit that Private Baz Outlaw was mobile—as all Rangers were expected to be. Two sheriffs in West Texas, both former Texas Rangers, Sheriff Pat Dolan from Jeff Davis County and Baz's old boss, Sheriff J.T. Gillespie of Brewster County, were clamoring for help. The call would not go unanswered. From Ranger headquarters the adjutant general ordered Captain Jones to handpick five Rangers, detailing them for law enforcing work in "that Section. . . ." If more Texas Rangers were needed, the man in charge of the detachment, Corporal J. Walter Durbin, was to make that assessment known.[10] On 25 April 1889 after marshaling the necessary supplies Privates Baz Outlaw, Charles B. Barton, John Reynolds Hughes and Charles Henry Vanvalkenburg "Charley" Fusselman mounted up and headed for faraway West Texas.[11] Corporal Durbin would follow by train later. That Private Outlaw, specifically mentioned in the Monthly Return, and his crew were to travel by horseback rather than rail was dictated straight out of the Ranger front office. The adjutant general was cognizant of the fact that a touch of favorable public relations and the corresponding degrees of authentic preventive enforcement could be had: "By scouting the country as they go along [with horses and wagon], they may render assistance to the civil authorities on the route and being Seen by everyone, their presence may have a good moral effect."[12] In the end, after being on the road eighteen days and covering 400-odd miles, Baz Outlaw and the detachment pulled into Brewster County, establishing a Company D satellite camp near Alpine on May 11, 1889.[13] Much to the detachment's chagrin or delight they quickly learned that their immediate boss, Corporal Durbin, had stepped off the train at Alpine's depot two days earlier after his leisurely trip by train.[14]

Private Baz Outlaw, having already pulled a stint as a Company E Texas Ranger in this section of the Lone Star during an 1885–1887 timeframe would forgo his state-paid salary, having been at Alpine less than a whole week. He could double his pay elsewhere; say, south of the border down Mexico way.

Captain Frank Jones' brother-in-law, William O. "Bill" O'Grady, was in a pickle. The mining executive, connected with the Fronteriza excavations taking place at Sierra del Carmen, State of Coahuila, Mexico, was desperately in need of firepower—in the form of gritty fighting men, true-blue and trustworthy. Whether he turned to his relative by marriage, Captain Jones, or simply penned a letter to J. Walter Durbin would, in the final analysis, only yield meaningless debate. It would be—for history's sake—the ultimate outcome that carried any major weight. Eyeing opportunity to fatten their wallets, J. Walter Durbin, Baz Outlaw, and John Hughes tendered their resignations to the State of Texas, accepting positions as single-minded and unwavering guards guaranteeing valuable wagon-loads of precious metal would make it to an intended destination unmolested.[15]

Unfortunately this phase of Ranger Baz Outlaw's tale has been sometimes and somewhat corrupted—perhaps unwittingly—but setting the record straight is obligatory. The three former Texas Rangers were working as autonomous hired-guns, with no longer an official connection to the auspiciously valuated Frontier Battalion. Therefore, any inference that this trio "as three of the toughest men in Texas" had been selected by Captain Jones to insure Company D tentacles reached across the border and deep into Mexico and that he had "named Hughes as head guard" is flat wrong—an instance of misleading mythmaking.[16] The three were acting as independent contractors, selling their services to private enterprise.

Prior to departing for the supposed profitable sojourn in Mexico, Corporal Durbin informally nominated Charley Fusselman as the man to fill his supervisory boots as the Alpine detachment's non-commissioned officer. Captain Frank Jones acquiesced and promoted Fusselman to the rank, though he did note to Captain Sieker that Charley was "a good man" but that he was "somewhat lacking in experience, he having been in the service only a year." Referring to the surprising resignations of Durbin, Outlaw, and Hughes, Captain Jones duly mentioned to Captain Sieker: "Three of my best men have quit."[17]

Herein and at this point it's but also fitting—compellingly germane from a truth-telling perspective—to dispel suppositional nonsense that because of Baz's sour and "quarrelsome disposition" his fellow Rangers of Company D "had no use for him."[18] With indisputable history as his witness, at least to this stage in Baz Outlaw's story, he had plenty of friends and the well-earned respect of the Texas Ranger hierarchy at headquarters. The demons haunting Baz Outlaw's life may have been present from the get-go, but they were yet to raise their ugly and destructive heads—consistently.

The ex-Company D Rangers had been instructed to put their saddles in a sack, bring their Winchesters and report to the mines pronto. At Eagle Pass, or rather across the Río Bravo at Piedras Negras, the privately paid buccaneers were held up a day trying to clear Mexican customs officials' "red tape." The trio was, at length, allowed to move to the interior on the railway, though they had to have "Stamps pasted all over our [their] Saddles to get them across." Some eighty-odd miles south of the Texas/Mexico border the three international travelers left the comforts and convenience of riding the rails, acquired wagon transportation, and struck out overland for Santa Rosa, some 160 miles to the west, and from there on to the mining complex. For that sparsely populated stretch of space and at that time they never had to gaze at any prickly wire fence or step down and open a gate as "it was all open country."[19]

When but six miles from their objective they faced a daunting geographic challenge. The mining company had expended $7000 blasting and cutting a roadway from the side of and over the top of a very high mountain. On the opposite side, the wagons had to scarily descend into a "deep Gulch." J. Walter Durbin would note that he and his pals, Outlaw and Hughes, could watch it rain at the mountain's base, while but not one drop would fall on top—and vice versa. Wearily arriving at the mines about supper time the voyagers were met and heartily welcomed by R.H. McCracken of San Antonio, Superintendant and General Manager.[20]

Baz Outlaw and John Hughes didn't leave written descriptions of what they saw in regards to the physical layout of their new home away from home but, thankfully, J. Walter Durbin did. Herein repeated with his unique and colorful markers, his personal brand not blotched by any persnickety editing:

> . . . they had fine mashinery all complete for crushing ore washing it out asseying and run in to Silver Bars this mine was new did not have it complete at that time also had a Saw mill attached and cut out fine lumber from Pine timber up in the mountains which cut and pulled to different places and start It down where it would run and slide for a mile the wood to run the furnice was cut Hauled and pitched down same way and re loaded at bottom and Hauled to the mine Some as pretty Senery in that Gulch as I ever saw the Sun did not shine but a few Hours a day in such a deep canyon. . . . there was also a little Mex town up and down the Gulch Aney place they could find big a nough to set a little Shach Sell Mex trinckets and muscal and all other Mex drinks. . . .[21]

Demographics of the mining operations should not come as any big revelation. Employed at the mine were about "500 Mexicans" and roughly "50 white men." The native Spanish speakers were paid in "mex money" which—when valued against the American dollar—was cheap labor. Proficient and practiced *vaqueros* drove in and "Killed beefs every day" to feed the ravenous workforce and the attendant populace living or leeching off the money-spinning boom.[22]

The work expected of the ex-Rangers was simple on its face—extremely perilous in practice. They had traveled across hard and lonesome country on their trip to the mines after leaving the last railway station at Barroteran. Now, their chore was to reverse course, insuring the richly laden wagons pulled by six-mule teams traversed that 160 miles back to the jumping off place, so the treasure could be safely transported by train to wherever and ultimately converted to cash. Between points A and Z was the home turf for cutthroats and unscrupulous co-conspirators with criss-crossed bandoliers stuffed plumb full. Previous shipments from the mine had been plagued by the prowling pirates.[23] It was not any job for timorous or fainthearted spirits, but it did pay "$60 american money a month."[24]

Keenly aware of the dangers in an isolated land where the reach of government and law enforcement was near nonexistent, the former Texas lawmen huddled and fashioned their plan. Atop each wagon loaded with silver bars weighing from 60 to 90 lbs. sat a dependable teamster capable of cajoling his half-dozen mules along the rudimentary roadway. The grand total of mineral wealth per wagon train was estimated—and it quite naturally varied—as being anywhere between $60,000 and $100,000. Supplementing the Mexican wagon-masters were a small crew of two or three advance guards, thoroughly trusted scouts who would as Durbin said, "look out all places where wee might be ambushed and fired on at close range without notice. . . ."[25] Hopefully, it was supposed, the departure dates being kept secret until the very last moment added an additional layer of security. Overseeing the movement of wagons and having each other's backs, the edgy band of ex-Ranger law-enforcing brothers had honed their protocols for protection. Subsequent to traveling hard for some forty or forty-five miles every day, as evening shadows began closing in, wagon drivers guided teams to a clear piece of ground, an opening not actually spotted on the roadway. Maintaining an obvious field-of-fire was never neglected. All campfires were extinguished at nightfall. Demonstrating there was not much expectation of treachery within, the Mexicans, who were "thoroughly armed" took their turns herding the livestock during the night. Closer in, Baz Outlaw, J. Walter Durbin, and John Hughes alternated keeping a watch over the wagons' valuable cargo. When not actually pulling their shift, the other two maintained readiness: "Slept with clothes Boots and cartge Belts and Six shooters belted on and winchester by side until wee reach Baretoran."[26]

Watchfulness was nourished twenty-four and seven. Negligence and/or inattention and/or plain sloppiness could extract a high price—a hard death could come easy. It was lonesome country for fortune-hunting foreigners on that rutted and jarring road connecting Sierra del Carmen and Barretoran. Writing that Baz Outlaw and John Hughes "had many narrow escapes from savage mountain lions and poisonous snakes," assuredly seems hyperbole ever so rich.[27]

Characterizing the job as "nerve-racking" might be an understatement. At any rate, upon reaching the depot and offloading silver bars the Texans were handed a written receipt acknowledging delivery. Prior to starting on the second leg of their two week round trip, a couple of days were spent relaxing men's backsides and resting the frazzled horses and mules. Then it was retracing steps to the mines, repacking the wagons, and returning to the grinding trek of guarding burdened wagons back to the forlorn railroad station. The thermometer of tension always registered feverishly high. The actual vomiting of bullets into bandits was scored as zip. The call for Outlaw, Durbin, and Hughes to grab their Winchesters and stand tall would be at the mine, not in the mountains.

Volatile labor unrest was and had been brewing. Though the drama associated with the expansion of organized trade unions in America is but scarcely cited in works chronicling the Wild West era, the labor movement was momentous—practically and philosophically, culturally and legally. Early on, before Baz Outlaw opted to gin money in Mexico, federal legislators at Washington, D.C. had enacted the Chinese Exclusion Act of 1882. The not insignificant Chinese workforce had been eagerly recruited and successfully immigrated into the United States to financially oblige American businessmen's insatiable demand for cheap labor during the furious development of transcontinental railway lines and the ensuing network of analogous rails feeding into them. Once the intense pressure on that front was somewhat relieved, Chinese laborers drifted into the arenas dominated by the heavily invested speculators concerned with exploiting the wealth an American West held underground and the flecks of promise washing about in her cold mountain streams. With treasures like gold, silver, and copper—and the premium deposits of multihued turquoise—the promise of riches was magnetic. Untold thousands crossed the Mississippi River chasing the rainbow's western tail end—and that big pot of delusionary gold. Afterwards, many with shattered dreams and empty pockets sat about toiling at back-breaking labor, employed by chance-taking capitalists and stockholders with money enough to invest in the costly machinery and manpower necessary for turning a profit—huge profits—by exploiting economic opportunity below ground. Threat of an economic stranglehold around necks of drudging workers pocketing a pittance spurred America's labor union escalation.[28]

The noise of collective bargaining north of the border bled into the psyche and imaginations of Mexican nationals toiling in open pits and underground mines: Properties nominally—in many instances—operated by American entrepreneurial executives and their staff of skilled and well-paid underlings. The disparities regarding issues of compensation were wide. Mexicans were paid with Mexican money, Americans earned U.S. dollars—a valuation 50% to the plus.[29] So, while Baz Outlaw, J. Walter Durbin, and John Hughes were on their second trip escorting wagon loads of richness across that 160 mile chunk of Mexico's treacherous and unforgiving and dangerous real-estate, busy minds were at work. Not exactly in the dark and dank underground mines but in the squatty adobe and picket hovels and *cantinas* and cathouse cribs scattered about on uneven ground in that aforementioned deep gulch: Dire whispers were echoing in the canyon. Big plans were on the drawing board, but not in the boardroom.

Strident voices had whipped the lower-tier employees—the Mexicans—into a grievance-settling frenzy. Shortly after their onerous two-week jaunt over the mountain and back, Company D's former Rangers met unstable and hot-tempered reality. The Mexican miners were on strike. To punctuate their displeasure with wages and working conditions the incensed demonstrators had "went to the Powder House and taken a lot of it" and then proceeded to ignore the shift whistle and staked their open-air headquarters on a hill overlooking the mine. Whether they had dynamite or nitroglycerin or both is not a matter of record, but the potential for an eardrum-busting and earth-shattering explosion was feasible. Bloodletting beyond that, well, that was anyone's guess. It was tetchy!

Superintendent McCracken was in no mood for such madness, nor were Messers Outlaw, Durbin, and Hughes—they were fighting men to the core. They'd back his hard play regardless the odds. With the tubular magazines of their Winchesters topped-off and empty loops in their cartridge belts filled, the trio, Colt's six-shooters at their side, accompanied the superintendent as he activated his three-prong battle-plan.

First, McCracken simply shut down the mills, no production: no wages in want of settlement. The majority of the men working in the mill houses "was white and was getting good pay." Secondly, given that those fellows would naturally side with management should fireworks detonate, and since the company had thirty Winchesters under lock and key, grave uneasiness was somewhat diminished. The armory was unlocked, the weapons were issued. The former Texas Rangers now stood with a private little army covering their play. Lastly, the company store was, if not padlocked, closed for business. No mining, no munching. For these three native sons of the Old Southwest—or imports—the colloquial Mexican Standoff was at hand. Bazzell L. Outlaw, John R. Hughes, and J. Walter Durbin didn't flinch or fade. They were hired guns, their nerves were forged from hard steel, their backbones ramrod straight.[30]

Time stood still. Despite any justifiable complaints and regardless any groundless grumbling, the striking miners had placed themselves in an untenable situation. Somewhat realizing the futility of doing nothing, the protesters picked a couple of spokesmen and sent them down the hill to palaver with Superintendant McCracken. The message he owned was clear: The strikers had no food, no guns, no hope of drawing money—even Mexican money—for idleness. Furthermore, they best get back on the job or they would be replaced with miners more thirsty for work than they. Too, if they really entertained any foolish ideas about blowing something up or testing his personal Rangers' resolve, especially when backed up by his Winchester-toting millhouse men, well, by God, let the snake strike! Zest for the labor strike wilted.[31]

For the Three Musketeers of this story, their gusto at pursuing leisure time pleasures seemed much stronger than the striking miners' eagerness for redressing any right or supposed wrongs. Though it does necessitate reading between the lines, J. Walter

Durbin particularly noted the quaintness and allure of Santa Rosa, then a village of about four thousand. In fact he graded the town as being "one of the prettiest little places that I have saw in Mexico." The enchanting site according to Durbin's remembrances had a clear stream running through—bisecting—the town with large fig trees shading its banks. Santa Rosa's charming plaza was surrounded by natural benches carved from native stone, and the little quadrangle was festooned with gorgeous plants and shrubbery. Indeed, it must have been a welcome oasis because, as the thoroughly impressed Durbin submissively reported, "wee always stopped off a day here on return to the mines."[32] Sound argument could not be credibly proffered that Santa Rosa wasn't charming and enticing. But one might register as naïve any belief that the boys laid over at Santa Rosa solely because of its aesthetic appeal. Celibacy and church, it's a pretty safe bet, was not the attraction. Sane men—smart men—never put to paper every detail. Sometimes, some things are best left unsaid. Santa Rosa was a nice place.

Sometimes Baz Outlaw wasn't nice. And it is at this juncture, while in Mexico, that the breakdown in good behavior emerged and, lamentably, it wasn't churned cream rising to the top. Bending to whiskey bottles' pull in his case would lead to hangovers, headaches, heartbreaks, and headstones. There is and has been a misnomer regarding Baz and booze. The dismal transfusion replacing his red blood with bourbon's amber current was not a single injection, an overnight transition. Deterioration by definition is progression. Though it's the bane of a storyteller's methodology, jumping into and out of correct chronology, temporarily pausing Baz Outlaw's tale is but decent. Many, if not most, writers chronicling his story suppose—assume—the last day of his life is the way he lived all days of his life—which is and would be a wrongheaded theory: Certainly an armchair hypothesis not creditably scaffold by fact.

There is, however, a hardcore reality to remember. Drinking and dumbness are not synonyms. Not all imbibers do imbecilic things. Not all abstainers are admirable. A blood/alcohol mixture does not automatically preclude someone from doing the right thing. During other cheerless occasions sour-mash and stupidity are bedfellows. A precursor for passably understanding—not necessarily approving—of Baz Outlaw's life story is plain. Sometimes he did drink hard liquor. Sometimes while drunk—or nearly drunk—he did good things. Sometimes while in his cups he may or may not have acted judiciously, decisions Ranger management and history would judge. And, yes, sometimes while in the bottle his behavior was atrocious, deplorable for any day. Certainly those dubious dustups that may be laid at Baz Outlaw's doorstep are the crux of a good Wild West story. Likewise, those very indiscretions and intemperate behaviors make for the underpinnings of a much broader storyline—upholding and maintaining discipline within an institutional framework.

Returning to the chronological story at hand, what follows most likely is true—at least to some extent—although an evident paper trail is elusive and probably nonexistent. With that caveat, Outlaw's south of the border gunplay will be replicated herein, as is generally penned by authors writing from secondary perspectives. Readers, like jurors sitting in the box, are allowed to weigh testimony and admissible evidence as they see fit.

Following the return from one of their trips, Outlaw, Durbin, and Hughes were given a few days of downtime to rest and recuperate, reclaiming a modicum of sanity from relentless caution. Durbin and Hughes remained at their quarters. Baz Outlaw, alone, wandered up the gulch and into a *cantina* or *casa*. The purpose of his visit is vague—left to imagination and speculation. What he found is unmistakable—trouble.

Whether the cause be a dark-haired brown-eyed beauty, the dexterous hand of a card-sharp cheat, or just a chip on someone's shoulder goes—in most renditions—unspoken and unwritten. Baz Outlaw had two Colt's six-shooters.[33] Pedro had a wicked looking and surely sharp knife. Moment by moment details of the interaction between Pedro and Baz are indistinct, excepting in all accounts the Georgia-born prodigal son was rip-roaring drunk. Fighting with guns is quite dissimilar to wanting to debone an adversary with blinding speed and the deft slice with a blade. Outlaw gunned down Pedro, before Pedro—likely drunk too—could close the gap and stick him. Then, Baz with six-shooters in hand and barking sour breath commands put the backs of Pedro's *amigos* against the wall.

Sometimes saddling and mounting the tiger is easy, getting off unscathed or uneaten is tricky. Pointing his pair of Colt's at the crowd, the hammers eared-back, Baz sidestepped the dead body and began backing his way toward deliverance. Assuredly those scared fellows with puckered posteriors pressed against the wall, hands held high, had not the slightest thoughts of heroism. Just to punctuate a sentence of intimidating warning, Baz Outlaw let loose a round into the floor—he wasn't joking.

Once outside, purportedly, Durbin and Hughes, who upon hearing the two gunshots had rushed to the hubbub, acted decisively. According to this version they "pinioned" Baz Outlaw's flailing arms and "twisted his wrists" causing him to release the tight grip on his six-shooters. Still unable to control their belligerent friend who was fighting them "furiously," either Hughes or Durbin—maybe both—thumped him on the head with one of his own Colt's and then "carried him quickly back to their quarters and placed him on a bunk."[34]

Not surprisingly, if one outright accepts the validity of this part of the story, the three privateers, knowing that Pedro's friends with lynch-mob mentality would soon surround their cabin, made ready for war. They would never, no matter what Baz Outlaw had done—fair and square or foul and mean—voluntarily give him over to certain death in front of a firing squad or dangling from a stout tree limb. No way *José*!

Dousing their light, the three waited for further developments which were not long in coming. A group of Mexicans assembled outside their abode's front door. With trepidation on the one side, apprehension on the other, finally, level-headed communication untangled misgivings. Plainly it seems that Pedro was not popular—was considered an evil man—and God had rightly called him home or sent him somewhere else. As far as Baz Outlaw and his pals were concerned there was no harm, no foul, and no sympathetic sniveling, but only good riddance to Pedro.[35] There was peace in the valley.

Interestingly, when J. Walter Durbin penned his memoirs he failed to mention this incident, which could lead down three divergent pathways: He simply and inadvertently overlooked it; there was, or would be some discomfort on his part vis-à-vis besmirching Baz's character for this episode; or, perhaps it didn't even happen in the first place. Durbin did, however, have this to say about Baz Outlaw, "I must say of all the bad men that I have knew he was one of the worst and most dangerous he never Knew what fear was."[36]

Feasibly some fellows that had been introduced to fear were the fellows heretofore harassing and robbing the shipments of silver leaving the mine or loads of supplies there destined on return trips. Since these no-nonsense ex-Rangers had answered the call for help, not a single wagon train had been approached, stopped, or high-jacked by bandits. Had the mere presence of the *Diablo Tejanos*—the Texas Devils—as Rangers were not lovingly known in South Texas and below the Rio Grande, had its salutary effect? Aside from Baz Outlaw's popping two caps and killing a Mexican—justifiably or not—the security detail's Winchesters and Colt's wheel-guns may have been oiled, loaded, and handy, but they had remained unfired. Not a single shot in anger or self-defense having been fired at a Mexican *mal hombre*.

Whether or not boredom was a factor is unknown. As would be if the to and fro trips over the mountain were just too taxing—physically or mentally, always being on alert around the clock: Sleeping in boots and belted twenty-four and seven with cartridges and a Colt's six-shooter as insurance. Anyhow, Baz Outlaw had seen enough of Mexico. Leaving Durbin and Hughes behind, Baz headed north, crossing the Rio Grande and making a show at Richmond, Fort Bend County. Captain Frank Jones welcomed him wholeheartedly. During their conversation Jones no doubt updated Outlaw about a few items of interest about the changing face of Company D and a couple of other matters, factors of worth then or in the future for Baz.

Perhaps first and foremost Sergeant Ira Aten was no longer a Texas Ranger. In what would go down in history as the Jaybird/Woodpecker War the county sheriff had been killed during a riot on August 16, 1889, shortly before Baz made his appearance at Richmond. The two political and warring factions had been at loggerheads regarding the temporary appointment of a sheriff, and Governor Ross—on the scene—demanded that they settle on Ranger Sergeant Aten who had an untarnished, though not always successful, reputation. On the twentieth day of August the fractious folks in Fort Bend County had a brand-new sheriff and the Texas Rangers of Company D were short a top-sergeant.

Baz Outlaw also learned that Captain Jones had promoted Charley Fusselman, yet stationed in the Big Bend Country, to replace Ira Aten as the 1st Sergeant for Company D. Although none could have possibly foreseen it at the time, Fusselman's upgrading within Ranger ranks would ultimately play into Baz Outlaw's thrilling and tragic Wild West narrative—in a big way. That Fusselman was deserving of promotion was undisputed. He was by any measure intrepid, racking up an impressive string of single-handed arrests and surviving a blistering shoot-out in which Mr. Badass bit the dust.[37] Sergeant Fusselman's stellar work was not only recognized at the company commander level—but the adjutant general was making note too: "I am glad to hear Such good report of Fusselman."[38]

At Richmond, during the recurrent Frontier Battalion's annual staffing and budgetary readjustments every September, Baz Outlaw had pledged he would reenlist in Company D on the first of the month. That Baz had been in Fort Bend County for the confab with his former boss is reasonably undeniable, as Captain Jones writing to the Ranger command staff from Richmond on preprinted letterhead stationery of The National Hotel on 29 August 29, 1889 expressly mentioned to the adjutant general, proudly it seems: "B.L. Outlaw will enlist again on the 1st of Sept. . . ."[39]

Company D's Monthly Return for September is just as explicit.[40] Four days later, if Ranger Private Outlaw made note of another personnel move, it is not a matter of record—but certainly he should have. Private James W. "Jim" King, who had previously seen hard service in more than one Ranger Company, including the perilous undercover duty in Navarro and Zavala Counties, messed up. Demon rum did him in—professionally. There can be little doubt it pained him to do so, but Captain Jones had been backed into an uncomfortable spot through no doings of his own. Ranger King was discharged for drunkenness, Captain Jones adding in his report to the adjutant general that "He has not been disorderly but is now too drunk to be efficient and it is impossible to Keep him sober."[41]

And therein, in that same missive to Texas Ranger headquarters at Austin, is one sentence that should—really does—dispel any notion that Ranger Private Baz Outlaw, at this point, had any widespread reputation as an out-of-control problem drinker or an alcoholic menace to good order and sound inter-company discipline: Captain Jones bragged, even after mustering in Baz Outlaw, "The balance of the men are sober and efficient and will reflect credit on the service anywhere they may be stationed."[42] Corrosion evolves over time.

What was not taking time to oxidize was the maliciousness and misbehavior of the previously alluded to Odle brothers. Though it took him time to brilliantly fashion his skullduggery after being transferred to the Williamson County jail at Georgetown, Alvin Odle successfully put his plan into play and skedaddled straight out of the calaboose and into infamy. The "spare made" and clean shaven Alvin would have—could have—blended well into ranks of the hundreds of nondescript cowboys herding cattle and riding the grub line, somewhat keeping a low profile and staying outside the law's notice. Alvin was different. The slightly cross-eyed twenty two year old was destined—by choice—to cut his notch in outlawry. By the time Baz Outlaw had reenlisted as a Company D Ranger, Alvin had joined his fugitive brother Will, and they were stealing and terrorizing that section known as the Texas Hill Country and ground west of there classified by geographers and geologists as the Edwards Plateau.[43]

Meanwhile, and it will become more than a little relevant, the goings on south of the border for J. Walter Durbin and John R.

Hughes were not newsworthy copy. Sure they trudged back and forth guarding the wagon trains, but journalists can hardly write about what didn't happen—and they surely had no spine-tingling stories to tell about standing off or shooting or scooting from any *banditos*. All and all their lives had turned relatively and disappointingly quiet: Markedly so for fighting men. Mother Nature would be their undoing.

Not too long after Baz Outlaw signed up once again with the Texas Rangers, the seasonal rains commenced to fall on guards Durbin and Hughes, and the wetness came with a vengeance. Runoff from high on the mountain cascaded down into the canyon, sometimes running and raging from two to ten feet deep and washing out the snaky little road so important to mine production and, correspondingly, for survival of miners and their families and/or the parasitical camp followers. Hinting that security men Durbin and Hughes had best rethink their pecuniary plight—perhaps being washed out of a job—was underscored in their minds by the fact that the mine was "shut down a bout half the time [and] men would not stay out there goeing and comeing all the time." Reading the admittedly damp tea leaves, J. Walter Durbin opted out, heading back to the United States. On the other hand, John Reynolds Hughes—for some less than prudent economic reasoning—chose to hang out and hang on, even after Outlaw and Durbin had changed course.[44]

While John Hughes was doing whatever in Old Mexico—and that might be an interesting substory within itself—Private Outlaw would be rather busy, the Company D Rangers had been ordered from Fort Bend County. They were to reestablish an operational base in Uvalde County. By mid October the repositioning had been completed. Company D's headquarters was now Camp Leona; the detachment supervised by Sergeant Charley Fusselman was yet in far-flung and precarious West Texas.[45]

That Private Baz Outlaw was trustworthy and apparently judicious enough to handle independent assignments could be extrapolated through his being sent, alone, to represent Company D in relation to official business in Tom Green County (seat San Angelo).

Private Outlaw's work in this instance, most probably but not absolutely particularized, was looking into the cow stealing problems a big-time and prominent ranchman was suffering. A former Company D Texas Ranger, W.W. Jones, was trying to obtain commission as a Special Ranger so he could gain fulltime employment on the ranch.[46] Sending Baz Outlaw to Tom Green County for an exploratory look into matters—and that seems to be the case—before Captain Jones would commit to writing a letter of endorsement was wise. Learning that there was, indeed, something for ranchmen to be concerned about, Captain Frank Jones gave his okay, writing to AG King that his former Company D private had been a "good Ranger" and with clear conscience he could and would "cheerfully endorse" his application.[47]

November 1889 was winding down for Rangers of Company D, Private Baz Outlaw included, and it perhaps seemed the holiday season would overtake and earn precedence over beating the bushes for badmen and burnt cattle.

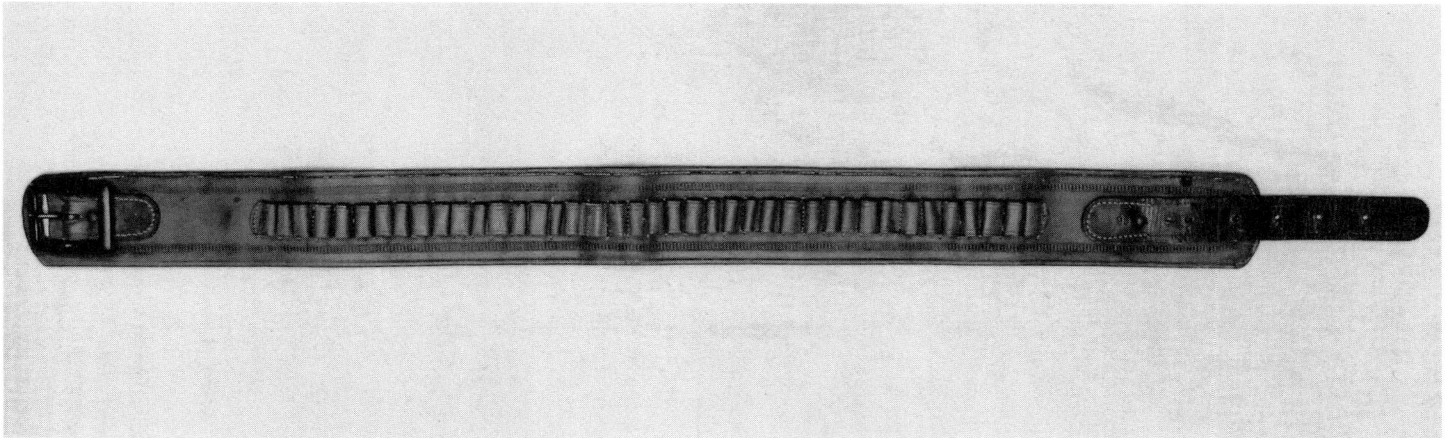

Examining even plain Ranger artifacts is fascinating and often supplements insight as to how the early day lawmen actually lived, dressed, and were armed. Herein is a first-rate example, the cartridge belt of Texas Ranger and Reeves County Sheriff Lycurgus S. "Kirk" Turnbo. Prior to the advent of speed-loaders, auto-loading handguns and their respective magazines, the daily carrying of six-shooters and a supply of ammunition could prove a "weighty" proposition, thus the necessity for a supportive wide belt. *Courtesy Tobin and Anne Armstrong Ranger Research Center, Texas Ranger Hall of Fame & Museum.*

Wood Saunders [L] and J. Walter Durbin assume a striking pose, an iconic image of how all Rangers looked—or were supposed to look—irrespective of humanity's unflattering anatomical trickeries. *Courtesy Nita Stewart Haley Memorial Library and J. Evetts Haley History Center.*

Herein is a delightful image of the Company D camp situated near the Leona River, Uvalde County. Note the sitting Baz Outlaw extreme right, seated next to John R. Hughes, and observe J. Walter Durbin positioned at the left hand of the standing Ira Aten with coffee cup in right hand. Rangers Outlaw, Hughes, and Durbin would all three try—unsuccessfully it would seem—to make a living in Old Mexico guarding shipments of ore. *Courtesy Jeri and Gary Boyce Radder.*

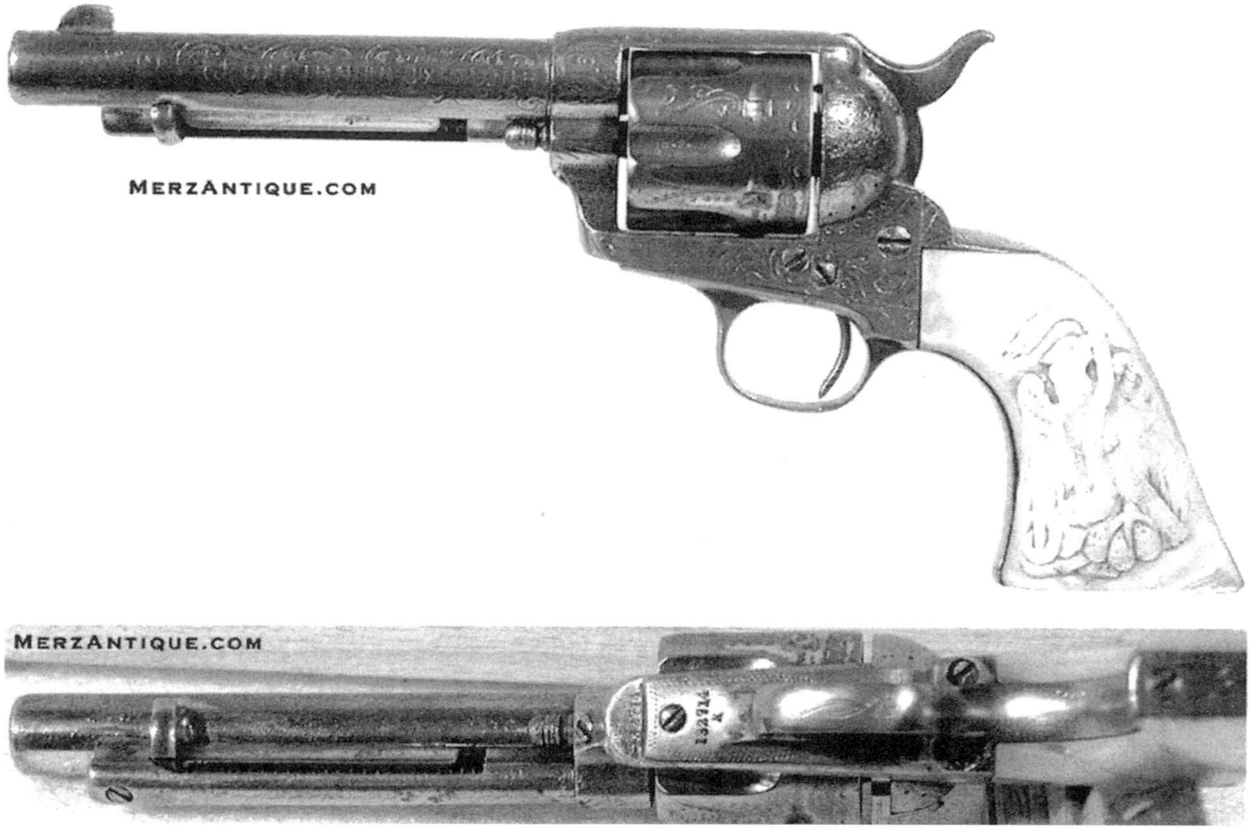

One of Baz Outlaw's fancy Colt's six-shooters: Provenance established by El Paso County court records. *PHOTOGRAPHIC IMAGE COURTESY LEROY MERZ ANTIQUE FIREARMS.*

This photograph of Company D Texas Rangers is certainly an iconic and well circulated image. Some of the Rangers pictured herein play significant roles in the unfolding Baz Outlaw drama. Standing, L to R: Jim King, Baz Outlaw, Riley Boston, Charley Fusselman, Tink Durbin, Ernest Rogers, Charles Barton, and Walter Jones. Seated, L to R: Bob Bell, Cal Aten, Captain Frank Jones, J. Walter Durbin, Jim Robinson, and Frank Schmid. *Courtesy Tobin and Anne Armstrong Ranger Research Center, Texas Ranger Hall of Fame & Museum.*

A remarkable photo of Texas Rangers. Standing L to R: J. Walter Durbin and Jim King. Seated L to R: George Parker and Robert McNamar. For the treatment in hand, it is especially germane to note that Private Jim King, while sometimes an outstanding Texas Ranger, was ultimately discharged from state service for too often sailing his ship on the Whiskey River. *From Texas Ranger Sketches courtesy the author, Robert W. Stephens.*

Pat Dolan, former Uvalde County Sheriff, Texas Ranger Lieutenant, and at the time lawman Baz Outlaw knew him in West Texas, he was sheriff of Jeff Davis County. *Courtesy Tobin and Anne Armstrong Ranger Research Center, Texas Ranger Hall of Fame & Museum.*

CHAPTER 6

Worth Two or Three Ordinary Men

THE ATTRACTIONS OF WORK OR DEARTH OF WORK in Mexico had lost their luster for John R. Hughes. Some time on that first day of December 1889 and somewhere in Uvalde County he raised his hand swearing an oath to the State of Texas and was once more a Ranger, a private in Company D.[1] Little did he realize it then but he had walked into a brewing administrative firestorm, divergent opinions about the rights and wrongs of cross-deputation. Though John Hughes and Baz Outlaw, at the time, would have had no comprehension about how such high-level disgruntlement would impinge on their lives—ultimately it would.

Paul Fricke, United States Marshal for the Western District of Texas, following the precedent of his predecessor, had continued the sagacious policy of deputizing particular Rangers. In this instance the controversy was swirling around his appointment of Sergeant Charley Fusselman. Captain Frank Jones—reading his interpretation of the law—thought the practice inappropriate. He asked that Charley Fusselman tender his resignation as a Deputy U.S. Marshal if, indeed, he wished to remain drawing pay from the Lone Star State:

> I instructed Sergt. Fusselman to resign his commission as Depty Marshal because from information I had rece'd, I deemed it

> hurtful to the interests of the State and am firmly of that opinion yet.[2]

Ever obedient and a Texas Ranger at heart, Sergeant Charley Fusselman tendered his resignation to Marshal Fricke. The federal lawman, in a nice way, was somewhat perturbed and refused to accept the resignation, opting instead to lay the matter in writing atop the adjutant general's desk. Excerpts from the U.S. Marshal's letter are self-explanatory:

> His duties as a ranger Kept him on a portion of the frontier, infested with Smugglers and "mescalileros" [liquor smugglers] and his services, since he received the appointment, have been valuable in the suppression of that class of violators of the law. . . . Of course if the duties of the one position conflicted with or were subordinated to the other, in any respect, I can see why there might be a ground of objection to his retaining the Commission but as a matter of fact such is not the case. On the Contrary it occurs to me that the two positions "dovetail" very nicely. . . . Fusselman is an active and valuable peace officer and I am informed that, since he has been a Deputy Marshal, there is decidedly less Smuggling and mescal, reducing horse stealing from Mexico, etc. than there was some months ago. . . . I make the request of you that you will permit him to retain his Commission and assist the Civil authorities of the U.S. where he can do so without detriment to the State Service. . . .[3]

Two days later AG King informed Captain Frank Jones that the matter niggling him was closed: "At the Solicitation of Mr. Paul Fricke, U.S. Marshal, I have authorized him to retain Sergt C.H. Fusselman as one of his deputies believing that the interest of the State will not Suffer while Sergt Fusselman acts both as Ranger and Deputy Marshal."[4]

Who were not acting in dual roles were the Odle brothers; they were apparently bad to the bone and hell-bent on following the Owl Hoot Trail, morality and lawmen could be goddamned. As early as

October 1889 Captain Jones had picked up speculative rumors and gossip, as well as quantifiable facts and hard numbers. In his jurisdictional sphere a crime wave had blown in with hurricane force. Particularly in Edwards County he noted there had been "an almost wholesale theft of horses."[5] To most everyday folks' way of thinking—certainly for area lawmen—the chief moguls for the across-the-board criminality were the notorious Odle boys, masterminds and masters at their craft.

Fugitives Will and Alvin Odle were young—and mean.[6] Their older brother John, after gunning a man down, was on the dodge—maybe in Arkansas, maybe in Mexico, for sure steering clear of any American lawmen and/or Mexican *Rurales*—wherever he hung his black hat. On the other hand Will and Alvin—their general whereabouts well known—were just slippery. They were constantly on the move, the two man crime wave for Edwards and Burnet Counties. Their repertoire for doing wrong was right full; burglary, livestock theft, assaults and, yes, even a coldblooded murder it was alleged, and that's not even counting their jailbreaks.[7] Riding a devilish trail lacking a trace of restraint, the boys were rascals through and through.

Their strategy for success was simple. Their energy and familiarity with the landscape, knowing every game trail, water source, above-ground overhang and underground cave, and which canyons were boxed in, not surprisingly served them well. They had, relatively shortly, maneuvered themselves into being first-class thieves and, like panthers, unafraid of the dark. During the dead of night they could steal horses or cattle and start them on the way to Mexico before roosters crowed, before owners were rubbing sleep from their eyes and hunting breakfast. A quick head start equated to a good getaway. The brothers Odle were fast. By daybreak, miles away, they could lay up in the cedar brakes and/or screening brush—the brasada—until the smiling Man in the Moon winked his okay for another midnight dash toward the Rio Grande. River crossings were countless. Will and Alvin were equal opportunists. South of the irregular Río Bravo, while Mexicans slept, the Odle boys executed a breakneck turnabout driving purloined livestock to the river's northern edge, where rather routinely the bargain basement prices trumped Bills of Sale. It was—were one fast and daring—a nifty racket.[8]

Stealing horses was Ranger business. Stealing horses was a county sheriff's business, as well. Owning a jurisdictional statewide reach, the county line meant nil to the Texas Rangers. Sheriffs' like counterparts within the criminal justice system, district attorneys, held jobs at an electorate's pleasure. Turf wars were troublesome, teamwork was practical. The lineup was taking shape. Ranger Private Baz Outlaw and his squad—county and state—would take to the field on the offense. The Odle brothers had the defense.

The outlawed Odle boys, however, were in the hole—a deep one. Unbeknownst to them, their supposed secret designs were fraught with a significant glitch—a snitch. Sheriff Ira L. Wheat was most fortunate in the fact that an Edwards County Grand Jury had returned indictments against a "prominent local rancher." The criminal charges revolved around the purchase of stolen cattle from the Odles. Cops and robbers is a hard game and Mr. Cowman faced a hard choice. He could give up Will and Alvin, or ride the bucking horse straight to East Texas and into the state prison at Huntsville. Squeal or stand pat, the choice was his.[9]

Sheriff Wheat, now in possession of the why, when, and where, summoned his chief deputy Will Terry filling in the blanks: Will and Alvin would, after nightfall on Christmas Day deliver stolen horses or, by another account, attend a party, at a site in the southeastern quadrant of what was still then Edwards County, near Bullhead Mountain.[10]

Word spread among honest men that there was somber work to be done, after sundown work. Reporting to Deputy Terry were Dan Crier and Paul Jones coming up from Barksdale, as had the Winchester-toting Jim Rhodes, outwardly disturbed but there nevertheless. Henry Wells, from the little community nearest Bullhead Mountain, Vance, had checked in as part of the posse. Whether it was afterthought or forethought is fuzzy, but Company D Rangers were there, too: Privates Baz Outlaw, Cal Aten, and John Hughes, who for this assignment was serving as the lead Ranger, in all likelihood a golden opportunity for Captain Jones to test his judgment and take measure of his managerial acumen—or lack thereof. There were others, but their names have been intentionally or inadvertently erased or forgotten in history's retellings. There may have been as few as the eight manhunters named, or as many as twelve or fifteen fellows foregoing Christmas at home that night.[11]

Perhaps private citizens of the posse would have phrased it differently, but lawmen's lexicon has terminology ever so applicable for this job. The Odle brothers "were bought and paid for." The wordy translation for everyday civilians or armchair thinkers would be something akin to this nice prattling justification: Since the bad boys were felonious fugitives known to have broken jail and had reportedly killed their brother-in-law, were actively and blatantly living a life of high crime, and had obviously chosen to mimic teeth-gnashing wolves rather than atone for their sins and face the music—it was most logically assumed they'd fight before surrendering. For lawmen wanting to go home or somewhere at day's end there was an underbelly premise about cuffing up dangerous men and hauling them off to jail against their will. Should they wiggle the wrong way or make a harebrained false move—shoot, several more times if need be. Survival mattered, sentiment didn't.

Cautiously and quietly skirting north past the little Nueces River community of Vance, the company Baz Outlaw was keeping caught a glimpse of the landmark marking their journey's end, the eastern base of 2,050-foot Bullhead Mountain. Prudently, before getting too close, the posse secreted their horses—far enough away so that any snorting or whinnying or pecking-order agitation would go undetected. Stealth was imperative. The setting sun's fading warmth would soon dissipate. Darkness draping around them would somewhat screen their movements but not short-circuit a December evening's blanketing chill. Once concealed, Winchesters across laps, thoughts of Christmas diversions gave way to what-ifs. Each man owned the privacy of his feelings and fears and fantasies. No matter, now was time to buck up inside, shed nervousness, readying for a real-time showdown if the Odles showed up. Trapping human-tigers at night was chancy at best. Getting it wrong—could—make someone graveyard dead.

Just how long good guys manned their lair would be guesswork, but what happened at eight o'clock that 1889 Christmas night isn't. Barefooted horses—unshod—soon go lame crossing rocky ground. Iron horseshoes were a necessity for riding the broken Nueces River country but they made music, notes ranging—dependent upon the horse's gait—from a scale barely audible to a crescendo of clinking and clattering. Unsuspectingly Will and Alvin Odle were generating a tell-tell melody as they approached the eastern foot of Bullhead Mountain, the route a supposed friend had suggested, one that would be free of sheriffs or Rangers that holiday night.[12]

The sound of hard metal clanking against white rock was a tune of forewarning, giving ample time for Privates Outlaw, Aten, and Hughes to remove the gloves warming their trigger-fingers. With hammers down the Rangers depressed the triggers on their Winchesters, noiselessly and carefully eared the hammers back to the full-cock notch, then let the triggers return to rest. They were then holding carbines made ready to fire absent a hint of that recognizable ratcheting sound.

Exactly how the identification was made is muddled, but someone must have or Lady Luck had stepped in to prevent a whopping mistake. Will and Alvin, horseback, had ridden into range. Preferably in keeping with idealisms' white-hat purity, the outlaws would have been afforded a chance to comply with a shouted plea that they must throw up their hands and humbly surrender. However, this was the real world and the lawmen were living in real time, and the notorious Alvin and Will Odle were real bad. Winchesters and six-shooters barked and spit bullets. For an instant, nighttime turned bright: Brilliantly illuminated by scorching orange muzzle flashes and blasts from the barrels of lever-actions and Colt's thumb-busters. Will's and Alvin's horses had suddenly jumped sideways at the initial crack of thunderous gunfire, rendering the desperadoes' accommodations in slick-forked stock-saddles precarious—at least for a split-second or two. Maybe Will heard the report that sent a bullet thumping into the horse's neck, killing it instantly. Perhaps he didn't. He lay dead on the Edward County's floor, an outlaw meant to rob no more. Alvin, too, was on the ground, nearby a wounded horse, head down, heaving and blowing pink froth from its nostrils while instinctively clinging to life. The highly sought and dangerous fugitives had had no time to panic. Hailstorms and hellfire come quick.

Jettisoning any creative claptrap—melodrama—so very often a part of Wild West narratives is but right. In this particular instance it is important, as well as revealing. First and foremost the lawman/posse were not glad-handing and guffawing, patting one another on the back and trading high-fives, while strutting about uttering braggadocios words of joy. In their minds, and there is a smattering of hard proofs, they had come to that east foot of Bullhead Mountain for a distasteful job and had done what the law demanded they do—a case of us or them—and better them! Purportedly, ranchman Jim Rhodes was so distraught he called an audience around serving as witnesses. In front of his God and everybody else, Rhodes rapidly worked the lever on his Winchester, ejecting the proper number of cartridges on the ground proving that he had not fired a solitary round at the dead Will, or the dying Alvin.[13]

Compassionately Ranger Private Cal Aten approached the wounded Alvin who was clearly struggling to hang on—a fellow fighting not to surrender his last breath. Cal Aten sat down beside Odle, gently raised Alvin's head "and held the dying outlaw in my [his] arms. One of the worst ever-known in the Southwest. Took his pistol out of his dying hand. . . . I was sorry for that boy. Just a few years older than I and I have often wondered what he would have done had our positions been reversed. Just rode off and left me like a dog, I think. . . ."[14]

Certainly Ranger Baz Outlaw was there, too. What he did or said, other than joining the others with unleashing the barrage and lighting up the night sky, officially goes unreported, but has been the fodder for foolish assumptions—at least foolish from a truth-telling standpoint. Assuredly, as already noted Baz and the bottle were not and would not be distant companions. That said, the following quotation about the tragic episode at Bullhead Mountain and Baz Outlaw is simply too rich: "One of his small hands held a Ranger issue .45 Colt. The other hand clutched a bottle of Edwards County stump juice that had been bought from an old gulley jumper who made it in a cavern called the Devil's Sink Hole."[15] True, there was a "sunken cavern" in Edwards County named after Lucifer.[16] True or not may be the writer's claim that the outlawed Odle brothers rode to their deaths just as Baz Outlaw "glanced down at the bottle. He was just going to uncork it for a quick one. . . ."[17]

What was true was that Will and Alvin Odle were dead. And it's also true, if taking the word of Cal Aten, who was one of the Ranger shootists is of value, that fellows finishing in second place for gunfights were losers, not winners. Not hiding behind fake sentimentality or false pity, the apparently somewhat bothered Cal Aten put his words—his version of the truth—to paper:

> I am responsible for [missing word] but you will understand that it pertains to the time when the Odle boys were assassinated. That is all it was just plain legal assassination. However, there would have been someone else assassinated if we hadn't got the first shots.[18]

What Calvin Grant Aten penned years after the episode, naturally, is intriguing and interesting. Likewise, the man in charge of the Edwards County detachment, Private John R. Hughes, rightly was duty bound to notify Texas Ranger headquarters what had just transpired. Plainly and provably Texas Rangers didn't kill somebody every day, though such truth tears the rug out from under a few impressionable romantics—and agenda driven detractors. Officialdom at Austin was due an accounting. On 25 December 1889, but two hours after the killings, Private Hughes took pen in hand and wrote the following:

> Ten O'clock P.M. With the assistance of Deputy Sheriff Will Terry and a few good citizens, We succeeded in trapping Will and Calvin

> Odel [*sic*] who are wanted for Murder and theft. They resisted arrest and made a hard fight and we had to kill them in self defence also Killed one horse and shot an other through the neck. It took place about 8 O'clock tonight. We will hold an inquest in the morning. Outlaw & C.G. Aten Were With me—[19]

As will soon become apparent, what Private Hughes did not say will generate a hiccup or two for Captain Frank Jones, an astute leader capable of tweaking the deficit. However, in the short term, the Company D commander was, no doubt, pleased and in a congratulatory mood when he made mention of the affair to Captain Sieker: "I guess you have seen in the paper where some of my men celebrated Xmas day by Killing the two Odles in Edwards County. It is a great strain off that country and the good people are rejoicing. John Hughes, Outlaw, and young Aten and some citizens did the work."[20]

Clearly Captain Sieker had spotted the shortage of key verbiage in Private Hughes' written recap of the shooting. Captain Jones, somewhat picked up the slack: "I have no particulars of the killing of the Odle's except that they drew their pistols when commanded to surrender and then the firing began. Hughes who is in charge of the Edwards County detachment simply stated that they made a hard fight and they (the Rangers) were compelled to Kill them."[21] Aside from the letters to Captain Sieker, the Company D Monthly Return for December 1889 identified Will and Alvin Odle as being wanted for Murder and were "Killed while resisting arrest."[22]

And even after all this, what was not being said was crucial. Understandably some of the back and forth was forevermore lost to history, but there was also a written supplemental report for the unit's Monthly Return, one particularly focused on the outlying Company D detachments in Sutton County (Sonora county seat) and Edwards County. Finally, at last, what needed to be said was said, and is herein quoted with emphasis added:

> Dec. 25—Private Hughes and two men with Deputy Sheriff and posse in attempting the arrest of Will and Alvin Odle wanted for

> murder *were fired on by them*. The *shots were returned* resulting in the death almost instantly of both.[23]

That touching such legal bases was imperative probably needs no further twenty-first century explanation, but at the time Texas Ranger Privates Baz Outlaw, Cal Aten, and John Hughes—as well as private citizens—were not guaranteed an exemption from answering to the state's criminal justice system for what had taken place during Christmas night at Bullhead Mountain. In fact, Private Aten's brother, Sheriff Ira Aten from Fort Bend County, would write a personal letter to Cal promising—pledging—if necessary to peddle his influence: "I will write to [Sheriff] Ira Wheat about not having you boys indicted in Edwards co. I wish I had time I would go up there & could tell in a short time which would be best, to have you indicted now or not. I expect Wheat would like to make some fees in the matter."[24]

Though somewhat of a misunderstanding, at the time many on-the-ground lawmen thought Bill of Rights protections as set forth in the Fifth Amendment regarding double jeopardy were applicable to grand jury proceedings. Their theory—an informal perception—was that if the grand jury took up the case, heard testimony, weighed the evidence, and chose not to return an indictment the matter was closed forevermore: No indictment, no worry. Quickly chatting with a lawyer would have clued them in to reality, legal reality. Prohibitions about being tried twice for the same crime meant just that, tried in a court of law. Indictments were only a step leading to trial. Sitting grand juries, especially after the presentation of new evidence and/or taking additional testimony had the luxury and latitude to bring forth an indictment at anytime. Sometimes, simply letting hot legal issues cool on their own, letting flame turn to embers, embers to ashes, ashes to the wind, was not unwise.

Captain Jones was a wise man. The shooting had taken place on Christmas Day 1889 and by the third day of January 1890 the Company D commander had decided the needs of the Ranger service could best be served by transferring Privates Outlaw, Cal Aten, and John Hughes to beef up Sergeant Charley Fusselman's understaffed detachment in West Texas. Captain Frank Jones' aboveboard reasoning was sound, and if there were other benefits, well, that was alright too. Captain Jones posted the adjutant general: "Sergt. Fusselman has only one man with him, and as the detachment in Edwards County is not especially needed there since the Odles are killed, I would suggest that they be withdrawn and sent to Presidio County."[25]

What plans Captain Jones had in the hopper for readjusting his manpower would be—at least for awhile—put on hold. Though eventually the three veterans of the Bullhead Mountain fireworks would wind up in West Texas there were, first, a few fits and starts as demands for Rangers were pouring into the governor's and adjutant general's offices. Particularly for moving Texas Ranger Baz Outlaw's story during 1890s first quarter are an item or two of general interest and importance.

Contrary to some whipsawing of the truth, Private Baz Outlaw was yet maintaining steady and commendable work habits, getting along with most everyone, and had assuredly earned the confidence of Company D's captain and, correspondingly, the Texas Rangers' headquarters staff. Particularly noting that "trouble is anticipated" at an upcoming murder trial to take place at Junction City, Adjutant General King ordered Captain Frank Jones to send a detachment of Rangers "to Keep peace and order at that point."[26] Unquestionably, had Private Outlaw been seen as a potential threat to Captain Frank Jones' overall standing as a first-rate leader and dutiful Texas Ranger he would have not chosen Baz to head up the three-man security detail sent to Kimble County for court, but he did.[27]

The following month a turn more telling took place. Corporal Jim Robinson, who had been in charge of a Company D detachment at Sonora, apparently in a tiff with management over something, resigned—voluntarily discharged—creating a spot on the company's roster for the promotion of a new noncom. Captain Jones didn't tarry: "I then appointed Private Outlaw in his place."[28] Privates Hughes and Aten may or may not have applauded the snappy personnel action; Baz was their pal, but they'd been skipped over.

Had not Robinson terminated his service with Company D there's little doubt—though it's not absolute—that Baz Outlaw would have been transferred to Presidio County along with Privates Hughes and Aten. Inasmuch as Captain Jones believed that a noncommissioned officer should always be attached to the company's headquarters camp—handling administrative and supervisory duties in his absence—Corporal Outlaw missed the reassignment to West Texas. Now, in the ever seesawing shifts of in-the-field Texas Ranger camps, Company D was at Cotulla, La Salle County—a hotbed of trouble for South Texas. But it would be in West Texas, far West Texas in El Paso County, that the real newsmaker and heartbreaker would take center stage. Texas and Mexico each knew halfway across the Rio Grande/Río Bravo as sovereignty's edge. Lawmen—it may be surmised—knew the river as Lucifer's Line. Though assuredly bilingual, for this chapter in Company D's story—and Baz Outlaw's—the Devil would snarl and speak Spanish between spitting bullets.

The morning of April 17, 1890, found Sergeant Fusselman wandering the streets of the town sometimes tagged "Hell Paso." He was killing time between court appearances or on standby at a judge's or district attorney's or grand jury foreman's order. He stopped by the county sheriff's office for a chat with the headman, James H. White, and/or his chief deputy, Frank B. Simmons. White was away, tending business of federal and state district court, while Simmons was holding down the fort at the jail's office. Also present was El Paso City policeman George Herold, who a dozen years earlier in Williamson County was generally credited with firing the shot tapping out the running lights of an incorrigible Sam Bass at Round Rock.[29] At this time, 1890, for the Ranger service represented in El Paso, Presidio, or Brewster Counties, if anyone carried a good name and a topnotch résumé it was Charley Fusselman, a twenty-three-year old holy terror when it came to making arrests and jugging lawbreakers.[30]

Rushing into the sheriff's office and interdicting the casual conversation was El Paso County rancher John H. Barnes. Bandits, one "a villainous looking Mexican whose appearance indicated that he meant to shoot if Barnes insisted on advancing" had killed and butchered a calf and stolen horses from his Munday Springs ranch in the Franklin Mountains eight miles north of town. Barnes wanted—and needed—help. Chief Deputy Simmons was unable to abandon his post, but Officer George Herold, age fifty, and Sergeant Charley Fusselman volunteered to do what lawmen are supposed to do—something. Fusselman, who had made the trip to El Paso by train, had no horse, and had left his Winchester in the hotel room. He quickly borrowed the sheriff's horse and a carbine from Deputy U.S. Marshal Bob Ross, who, like James White, was hamstrung by tending to matters already scheduled for a court's docket.[31]

What ensued would be a real game changer for two Texas Rangers, Sergeant Charley Fusselman and Corporal Baz Outlaw. The long and short of the first part of that sad story unwinding in those mountains above El Paso is loud—and bloody. Sergeant Fusselman, policeman Herold, and rancher Barnes had overrun the bandits' noonday camp, inadvertently and shockingly riding straight into Hell. One of the desperadoes' bullets whizzed past Fusselman's head, not fired as a warning, but merely wide of the mark. Tougher than a Bois D'Arc stump and as tenacious as a wolverine, showing the white feather was not in Charley Fusselman's psyche. Not having time to unsheathe the borrowed Winchester from its saddle-scabbard, the Ranger sergeant quick drew his Colt's six-shooter, simultaneously screaming, "Boys, we are in for it, and let's stay with it." The next bullet was unheard by Charles Henry Vanvalkenburg Fusselman. That squeeze of the bushwhacker's trigger had sent a bullet plowing through the sergeant's right temple, carrying "away with it nearly the whole of the right lobe of the brain." Before falling from the saddle a second missile of spiraling hot lead tore through his neck, under the chin, exiting through his left ear. The Grim Reaper smiled; Charley Fusselman was dead. For the moment, understandably incapable of a survivable outcome in the crosshairs of an unrelenting bombardment, George Herold and John Barnes went one way—to attain reinforcements—while the murderous miscreants went the other, to attain sanctuary Mexico promised.

During the same timeframe this tragedy uncorked in El Paso County, Corporal Outlaw had been busy with a manhunt in Zavala County. Former Texas Ranger Jim King had been murdered during February 1890 and the investigation and hunt for his killer or killers was yet underway. Captain Jones had called attention to the matter earlier, reminding headquarters:

> The man J.W. King who I discharged at Richmond for drunkenness was foully assassinated in Zavala County on the 11th of this month [February] by parties who I am thoroughly convinced thought King was yet a Ranger and on detective work. Sometime before I went to Fort Bend County I sent King into that section as a dishonorably discharged man, to try and work up some cattle stealing. He said at the time that if he was suspicioned that he would undoubtedly be murdered. Since then it was known that he was in the Company and they evidently thought he was trying to play the same game again. I shall do my best to ferret out the murderers and see that they are punished.[32]

For the Texas Rangers it was not necessarily a high-profile case publicity wise, even though the governor had authorized the posting of a $250 reward for the arrest and conviction of Jim King's killers. However, institutionally they were bound and determined—driven—to offer any and all possible assistance to Zavala County Sheriff C.C. Akers at the then county seat, Batesville (now Crystal City).[33] As late as April—the same month Sergeant Fusselman was murdered—Corporal Baz Outlaw had been in Zavala County. Before returning to the Company D camp at Cotulla, he had assigned a private to stay behind and assist Sheriff Akers.[34]

Whether or not Captain Jones had specifically ordered Corporal Outlaw back to Company D's headquarters camp is hazy and, in the big biographical picture—inconsequential. Conversely, for Baz Outlaw the captain did own two pieces of information of consequence which would impact his life—and his story. First and foremost he was a corporal no more. For Captain Jones, filling the vacancy created by Fusselman's tragic and untimely death was actually a no-brainer. With at minimum a tacit nod from Austin or maybe a hearty expression of their approval, Baz Outlaw was promoted to 1st Sergeant, Company D.[35] Once again, for the second time, Captain Frank Jones—and maybe the top brass—had not at all hesitantly opted to promote Baz Outlaw ahead of John Hughes, or any Texas Ranger then serving in the company. At the time, indisputably based on Texas Ranger Baz Outlaw's past—not future—law enforcing performance, Captain Jones' estimation of the newly selected top-sergeant was optimistic, fed at least in part by his deliberative personal assessment: "he was a man of unusual courage and coolness, and in a close place is worth two or three ordinary men."[36]

Although editorial salvation or condemnation should be somewhat cropped within the nonfiction context, in light of what's been previously penned regarding Baz Outlaw's character flaws, a short comment about his promotion cries for a hearing—one not preprogrammed by knowledge about how his story will end. Rest assured, at the time Captain Frank Jones elevated Baz Outlaw from corporal to sergeant, his services as a Texas Ranger "had been outstanding" and the company commander "placed special confidence in his abilities." Importantly—and it is more than highly unlikely—that Captain Jones would have awarded the promotion to a Ranger who owned a "quarrelsome disposition" and was an agitator constantly "embroiled with the men of his company."[37] No, true stories and biographies unwind in a natural order, from beginning to end. What happens in between is where meat is put on the bone. When placed on the butcher's block, newly sliced and trimmed, it's near always fresh, but even choice cuts can rot over time. Baz Outlaw's tale starts—continues—and stops.

Backfilling behind Baz Outlaw's vacated spot, John Hughes figuratively sewed on the corporal's stripes. Corporal Hughes, at the time, was and had been, the man placed in charge of the five-man Company D detachment in Presidio County.[38] Corporal Hughes before the month of May 1890 was history, had relocated his detachment from Marfa to Presidio, the Texas town straight across from Mexico's northern frontier village of Ojinaga.[39]

The other news of import for now-Sergeant Outlaw should have come as no bombshell. Company D was to be redeployed—again. The message straight out of the adjutant general's office left no wiggle room for misunderstanding. Captain Jones was told, "Further demands for rangers come from Presidio County and it has been decided to Send your Company to that Section."[40] The marching orders couldn't have been any clearer than that. On May 30, 1890, Captain Jones and the Company D Rangers not on detached duty, broke camp in La Salle County and headed northwest.[41]

Somewhat naively and, certainly incorrect by implication, it's been tendered the Company D Rangers' work in La Salle County "had been so effective that their efforts would now be better spent elsewhere."[42] The truth of the matter is not the least bit elusive. Under direct orders from the adjutant general, Company F, then led by James A. Brooks, since promoted to captain, was to fill the vacuum created in La Salle County by relocating the command of Captain Jones.[43] Asserting—by omission or implication—that the Company D Rangers had almost overnight cleaned up the mischief and madness in La Salle County is belied by the remarks of Captain Jones, who declared: "There is a great deal of work to be done in this and adjoining Counties. Affairs are in worse condition in this section than I have ever Known in nine years service in different Counties of the State. Men are afraid to be seen talking to me and want to sulk off in a dark corner and then swear me to secrecy. It seems hard to infuse any self reliance, or confidence in any legal redress. I shall use the utmost means in my power to right matters while I am here."[44] Undoubtedly when he had penned those words Captain Jones had no idea how short his tenure in La Salle County would be.

Now, the Company D Rangers were again on the move, directed to proceed to their old camp near Uvalde first, and from there travel by train. Quite entertainingly now, but not amusing to rank and file Rangers then, was the indifference Ranger headquarters paid to their comfort, telling—not suggesting—that Captain Jones should "enter into correspondence with the officials of the Sunset route, as to Special rate to carry your Wagon, horses, baggage & from Uvalde to Marfa You will probably need two Cars and the men can ride with baggage & Camp equipage."[45] Captain Frank Jones—faithful to the core—jumped to, dutifully notifying the adjutant general: "I have torn down and am anxious to get off."[46] Reasonably speaking the train trip was real quick.[47] Company D Rangers detrained at Marfa's depot, making themselves ready for war or whatever.[48]

That many of the prominent folks looked upon their home county as a warzone is not hyperbole meant to juice a Wild West narrative. Company D's deployment to Presidio County was the direct response to distressed citizens' petitions to Austin. One, a typewritten plea to the governor of Texas, L.S. Ross, will serve as an example of the catalysts that politically propelled 1st Sergeant Baz Outlaw and Company D to the Big Bend Country:

> Now, therefore, we humbly and confidently prey to your exellency that you will cause to be placed at this town of Presidio, in this county, a force of rangers of not less than ten men, with orders to continually scout the river front of this county, for at least one year; that you will use your influence to have troops removed from interior posts, and placed on the river where they may be of service to the settlers, who are so honestly and energetically trying to build up and fortify the border, and make west Texas what it should be, the garden, and not the slaughter house of the United States.[49]

Whatever alluring sights to be seen, innocent pleasures to be had, or delicious sin to savor while at Marfa would be put on hold—at least temporarily so. At Captain Jones' command, Sergeant Outlaw ordered the Company D Rangers into the saddle. They would scout the lower reaches of Presidio County familiarizing themselves with the lay of the land, its people, and their problems. They, too, would catch up with Corporal Hughes and his small detachment, which had relocated to the Rio Grande town of Presidio the previous month. No doubt Corporal Hughes would have an earful for his supervisors, Sergeant Outlaw, and Captain Jones.

Though admittedly a posed photographed this image of Company D Rangers near their Uvalde County camp is somewhat unique in that—to date—it is the only known instance wherein Baz Outlaw is seen atop a saddle-horse. Sergeant Outlaw is more or less in the center foreground, seventh from the left. *Courtesy Jeri and Gary Boyce Radder.*

Bullhead Mountain in scenic Edwards County, the site where two of the Odle brothers, Will and Alvin, were killed by Texas Rangers and a sheriff's posse. *Courtesy Chris Robinson.*

Calvin Grant "Cal" Aten, brother of the former Company D 1st Sergeant but at the time of Cal's signature gunplay, Ira was serving as the Fort Bend County Sheriff at Richmond, Texas. *Courtesy Bobbie Walker in memory of Sally Walker, Cal Aten's granddaughter.*

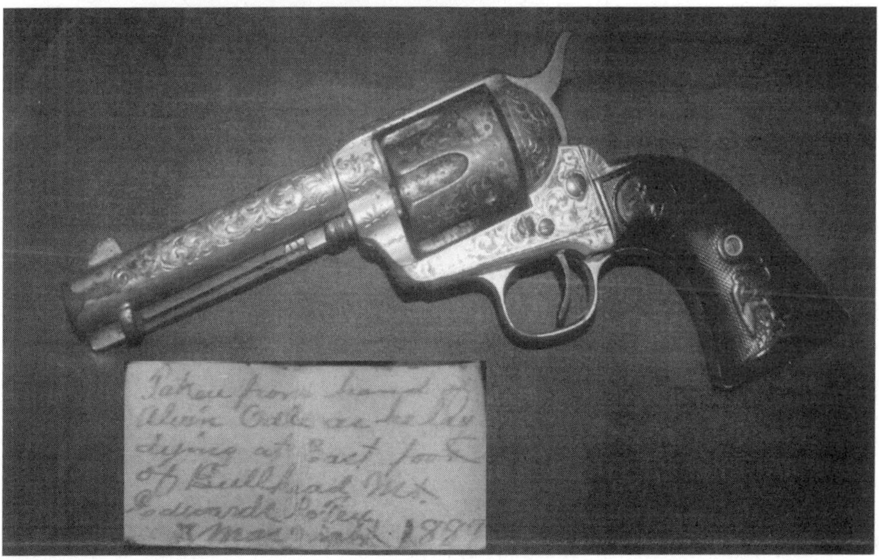

The engraved Colt's six-shooter taken from the dying hand of Alvin Odle by Ranger Private Cal Aten subsequent to the blistering 1889 Christmas Night gunplay at Bullhead Mountain. Ranger Private Cal Aten penned a note, placing it inside the Colt's grip panels by the mainspring. The handwritten pencil note reads: "Taken from the hand of Alvin Odle as he lay dying at East foot of Bullhead Mt. Edwards, Co. Tex. X Mas Night 1889." *Courtesy Joseph Trobaugh II.*

Charley Fusselman, a crackerjack frontier-era Texas Ranger with no deficit of guts and gumption, would unluckily be killed in the Franklin Mountains north of El Paso while chasing treacherous *mal hombres*. *Courtesy Tobin and Anne Armstrong Ranger Research Center, Texas Ranger Hall of Fame & Museum.*

Whether or not El Paso Policeman George Herold used this particular Colt's six-shooter during the blistering gunplay at the time Sergeant Charley Fusselman was murdered is indistinct. Nevertheless this revolver did belong to Herold. Note the front sight has been filed off, making it handy for up close and personal work when a fleeting split-second could be the difference between first place—and dead last! *Author's photo courtesy the James H. Earle Firearms Collection.*

58. Donald M. Yena's riveting *Downed by the Colt .45* is a truly masterful visual image illustrating the horrors and heartbreaks and potential headstones attendant to real time, real world gunplay. *Courtesy the artist, Don Yena.*

CHAPTER 7

Couldn't Leave Liquor Alone

CORPORAL JOHN R. HUGHES seemed to have had the state of affairs along the Rio Grande pegged tight—and right—noting there had been "so much lawlessness at & near Presidio" that he thought it best to maintain a camp there for at least a month's duration. Past that timeframe, well, he was decidedly sure that it wasn't such a good idea "to stay long in one place, especially in Presidio as the mexicans [*sic*] can watch us pass out & in the town."[1] Particularly Corporal Hughes updated his war-chiefs, Sergeant Outlaw and Captain Jones, regarding real time reality: The presence of his detachment at Presidio had driven "six or eight" fugitives across the river into Ojinaga, where they were giving local lawmen the slip. For near a month, employing his best law-enforcing efforts Corporal Hughes and his men had been trying to "decoy" the wanted men into crossing the river and capturing them in the Lone Star State, rather than effecting a midnight extradition—kidnapping—in the State of Chihuahua. Thus far the corporal had been unsuccessful, but hope springs eternal for Rangers, too.[2]

Not leaping out of the way of Texas Rangers were a few ne'er-do-wells intermixed with the hard laboring and multicultural workforce eking out a living at Shafter, a settlement but eighteen miles north of the Rio Grande and its confluence with the Río Conchos.

Staked along the banks of Cibola Creek and in sight of the Chinati Mountains, Shafter was an island in the sea of desert sands, rugged mountain peaks, and winding arroyos sometimes dry, sometimes flashflood rich with wetness.[3] There was an aurora of affluence at silver ginning Shafter, especially in the minds and pocketbooks of executives and shareholders linked to The Presidio & Cibola Mining Company. Demographically the floating population at Shafter was lopsided in favor of the folks of Mexican ancestry employed in the mines. As elsewhere in the American Southwest, there was a glaring pay gap between native speakers of Spanish and overseers speaking the King's English—or trying to.[4] Men, primarily single men, or men with wives and families elsewhere, lived where they could, while the upper-level Anglos associated with the enterprise occupied "comfortable stone and adobe houses."[5] Financially, mining moguls had the everyday working class outstripped and a few saloon owners and prostitutes were eagerly competing for the leftovers—trading in sour mash and warm beer and personal services, turning desire into dollars. Payday was frolicsome at Shafter—at least while money was changing hands, for the little hotspot was where "gamblers, roughs and lewd women routinely congregate."[6]

Ranger Private Cal Aten, who was a part of Corporal Hughes' detachment, particularly noted that the neighborhood—all of the Big Bend area—was overstocked with a populace consisting of "a lot of cowardly thieves and murderers in which this country abounds."[7] Though he was at faraway Austin, even Adjutant General Wilburn Hill King's idea about the region seems to comport with Private Aten's gloomy assessment: "The detachment in Presidio [County] had an immense territory to control, the country very broken, sterile and dry in many parts, and much of the population an ignorant and dangerous class of Mexicans, with a mixture of desperate whites."[8] Understandably the section's proximity to the Rio Grande was problematic for lawmen, local, state, or federal, prompting one Ranger to write: "Since Aug. 17, 1889 there has been 7 murders committed in & near Presidio Co. & the murderers taken refuge in mexico & some of them American citizens & no steps can be taken to get them, the mexicans in Mexico seems to uphold them."[9] By any man's measure—Texas Ranger or not—Presidio County, notably the southern stretch, was damn hard country for yielding any bad men or *mal hombres* into the hands of lawmen.

Naturally, not everyone at Shafter was bad—even part of the time. There was a priest, Catholic church, and school, along with stores for purchasing items hauled overland from the county seat at Marfa, forty-two miles to the north. There was even a U.S. Post Office at Shafter. And that plays directly into Sergeant Baz Outlaw's compelling narrative—coughing up both good and bad subchapters. By at least one relative's account the postmistress at Shafter was the widow Laura Carr Hay, a genial and free-thinking spirit who would come to know and grow quite fond of Baz Outlaw—and later, another gutsy and self-confident Ranger.[10]

Sergeant Baz Outlaw for the month of July 1890 was assuredly not idling away his hours sitting around Company D's headquarters camp outside Marfa. Nor at this time is there reason to suppose, suggest, or spew that he was a regular habitué of gin-mills and taprooms. No, Sergeant Baz Outlaw was busily engaged leading scouts throughout the Big Bend Country, showing the Texas Ranger flag and hunting for cow thieves and horse thieves. Along the treacherous river where the Rio Grande does in fact make its sweeping big bend, Sergeant Outlaw, riding at the head of a three-man detachment, investigated a reported case of "Cattle Killing by Mexicans." For the month, he was away from camp for a minimum of a dozen days, forking a saddle and covering somewhere near 350 miles horseback.[11]

Pinpointing the exact spot Sergeant Baz Outlaw was occupying on the fourth day of August is but guesswork—reasoned guesswork—but likely it was at the Company D camp two miles from Marfa.[12] At any rate when the horrendous news broke at camp, Captain Frank Jones ordered his top-sergeant to roust the men and saddle their horses—a Ranger had been killed at Shafter.[13] The morning sun was already peeking, but by ten o'clock, the captain, sergeant, and five privates were "splendidly mounted" atop horses that could cover a "hundred miles in one day." Six hours later they reined in to Shafter tired but energized by adrenaline's rush.[14] Somebody or some bodies were going to jail or Hell.

Ranger John F. Gravis, twenty-two, had been gunned down—by most accounts mercilessly.[15] During the preceding night he had been partnered with Isaac N. "Ike" Lee, a fulltime deputy sheriff for Presidio County Sheriff William "Bill" Russell and a part-time (dually commissioned) Deputy United States Marshal.[16] Sometime during the wee morning hours, for some reason—professional or private—Ranger Gravis and Deputy Lee were in attendance at a wingding primarily composed of Mexicans and Mexican-Americans, but Anglos were also part of the mix.[17] Booze and bullets make for a perilous concoction, stir in some *machismos* and it's poisonous. When a six-shooter came out, Ranger Gravis stepped in. When the shooting stopped Gravis lay dead on the floor, Deputy Lee wholly incapacitated, carrying a nasty gunshot wound, luckily not mortal.[18]

As with most police shootings—good and bad—controversy swirls with herculean intensity. The bone of contention was predictable. Was Texas Ranger Gravis on duty, trying to make a lawful arrest and the situation spiked Western, or was he off-duty—drinking and partying—and for an undisclosed reason the brouhaha netted bloodshed? Newspapermen from faraway places were never in doubt. Writing for the *Luling Signal* in Caldwell County an opinionated editor enlightened his readership: "A row occurred at Shafter mines near Marfa, last Monday between a lot of drunken Mexicans on the one side & State Rangers and miners on the other, in which a number of Shots were fired."[19] A journalist writing for the *Brooklyn Daily Eagle*, too, had his story typeset: "News was brought in yesterday morning by J.E. Ontbes, foreman of the mines at Shafter, of a killing which took place at 2 o'clock that morning. It seems a crowd of Mexicans had got on a spree and were firing off their weapons when several of the white miners, rangers and deputy sheriff went down to see what was the matter. Suddenly they were fired upon from ambush and State Ranger J.F. Graves [*sic*] was instantly killed and J. Lee, deputy sheriff and deputy Untied States marshal, was seriously wounded in the arm. The fire was returned and it is believed one Mexican was killed and several wounded. A physician, Captain Jones, several rangers and deputy sheriffs have left for the scene. Trouble has been brewing with the Mexicans at Shafter for some time, and it is believed that the intention was to rob and burn the mine. Graves, the dead ranger, belonged to company D and was very highly thought of by his fellow rangers."[20] Killing a Texas Ranger was not smart!

Subsequent to their arrival at Shafter the Rangers were in no mood to idly waste time, letting the fine points of Probable Cause stand in their way: There had been a riot and rioters had rooms reserved at Presidio County Sheriff Bill Russell's *hotel de lockup*. Wording for the Company D Monthly Return was plainspoken:

> Captain Jones and six men went to Shafter to investigate killing of Private Gravis during a riot at that place. Returned on the 7th with seven Mexicans charged with murder. . . . Privates Barton, Jones, Kipling and Mayfield, assisted by citizens, arrested 12 Mexicans charged with riot and murder and assault to murder. . . . Private Kipling then came to Marfa with body of Private Gravis and shipped it to Laredo by request of his family. . . . Private Kipling assisted by Deputy Sheriff arrested near Marfa three Mexicans charged with the Shafter riot and murder. . . .[21]

For public consumption the adjutant general took great exception with U.S. Army Lieutenant T.R. Rivers' accusations that perhaps, just perhaps, the dead Ranger and wounded deputy had bought into their own misfortune by misbehavior: "Lieutenant Rivers was evidently misled by partial reports [hearsay] of this transaction and being misled he did an unintentional injustice to the character of the Ranger who was killed, and indirectly to others."[22] Privately, the adjutant general had some implied words of wisdom for Captain Jones, Sergeant Outlaw, Corporal Hughes, and all of the Rangers in Company D: "Whether these assertions are true or not, it becomes necessary to put you on guard, So that you may caution the members of your Company against the danger of promiscuous meddling or mixing, either for pleasure or otherwise, with an element over which

& with which, you are likely at any moment to come in contact."[23] Or, in other words, watch who you play with today, for you may arrest, fight, or kill them tomorrow. History will bear witness—*some* Rangers heeded the warning.

As summer began giving way to cooler nighttime temperatures at Marfa during mid-September, Sergeant Baz Outlaw would not find himself at camp or down along the Rio Grande. He and three Rangers had headed northeast into Pecos County, charged with keeping the peace at the county seat, Fort Stockton, during a scheduled session of District Court. All was not peaceful at historic Fort Stockton, but it wasn't the hardened felons or petty criminals or slobbering drunk cowboys that would catch Sergeant Outlaw's notice. He had bigger fish to fry. Though tempting it would be—making the chronological jump and identifying the irony—real time unwinds at its own pace and journalistic leapfrogging is wrong. Quirks of fate will play out in due time. Meanwhile, at Fort Stockton, Ranger Sergeant Outlaw did not shirk responsibility, whine, or make lame excuses. He was gutsy, and some gutsy work was in want of doing. A run amok and intoxicated county sheriff, Colt's .45 six-shooter in hand, was sparking a bleary-eyed tear, threatening—promising—attempting—to "Kill a man." There was not the slightest doubt the sheriff was drunk and dangerous. Too, there was not room for even a whisper of skepticism as to whether or not Texas Ranger Sergeant Baz Outlaw had sand. What words were spoken is not a matter of record. That the sheriff was "disarmed" is. There is no mention that the sheriff was locked into the Pecos County Jail, the humiliation may have served as punishment enough—or patent professional courtesy trumped formal charges.[24]

Apparently the run in with an inebriated sheriff had been the most noteworthy event for Sergeant Outlaw and his detachment during their visit to Fort Stockton. Pedro Valeas would not be near so lucky. Sergeant Outlaw and his Company D Texas Rangers had made the eastward trip to Fort Stockton by train—or a least part of it. While returning to Marfa, either on the train or at the Haymond Station east of Marathon and west of Sanderson, Pedro, for reasons yet undisclosed, caught Baz Outlaw's notice. Employing the technique law enforcers refer to as a "field interrogation," Sergeant Outlaw somehow determined that the subject of his inquiries was in fact running from a murder investigation—and had been creatively ducking and hiding from frustrated lawmen for more than half a dozen years. Pedro was arrested. At Alpine the Pullman coach was short one passenger, while Brewster County Sheriff John Rooney's headcount at the jail was to the plus side by a factor of one.[25]

Keeping with the spirit of continually readjusting campsites to advantage themselves of readily available firewood, water, and adequate grazing for their livestock, Company D repositioned—again. On the first day of October 1890 the company's headquarters camp shifted from Marfa, Presidio County, to five miles outside Alpine, Brewster County. Captain Jones had been particular not to relocate too close to municipality's limits, because, to his way of thinking he did "not like to have the men loafing around any town."[26]

Unfortunately within the scope of his jurisdictional complex there was one town that the captain thought required an everyday presence of Rangers—Shafter. For this particular and delicate duty he needed a topnotch noncom to lead the five-man Ranger detachment and, one more time, decided that Sergeant Baz Outlaw would be better suited for the assignment than Corporal John R. Hughes.[27] The end of the month return was explicit: "Sergt Outlaw was sent to take charge of the detachment near Shafter, Corpl Hughes returning to Headquarter Camp."[28] Had Captain Jones availed him self of Tarot Cards or the misty wisdom swirling around inside a fortune teller's crystal ball would he have judiciously made that same personnel decision, the prerogative of company commanders?

Regardless what the future might hold, Sergeant Outlaw was seemingly incapable, not always smartly though, of sidestepping big trouble. He was not cast from molds of tentativeness or fearfulness. Captain Jones had been right as rain about one thing, however: Shafter was a tough spot. The same month he dispatched his top-sergeant to the settlement, October 1890, Captain Jones updated Captain Sieker about the "street fight there the other day between two Americans resulting in the serious, if not fatal wounding of one, and this has engendered a good deal of bad feeling. It is deemed absolutely necessary for Rangers to be right in town."[29] One of the alleged shooters, Jim Humphreys, made tracks for the Rio Grande and the supposed sanctuary Mexico might offer if bothersome lawmen interjected themselves into the soap opera shenanigans at Shafter. After all, it was West Texas and settling some matters with six-shooters was but par business—Penal Codes could be damned.

Never hesitant to act, Sergeant Outlaw immediately took the bull by the horns and at Presidio disarmed and arrested Jim Humphreys, the Assault to Murder suspect, hauling him to the county lockup at Marfa.[30] The tale had not ended. Jim Humphreys apparently posted bail or paid a fine and was turned out of the Presidio County Jail—heading straight back to the sin and sensuality Shafter promised. His stay was short. A local whore, Maria, last name unknown, wasn't any too happy with Mr. Jim Humphreys, so she killed him. Captain Jones again posted Captain Sieker: "A Mexican woman prostitute Killed an American at Shafter last night. He was no loss to the Country, but more Killing may follow."[31] Sergeant Baz Outlaw promptly arrested Maria "for murder of Jim Humphrey," handing her over to a deputy sheriff so he could transport her to Marfa—the appropriate lockup for Presidio County's felons.[32]

Although it might knock sideways some previously penned characterizations of Baz Outlaw, at the time (October 1890) he was in pretty good standing with the company commander and the Frontier Battalion's front office at Austin. Captain Frank Jones had respectfully asked for an extended leave of absence—several weeks—for having a medical problem dealing with his hearing checked.[33] That his request was approved should not come as a surprise, but the adjutant general's additional instructions to Captain Jones might—for those harboring preconceived notions about Baz Outlaw: "Instruct your 1st Sergeant to open your official mail & act as you would yourself in all matters of public service."[34]

That Sergeant Outlaw was committed to public service seems but a foregone conclusion. However, it is at Shafter (and/or elsewhere) when a certain ugliness—maybe demons he'd always owned—surfaced. Sergeant Baz Outlaw had a personal problem—a drinking problem. "Evidence indicates that Outlaw was serious while on duty, but tended to cause trouble when off duty and drinking."[35] Although what follows is but an anecdotal account, in light of latter established facts it rings quite true. The aforementioned postmistress at Shafter—the widowed mother of three—Laura Hay, knew Baz quite well, often entertaining him in her home for Sunday dinners and charming visits—and whatever, she being single at the time.[36] Laura was not so foolishly infatuated with Mr. Baz as a stalwart Texas Ranger or as an available bachelor that she was blind to hardcore reality. She duly noted—and later wrote—that once Baz Outlaw had consumed "several drinks [it made] a beast of him." And, when word got out that he was drinking, well "the doors were locked, children brought in off the street and all of us kept silence and hoped for the best."[37]

Purportedly, during one spree, Sergeant Outlaw and some cowboys, at Shafter or somewhere else, decided that the world would be better off absent a certain Chinaman, the one operating a laundry business. For some reason, perhaps he trusted the mail lady if that part of a daughter's story is right, the "inoffensive" fellow sought refuge at Laura Hay's residence—and thankfully so. There was a small trapdoor leading to a root cellar, and there she motioned for the Chinaman to hide. He squeezed through, Laura easing the door back to the floor behind him. Then, rather ingeniously she placed her sewing machine and dress-making materials atop and stood ready to rebuff any inquiries. When the ill disposed Baz Outlaw—obviously in his cups—arrived with his equally inebriated henchman they were cordially invited to search the house if they really thought a hardscrabble working-class Chinaman was foolish enough to seek sanctuary with a white lady. The search netted naught. Dejectedly the men left to hunt for the Chinaman, or someone else to harass—or another drink. Laura Hay breathed her sigh of relief—she really liked, admired, but admittedly too, pitied, Baz Outlaw.[38]

Baz Lamar Outlaw was, apparently, by this time in his adventuresome life an alcoholic—a qualified alcoholic, a functional alcoholic.

When sober, which was most of the time it seems, he was a reasonably likeable person and a damn good frontier-era lawman—in fact better than most. What he was not, was a social drinker—one or two and quit. Pulling the bottle's cork was the opener. Putting it back in the bottle—for Baz Outlaw—was hopeless. Good intentions are appreciated but actions accrue. There's little doubt—and some evidence—Baz Outlaw was more than anyone aware of his character flaw—as most addicted personalities are. Even knowing that his first drink mollified inhibitions and would lead to a second pull from the bottle—and a third—and a fourth—and many more, that knowledge didn't temper his bad behavior or battles with booze and blackouts. Baz Outlaw was a mean drunk, too. He assuredly was dangerous when sober, treacherous and wholly wild when under the influence of liquor, a condition one Ranger put into words. Declaring that Baz, notwithstanding his many admirable traits, had "but one weakness that—at last—proved to be stronger than all his virtues. . . . [he] couldn't leave liquor alone." And when he was drunk he was simply a "maniac" and no one "could handle him" nor could anyone "reason with him." His steadfast friends and uneasy Texas Ranger comrades just "stayed with him until he sobered up."[39]

Getting drunk is easy, hangovers are miserable. Though several episodes of Baz Outlaw's drunkenness have been cited—and others will follow—the record is silent about the morning-after wretchedness. Baz Outlaw, unless he was superhuman, may have over imbibed with gusto but he could not escape the amber current's vengeance. Alcohol-induced euphoria is fleeting. Today's yummy hot *tamales* taste better going down, than coming up cold and sour tomorrow. There is no melodramatic niceness about puking one's guts and toenails up, wiping vomit off boots and piss off pants' legs and involuntarily retching—the dry heaves—even after stomachs and bladders have emptied. Painful cramps and throbbing heads and cottony mouths reeking of vile boomeranging odors are not fun. Hard to describe is that tightfisted monkey of addiction reaching into sockets and squeezing the last milliliter of juice from bloodshot eyeballs, but he's there, never on vacation. And that's not counting teeth and bone and muscle hurting to the core: Nor gauging pin drop noises resonating with the thunderous bang of a shotgun blast in a boxcar. The sickening and cruel lure of liquor is—for some folks—as unexplainable now as it was then. Baz Outlaw was a victim and a victimizer. Why would anyone court misery, time after time? Hangover's hostages pledge ransoms of abstinence—never to do it again—on Sunday mornings while choirboys are singing hymns of righteousness and piousness, but by evening the closing shadows of that same Sabbath are slyly winking at promises made under duress. That said, law enforcing is no game, and there's no place for an ounce of chemically induced bad behavior or mind-altering fuzziness. Texas Ranger Sergeant Baz Outlaw had a bad problem with no good defense—and none is proffered herein, none whatsoever, There are, though, two sides to coins. Baz Outlaw was not drunk—or near drunk—twenty-four and seven. So, when sober he was real good. When drunk he was bad. And, over time, soberness seemed to surrender more than win. In the case of Bazzell Lamar Outlaw, simplicity is easily reachable: What it was, is what it is! Hard drinkers damn sure understand. Teetotalers and tea sippers, well, they just live in a better world.

Local elections in the Lone Star State were fertile ground for mischief and during the latter quarter of the nineteenth-century in many counties, especially South Texas and West Texas, the presence of Rangers was requested by one side or the other at polling places. Though Rangers from Company D were disbursed widely throughout the region and assigned to more than one voting precinct, West Texas' electorate was relatively well-behaved during the November 1890 election cycle. Of particular interest to the fellows of Company D was the changing of the guard in gargantuan Brewster County. One of their very own, so to speak, former Texas Ranger James Buchanan Gillett now owned the honor and the office as Brewster County's new sheriff.[40] Gillett's ascension to sheriff will play a not trivial part in the rich saga of Bazzell Lamar Outlaw—several times over.

On the law-enforcing front at Shafter, seemingly, Sergeant Outlaw and his detachment were reasonably efficient with the overall strategy of preventive enforcement—proactively being seen. For that month of November at Shafter there had been but one arrest, and it had been executed by Sergeant Outlaw himself: Marcus Padreas for Assault & Battery.[41]

Presidio County Sheriff Russell may have been ready to wind down as the Christmas holiday season of 1890 approached: Sergeant Baz Outlaw wasn't, he was hardwired and wound tight. The two lawmen would clash over police business, not monkey business but, still, it was foolish. And not surprisingly so it seems, Sergeant Baz Outlaw was "under the influence of liquor."[42] Were the report half true, and there's hardly justification in disputing it or proffering an inane excuse, it doesn't speak too favorably of Company D's 1st Sergeant. The unfortunate—and preventable—brouhaha had its genesis with several apprehensive civilians' implementation of a "citizens' arrest" at Shafter. A "Mexican" had stolen something and was being detained until legal authorities could take charge of the prisoner. Sergeant Outlaw assumed custody of the alleged thief, then set him free, declaring that criminal charges against the scared man were insufficient—for one reason or another. The local deputy sheriff (and future sheriff) in charge at Shafter, Samuel R. "Sam" Miller, an English born Texas frontiersman and bona fide Indian fighter, rearrested the Mexican intending to send the suspected thief the forty odd miles to Marfa, have him locked away in Presidio County's Jail, and let the state District Court unravel the truths and mete out justice.

Sergeant Outlaw was royally pissed and already primed with pulls from the hip-pocket flask. On the outskirts of Shafter, Deputy Sheriff Joseph Sprunk and his partner, ex-Ranger Charles B. "Charley" Barton, with prisoner Louis Gardia in tow, were overhauled by the hard-riding and somewhat tipsy Sergeant Baz Outlaw and his partner, Ranger Private E.S. Fisk. At this point in the ongoing saga, purportedly, the two Texas Rangers pulled their six-shooters and "compelled" the two local officers to "convey the prisoner back to Shafter, the place from which they had started. . . ."[43] Thankfully there had been no shooting, but there was a war—of sorts.

The prickly matter was quickly brought to the attention of Captain Frank Jones by the assistant superintendent of the Shafter mines, who punctuated his displeasure with Baz Outlaw by asking for disciplinary action—with a caveat. Area citizens, according to this account, did not want Sergeant Outlaw actually discharged from the Texas Rangers—but transferred elsewhere. There was quite possibly sound reasoning behind their entreaty: "good citizens of Shafter, fearing violence at the hands of said Outlaw, requested Capt. Jones not to discharge him and leave him. . . ." at Shafter "in their midst."[44] They wanted him gone.

After learning of the embarrassing hubbub Captain Frank Jones made a personal on-site investigation, on paper noting that he had traveled south from Company D's camp in order to conduct "official business."[45] At Shafter he learned that his top-sergeant had acted with good purpose, but injudiciously. Reduced to writing, Captain Jones advised Ranger headquarters of Baz Outlaw's rationale, but did not excuse his intemperate demeanor, acknowledging that "Outlaw has at times drank to some excess, but has given me no trouble."[46] Sergeant Outlaw's reasoning is herein reported through the filtering of Captain Jones' writings:

> Outlaw and E.S. Fisk followed and overtook them and told them the Mexican must be tried in Shafter and that Marfa was not the place to have a preliminary hearing. They then returned to Shafter and the man was delivered to the Justice of the Peace.[47]

The Company D commander had listened, then acted absent an endorsement of disciplinary punishment, an astute solution for problem resolution—but unintended consequences lurked in the darkness of administrative tiptoeing and sidestepping. With relative tranquility at Shafter—a subjective appraisal—Captain Frank Jones once again readjusted his manpower deployment model, having Sergeant Baz Outlaw return to the company headquarters, Camp Hogg, with Corporal John Hughes backfilling at Shafter.[48]

Sergeant Outlaw, certainly not confined to camp, more-or-less hit the ground running as the holiday season was upon West Texas, arresting one fellow for Unlawfully Carrying a Pistol and another for Theft of Property. Both prisoners were carried before a local justice of the peace for appropriate adjudication. Less than a week before Christmas, Sergeant Outlaw was in the saddle, accompanied by only one Ranger, hunting hard for a murder suspect haunting the striking mountain country around Fort Davis, Jeff Davis County. This time the Texas Rangers failed to get their man. But such would not be the case for Sergeant Outlaw on Christmas Eve. Traveling by railroad east to Sanderson (now Terrell County but then Pecos County), the Company D sergeant located and arrested murder suspect Magil (perhaps Miguel ?) Alahan, then securely hauled him northwest to Pecos and "Put him in Jail."[49]

As the new year of 1891 was near at hand, someone not in jail was Finus "Fine" Gilliland, the prime suspect in the murder of Henry Harrison Powe, "an old one armed ex-confederate soldier."[50] Gilliland and Powe had argued over ownership of "a brindle bull yearling."[51] As to just who was right is neither here nor there: Henry Powe lay dead and Fine Gilliland was on the run, while every member of Company D was scouring the mountain and desert country of far West Texas trying to scoop him up or shovel him under.[52] Sergeant Baz Outlaw, leading a "prospecting scout" accompanied by three Ranger privates hunted hard for Gilliland or any other fugitive that may have chosen to escape notice along the Rio Grande's hidden banks southeast of Marathon and along the river north of Boquillas Canyon. Though there's little doubt they were worn to a nub, averaging thirty miles between sunup and sundown during that nine-day sojourn in the saddle, the end result was zip—no fugitives, no fights, no funerals.[53]

The following month, February, while Sergeant Outlaw and one man were returning from another hunt after Fine Gilliland in Brewster, Jeff Davis, and Pecos Counties, another Ranger from Company D had hit the jackpot—and it spit lead, not silver coins. Arriving at Company D's Camp Hogg on February 2, 1891, the Ranger posted his captain about what had taken place on the last day of January. Fine Gilliland had been run to ground in the Glass Mountains north of Marathon by Texas Ranger James Mitchell "Jim" Putman and a Brewster County deputy sheriff, Thalis Tucker "T.T." Cook, a former and future Ranger capable of breathing fire when situations turned Western. The somewhat unexpected encounter spiked hot, Gilliland opening fire with his Winchester and with the first two shots had wounded Deputy Cook and killed his horse. Trying to stay atop his gyrating horse, Ranger Jim Putman had returned the compliment, killing Fine Gilliland's horse outright and dumping the fugitive onto Mother Earth's floor. His Winchester flying as if it had sprouted wings, in a fluid motion Gilliland had deftly whipped out his Colt's six-shooter and using his dead horse as a breastwork, began popping rounds at the Ranger. As far as marksmanship and luck was concerned, as the eagerly listening Captain Jones learned, it had really been no match. Jim Putman had cashed Gilliland's ticket—a Winchester's payday bullet square between his now lifeless eyes. Jim Putman's horse had also caught a round, rendering it wholly useless and unserviceable—plus suffering. Captain Jones ordered its merciful destruction. Unmistakably it had been a desperate gunplay.[54]

Although it may once again somewhat shatter the legendary spin sometimes put on paper about Texas Rangers, Captain Jones was desperate on another front, too. The parsimonious state legislature was still paying but a dollar a day—cowboy wages—and the turnover rate within the Frontier Battalion ranks was, perhaps, just somewhat short of atrocious. Not everyone wanted to be a sure enough standup six-shootin' Texas Ranger. On January 6, 1891, Captain Frank Jones had made such actuality known to the incoming adjutant general, Woodward Heywood Mabry, who had replaced Wilburn Hill King: "I am of the opinion that it would be an impossibility to enlist more than 5 or 6 good men out here. Men are paid $30.00 per month and furnished [room and board] for ranche work and the best class are employed."[55] Certainly Private Homer L. Nix was not overawed with Ranger work; he resigned to accept employment as a store clerk at Shafter.[56] Private A.H. Jones also wanted a discharge.[57] John Woodard Saunders, a dynamite fighting Texas Ranger with a long history of comings and goings in state service, sometimes discharged for drunkenness, but seemingly always on the bandwagon of reenlisting after all was forgiven or forgotten, this time, wanted out at his own request: "having been offered a good position with better wages. . . ."[58] With regards to another, the adjutant general specifically asked Captain Jones: "Write me what you may know about Albert Costley who once serve [*sic*] under you. He is an applicant for enlistment in new Company."[59] Never accused of mush mouthing, Captain Jones laid bare his opinion:

> In regard to Albert Costley, will say that I would not enlist him again. He, generally either has as a sick headache or the rheumatism troubles him, and then he is disposed to be insubordinate to any non commissioned officer or Private who may be placed in charge. He has sufficient courage & intelligence. His brother, Solon Costley, I can heartily recommend.[60]

Other Company D personnel actions will play into Sergeant Baz Outlaw's story, directly or indirectly. Private Ernest St. Leon, according to the Monthly Return and specific correspondence directed to the adjutant general's office—at least on paper—was dishonorably discharged from Company D "for committing petty thefts from the commissary."[61] There might be a case made arguing—in this instance and in light of later events—that this dismissal was or could have been part of a synchronized investigative strategy providing an undercover operative a good cover story—a disgruntled Ranger—as had been done earlier with Private Jim King.[62]

Another matter of administrative decision-making will, in due time, play significantly into the factual side of Baz Outlaw's story. On February 21, 1891, Captain Jones acquainted the adjutant general as to just who, in fact, was being carried on the Company D roll as Special Rangers. Intermittingly he had been specifically ordered in the past to place names on the roster. Now with a fresh face in the headquarters command, Captain Jones elected to suggest "those who I think will perhaps be an advantage to the public to retain." Of the sixteen Specials carried on the Company D books, Captain Jones "marked" but five as worthy of retention.[63]

Captain Frank Jones was really concerned on another administrative front: What to do with deadbeat Texas Rangers. Although just who and just how many of the Company D fellows were strapped for cash falls into the generalized realm of guesswork, one Ranger's real deficit doesn't. An Alpine merchant had contacted the captain regarding Sergeant Baz Outlaw's indebtedness. Undoubtedly the matter—the way it was being handled—rankled the overextended lawman: "Captain Jones was telling me that you were inquiring of him into my financial condition. I only write to say to you that, just as soon as I possibly can, I will settle what I am due your firm. As I told Mr. Humphries & Just as quick without you prying into my affairs as without, if not sooner at any rate. I can't do it until I get the money to pay with, which I will do Just as soon as I possibly can. I am Sorry that I can't do it now."[64] There may be little doubt that the area businessman taking the matter up with Frank Jones triggered the captain's concerned missive to Frontier Battalion headquarters at Austin, noting that complaints were sometimes made that "individual Rangers are contracting or have contracted more debts than his pay amounts to." And in his no-nonsense opinion: "When a few Rangers spend more money than they make it inures to the detriment of those who do, and can pay their indebtedness, and gives the Company a bad reputation."[65] Adjutant General Mabry agreed. Clear were headquarters' orders to Captain Jones: "If a ranger of your Company persist in contracting debts which he Knows he cannot meet—you will discharge him."[66] Undoubtedly Captain Jones and AG Mabry were steadfastly trying—proactively—to put the Texas Rangers on the right foot with regards to professionalism and public perception.

On the first day of March 1891, Alonzo Van "Lon" Oden enlisted as a private in Company D. Rather out of character for a routine enlistment, Captain Frank Jones made particular note to the adjutant general about his new man: "Today I enlisted A.V. Oden. He is from Frio County and comes well recommended and I think will make a good efficient Ranger."[67] Never inclined to dawdle, Captain Jones was normally perceptive about borderland reality, making his thoughts and decision known to the front office: "There seems to some alarm felt at Shafter that there might be a recurrence of the trouble experienced there last August. In view of this fact I will, at once, send Private Oden there to take the place of the man just discharged."[68] Adjutant General Mabry was, too, focusing on the same target as Captain Jones, that little settlement eighteen miles north of the Rio Grande. He concurred with Jones' judgment to "enlist a man to fill the place of private Nix. . . ." And to be ever watchful of "the situation at Shafter and prevent any occurrence of former troubles."[69]

It may be written with absolute clarity that Baz Outlaw and Lon Oden would become fast friends.[70] Captain Jones referencing that his new hire was from Frio County is intriguing, as Baz's uncle Y.P. Outlaw during 1882 had migrated to the community of Moore, Frio County. Could Baz and Lon have known each other before either one—or both—became Rangers? Could Lon's ringing endorsement as stated by Jones, that part about coming "well recommended" have been some personal personnel handiwork on the part of his top-sergeant? Or, perhaps J. Walter Durbin put in a good word: He was living there and would become the county's sheriff.

Sergeant Outlaw would close out the summer of 1891 with more-or-less routine assignments. During July he led a three man scout along the Rio Grande, finding a dead horse and some dead and butchered cattle, "Killed presumably by Mexicans living in Mexico," but returned to camp ten days later. The following month, Sergeant Outlaw was dispatched to make an apprehension in El Paso County. After diligent investigation Company D's 1st Sergeant determined that the man he had been sent to arrest was "found to be the wrong man" and he returned to Camp Hogg. Law enforcers' reprieves from boredom are short lived. For the remainder of the year—starting in September—Sergeant Outlaw would chase newsmakers and be a newsmaker.

A wonderful and seldom published photograph of Company D Rangers. For this treatment, particularly note Captain Frank Jones seated front and center and Sergeant Baz Outlaw to his left. *Courtesy Tobin and Anne Armstrong Ranger Research Center, Texas Ranger Hall of Fame & Museum.*

Thalis Tucker "T.T." Cook, sometimes Ranger, sometimes deputy sheriff, but at all times utterly fearless. Though critically wounded, he survived a deadly gunplay wherein fugitive Fine Gilliland bit the dust in the Glass Mountains north of Marathon with Ranger Jim Putman's Winchester's bullet square between his eyes. *From Texas Ranger Sketches, courtesy the author, Robert W. Stephens.*

Marathon, Brewster County, for a time one of the leading livestock shipping points for far West Texas. Texas Rangers were in and out of town often, traveling by railroad with their horses and pack mules in search of desperadoes. Marathon, too, was a jumping off spot for heading south to the Rio Grande. *Courtesy Archives of the Big Bend, Bryan Wildenthal Memorial Library, Sul Ross University.*

Alonzo Van Oden, perhaps Baz Outlaw's closest personal friend and fellow Texas Ranger.
Author's photo courtesy the late John D. Tanner, Jr.

A striking image of Pearsall, Frio County, Texas. Texas Ranger Lon Oden, living with relatives would sometimes call Frio County home, as would Baz Outlaw's uncle, Y.P. Outlaw, who had taken up residence near the community of Moore. *Courtesy the Donald M. and Louise Yean Collection.*

Pictured in this neat and heretofore unpublished photograph is a seated J. Walter Durbin, later in life, who aside from earlier being a celebrated Texas Ranger would also serve as the multi-term elected sheriff of Frio County. *Courtesy Roberta Durbin Gutierrez.*

Another delightful old-time Frio County area photograph: Pictured here is the 1,325-acre homeplace and birthplace of Mary Permelia "Mollie" Burden, the daughter of Joseph Louis "J.L." and Eliza Jane (Franks) Burden. Mollie would become the wife of J. Walter Durbin and mother of their three children, Julia, Marshall, and Herman. *Courtesy Roberta Durbin Gutierrez.*

The spirited Texas Ranger detail temporarily stationed at Shafter, Presidio County. Standing, L to R: Private Robert "Bob" Speaks and Private Jim Putman, the latter having killed fugitive Fine Gilliland during a vicious shootout in the Glass Mountains north of Marathon. Seated, L to R: Ranger Private Lon Oden, and Corporal John Hughes, a future Company D Captain. *Courtesy Tobin and Anne Armstrong Ranger Research Center, Texas Ranger Hall of Fame & Museum.*

CHAPTER 8

Insulted in the Presence of Ladies

DURING WEE MORNING HOURS of September 2, 1891, at about four o'clock, the engineer on the westbound Galveston, Harrisburg & San Antonio (Southern Pacific) Railroad's No. 20 noticed something unfamiliar and out of the ordinary—debris had been piled onto the railroad tracks. Quite successfully—and luckily—he applied the locomotive's air brakes, bringing the train to a safe stop roughly a mile from what was then known as Samuels Siding (now Pumpville) at Horseshoe Bend just inside Val Verde County's western and just outside Pecos County's then eastern boundary line.[1] It was by any standard lonesome country. However, the train's crew had bad-mannered company: Four masked and menacing fellows carrying Winchesters. With threatening words and carbine muzzles poked into their ribs, the engineer and his fireman were marched back to the Express Car.[2]

Outside, the train robbers demanded entry. Inside, J. Ernest Smith, Wells, Fargo & Company's express messenger "barred his doors" and made ready for war; he'd undergone holdups before. And, in fact, during one such crime gone awry near El Paso four years earlier he had killed would-be bad men Jack Smith and Dick Myers when they tested his resolve.[3] This time, it was different, the robbers had an Ace—a bundle of red-wrapped sticks with a fuse. J. Ernest Smith offered commentary: "My idea was to watch and get a dead shot at them, but they were no novices and remained down under the side of my car, and I'm glad now I did not get a shot for there was a regular army of them. Only six showed up, but others could be heard talking in the bushes. I was ordered to come out, but refused and heard the captain of the gang give orders to shoot into my car, and immediately they proceeded to pump lead in to my apartments. I started across the car to get behind my safe. The captain called to me: 'Open up and come out of there or I will blow the blamed car up.'" Boastfully and quite truthfully it seems, one of the outlaws hollered that "they had a whole jackass load of dynamite" and by damn, entry they would own. Bravely, J. Ernest Smith stood pat—for a little while.[4]

The thunderous explosion knocked him off his feet. Or, as a witty newspaperman writing for the *San Antonio Daily Express* expressed it: "Express Messenger Smith, had his anatomy pretty well shaken up by the dynamite bombs. . . ."[5] Though his ears were ringing, the chief robber's command was audible; be blown to smithereens or surrender—they had plenty more dynamite. While somewhat addled by the explosives' concussion, Mr. J. Ernest Smith was not stunned into stupidity. He submitted. Halfheartedly he opened the Express Car door and "jumped out." Smartly a brigand took Smith's Colt's .45 six-shooter and explained the situation fully: J. Ernest could give up the combination for the local/way safe or give up the ghost. It would be, although personally humiliating, his eventual choice to make.[6] While waiting for his decision—which was a foregone conclusion—the impatient crooks rifled canvas bags filled with the U.S. Mail—a federal violation—as they had already taken William Lytle, Postal Clerk, from the "car and bound him while the robbery was being committed. . . ."[7] Little did they realize it then, but this bunch of train robbers would cut their little notch in the history book of criminality. Messenger Smith did not have a combination for the through safe, a lockbox that could only be opened at each end of the train's trip. No problem. Busily the robbers rigged explosives to serve as their key to the vault—boom! Such a dynamic entry was the very first instance in documented American banditry that "train robbers opened an express safe by blasting it with dynamite."[8] With safe doors standing wide open the highjackers eagerly tallied their take: $3,600—currency and coin—plus what ever loot might be tucked in envelopes of the registered mail. Assuredly it wasn't the largest haul in the history of Old Southwest thievery, but divvied for a four-way split, $900 apiece wasn't paltry—those damn pesky Rangers and deputies that were sure to follow couldn't sneeze at that, not when they were banking but $1.00 per day.

Adopting a decided Robin Hood-type flair, the chief mogul of the gang vociferously declared that the passengers' purses and wallets were off limits—as were their watches and jewelry, and that went for the train's crew, too. During their banter one of the robbers chimed in with an excuse for this criminal misbehavior, saying that "cattle were so poor and grass so bad, that the animals were not worth skinning."[9] They only robbed corporations, not hard-working folks like themselves or passengers or trainmen scratching for scarce dollars, daily living hand to mouth. Well, excepting for J. Ernest Smith's six-shooter: They would have to keep that particular pistol for self-preservation's sake. In keeping with the congenial spirit of being a "jolly good fellow" the gang's big boss, before they marched the crew 100 yards from the train so as to make a clean getaway, proffered his hospitable invitation to Mr. J. Ernest Smith, not having an iota of an idea he'd already cashed two foolish train robbers' tickets east of El Paso with a double-barreled 10-gauge, saying: "You are a damn plucky fellow and if I had a bottle we would drink but it is too dry here for even water. We will treat you boys, the first time we catch you in San Antonio."[10] Then they were gone.

Even in the desolate and rocky and rattlesnake-infested West of the Pecos Country big news travels fast. At Del Rio, the county seat of Val Verde County, a near dozen-man posse was hastily fashioned by Sheriff August H. Kieffer. Loading their "horses and accouterments" onto a westbound train the sheriff and his men hastened to the crime scene. They were there joined by another small posse, this one captained by none other than the ever waggish Judge Roy Bean, the justice of the peace at Langtry operating out of his notorious Jersey

Lilly Saloon.[11] Clearly robbers were headed for the Rio Grande, only a few short miles south of the crime site. The yahoos' backtrail was carelessly littered with "cigar stumps and peach peels," byproducts of their pilfering a newspaper vendor's box of goodies kept for sale to passengers.[12]

Pulling up at the Texas edge of the Rio Grande, Sheriff Kieffer and Judge Bean huddled for but a moment then made their decision known to their respective troops—they'd not breach the river. This was a job for the Texas Rangers and a telegraph message had been sent to the nearest command, Captain Frank Jones' Company D. At least for the time being they would wait for the Rangers. Splashing into Mexico could prove—besides dangerous—politically dicey business for local lawmen absent backing—prearranged backing—from the statehouse at Austin. They didn't have any such arrangement and certainly weren't privy to some very special instructions from the adjutant general to Captain Jones regarding such potentially touchy issues. Just the month before—prior to the train robbery—AG Mabry on a like matter had made his thoughts known to the Company D commander: "Be careful how you cross over into Mexico with an armed force, and, don't be too long from Communication by this office."[13]

Meanwhile at Camp Hogg outside Alpine, the Company D Rangers were astir, fast gathering horses and suitable rations of Arbuckles, air-tights (canned tomatoes, corn, peaches, and condensed milk), and ammo. A sure enough manhunt was on tap. They would, under the direction of Sergeant Baz Outlaw, load everything, horses, gear, and men into livestock cars of a specially requisitioned train, and notify Captain Jones all was good—they were ready. Perhaps hearing from the captain, unedited, is fitting:

> On the morning of the 2nd inst with 5 men I went on a special Car to where the Sothern Pacific train was robbed in Val Verde County. Arrived at the scene of the robbery about 4 p.m. and with 4 citizens of Val Verde County and one of Brewster took up the trail which led in the direction of Mexico. I followed the trail to the Rio

Grande that evening and tied up our horses without any grass at all. The next morning as soon as it was light enough I found where they had crossed into Mexico and there was 5 of them as each horse track showed plainly in the sand all of them shod all round. They took a southeast course after crossing the River for about ten miles and then all scattered. I followed a single horse trail and soon discovered they had turn North. About 8 miles from where they separated they came together and burned quite a lot of papers as the ashes showed and unshod their horses. The trail then lead back to the river and re crossed to this side and again scattered. We again followed on track and found where they came together and camped. We followed the trail in this way, they separating every few miles and going across the roughest Country on the route, always leading up the Rio Grande. On the 5th day we found where they had reshod their horses and then they staid together. On the 6th day we found their camp in a dense cane brake on the Mexican side of the river. One of their men out as a scout or looking after stock discovered us about 4 miles below their Camp and although we chased him he had too much the start and got into Camp and gave the alarm. After we chased this man we continued on up the River until we came to the cane brake and some dogs Came out to meet us. We then scattered out and tried to look through this Cane but I soon saw it was too dense and was besides very dangerous. I then surrounded the brake as well as I could and set fire to it in several place and closed in as it burned. We then located the Camp and closed in on it but the men had mounted fresh horses and fled. I found a camp that has evidently been there for several months with quite a lot of plunder. There was 3 extra saddles in this Camp of men who must have been murdered. This was the Camp of a man named John Flynt who has some stock on this side of the river. The only way for the Mexican authorities to get at his Camp would have been to cross to this side. We found a great many stolen Cattle there and letters that prove they were regularly in the business. After leaving this Camp I trailed them to this side and then back into Mexico. At a point when they left their horses and again

> went into the Cain. I spent 3 days beating and burning out the brakes on both sides but failed to ever Catch them. Three of them are well known in this section. There is no Mexican settlement any where in that region and Flynt has murdered several on the other side and they don't dare Come near him. If we had not found the robber Camp we would have been without rations for several days. I demolished their roost entirely and am satisfied hunger will drive them from the River. Now Genl I wanted you to know, through me, that I had crossed into Mexico and Chased these men but there is a reward I am told offered by the Mexicans for some of these same parties for thefts committed from them. Of course I would not cross into Mexico where there are settlements and would be any danger of stirring up any international trouble. You would do me a favor by stating this matter to Gov Hogg as it really is as he might hear through the papers of my crossing. My horses are completely broken down. I returned to Camp today. The robber camp is about one hundred miles from here.[14]

Captain Frank Jones' mention that there were rewards offered due to this gang's crimes in the State of Chihuahua might have had merit. On the Texas side of the river it was categorically true. The train robbers were worth money, the bounty totaling $1,750 a head, stone-cold dead or alive and kicking: For trifling with the U.S. Mail the federal government chipped in $1,000 per robber; Wells, Fargo & Company $250 per head; and the railroad upped $500 apiece for the pot.[15] There was, too, another part of the financial story, rumors and gossip that as much as $50,000 had been taken during the robbery and that the wily corporate executives were downplaying such a whopping loss. Such would be not only uncomfortably embarrassing—but bad for business.[16] True though it wasn't, the buzz persisted.

Subsequent to their return to Camp Hogg, Sergeant Outlaw outfitted another scout after the train robbers. Riding as headman for the eight-man patrol, the top-sergeant struck a southeasterly course for the Rio Grande—a particular section of the river that would quickly become known as *Las Vegas de los Ladrones*, The Meadows of the Bandits. This distinct piece of ground "lies on both sides of the Rio Grande. . . . The narrow, discontinuous vegas extend downriver below the point where Maravillas Creek empties into the Rio Grande and are covered with dense thickets of Carrizo, a tall cane grass which may grow as tall as a man on horseback. In this stretch of the river the Rio Grande occupies a valley one to two miles wide and about two thousand feet deep. The valley walls consist of steep rocky slope below high cliff of massive limestone layers. The vegetative assemblage of the lowland and slopes is typical of the Chihuahuan Desert and consists of creosote bush, lechuguilla, sotol, yucca, mesquite, cacti, and chino grass. The area is, and has always been, virtually unpopulated—because of the rugged topography and aridity."[17] This section of the river's borderlands is where Captain Jones and Sergeant Outlaw had demolished John Flynt's campsite, now a prime suspect in the Samuels Siding heist.[18]

Working out of a subcamp southeast of Marathon, near Little Wood Hollow, Sergeant Outlaw and his squad of gritty and grimy and gutsy Texas Rangers hunted hard for the outlaws for nine wearisome days—unsuccessfully before returning dejected and downtrodden to Camp Hogg.[19] They, however, had not been searching for an unknown commodity. Through reasonably astute investigative work at the abandoned campsite and elsewhere, the Company D Rangers had the identities of the train robbers pegged—at least for the most part it was presumed. They were looking to arrest the aforementioned John M. Flynt, a thirty-one-year-old, originally from Gonzales County due east of San Antonio, "brave and fearless as a lion, and when aroused was a very dangerous man," having drank and gambled heavily for about six months, he was now "desperate"; John "Three-Fingered Jack" Wellington, thirty-five, a Val Verde County horse raiser and horse trader; James "Jim" Lansford, twenty-two, with a "long and gaunt" look, and with his clean shaven face, casting hardly the appearance of a daring cow country criminal raised amid South Texas' brasada in La Salle County, but he undeniably was a hardened and leathery fellow "of the rough cowboy element"; and Tom Strouts, aka Tom Fields, just short of his fortieth birthday, now a Brewster County cowboy, but one owning a criminal history in Williamson County regarding the "ownership of a mule," and certainly as a newspaperman declared, "a reputation not to be proud of."[20]

News of the train robbery and hunt for its architects had not only captured notice of print media correspondents, but the Rangers' big boss, Adjutant General Mabry, was paying particular attention to the twisting and turning drama playing out in the West Texas borderland country. Mabry was reasonably confident of success, predicting to Captain Jones: "This department is anxious to have these fellows caught, and since most of them are Known to you the capture is made somewhat easier." The adjutant general wasn't on the ground. Catching crooks in the office—in one's mind—is somewhat easier than running them down in the field. Peculiarly, but understandably in light of Company D's hard-hitting reputation, was AG Mabry's further remarks to Captain Jones: "I have information that they desire to Surrender but I do not give credence to such report. I think they desire to create this impression so as to stop pursuit—Thus enabling them to get out of the Country—They claim that they will surrender, but not to you. . . ."[21] At the time it seems there was an undercurrent of animosity, especially between fugitives Three-Fingered Jack Wellington and John Flynt on the one side and Captain Jones and his Texas Rangers serving under the command structure of Sergeant Baz Outlaw on the other. Purportedly death threats either had been made publicly or a murder plot was somewhere on the conspiratorial drawing board.[22]

Sergeant Outlaw and his men had returned to the camp near Alpine on the first day of October 1891 and shortly Captain Frank Jones was at El Paso, scheduled to make an appearance before the federal grand jury regarding the train robbers' tampering with the U.S. Mail. Meanwhile, idleness was not playing out in Val Verde County. Big doings were also unfolding regarding the train robbery. First but not necessarily foremost was the return of state court indictments charging the above mentioned—and known—perpetrators of the Samuels Siding caper. The quartet of ne'er-do-wells was now wanted by the law—officially, warrants had issued. There was, however, an item of more immediate interest than legalities, namely the fugitives' whereabouts. Shelf-life of that mystery would be short.

Deputy Sheriff Joseph Russell Sitter, then working for Sheriff Kieffer, but later a Ranger and still later a U.S. Mounted Customs Inspector, was on the train robbers' trail forty miles due north of Comstock near the tiny settlement of Juno. He had picked up intelligence that the fugitives had visited Henry Stein's store, and with $20 gold pieces which appeared somehow scorched, had purchased "clothing, undershirts, and slickers." Purportedly the fugitives had ridden west of Juno and gone to ground, setting up a temporary campsite. Asking or ordering fifteen-year-old Joe Bendele to pilot him to the spot, Deputy Joe Sitter had taken up what he figured was the outlaws' trail—after finding discarded old clothing and a freshly butchered calf he knew he was right. Another dozen or so miles further west, at Johnson's Draw (or Johnson's Run), Joe Sitter and his apprentice lawdog sniffed out "fresh tracks of horses where the robbers had them hobbled." Wisely, Sitter and Bendele stealthily retreated, heading back to Juno for reinforcements. Unfortunately, as Deputy Sitter learned, there was no help to be had. Joe Bendele went home. Joe Sitter scooted for the nearest telegraph station, Comstock, where, at long last, he finally got word to Captain Jones—who, with Sergeant Outlaw and two privates, was actually traveling by train to El Paso—but notification of the Texas Rangers had been achieved.[23]

Captain Jones, elated to get such valuable intelligence, assured Joe Sitter he would make double quick time to Val Verde County with the necessary manpower, but in the interim don't dare let the cunning fugitives give him the slip and make all of his hard work count for naught. The Texas Rangers by anyone's calculation were near two days away, at best. Leaving word at Comstock for Rangers to follow him to Juno, Joe Sitter fast backtracked the forty miles to Juno. There, hurriedly he provisionally deputized ranchman Bob

Stockman and young Joe Bendele, again leaving word as to their course so Rangers could—in time—overtake them.[24]

Admittedly there is a degree of haze concerning the particulars, but whether it was in regards to indicting the train robbers or a mandated appearance in either federal or state court at El Paso for another criminal case, or simply because of legal formalities and/or prosecutorial necessity, Sergeant Outlaw was to remain in the city while Captain Frank Jones caught the eastbound Galveston, Harrisburg, & San Antonio for Alpine. From there, after marshaling manpower and loading saddle horses and pack mules onto a hastily prearranged train with railroad officials' blessing—and encouragement—Captain Jones was to hasten to the picturesque but not so angelic Devils River Country in Val Verde County northwest of Del Rio. Once there, somehow and somewhere in that big land of sparse population and even scarcer communication lines, he was to make contact with that ever tenacious man-tracking deputy, Joe Sitter.[25]

Slow trailing, Joe Sitter and his lightly armed crew—Bendele only had an old pistol—again were fortunate in finding another slaughtered steer, and even the charred forked sticks the hungry hoodlums had used to broil meat over the open-flame cookery.[26] Traveling north, the manhunters, leaving Val Verde County on the backtrail, crossed into Crockett County (Ozona) which had been surveyed on paper since 1875, but only formally organized two months before the train robbery, with John C. Perry holding down the sheriff's job. Although he had no jail at the time, at the very first county commissioner's session, meeting under a "large live oak tree," the county's administrators did willingly agree to furnish the newly elected sheriff with a pair of handcuffs and leg-irons.[27] Deputy Sitter and his party, after crossing into Crockett County, began angling northwest toward historic Howard's Well near the crumbling ruins of old Fort Lancaster. Like some of the Big Bend Country, at the time Crockett County was but thinly populated and the topography was rugged and rocky. Faint-hearted folks went elsewhere. Finally, after a respite of rest and recuperation for themselves and their jaded horses at an area sheep ranch, Deputy Sitter and his two troopers were overtaken by Captain Frank Jones and five Rangers, who had offloaded their animals at the Comstock station, and were now mounted, riding-hard for a conclusion with the dodging desperadoes.[28]

After hooking up with the Rangers, Joe Sitter moves the story forward: "We then took up to follow the trail to where they camped after leaving Howard's Well, about ten miles distant, where they had nooned. About ten miles further on they had camped for the night. From there we trailed them over to the 77 Ranch on the head of Live Oak Creek."[29]

Quite appropriately and tactically smart, the Rangers surrounded the headquarters house at the 77 Ranch. Were they inside, cutting off the robbers' escape was imperative. Accompanied by another Ranger, Captain Frank Jones boldly entered the residence Colt's .45 six-shooter in hand. The ranch owner's wife, Mrs. Roy, home alone was sleeping in the master bed, wholly unawares that she had uninvited male company—scruffy-looking and gun-carrying guys—in her bedroom. It should come as no real shocker, when Mr. Roy's better-half was awakened she was shocked, "scared very badly," so much so that "she could hardly talk."[30] After the apologies and when Mrs. Roy gained her composure, the pursuing lawmen were tickled pink with what the ranching lady—a Northern woman—had to say. Yes, she had seen four fellows fitting the description. And fortuitously, at that very moment in time, they were negotiating trading horses with a cowboy working the 77 Ranch: He had a string of personally owned mounts. And, too, if the Texas Rangers really wanted those mean boys, well, the transaction was taking place over in the "next pasture," some eight or ten miles from her house.[31]

Stepping into the stirrup and setting out, Captain Frank Jones was strong-minded in his belief that when the sixteenth day of October 1891 shut down, his Rangers and the Val Verde County crew would be assigned duties as guards or gravediggers. This train robber chasing had worn thin. Subsequent to covering eight miles at a gut-wrenching clip, the lawmen pulled in for a quick dinner break (lunch) and to let fatigued horses blow. Hardly had they stopped before a fellow "hallooed" their cold camp and rode in—no doubt to the tell-tell tune of ratcheting clicks as Colt's hammers were eared back to the full-cock notch. The inquisition was quick and painless. The young 77 Ranch cowboy was near speechless, but he did manage to blurt out that he had just partaken of dinner and traded horses with four strangers—just about three or four miles further up the canyon. He described his luncheon partners. Captain Frank Jones nodded in agreement: The boy had just dined with train robbers. Excitedly, but appreciatively, the cowhand coughed: "My God, I'm sure glad you didn't run on them while I was there."[32] Hurriedly and quietly the lawmen began tightening cinches—their innermost thoughts about what could happen, might happen, were private—but everyone was up to snuff, now was the time "to run on them" and the Grim Reaper isn't a reliable team player. Nevertheless, good lawmen do what good lawmen do: Something!

It turned Western at one o'clock in the afternoon. Rangers spotted the four bandits leading a packhorse about a mile away. Captain Jones ordered the men into the bed of a dry creek, which if his calculations were correct, would parallel the outlaw's direction of travel—getting them ever closer without being detected. The Rangers set off at the trot, spitting dust from dry mouths and worry from their psyches—this was no time for nervousness. In short order the Rangers closed the distance to a half mile. Then they topped out of the shielding creek bed ready for whatever: Peaceful submission, or desperate gunplay or panicky flight. Four crooks would have the option. Incredibly, the pursuers were steadily closing the gap while their quarry lazily ambled along. Shortly, however, the outlaws' horses perked their ears and whinnied, herd instinct kicking in. Turing sideways in their hulls, and spying bad trouble at their left flank, the fugitives put iron to their mounts, drawing Winchesters from saddle-scabbards as they took flight, burning the wind. Hollering loudly Captain Jones issued the required command: Stop! They didn't. His orders to his men were explicit: "kill their horses, and try to arrest the men alive—if possible."[33]

Jim Lansford got the message right fast, bringing his horse to a sliding stop and throwing his hands in the air—reaching for the sky and salvation—not from God, but bullets. Tom Stouts (still known as Fields) spurring madly soon felt the horse beneath his legs falter, fagged and gasping for air. He, too, threw down his Winchester and surrendered. Not choosing to forfeit their freedom, the strong-willed John Flynt and Three-Fingered Jack Wellington entertained no silly thoughts of quitting.[34]

Captain Jones, Joe Sitter, and Bob Stockman gave chase, while the others were guarding the two prisoners, and rounding up pack animals, theirs and the guttersnipes. According to posse member Joe Sitter, the bad guys were firing at them, and they at them, and the shooting had become "promiscuous and lively."[35] Suddenly Wellington went to ground, his horse having caught a round, lurching, then lumbering—immobilized. Captain Jones shouted for Sitter and Stockman to keep after Flynt, "until they ran him in some hole" and that as soon as he captured or capped Wellington he would follow.[36] Company D's captain, captivatingly picks up what happened next—at least as he saw it:

> When he [Wellington] dismounted I was sure that Flynt would too and that they would fight to the death. I dismounted and shot at Wellington 3 times but it was at a long distance and I undershot him. He had a much better gun than mine, it being a large long range rifle with cartridges as long as your finger. I knew that he was a famous shot and at long range had a decided advantage. . . . I remounted my horse and ran up to about 100 yards of him where I felt pretty sure I could kill him the first shot. I then called out to him that I was an officer and did not wish to hurt him and he surrendered. . . . There had been so much talk about Wellington that I was anxious to try conclusions with him and I guess we would have had a regular Winchester duel only he saw some of the men coming on up the flat and knew that in case he killed me he could not get away with his life. He was not a particle unnerved.[37]

Conversely the frantically fleeing John Flynt was unnerved. For as long as he could—about seven or eight miles—Flynt was "riding like fury" and exchanging shots with Joe Sitter and Bob Stockman. The actual chase came to an abrupt end when the hare jumped off his horse taking cover in a ravine, and the two hounds did likewise at a safe interval. Somewhat surprisingly Flynt popped out of the ditch, racing for the saddlebags on his winded horse, then scampered back to concealment. Moments later a solitary shot rang out—robber John Flynt had "suicided." Cautiously but daringly the lawmen approached the spot and found Flynt dead, laying on his back, a self-inflicted gunshot wound to his right temple and his inoperative Winchester beside him "choked with a cartridge in it." The hastily scribbled suicide note—bequeathing all of his personal property to his brother—was found in the top of his boot.[38]

Captain Jones ordered an inventory of property and recovered most of the money taken in the robbery and, of important evidentiary value, Rangers also recovered the six-shooter once owned by Express Messenger J. Ernest Smith, though the serial numbers had been filed off. Subsequent to making arrangements for a rough country burial for Flynt, the Rangers escorted the three prisoners to Comstock—where a squabble sapped most good cheer from the capture. Sheriff Kieffer demanded custody of the prisoners. Captain Jones refused. They were to be prosecuted in federal court—and that meant removal to El Paso.[39] Captain Jones won the day.[40] However, despite hard and provable truths, two hot topics spun on tornados of gossip swirling throughout the region—and elsewhere: Number one was that John Flynt had been murdered by Rangers. Number two played into the cockamamie cover-up story, in that those damn sorry big wig executives had lied about the amount of money taken in the first place and somewhere out in the desert and mountain Big Bend County *mucho dinero* was buried. A correspondent writing for the *San Antonio Daily Light* wasn't speciously spreading unsubstantiated rumors for any treasure hunter's gristmill of misinformation, but he did seem to have a smidgen of deference for a good boy gone wrong—real wrong:

> Flint [*sic*] the suiciding express robber, was the right kind of a thief. If a man is going in for that kind of thing and proposes to defy law let him have the courage of his actions and not squeal when it comes to taking his gruel.[41]

On the other hand, at El Paso, prisoner Lansford squealed like a pig with one foot caught in a fence's wire gate. It had been expected—from the get-go—that he would be first to "limber up." Quickly the scared and weak-kneed defendant turned state's evidence and "unbosomed himself" to federal prosecutors. Ultimately (an uneasy but crucial chronological leap to 1892) with legal skills and trial guidance of Prosecuting Attorney Jack Evans—and the fundamental testimony of Captain Frank Jones and Sergeant Baz Outlaw—along with others—as well as the introduction of physical evidence such as the express messenger's Colt's revolver, "empty shells, horse shoes and other relics of the battle which [were] picked up at Samuel's siding immediately after the event," the train robbery saga was but old news.[42] Lansford had "walked," no hard time in the big-house, while Wellington and Stouts each pulled a dime—ten years to do as prisoners in the House of Corrections at Detroit, Michigan, where many federal inmates were kept, guaranteeing imposition of the U.S. Courts' sentences and setting examples for other erstwhile cowboys thinking they owned enough derring-do to mess with cooperate America's money.

Back on chronological track, while all the drama had been playing out east of Camp Hogg during October 1891, Sergeant Outlaw had been steadily—and competently it seems—holding the fort, communicating and updating the adjutant general's office regarding his personal activity and trying to pinpoint Captain Frank Jones' exact geographical location for Frontier Battalion headquarters.[43] Had Sergeant Baz Outlaw been overtly misbehaving, carousing and carrying on in Alpine's barrooms and billiard halls and bordellos while the company's big boss was away, it goes unspoken—perhaps successfully swept under the rug—but truly unrecorded nonetheless. But, that was quick to change.

On the second day of November 1891 Sergeant Baz Outlaw and a couple of unnamed Rangers went to town intent on having some fun, innocent fun. There was to be a scheduled performance at Alpine of Zamloch's Congress of Wonders, a San Francisco-based exhibition traveling the Southwest.[44] Billed as the "World's Greatest Magician," Anton Zamloch aka Professor Zamaloch, had earlier closed a six-night engagement at Rische's Theater on Houston Street in San Antonio and was headed home to California, working one night shows along the way to make money and defer expenses. The *San Francisco Chronicle's* journalist dealing with matters of amusement, picked up by the *San Antonio Daily Light*, strongly touted the extravaganza: "No wonder this great show attracts immense audiences. It is the most magnificent in all its parts. A more tasty stage or a finer paraphernalia we never saw."[45] Anton Zamloch's sales pitch philosophy was tagged at the bottom of his promotional posters:

> Enjoy Yourself While You Live for You Will Be A Long Time Dead

There's not too much room for any thoughtful dispute, at one of Alpine's wet ports Sergeant Baz Outlaw had launched his canoe on a whiskey river, and was fast drinking and paddling not to be late for the evening's show time. At the ticket gate, the unnamed Texas Rangers forked over their money and were granted entrance to what promised to be an electrifying night. At the figurative turnstile Baz Outlaw purportedly brushed passed the show's general manager, C.E. Van Horn, without paying. Somewhat imprudently since he had no idea he was grabbing a hair-triggered tiger by the tail, Mr. Van Horn reached out and grasped Baz Outlaw by the elbow, tugging him to an abrupt halt. When braced about his supposed free ride Sergeant Outlaw "made threats of what he would do if there were not ladies present, making so much noise that Professor Zamloch left the Stage and came to the door to see what the mater [*sic*] was." Sergeant Baz Outlaw claimed he was not accustomed to paying at such venues—he was, after all, a Ranger—and furthermore he wasn't going to pay—not one damn red cent.[46] As the saying goes, the show went on, as did the stewing discontent of the Californians' perceived shabby treatment by a lawman, a Texas lawman at that! That would not stand.

Perhaps, had the unpleasantness remained behind at Alpine, time would have soothed ruffled feathers and a drunk Texas Ranger would have sobered up. Such was not to be. Zamloch's Congress of Wonders set sail—on the railroad—for Marfa, but twenty-five miles west of Alpine. Sergeant Outlaw's whiskey watercourse flowed in that direction, too. And he was still furiously paddling. On a Marfa street Mr. Van Horn and Sergeant Outlaw met for a second time—and it did not go well that fourth day of November. Purportedly Baz was still liquored up and "commenced his abuse and making threats." Area citizens, though unidentified, approached Van Horn advising him to use extreme caution and to "keep away from him as he is a bad man and has killed several men in the same way. . . ." Mr. Van Horn took the advice to heart, though he was not about to let the matter rest, allowing some malicious and mean-spirited and goddamned arrogant Texas Ranger run roughshod over him.[47]

Sitting down at the Marfa hotel's desk, pen in hand, Van Horn wrote James Stephen Hogg, the first Texas-born governor of the Lone Star State. His message to the Chief Executive was clear, plainspoken—and carried a threat. He wanted Baz Outlaw kicked out of Texas Rangers, or else, since he was connected with a Bay Area newspaper, he would "give the State of Texas and her Peace Officers the benefit of an article and a Cartoon." The good governor had four weeks leeway, that's when Van Horn would be returning home to San Francisco and when he "would be glad to hear of Mr. Outlaw's discharge."[48] Not to be neglectful in his formal complaint, the perceptibly upset Mr. Van Horn also wrote a bitching letter to Captain Jones—that way he was on record, any brother-in-law type whitewashing would not go unnoticed.[49]

From top echelons of governmental bureaucracies bad stuff characteristically rolls downhill. In this instance, Captain Frank Jones was at the bottom. He was charged with making an internal investigation into Van Horn's allegations and then to report his findings to the adjutant general. Though a headache it was, Captain Jones conducted an inquiry. First he took statements from the men "who were with Outlaw" regarding the incident at Alpine. And, not surprisingly, those Rangers figured that and were in agreement, "the matter is very much exaggerated. Said, that Outlaw made no effort to crowd in and did not Create any disturbance. Simply told the man he was in the habit of going into such places without paying, but make [made] no contention over the affair as ladies were present."[50] Captain Jones also interviewed Brewster County Sheriff Jim Gillett, who was actually there and "who saw it." According to the sheriff, Van Horn had "seized Outlaw by the arm and pulled him backward in a very rude way." Sheriff Gillett candidly told Captain Jones "that Outlaw would have been justifiable in knocking him down on the spot."[51] The ever dutiful—and fair minded—captain then moseyed over to Marfa, following up on what was said to have happened there.

Frank Jones visited with the Presidio County Judge, B.F. Adams, who not hesitatingly backed up the story of Mr. Van Horn, telling the captain that it was "substantially true."[52] According to Judge Adams the exchange between Van Horn and Outlaw at Marfa was off-color, verbiage that was biting and blue. Among other things Sergeant Baz Outlaw told C.E. Van Horn that he had been insulted in the presence of ladies at Alpine and couldn't then do anything about it. But now, he would tell him what he thought of him—"that he was a horse's ___ and that he would knock the ____ out of him—that he was a d____d blue belly & c." Deftly Captain Jones had toned down the scorching rhetoric with several of those fill-in-the-blank spaces when reporting Sergeant Outlaw's tirade to the adjutant general: "This language is not choice but I thought it best to give it to you as it occurred so that you can judge the matter as it is."[53]

In a sense of playing fair, Captain Jones offered Sergeant Outlaw the chance to tell his side of the story. In Outlaw's mind the incident at Alpine was way overblown, especially regarding his attending the performance without paying. On the other hand, at Marfa, well:

> Outlaw now says that he is sorry he ever said anything to him but accidently met him and felt so outraged that he could not resist the

> temptation to tell him his opinion of how he had been treated in a place where he could not resent it.[54]

Captain Frank Jones was somewhat betwixt and between. Though it goes unsaid, there can be little doubt he was somewhat amused at Mr. C.E. Van Horn's self-assured pronouncement that he "had to submit to an abusing [by Outlaw] as he was unarmed." That day somebody's God was looking after a Californian. There was no shortage of Colt's six-shooters or Smith & Wesson belly-guns or Winchesters in the Big Bend Country and he could have laid his hands on firepower real fast. Van Horn's resorting to settling Baz Outlaw's hash with paper and pen, rather than pistols and projectiles, speaks to good sense. Odds are, had he actually pulled for a pistol, Sergeant Baz Outlaw would have been found *Not Guilty* of murder, a West Texas jury buying into a claim of self-defense.

On the other hand Captain Frank Jones' dilemma was epic: Balancing the scales of discipline with the weights of past performance. What wrongs wipe out what rights? Who held those thorny and hard to come by answers? If truth be told—and it certainly should be—in this case Texas Ranger headquarters at Austin didn't. Lofty idealism is fine—from the armchair and from afar. On the decision making ground, in the real world and in real time, life is much more nuanced. Adjutant General Mabry revealed as much:

> If you find no palliating circumstances to excuse Sergt Outlaw for conduct prejudicial to the good of the service you will discharge him from the service—Every Ranger must so deport himself as to reflect credit upon the force—To compel that respect which is due from the people to every conservator of the peace. The position of a Ranger is one of trust and when any member of the force fails to appreciate this fact, and shows by his example his disregard of the importance of such trust he should be relieved of it.[55]

Pretty well cut and dried—simple? Maybe not!

> If Sergt Outlaw has made a faithful Ranger and a conscientious officer in the performance of his duties heretofore, same should be

> taken into consideration. If he was provoked by certain extenuating circumstances he should have the benefit of such and you will reprimand him and assure him that any more of such Conduct will cause his dismissal from the service. The above will guide you in your action and same is left largely to your discretion, feeling that you will act for the best interest of the service.[56]

Although the actual depth of Captain Frank Jones' admonishment to his top-sergeant is or has thus far remained undisclosed, it's not unreasonable to suggest a stern verbal warning ensued regarding Baz Outlaw's run-in with C.E. Van Horn. Not a blow had been struck, nor had a six-shooter been unleashed, only belligerent hot talk punctuated with blistering streaks of profanity. Was that, standing by itself, justification enough to wash overboard the several years of outstanding and courageous service rendered by Baz Outlaw? For managerial folks and, Captain Frank Jones was one, the uncomfortable quandary was legit—the disposition to be addressed with circumspection. There's little doubt the pros and cons of divergent disciplinary actions were seesawing in the captain's mind—what was enough, what was too much. So, what was or wasn't said is cloudy. That Sergeant Baz Outlaw was not cashiered out of the Texas Rangers or demoted is more than transparent.

Even after Mr. Van Horn's complaint was made known, Sergeant Outlaw arrested Bill Storis for Assault to Murder at Marfa, and then continued hunting for a "Mexican" wanted for killing another fellow somewhere around Shafter. On the twenty-sixth day of November 1891, the Company D 1st Sergeant led four Ranger privates on a scout into Presidio County searching for another "Mexican" being sought for tapping out someone's running lights—for keeps. The victim, according to Captain Jones, was "a prominent ranchero of Jeff Davis County." By the time Sergeant Outlaw and his detachment arrived in Presidio County the wanted fellow had already voluntarily surrendered or had been taken into custody by the sheriff. But that Wild West story was far from playing out. Speaking to his demonstrated competency and indicative of the trust Captain Jones still held, on the twenty-ninth day of November, Sergeant Baz Outlaw was entrusted with a sensitive double homicide investigation near Fort Davis.[57]

The crime's genesis may be traced to mulishness over donkeys. The "prominent ranchero" referred to by Captain Jones was William T. "Bill" McCutcheon who, at his picturesque place near Seven Springs in northeastern Jeff Davis County, maintained a carefully irrigated and manicured field of alfalfa. José Ceniceros, freighting out of Fort Davis, and his burdened caravan frequently made overnight stops near McCutcheon's prized patch of alfalfa. Not infrequently it seems, José's donkeys found the alfalfa too alluring to resist, and their owner either couldn't or wouldn't take preventative steps to keep them from trampling and munching the deliciousness. Purportedly, and it's easy to believe, Bill McCutcheon had forewarned José Ceniceros that inattention to his livestock's wanderings would extract a heavy toll. On November 26, 1891, the donkeys tromped into the field of alfalfa and ranchero Bill went ballistic. Grabbing a gun he charged out of his house and started shooting the burros. José and his freighters—numbering two—were also armed and they or their rifles were not inoperative. Bill McCutcheon's blood painted the lush greenery beneath his form red, until it ran dry—then he was an artist no more, just dead. Thinking it was his handiwork that had done the trick, Ceniceros made tracks for town, leaving his compadres to round up surviving donkeys, repack, and finish the trip.[58]

The word-of-mouth grapevine had put Sheriff Joseph Randolph "J.R." Chadborn and Deputy Charlie Owens on the alert, and they were right fast horseback, making tracks for the scene of the madness and mayhem. Galloping through Limpia Canyon, the near breathless lawmen made a gruesome discovery—two for sure breathless bodies sprawled in the roadway, buzzards circling overhead.[59] That was one version, slopping around: that an unnamed field deputy and a citizen had started for Fort Davis, prisoners in tow, when circumstances turned to hell in a hand-basket. Captain Frank Jones' report to the adjutant general spun his rendering, apparently with a huge question mark: "After McCutcheon was Killed 2 Mexicans thought to be implicated in the same Killing were arrested and 2 men, one of them a Deputy Sheriff of Jeff Davis County, started to Fort Davis with them. On the road, so they say, they were confronted with armed men who demanded their prisoners. They gave them up and they were shot to death."[60]

Sergeant Outlaw, seemingly sober as a judge, had been "at once" dispatched to Jeff Davis County to investigate the double killings, and "see if any clue could be obtained as to who the guilty parties were." Unfortunately, though certainly somewhat predictable, his sleuthing earned nil due to the cold hard facts of partisanship—cultural bias: "He found every one disinclined to talk and could learn nothing. . . ."[61] The double slaying as a result of vigilante injustice would forevermore remain a "cold case." If there was any smidgen of consolation—a slow drip—the Jeff Davis County Grand Jury would later suggest that the deputy sheriff in charge of the slain detainees, "should have made a greater effort to protect the lives of his prisoners and they recommended that the Sheriff appoint better men as deputies."[62]

John Humphries, proprietor of the Big Bend business house of Humphries & Company dealing in "General Merchandise and Ranch Supplies," had a perplexing quandary of his own, one concerning Company D's 1st Sergeant. Reconstructing this financial arrangement may or may not reflect badly on Baz Outlaw, but certainly for a period of time John Humphries was anxious, maybe irritated. From what sparse evidence is available it seems that Baz Outlaw had made an arrangement with one of Humphries' store managers either at Marfa or Alpine to draw and write checks on the firm in lieu of Captain Jones turning over the top-sergeant's quarterly pay voucher to the business. And, in fact, there are a collection of preprinted checks drawn on Humphries & Co. to various individuals in varying amounts signed by "B.L. Outlaw," none exceeding twenty dollars, the majority for five or ten dollars.[63]

Either with a fiscal responsibility of clarifying or canceling the arrangement, John Humphries corresponded with Captain Frank Jones, seemingly leaving Sergeant Outlaw out of the loop. Not surprisingly, once again, Baz was more than miffed with the approach, but not necessarily bent toward apologies for any shortfalls or inconvenience resultant from the arrangement—even if such was justly due. In Baz Outlaw's mind, rightly or wrongly, they had a deal. And, not too much of a shocker should it be, on Buckhorn Saloon letterhead stationery Sergeant Outlaw made his personal thoughts known to Mr. Humphries, in part saying, "if you want to go back on your contract or agreement that we made heretofore—why you give me the opportunity to do the same, the agreement is understood between the Captain & myself, the same as it is between you & I. . . . While it is an accommodation to me for you to advance on my vouchers it is a Business transaction & you get good interest—besides a proffit [*sic*] on what goods I purchase of you. . . . I think that you should Stick to your contract & agreement for this quarter & if you don't wish to do so Any more why all right please let me know at once about this matter So that I can make arrangements accordingly. . . . if you are getting uneasy about anything all right but I will tell you now, unless you give good reason for going back on your agreement & undertaking, Why I will claim the privilege to do the Same & countermand the order [to have pay vouchers forwarded to Humphries & Co.]."[64] How or if John Humphries' inquiry—or dispute—was resolved is at this point somewhat unsettled, but history will bear witness that the big-time mercantile man would in the not too distant future turn to Big Bend Country lawman Baz Outlaw.

Clearly Captain Jones had bent to benevolence, giving Sergeant Outlaw the benefit of the doubt for past performance and pledges of future good conduct as 1891 faded from the calendar. Father Time, ushering in the New Year, would not be so compassionate.

Donald M. Yena's captivating *Texas Trail to Train Rails* skillfully weaves together technology and tradition. Coming of the railroad—from the law enforcement perspective—afforded Texas Rangers newfound mobility with regards to chasing after desperadoes. Unfortunately those same spider-webs of steel track also harkened a new breed of outlaws—train robbers. *Courtesy the artist, Don Yena.*

Though decked out here in fancy "city clothes" and spiffily posed in a photographer's studio, make no mistake, Captain Frank Jones was the real McCoy, in the eyes of his subordinates a Ranger's Ranger. *Courtesy Suzanne Giffin-Garcia.*

Judge Roy Bean. The ever waggish Justice of the Peace, the "Law West of the Pecos," headed up a posse chasing after the Samuel's Siding train robbers—for a little while. *Courtesy Nita Stewart Haley Memorial Library and J. Evetts Haley History Center.*

Joseph Russell "Joe" Sitter [L] and a pal seem to be having one whale of a time, though the extent of their sobriety—or lack thereof—is blurry. What may be said with clarity is that Sitter, as a Val Verde County deputy sheriff, Texas Ranger, and U.S. Mounted Customs Inspector, would be one of the better known borderland lawmen. *Courtesy Jake Sitters.*

Another—and definitely more flattering—photograph of the ever audacious lawman Joe Sitter. During the timeframe Texas Ranger 1st Sergeant Baz Outlaw was working with Sitter, he was favorably known as an amazingly proficient man-hunter, which logically correlates to his having had not just a few enemies. *Courtesy Jake Sitters.*

John Flynt, a carefree Big Bend borderland cowboy turned train robber. Rather than smartly surrender to Texas Rangers and local lawmen, he "suicided!" *Courtesy Archives of the Big Bend, Bryan Wildenthal Memorial Library, Sul Ross University.*

Alpine, formerly Murphyville, Brewster County, geographically the largest county in the Lone Star State. Note the locomotive and coaches at center. This train—or one like it—brought Zamloch's Congress of Wonders to Alpine, and it's yet a small wonder Ranger Sergeant Outlaw's dustup with the show's manager made no work for the local mortician. *COURTESY ARCHIVES OF THE BIG BEND, BRYAN WILDENTHAL MEMORIAL LIBRARY, SUL ROSS UNIVERSITY.*

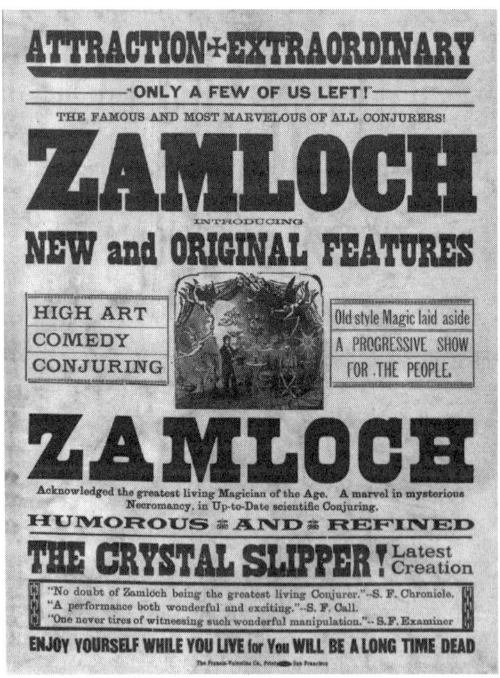

An advertising poster for what at the time was billed as the World's Greatest Magician, Anton Zamloch. During a show at Alpine, Baz Outlaw allegedly misbehaved, drawing ire of the show's general manager, C.E. Van Horn. Particularly note the promotional tag line at the bottom of the poster: "Enjoy Yourself While You Live for You Will Be A Long Time Dead." Professor Zamloch had Baz pegged right and tight. *COURTESY LUPE NIELSEN, THE NIELSEN MAGIC POSTER COLLECTION.*

CHAPTER 9

Simply Cannot Control Himself

ASSUREDLY THE GRIM REAPER HAD NOT BEEN ASLEEP during that first month of eighteen-hundred and ninety-two: Not in the Big Bend Country, Company D's territory. Subsequent to slick undercover work, Diamond Dick St. Leon, the former-Ranger, had infiltrated and ingratiated himself with a nasty gang of Mexican ore thieves at Shafter. Surreptitiously, after talking with Diamond Dick, Corporal John Hughes and Private Lon Oden knew where to take a tactically advantageous position on that twelfth night of January. St. Leon would be acting as the rear guard for the gang's pack-train of stolen ore, treasure being shipped under the cover of darkness from Shafter to the Rio Grande—and across. Unbeknownst to Matilde Carrasco, José Villeto, and Quinlino Chaves they would never see or feel the warmth of Big Bend Country sunshine again. The ambush—law enforcement interdiction—had been blueprinted with buckshot perfectly. Whether or not the challenge to throw up hands and surrender was hurled before or after the Rangers' shotgun blasts is somewhat irrelevant now, certainly not of any concern for Villeto and Chaves—they were sledgehammer dead. During the initial gunfire Carrasco had been wounded and might have survived had he not opted to fight a little longer. Apparently it had not even dawned on the cleverly duped Matilde that Diamond Dick was really not his friend. So, almost effortlessly when Carrasco repositioned himself to pop a few caps at the two suitably concealed Texas Rangers: "St. Leon rose up and shot him between the eyes."[1]

Just short of two weeks later, in the imposing Glass Mountains north of Marathon, Captain Frank Jones, accompanied by three privates became caught up in an another arrest scenario gone awry. Quite proficiently they took into custody José Blanco and a man identified only as Eduardo. Quite proficiently they killed Pedro Eureto—who had most foolishly failed to think before resisting arrest.[2] The company commander really was somewhat distressed about his Rangers having killed four people in a single month, soulfully informing Adjutant General W.H. Mabry: "As you will see by report we have been compelled to do some Killing which I regret. I have no desire whatever to get up a 'bloody record' and have always considered it far more creditable to Capture than to Kill."[3]

For Sergeant Baz Outlaw that first calendar month of 1892 was more-or-less rather mundane, not even a mention in the Monthly Return for Company D. However, the following month was more active. Riding as headman for a three-man scout, Sergeant Baz Outlaw and two privates hunted hard east of Camp Hogg and, after covering an even 100 miles, finally were successful in tracking and capturing two fellows only identified as Sanchez and Andreas, both wanted for Conspiracy to Murder. They hauled them to the jailhouse. Shortly thereafter, Sergeant Outlaw and three Ranger privates expended six wearisome days away from camp trying to find a herd of suspected stolen or smuggled sheep. In this instance they did not triumph, returning empty handed to Camp Hogg on February 13, 1892. Clearly after such an arduous and exhaustive excursion many a hot-blooded fellow would welcome the chance to cool off, sampling some liquid libation. Baz Outlaw was a good-timing Ranger.

During evening hours of the thirteenth Sergeant Baz Outlaw climbed back in the boat, feverishly paddling upstream in those seductively promising climatic moments of escape and ecstasy on the whiskey river. Through bloodshot eyes Baz had obstinately mapped his destination, the dock at Alpine, the one illuminated with red-lights. What was on his mind when he first started tipping the bottle that night evades any preciseness. However, after pickling his brain with hard liquor for awhile—a little while—Sergeant Outlaw's euphorically induced alcohol dreamscape had been sinfully sidetracked by testosterone's temptations. Sergeant Baz Outlaw wanted—was in dire need of—some sugar, and not the purely refined kind inside an intricately painted china bowl on Mama's kitchen table. No, in this instance the raw product—the rawer the better, in fact—would do quite well.

On the outskirts of town, at what some classed as an iniquitous address, Company D's 1st Sergeant, hopelessly inebriated, made his presence loudly known at the house of J.M. Watts, a black man with somewhat of an unsavory reputation due to his partying and pecuniary pastimes with prostitutes. The night for Sergeant Outlaw was yet young, though the same could not be said for the questionably engaged and perhaps somewhat sleazy Watts; he'd already donned his bedclothes and turned in. Pimps and prostitutes do need to sleep—sometime. Outside Watts' abode stood Baz Outlaw, Winchester in hand, with hot words escaping from his lips after being slapped around inside his mouth by a thickened tongue. Slobbering and slurring, Sergeant Baz Outlaw had—at last—awakened J.M. Watts. Company D's top-sergeant wasn't doing police business, but erotica was on the night's program—in his mind. The only fugitive he was hunting that night wore a skirt and silk stockings—at least for a minute or two. Outlaw made his demand known: the whereabouts of a particular whore's crib. But, since he was actually there—staring into the foreboding abyss of a lever-action carbine's muzzle—perchance hearing from the good, well, sometimes bad Mr. Watts is not out of place:

> Outlaw came to my house after I had retired and called me. I came to the door and he wanted me to go with him and point out the house of a prostitute. This I declined to do saying I was not well and was besides undressed. Outlaw who was holding his gun (Winchester) in his hand suddenly pointed it at me saying what are

> you doing with your hand behind you. I then closed the door and locked it when he began cursing me saying he would shoot me and would put a rope around my neck and drag me out. Then he fired, the ball striking the door facing about a foot from the ground. Finally he mounted his horse and left, returning in a few minutes saying that he wanted me to come out and that he was not angry with me. This I refused to do when he went to the house of a prostitute and forced her to allow him to remain with her which he did until broad day light.[4]

This time Sergeant Outlaw had stepped in it—maybe? From the best evidence at hand it does seem that Captain Jones was not out on a scout, visiting at his home in Boerne, or hobnobbing with hierarchical Texas Ranger bigwigs at Austin. No, most likely he was at Camp Hogg when Baz Outlaw excused himself for some rest and relaxation and a rumpled sheet romp at Alpine. Admittedly there is room for some chronological fog as to exactly when Captain Jones learned of Baz's latest imbroglio. Nevertheless, learn of it he did. Therein, and once more, the company commander was placed in an awkward position through no fault of his own, but the demand for an explanation or excuse or extenuating circumstances was forthcoming. Sergeant Outlaw didn't deny his drunkenness—he was off duty—but discharging his Winchester had simply been an accident, no harm, no foul, just carelessness. As far as "forcing" himself on the favors of a whore, that was utterly preposterous. Captain Jones had received no complaints from anyone about Baz reneging on any promises to pay for play—had he?

Again, Captain Frank Jones was the one uncomfortably "forced" to look at real time reality. Assuredly the captain's thought processes are his, but there are suggestive clues and hard facts which provide—at least to some degree—reasoned insight. Certainly that previous brouhaha with C.E. Van Horn at Alpine and Marfa had been an embarrassment and, yes, he seemed a reasonably credible fellow, but the weapons of war between him and Baz Outlaw were but words. No six-shooter, no Winchester, no knife, or brass-knuckles had been indiscriminately taken up. Assuredly Mr. Van Horn had been—not outclassed—but overmatched in what materialized as but a one-sided cuss fight, Sergeant Outlaw racking up the win for asininity.

On the other hand, the run-in with J.M. Watts at Alpine's fringe was a horse of a different color. Captain Jones was well aware of the fact Mr. Watts had not sought him out to make any official personnel complaint. In fact, it had been the other way around. For Frank Jones' way of thinking, any grievance or grumbling coming from Watts would have to be dissected carefully because as the captain had it figured "he is a negro who keeps a low dive in the outskirts of town laying up with a white woman himself."[5] The antipathy and amity between purveyors of traditional vice and enforcers of the law is a tricky dichotomy to understand and even harder to explain. This time around though, it was thorny: Sergeant Baz Outlaw for whatever the lameness of his excuse had discharged his gun—and bullets are uncompromising wherever they go. Was the sergeant really now on a downhill slide, deteriorating from a fun-loving occasional drunk, into a dangerously troubled Texas Ranger with internal demons pulling at his very soul and erasing all restraint? Were mental blackouts now precursors to black deeds? Was Sergeant Outlaw lost forevermore? Though but guesswork, Captain Frank Jones had to be perplexed.

Personally troubled though he might have been, and reservations he may have been holding, nonetheless Captain Frank Jones—as far is now known—did not swing the switch of discipline at Sergeant Outlaw for what was, indeed, full-blown unpleasantness at Alpine with the purported pimp and/or "Watts' prostitute."[6] Sergeant Outlaw was embroiled in the middle of another row, right there at Camp Hogg—this time not with a civilian townsmen—good or bad—but another Texas Ranger, M.R. Danniel.

Seeing service with Company D for a term not exceeding three months, having only enlisted the day after Christmas 1891, Private Danniel had already been credited on paper with killing Pedro Eureto during that January shoot-out in the Glass Mountains.[7] Whether that enforcement action had emboldened him or not is really unknowable—and immaterial. Private Danniel was at the bottom-end of the pecking-order, and therefore in theory and practice answered to senior Rangers, noncoms, and commissioned officers. Captain Jones was thoroughly appreciative of the man's sense of integrity and honesty, but assessed Private Danniel as not being exceptionally smart and owning but "little intelligence." There was—positively—a problematic downside, too. Private Danniel, according to Captain Jones, was a man of little or no discretion, capped off by a "most ungovernable temper."[8] Sergeant Baz Outlaw's temperament when sober was good: When in his cups that disposition morphed to madness and, progressively, to psychotic episodes. Mature bulls lock horns, gamecocks rake sharp spurs, fighting curs go for the jugular, so there's not room for any real surprise, Sergeant Baz Outlaw and Private M.R. Danniel—cautiously eyed each other—already preset at the half-cock notch.

To be sure there is a certain romanticism associated with a working career spent outdoors. There are, too, routine tasks to be handled if a reasonably clean and healthy camp is maintained. Camp chores need doing and supervisory personnel are permitted to delegate who does what. Sergeant Baz Outlaw either nicely or nastily detailed Private Danniel "to assist in sweeping out Camp." Somehow, either with the task itself or the bearing with which the order was issued, Private Danniel "became offended with Sergt Outlaw." Rather than take the matter up with the company commander, Private Danniel "put his pistol under his coat to conceal it" and there it remained for the next several days while the thoroughly disgruntled and damning Texas Ranger bitched and moaned about operational, administrative, and supervisory matters at Company D's headquarters camp. Private Danniel was not a happy camper! Captain Jones, generally agreeable and understanding had had enough, a belly full: "I had him down to my quarters for the purpose of reprimanding him about some talk he had made in Camp relative to the management of the Co. and since learned he came secretly armed. . . . I don't feel secure with him in Camp. Am afraid that he will get in to some trouble with some of the men. I want no Ranger in my Company who carries concealed weapons around the Camp where men should feel toward each other almost as brothers." No doubt having the best interest of the rank and file and the service at heart, Captain Frank Jones figuratively booted Mr. M.R. Danniel out of the Frontier Battalion—a Ranger he was no more.[9] When that news broke across the top of the adjutant general's little maple desk at Austin, he not surprisingly backed the captain.[10]

Baz Outlaw's quarrel with an enlisted man regarding compliance and/or noncompliance with a rightful order had not diminished the captain's reliance on his top-sergeant. Frank Jones was not a martinet nor was he blind to reality. When sober, Baz Outlaw was a dynamite lawman: While drunk Baz Outlaw was brutish, belligerent, and bad—not worth spit or the powder to blow him up. Psychological evil washed over his consciousness and conscience during those recurrent bouts with the bottle, drowning sanity and sensibleness. He knew better, was raised better, yet he just couldn't—or really wouldn't—leave liquor alone. Addiction is weird; easy to condemn; difficult to describe; near impossible to manage—and damn hard to cure or overcome. And there was not room for compromise, one drink or two, even if such an idea had been sparked at the outset of a tranquil trip to town. Sergeant Baz Outlaw's first drink always unlocked whiskey river's floodgate.

Sergeant Outlaw's ownership of some not so nice personality traits—normally traced to the amber current—had not sidetracked his enforcement duties. He still had value to Company D, particularly in the eyes of the captain, who was bending over backwards to counsel a friend. Shortly after the dustup with M.R. Danniel, Sergeant Outlaw, working by himself, traveled into Pecos County conducting an investigation of stolen livestock. The following month, May 1892, and clearly showing that he had not lost management's confidence as a crackerjack lawman, is the fact Sergeant Outlaw took three privates and raced back to Pecos County at the "urgent" request of Sheriff W.P. Matthews. The 1st Sergeant had been hastened to the county because, "The Mexicans are in some force on a ranche and the Sheriff is afraid to attempt some arrests without assistance."[11]

Sheriff Matthews had every reason to be concerned, and the fact Sergeant Outlaw was trusted with the delicate assignment should put to bed any assertion he was drunk from dawn to dusk, everyday. Baz Outlaw was a spree drinker—sometimes sober, sometimes flooded to the gills. The situation in Pecos County spun around Andrew Jackson Royal and his fatally gunning down of Apollinar Mendoza on the twentieth day of May, while in front of Fort Stockton's Koehler Saloon. With this killing, Royal, a future sheriff of Pecos County, had cemented his reputation as a hard, dangerous, and uncompromising man. In fact, during the next day's Inquest, Andy Royal sat in the justice of the peace's courtroom facing witnesses as they testified—"with a double-barreled shotgun across his lap and a pistol in his scabbard." Understandably, amid a racially charged atmosphere choked with "hearsay, circumstantial, and conflicting" testimony—or interpretation of testimony—was up for dispute and/or impeachment. Much of the contradictory accounts gyrated on the axis of an ongoing feud between Royal and a number of "Mexicans" who may or may not have been plotting his premature death. There were charges and countercharges and many unasked, as well as a slew of unanswered questions. Putting Andy Royal under a $1000 bond, awaiting investigation and legal action of the next scheduled session of a grand jury, somewhat defused the volatility of the sheriff or Baz Outlaw and his Rangers having had to go to war with one faction or the other.[12]

During the trip to Fort Stockton, however, Sergeant Outlaw and his detachment were not sitting on their hands, waiting for more madness to unfold. They arrested W.P. Anderson, aka Cobert, and Juan Posterd, the former for a livestock theft incident in Atascosa County, the latter for allegations of cow stealing in Reeves County. Both prisoners were handily turned over to Sheriff Matthews, to be held until proper authorities could come to Fort Stockton and take charge of their unlucky fugitives from justice. From start to finish, Sergeant Outlaw and crew were away from Camp Hogg for eleven days, roughly covering 170 miles.[13]

Elsewhere in the wild sphere of jurisdiction administratively assigned to Company D an enforcement action jumped from routine—if ever they are—to scorching, sizzling lead flying. Corporal Hughes, assisted by Privates Lon Oden and Jim Putman, were along the Rio Grande, upriver from Presidio by some fifty miles near what's now the village of Candelaria on the Texas side, and San Antonio de Bravo, a former Mexican penal colony on the Río Bravo's opposite bank. Haphazardly situated underneath the Sierra Vieja and Candlaria Rims this section of borderland was lonesome and chancy country for near anyone—especially Lone Star lawmen. For the moment at hand the little detachment was hard searching for Desidario Durán, a fugitive charged with raiding the section house at Chispa in Jeff Davis County. Quite fortunately in one regard the Texas Rangers nabbed their man; inopportunely though, Desidario Durán had good friends—mean men—in that neighborhood, and they were not the least scared of this Ranger trio, one so far from home and so insignificant in number. One of the arrested man's *amigos* was Florencio Carrasco, brother by blood and badness of Matilde Carrasco, the ore thief killed at Shafter by the demonstrably handy marksmanship of Ernest St. Leon. Florencio owned pending criminal charges himself, at least one warrant for Murder. Understandably though not excusably, Florencio had not a smidgen of sympathy for John Hughes and Lon Oden, they were the upfront faces involved with his brother's death—coldblooded murder in his warped mind. Texas Rangers taking Durán back to Marfa in irons would not stand. Florencio Carrasco started the hot fight with Rangers and ended up dead—either one, or all of them, having killed him with unerring accuracy and fast spiraling bullets: An irrational bombardment he asked for but couldn't outlive. Captain Frank Jones, in recounting the event for the front office, showed not the least sympathy either, declaring that Florencio Carrasco was "the worst Mexican on the border and his death is hailed with delight by all good citizens."[14]

For those eleven days Sergeant Outlaw spent in Pecos County, he may have been gone from camp but he certainly was not forgotten—not by civilian M.R. Danniel. Contacting a lawyer the thoroughly disconcerted ex-Ranger turned the skunk out of the sack, unburdening his psyche about all he knew or thought he knew about his former 1st Sergeant's misdeeds and madcap binges. With his formalized multi-page complaint fastidiously typewritten—replete with wordy legalese—Danniel forwarded it and his cover letter to the adjutant general: "I herewith enclose and respectfully present for your consideration certain charges against one B.L. Outlaw, now 1st Sergeant of Company D, Frontier Battalion. I also request an honorable discharge from the service of the State, for myself."[15] The litany of censurable complaints against Sergeant Outlaw summarized Baz's clash with Presidio County Sheriff Miller and deputies Joe Sprunk and Charley Barton at Shafter; the drunken disruption at Alpine with Zamloch's Congress of Wonders show manager C.E. Van Horn, and next day's tirade and threats against him at Marfa; and the Winchester discharging disturbance at the home of J.M. Watts regarding a sought-after whore's whereabouts.[16] What the adjutant general and/or the company captain did or did not know beforehand and to what extent was now reduced to writing and a part of the battalion's official correspondence files. Within the framework of generalization, from this point forward overlooking repetitive bad behavior could—might—prove publicly embarrassing for the Texas Rangers as a professional outfit and detrimental to its good order and maintenance of discipline. Metaphorically speaking Sergeant Baz Outlaw may have previously been skating across whiskey river's frozen surface, but now the ice was thin.

Summertime of 1892 would yet find Sergeant Outlaw hustling. Leading a scout with three privates, he rode out of Camp Hogg heading for the now quite well known Stillwell Ranch on the Rio Grande. The Rangers were hunting hard for W.S. "Will" Henderson, the prime suspect in a case revolving around the thefts and smuggling of stolen horses. The disappointed Rangers returned to camp on July 22 empty-handed. After but a short stay in camp, Sergeant Outlaw, acting alone or in concert with other Company D Rangers, did on the second day of August manage to locate and arrest Henderson somewhere in Brewster County. Charges against Will Henderson were to be prosecuted in federal court. Therefore, Sergeant Outlaw delivered his prisoner to the U.S. Commissioner (Magistrate) at Marfa "who fixed his bond at $1000." But a few days later Sergeant Baz Outlaw was back in the saddle so to speak—really on a train—traveling back to Pecos County in hopes of nabbing Elsie Brown, who had been charged with Theft of Cattle. Unfortunately for Sergeant Outlaw and his unnamed Ranger partner, the five-day trip netted but a goose egg—not a prisoner.[17]

September of 1892 would prove to be the most eventful month in the Texas Ranger career of Sergeant Outlaw—it started off chipper but ended on a sour note. Again illustrative of the fact Baz was never far removed from designated supervisory responsibilities and assuredly not lazy and most definitely not too drunk to mount a horse and lead a scout, may be logically drawn from the Monthly Return of Company D for September. He and three men absented themselves from Camp Hogg for five days chasing after and trying to overtake and temporarily seize another suspected herd of smuggled and stolen cattle. The challenging but unproductive search burned up the month's first week.[18] By mid-month the insensitive devils or demons lurking somewhere inside Baz Outlaw's troubled psyche were thirsty. Increasingly immune from unbroken streaks of good judgment, Baz once again bent to stupidity—deciding to slake those inner beasts' dryness. He climbed back into the boat of disillusionment—thinking a jigger or two of tarantula juice would tame the monsters—setting sail for Alpine and one of its landmark emporiums, the Buckhorn Saloon.

Although nonprofessional psychological comments from afar are decidedly questionable, there does seem to be two dimensions, two courses of Baz's mindset when boisterously drunk: The 1st Sergeant was geared to proving he was either a lover or a fighter, an amorous rake or an agitating foe. During this trip to Alpine the ever feisty Baz Outlaw had fight on the brain, and it took precedent over passions of the personal persuasion.

Amalgamating the several different versions of what happened next into one coherent story is not out of place and, from the historical perspective, nothing is lost. Baz was damn drunk again. Outside the Buckhorn Saloon an obviously inebriated Outlaw unlimbered his Colt's revolver and discharged a round or two or three, whooping it up, howling at the moon and daring anyone to spank him for being bad. He had no takers. Then he stumbled through the Buckhorn's swinging doors and bellied up to the brightly polished mahogany bar—a carafe of your best, if you please. The Buckhorn's barkeep was no dummy; forthwith he set up the shot-glass and bottle. Bending his elbow and tossing one down, his terrorizing the town may have even gone unnoticed and/or unappreciated by Baz—sour mash blackouts are like that. Though one fellow wasn't in the dark about what he had heard and what he was being told. Sheriff Jim Gillett was marching to the hullabaloo and he too pushed through the Buckhorn's doors. There, by several accounts, Sergeant Baz Outlaw was squared off with Abraham "Abe" Anglin, former Texas Ranger but then the county tax assessor, the fuse fast burning toward tragedy. Whether Colt's six-shooters were in hand or holstered is up for grabs—the outcome isn't.

If Sergeant Baz Outlaw yet had his six-shooter in hand, Sheriff Gillett unsmiling and promptly told him to put it away right now—else, he could just unchain his bad ass grizzly bear. Sensing the earnestness in the sheriff's tone and seeing the sternness in his cold unblinking eyes, Baz Outlaw began making light of the situation's seriousness and began fumbling for money in his pocket to buy Sheriff Gillett a cordial drink—notwithstanding that half-full bottle on the bar. Then by deceptive design or simply an accident attributable to numb fingers Baz Outlaw dropped a coin to the hardwood floor. Baz feigned picking up the coin, "then straightened suddenly as if to go for his gun, but he looked hard at the sheriff, checking to see if Gillett planned to shoot him."[19] Assuredly tuned into the volatility of dealing with drunks—and in this case one with a hair-trigger detonation point—Sheriff Gillett's mental wheels were turning fast, but he was not rattled by Baz Outlaw's recklessness. With cucumber coolness Jim Gillett, his eyes never averted from those of his wobbling adversary, stooped down and picked up the coin, pitching it onto the bar. Purportedly Sheriff Gillett said, "Now you remember what I told you. It's a fine thing when a Ranger has to be ordered to keep the peace."[20] Even if such quotation is not flawlessly exact, the meaning and end result are clear: Baz Outlaw wilted.

Pinpointing where Sergeant Outlaw lay his head down that night—if he did—thus far is not a matter of record. What happened next is. While this silliness and stupidity laced with potential for disaster had uncorked, Captain Jones had been away from camp tending to personal and company affairs at Ysleta the site of his upcoming wedding (his first wife died in 1889) to Helen Baylor, the daughter of George Wythe Baylor and, interestingly, the ex-wife of Sheriff Jim Gillett.[21] Though it was news he regretted hearing, upon his return to camp Captain Jones got an earful regarding the unbecoming conduct of his top-sergeant.

There was no quandary of worth for the let-down captain. What had to be done he would do. Although the action would individually be distasteful, due in large part to Frank Jones knowing and admitting that Baz was a man with more courage than "two or three ordinary men," and that he had "always felt a warm personal feeling for him," duty trumped inertness.[22] Captain Jones had been backed into the proverbial corner: He could buck up to sad reality about his friend and do the right thing, or he could bend again to those false promises of abstinence—though perhaps given with good intentions when made—but yet false nevertheless. Hangover atonement is generally seriously spoken but habitually subverted. Alas, now, it had come down to stepping up. The good name of the Texas Rangers—Captain Jones' Rangers—came first and foremost above the special interest of any one man—regardless of past performance or personal partiality. In the short term, Sergeant Baz Outlaw, too, could do the right thing. Captain Jones explains:

> Sergt. Outlaw has requested a discharge which I have done. This request has been made in view of the fact he "got on" a spree and acted disorderly in town. I have allowed him the privilege of requesting this discharge on account of his long service to the State

> and many good qualities. He simply, cannot control himself when away from my influence. As a fearless officer he has no superior in the State service, and while I am sorry to lose him, consider it best for the service.[23]

Deeming it "best for the service" was no understatement.[24] Even one of Baz's closest personal friends within Texas Ranger ranks acknowledged the possibility of trouble—bad trouble—on Company D's horizon regarding the 1st Sergeant's irresponsible indulgence, even though he knew Baz "was so brave and kind; who could laugh louder, ride longer, and cuss harder than the rest of us; and who could be more sympathetic, more tender, more patient than all of us when necessary." Then his pal, Lon Oden, mentioned the downside regarding Baz's "one weakness," the unrelenting lure of liquor, and that "proved to be stronger than all his virtues."[25] At Austin the adjutant general—perhaps growing somewhat tired of continually learning about this or that allegation about a specific Ranger company's problem noncom—endorsed Captain Frank Jones' decision in a single sentence, he needed to hear no more justifications, no more tasteless excuses. Baz Outlaw had burned—time and again—second chances: "Your action as indicated in your favor of the 18th inst discharging Sergt B.L. Outlaw from the Service is approved."[26]

Quite naturally the resignation—semi-forced resignation—created a vacuum in Company D. There was need for a new 1st Sergeant. Subsequent to his tutorship first by Sergeant Ira Aten, then Sergeant Charley Fusselman, and finally Sergeant Baz Outlaw—all the time under overall leadership of Captain Frank Jones, Corporal John R. Hughes, now with five years' Ranger service under his belt, was ready for advancement. He had proved beyond doubt he was willing to pull a trigger during darkness or in daylight. Had they been able to, the Odle boys, a couple of Shafter ore thieves, and Florencio Carrasco could have attested to that. Private John R. Hughes, as a neophyte Ranger, had by now registered several of the finer points of forensic investigation; those demonstrated by his supervisor Sergeant Ira Aten during that horrendous quadruple homicide wherein defendant Dick Duncan bought his nonrefundable ticket for a date with death atop that towering wooden scaffold in borderland Maverick County's jail yard at Eagle Pass. Character-wise, Corporal John Reynolds Hughes was made of the right stuff. John Hughes had to some extent learned and, was continually incorporating into his individual workplace portfolio, those sometimes mundane but nonetheless mandatory pieces of minutiae required for managing and logistically maintaining a Texas Ranger company—one staffed with divergent personalities—all carrying Colt's .45s, Winchesters, and great big razor-sharp belt knives. Captain Frank Jones, but one day after Baz Outlaw's discharge from Company D, with or without a second thought, awarded John Hughes with the top-sergeant's line on the Muster & Payroll. Also on that day, September 19, 1892, the captain backfilled the corporal's position with the merited promotion of a true-blue native Texan, twenty-four-year-old Carl Kirchner.[27]

Amid all the intra-company turmoil and procedural matters relating to promotions, dismissals, and recruiting Company D to its authorized strength, geographical concerns such as the perpetual need for plentiful wood, potable and ample water, as well as nutritious grass for the Rangers' horses and pack mules prompted Captain Frank Jones to relocate some thirty miles east of Alpine. Camp Hogg was no more. Now Company D Texas Rangers were headquartered near Marathon, in an encampment officially designated as Camp Cleveland.[28]

Being given an option to quit ahead of being fired—sacked—is not a plus for one's résumé, but frequently it's about at this point in storytelling time that hard fact and more suppositional melodrama are infused into ex-Ranger Sergeant Baz Outlaw's admittedly wild, Wild West biographical profile. Sometimes truths are troubling.

Though the back end of the story is hazy—an adjudicated legal disposition—the front part of the tale should not come as a surprise. On the fifteenth day of October 1892, subsequent to forfeiting his regular Ranger commission, a drunk and disorderly and disruptive Baz Outlaw was the center of attention in a "public place" at the city of El Paso. There he was "unlawfully and willfully," and very rudely displaying a pistol, to wit: a Merwin and Hulbert, SN 195. According to court papers Outlaw was doing such in a manner calculated to "disturb the inhabitants of said public place." Local lawmen disarmed Baz Outlaw—and the El Paso County Sheriff retained the pistol pending the legal outcome. Whether the misdemeanor case was settled by fine or jail time is muddled, but the ill-omened Baz Outlaw lost the pistol forevermore.[29]

Not infrequently it's been written in a few trendy popular periodical articles that somewhat despondent and dead broke, and after borrowing a specifically identified 1873 Winchester from Jim Gillett, the former top-sergeant, head and spirit submerged in a whiskey bottle, roamed the gigantic and lonesome Big Bend Country, especially that section straddling the Rio Grande known as *Las Vega de los Ladrones*. By those accounts the jobless Baz Outlaw was obsessed with recovering the loot—the supposed $50,000 worth—secretly buried before the Samuels Siding train robbers were caught and John Flynt had opted not to squeal and in a last meal eat his gruel—suicide cereal seasoned with gunpowder. Repeatedly, for days at a time, the treasure-hunting ex-Ranger would absent himself from Alpine, tirelessly riding the backcountry alone and secretively search for the train robbing pirates' end of the rainbow pot of gold doubloons and real Yankee dollars. And it was there, in that dogged pursuit of elusive wealth that many—at least a few—local folks started referring to ex-Sergeant Baz Outlaw as the "Little Wolf" or the "Lone Wolf." The nickname might have been apt regarding Baz Outlaw's never finding need to impregnate his reservoir of raw nerve with company to back his plays, but a compulsive treasure hunter—in reality—he seems not to have been. There's yet plenty of room for circumspectly looking at Baz Outlaw's legit Old West history.[30]

Regardless, even if civilian Baz Outlaw was sometimes looking for a buried fortune, primary source records unmistakably reveal he wasn't too far removed from the law enforcing game, and certainly not too long uninvolved. Absolute precision is somewhat hazy, but before 1892 was history, Baz Outlaw was yet making his mark as a bona fide lawman. He had been appointed as a field deputy by Paul Fricke, U.S. Marshal for the Western District of Texas, the same man that had earlier dually commissioned Ranger Sergeant Charley Fusselman, killed in the line of duty in El Paso County. It will be recalled that upon Fusselman's death, after mulling over potential replacements, Captain Jones chose and promoted Baz Outlaw as 1st Sergeant of Company D.[31] There's little room for speculative doubt that Baz Outlaw's imprudent escapades—at least some of them—were common knowledge. On the other hand, still at this time—when sober—he was widely recognized as an altogether competent and utterly fearless West Texas peace officer, now charged with investigating and apprehending those alleged to have committed a federal crime. Any assertion that Baz Outlaw was universally unpopular and shunned by everyone except wicked degenerates and decadent habitués of Alpine's barrooms and bordellos is out-and-out nonsense. A hard truth somewhat buttressed by his own hand in a letter to Adjutant General Mabry on the last day of December 1892:

> As I am working for Several Stockmen of Brewster, Foley & Presidio County I will respectfully request that you Enlist me as Special Ranger of Capt Jones Company. I am traveling about a great deal & think that I can help to make a good report & also assist Captain Jones & his men. I could be appointed Dept. Sheriff of Brewster or Presidio co. but I have a big Scope of country to work in and would prefer to be a Special Ranger So that I can act in any county in the State. Enclosed please [find] petition from Citizens of Brewster & Foley counties & also Capt Jones approval. [signed, B.L. Outlaw, Dept. U.S. Marshal][32]

Folks endorsing Baz's appeal to become a Special Ranger were not nitwits and ne'er-do-wells. Perhaps quite surprisingly in light of previous writings, they comprise a rather wide array of public and private citizens, including County Tax Assessor Abe Anglin who Baz purportedly had the near catastrophic tête-à-tête with, the county clerk, a druggist, an entrepreneurial merchant, school teacher Ben

Fly, former county sheriff Jim Gillett, and the brand-new Brewster County Sheriff, as of the eighth day of November 1892, D. W. "Doc" Gourley, as well as another staunch ex-Ranger, Lavoizare Blair "L.B." Caruthers. Too, there was a rather healthy sampling of Big Bend Country ranchmen typically identifying themselves as "stockman." And, conceivably the most astounding of them all, giving his stamp of approval was Company D Commander Frank Jones. He also had endorsed Baz's formalized petition for appointment as a Special Ranger.[33] There is not room for ambiguity, at this time, despite his episodic drunken and disorderly sprees; Deputy U.S. Marshal Baz Outlaw was no pariah.

There was something going on in Captain Jones' mind aside from endorsing Baz Outlaw's try at becoming a Special Ranger—an endorsement of his own. Changing of the presidential guard at Washington, D.C. had opened the gateway for routine awarding of patronage appointments. And for lawmen nationwide those reoccurring U.S. Marshal's vacancies were political plums worth plucking. Captain Frank Jones wanted a taste, was salivating with anticipation, and wasn't bashful about telling the boss he was hungry: "If you have no objection I would like to visit Austin about the 6th of January on some business connected with my candidacy for the Marshal's office. I am very anxious to meet some parties who will be in Austin when the Legislature convenes."[34] The adjutant general nodded his approval, granting Captain Jones permission to visit Austin when the legislature met, but with a single caveat: The captain's personal trip must not interfere with his public duties.[35]

Politics—not necessarily bad politics—however did interfere with his personal plans and aspirations. Frontrunner for the U.S. Marshal's position for the Western District of Texas was Richard Clayton "Dick" Ware, ex-Texas Ranger and former elected sheriff of Mitchell County (seat Colorado City) and, perhaps, most notably a popular veteran of the horrific 1878 gunplay at Round Rock: The one wherein a notorious and much wanted desperado named Sam Bass had his last earthly ticket punched.[36] Captain Jones, though exceptionally well liked throughout the state, and widely recognized as a Ranger's Ranger, didn't own the political horsepower to outright land the job—neither did Dick Ware. That final decision would for awhile be suspended in the time-warp of a federal government's limbo—as many if not most of their final actions and pronouncements do—and did. During that psychologically torturing interim, neither Company D's commander or Deputy U.S. Marshal Baz Outlaw were idle.

Sometime during January 1893 Captain Jones, by the best information at hand, had conferred with the Lone Star State's adjutant general about commissioning Deputy U.S. Marshal Baz Outlaw a Special Ranger. Exactly what words were exchanged between Jones and Mabry is lost to history, though the interpretative message the captain carried was assuredly not mush mouthed and didn't necessitate the services of a psychotherapist: That most if not all of Baz's tribulations paralleled his unstopping the bottle and throwing the cork away was evident not only to his former Ranger bosses, but for Baz as well. Somewhat sheepishly—definitely self-servingly—in written format he more or less whined to AG Mabry. Acknowledging that there had, indeed, been derogatory letters and official battalion reports regarding his bad behavior, Baz Outlaw justified—or tried to: "I was wrong only in one thing, and that was drinking too much Some times, but not when I was on duty, for it never caused me to neglect any Business." For Baz Outlaw, salvaging status as a Texas Ranger—even Special Ranger—was ravenously eating at his insides, else he might have not gambled on such long odds, signing such a near impossible pledge: "I went before the county Judge this morning and took an oath and it is on file at his office, not to drink liquors of any kind for the next five years & I intend to Stick to it for I realize that it has already injured me financially and otherwise."[37]

On the sixth day of February 1893 in somewhat of a whopping understatement Baz Outlaw declared that he was "sober and temperate" in his habits, and that he had never "been convicted of any crime," then signed his application for appointment as a Special Ranger. Four days later, Brewster County Judge W. Van Sickle instructed Baz Outlaw to hold up his right hand while he administered the legally obligatory Oath of Office. Looking on and executing their signatures were Ranger Captain Frank Jones, powerhouse lawyer and state legislator and West Texas livestock raiser William Ward Turney, as was A.S. Garza, one and all meaningfully vouching "for the good character" of the hopeful applicant. It was then marked as official: U.S. Deputy Marshal Baz Outlaw could also now legally claim status as a Special Texas Ranger.[38]

Although not receiving funds from the state, even Special Rangers were obligated to each month update the adjutant general with the names and numbers of persons arrested, as well as the nearest U.S. Post Office where they could receive the state's correspondence and/or orders. Ostensibly in Baz Outlaw's capacity as a Special Ranger he hit the ground running during March 1893, giving AG Mabry an explanation as to why his compulsory monthly report was in arrears: "On account of being on trail of a man wanted in Llano co. wanted for theft and Murder—I failed to report to you on the 1st of April. I arrested Ed Oatman on 1st of April in Reeves County & put him in Jail at Alpine. Everything quiet here but I understand that Mexicans between Valentine & El Paso are Stealing cattle & Horses continually from Stockmen in that vicinity. My P.O. will be Alpine during this month."[39]

For several weeks—two according to his report—Special Ranger Baz Outlaw had been somewhat under the weather—sick—and unable to perform any law-enforcing duties. He, too, it's presumed, would have been prevented from absenting himself from Alpine in the lonesome quest of scouring that gargantuan Big Bend Country hunting for any rumored buried treasures.[40] Speculatively though, a tidbit of hard news wafting his way must have cheered him up. On the twenty-fifth day of April the appointment of Dick Ware as U.S. Marshal for the Western Federal Judicial District of Texas came through.[41] The newly named U.S. Marshal was living in real time, with not the slightest iota of an idea as to what horrors or happiness the future might bring. Due to Baz Outlaw's immense popularity with many folks in Presidio and Brewster Counties and for whatever other reasons, Dick Ware did not revoke but continued Baz Outlaw's commission as a Deputy U.S. Marshal.[42] And, at that time, it seemed a prudent decision. You see, on the twentieth day of May 1893 in one capacity or another Baz Outlaw figuratively lassoed and tripped and literally handcuffed George Johnson one of the prime suspects for robbing a Southern Pacific train near Kent Station, then El Paso County, now Culberson County (Van Horn).[43]

Troubling as it might be for modern-era scribes wanting to tar and feather Baz Outlaw with all-embracing condemnation, at this point in his life's story he was not across-the-board disliked or ostracized. Truthfully speaking Baz lived at a place and time often winking at distilled spirits' bribery. After all, it was indeed yet a Wild West theater where "nearly all men drank nearly all the time, which made nearly all men more or less drunk most of the time."[44] Baz was paddling toward decadence and depravity, but the calendar owed him a few more good days.

Though the obviously favorable impression would shortly change, this brilliant sketch of prominent Frontier Battalion personnel appearing in the June 15, 1892, edition of *The Texas Volunteer* offered not even a hint as to Sergeant Baz Outlaw's recurring bouts with the bottle and/or brothers of the badge. *Courtesy Texas State Library and Archives.*

Brewster County Sheriff James B. Gillett, pictured here later in life, had a nasty tête-à-tête inside the Buckhorn Saloon at Alpine with an inebriated Sergeant Outlaw. Luckily, Baz showed good sense by not testing the sheriff's six-shooter resolve, but unluckily the self-imposed madness cost him his Ranger job. *Courtesy Archives of the Big Bend, Bryan Wildenthal Memorial Library, Sul Ross University.*

As with most lawmen, then or now, the fascination and utility of firearms is ubiquitous. Pictured here is another of Baz Outlaw's handguns, a Merwin & Hulbert Pocket Model revolver. Unfortunately for Baz, during one of his misbehaving outings at El Paso, county lawmen seized the revolver—never to return it. *AUTHOR'S PHOTO COURTESY THE JAMES H. EARLE COLLECTION.*

Renowned collector Jim Earle, with the Merwin & Hulbert once owned by Baz Outlaw. *AUTHOR'S PHOTO.*

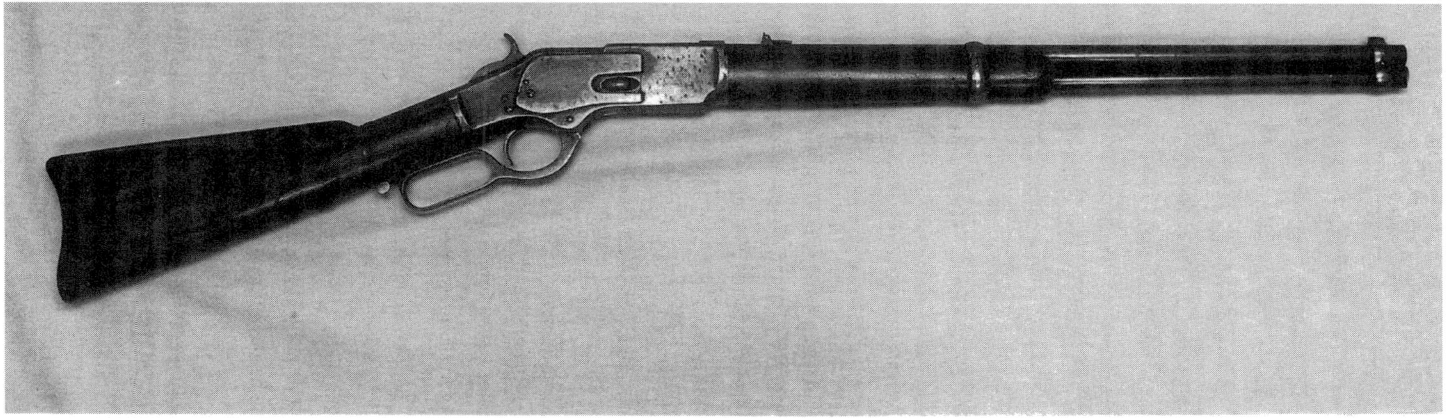

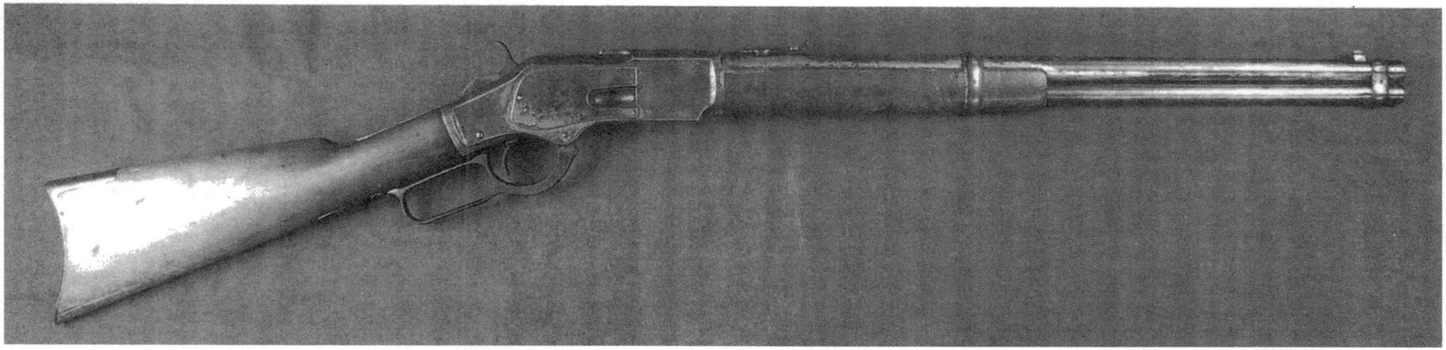

Top: Sheriff J.B. Gillett's personally owned 1873 Winchester, purportedly from time to time a carbine borrowed by a financially destitute Baz Outlaw; an assertion falling far short of any factual framework. *Courtesy Tobin and Anne Armstrong Ranger Research Center, Texas Ranger Hall of Fame & Museum.* Below: What may be said with clarity is Baz Outlaw did have an 1873 Winchester, one of his very own. That saddle-ring carbine is pictured herein. Provenance for this particular Winchester, as with his engraved Colt's six-shooter, his Merwin & Hulbert Pocket Model revolver, and a Colt's short-barreled "slip-gun" is justly established by a reasonably documented paper trail. *Courtesy Frank Jardim/Frazier History Museum Collection.*

Though but folklore, it's often been penned in popular periodicals that following Baz's semi-forced resignation from the Rangers that in a fit of denunciation and despair he wandered the vast Big Bend region hunting for a supposed cache of buried loot taken during a train robbery, therefore earning a nickname: "The Lone Wolf." Donald M. Yena's captivating painting represents personification of the legend, though he thoughtfully preserved anonymity for his subject when brush was put to canvas. *Courtesy the artist, Don Yena.*

Richard Clayton "Dick" Ware, ex-Ranger and veteran of the 1878 shootout with Sam Bass at Round Rock, Williamson County, Texas, former elected sheriff of Mitchell County (Colorado City), and as the newly politically appointed United States Marshal for the Western District of Texas, Baz Outlaw's boss. *From Texas Ranger Sketches courtesy the author, Robert W. Stephens.*

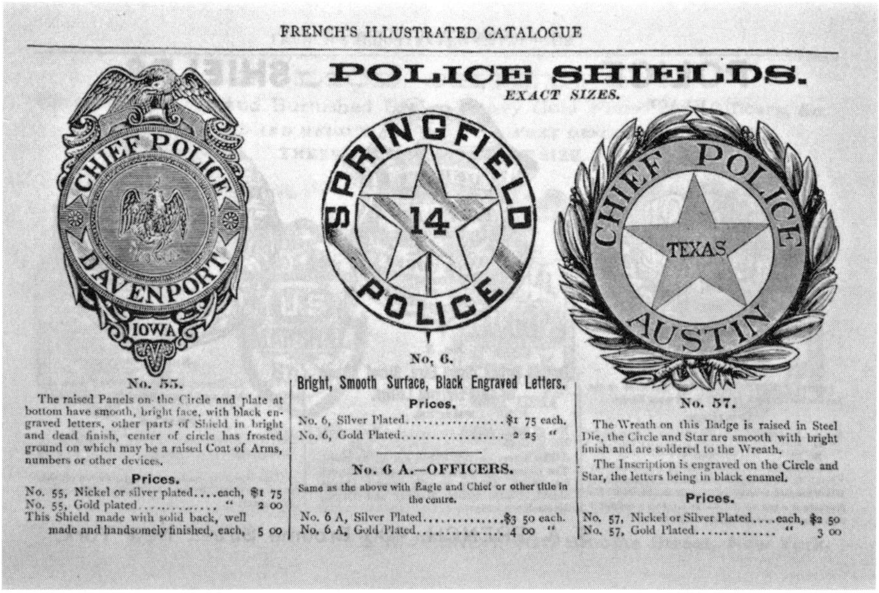

FRENCH'S ILLUSTRATED CATALOGUE

POLICE SHIELDS.

EXACT SIZES.

No. 55.

The raised Panels on the Circle and plate at bottom have smooth, bright face, with black engraved letters, other parts of Shield in bright and dead finish, center of circle has frosted ground on which may be a raised Coat of Arms, numbers or other devices.

Prices.

No. 55, Nickel or silver plated....each, $1 75
No. 55, Gold plated.............. " 2 00
This Shield made with solid back, well made and handsomely finished, each, 5 00

No, 6.

Bright, Smooth Surface, Black Engraved Letters.

Prices.

No. 6, Silver Plated..................$1 75 each.
No. 6, Gold Plated.................. 2 25 "

No. 6 A.—OFFICERS.

Same as the above with Eagle and Chief or other title in the centre.

No. 6 A, Silver Plated..............$3 50 each.
No. 6 A, Gold Plated............... 4 00 "

No. 57.

The Wreath on this Badge is raised in Steel Die, the Circle and Star are smooth with bright finish and are soldered to the Wreath.

The Inscription is engraved on the Circle and Star, the letters being in black enamel.

Prices.

No. 57, Nickel or Silver Plated....each, $2 50
No. 57, Gold Plated.............. " 3 00

Texas Rangers would not be issued badges by the State of Texas until 1935 upon creation of the Texas Department of Public Safety. Many Texas Rangers, however, owned and sported badges, ones they had ordered from a catalog, jeweler, or had one personally hammered from a Mexican *cinco peso*, the near iconic star-in-wheel badge. Upon reviewing this catalog ad there is little doubt as to where Captain Frank Jones turned for his striking badge. *COURTESY KURT HOUSE COLLECTION ©PAUL GOODWIN CREATIVE SERVICES.*

Frank Jones' neatly crafted badge, the initials standing for Frontier Battalion. *COURTESY KURT HOUSE COLLECTION ©PAUL GOODWIN CREATIVE SERVICES.*

Other early day Rangers, perhaps not financially capable of or inclined to order from a catalog, displayed less artfully crafted badges, such as this one. *COURTESY TOBIN AND ANNE ARMSTRONG RANGER RESEARCH CENTER TEXAS RANGER HALL OF FAME & MUSEUM.*

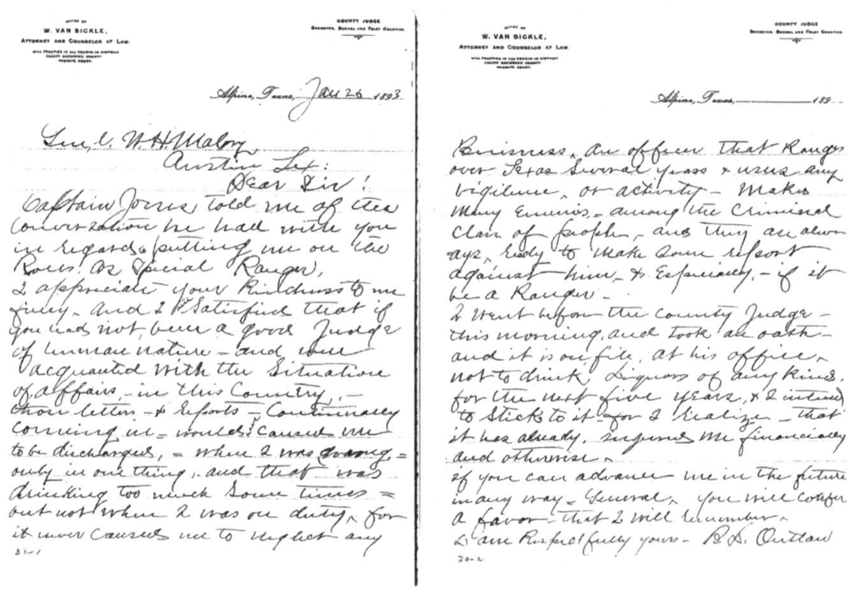

W. VAN SICKLE,
ATTORNEY AND COUNSELOR AT LAW.

COUNTY JUDGE

Alpine, Texas, Jan 26 1893.

Genl. W. H. Mabry
Austin Tex:
Dear Sir!
Captain Jones told me of the conversation he had with you in regards putting me on the Rolls. As Special Ranger, I appreciate your kindness to me fully. And I [am] Satisfied that if you had not been a good Judge of human nature — and well acquainted with the Situation of affairs, — in this Country, — those letters — & Reports — Continually coming in — would have Caused me to be discharged, — when I was wrong only in one thing, — and that was drinking too much Some times — but not when I was on duty, for it never Caused me to neglect any

W. VAN SICKLE,
ATTORNEY AND COUNSELOR AT LAW.

COUNTY JUDGE

Alpine, Texas, 189

Business. An officer that Ranges over Texas Several years & uses any vigilence, or activity — Makes Many Enemies, — among the Criminal Class of people, — and they are always, ready to make Some resort against him, — & Especially, — if it be a Ranger. —
I went before the County Judge — this morning, and took an oath — and it is on file, at his office, — not to drink, Liquors of any kind, for the next five years, & I intend to Stick to it — for I realize — that it has already, injured me financially and otherwise. —
If you can advance me in the future in any way — General, — you will confer a favor — that I will remember. —
I am Respectfully yours — B. L. Outlaw

The letter from U.S. Deputy Marshal Baz Outlaw to Texas Adjutant General W.H. Mabry, wherein he pledges to refrain from drinking "Liquors of any kind for the next five years & I intend to Stick to it—for I realize that it has already injured me financially and otherwise." *COURTESY TOBIN AND ANNE ARMSTRONG RANGER RESEARCH CENTER, TEXAS RANGER HALL OF FAME & MUSEUM.*

Chapter 10

Undaunted Courage and Fine Generalship

SPRINGTIME OF 1893 HAD CLOSED finding U.S. Deputy Marshal/Special Ranger Baz Outlaw sitting in a reasonably good position career-wise. Certainly, despite the intermittent drunken and messy imbroglios of the past, maybe his word about foregoing taking a drink would stand good. Unquestionably, several Big Bend Country folks thought he was yet the man to turn to in a crisis. John Humphries, the storeowner previously advancing Baz cash in lieu of Captain Frank Jones forwarding Outlaw's quarterly pay vouchers, apparently had forgotten and/or forgiven—or it never had amounted to too much in the first place. Subsequent to some intricate consultations of a serious nature, John Humphries carried the message. Civilian Humphries wrote to Baz Outlaw enjoining him to exercise his authority as a federal officer: Proclaiming to the deputy marshal that the "Mescal business" at the Chispa Coal Mines must be stopped. The novice would-be lawmen had concocted what they believed was an ingenious plan. As it was spelled out to the Deputy U.S. Marshal, they would furnish him—loan him—a Winchester, horse, and saddle for the job.[1] Then he could

> go out dressed as a miner and loiter at the mining camp [manager's camp] during the heat of the day, so as not to get into [the

> laborers'] camps till after dark on Thursday, Then Friday and Sat night you can lay for them across the Canyon. . . .[2]

There was nothing ambiguous regarding the request or about asking Baz Outlaw—the well known and well liked Big Bend area lawman—to fix the perceived or real smuggling problem. That he had been exiled from the thought processes or physically banished from the region by several of the Big Bend Country's movers and shakers would register as an oversized misnomer, as gigantic as that picturesque Far Wild Country itself. At the time, while grading his scorecard about challenging whiskey river's rapids would have earned dismal marks, Baz, as everyone at Alpine and Marfa and along the Rio Grande knew, had undertaken a pledge to paddle his canoe through calmer waters. Should he stand tall, honoring that promise there no doubt would be good days in store for the reformed—abstainer—alcoholic Baz Outlaw. In another book, on another page, good days were numbered for Captain Frank Jones.

Subsequent to his marriage to divorcee Helen Baylor Gillett and after thoughtful analysis of the myriad of pleas and petitions that a company of Rangers be deployed to El Paso County, the Company D headquarters camp had been shifted to Ysleta. Sergeant Hughes remained behind in the Big Bend Country with a little detachment to cover a lot of ground. At this time the principle evildoers along El Paso County's portion of the Texas/Mexico borderlands were the Olguins, a bloodline crime family leading what was commonly referred to as the Bosque Gang. Consulting a dictionary is not necessary, but were one so studiously inclined it would be quite evident that by simple definition members of a gang—are gangsters. From the gang's patriarchal leader, Clato Olguin, somewhat semi-retired due to age, the family tree was choked with sons and grandsons owning prison records and thefts and murders and at least one conviction for rape to their heinous credit. Too, a horde of minions unrelated by blood were also part of the setup, and with blood on their hands had proved themselves worthy of initiation into the despicable outfit. Through and through they were one and all, gangsters to the core.

They, too, were nonpartisan, sadistically preying on Texans, *Tejanos*, and Mexicans alike. Company D's first major thrust following the June 1893 transfer into El Paso County was to step on the Olguins' necks: Figuratively if possible, literally if necessary.[3]

Lamentably on the thirtieth day of June it was the Olguins and their crew wearing the boots of dominance, not the Texas Rangers. Shifting Rio Grande sands had confusingly channeled an island, Pirate Island, a piece of real-estate with an iminagary line down the middle separating the sovereignty of Texas and Mexico. And it was there, that Captain Frank Jones and Corporal Carl Kirchner, along with Privates Eddie Aten, T.F. Tucker, Wood Saunders, and Ed Bryant were kicked hard, the life figuratively stomped out of Captain Frank Jones when bushwhackers' bullets ripped into his body—a dead man on Mexico's side of the line. The Rangers' retreat was not pretty, but it was compulsory. Mexican soldiers were riding hard due to verbal reports and cracking sounds of gunfire; armed Texans had invaded their country—bullets not diplomats would settle the score. And so, the living Texas Rangers shrewdly skedaddled.[4]

Though much can be and has been written about Baz Outlaw with negative connotations and, for particular episodes rightly so, he hardly ever was or could be criticized with characterizations of being a wallflower. At once, upon learning of the Pirate Island shoot-out and Frank Jones' demise, wearing his Special Ranger hat Baz Outlaw sent a telegram to the adjutant general with his itinerary: "Capt Jones was Killed near Ysleta by thieves today will go up on first train do all I can to capture murderers."[5]

Even with the understandable chaos and turmoil, Special Ranger Outlaw—either on the train or at his room in the Lindell Hotel at El Paso—realized he still owed Texas Ranger headquarters his monthly report for June. Taking pen in Special Ranger Outlaw posted the adjutant general with compulsory mention of an arrest and other tidbits of news he supposed would be of interest to the Frontier Battalion's headman: "On acct of leaving Alpine to assist in recovering Capt Jones body I am late in Sending report. Arrested Wm Louis in Brewster Co on 15th June, Assault and Attempt to Murder. I arrived at Ysleta yesterday with Seven Men but was too late to get to the River before the Mexican authorities had delivered the Captains body—Which was intered [*sic*] yesterday at Ysleta with Masonic honors! His wife is in very delicate health and I think it doubtful about her recovery from the Shock! There is a hard gang of Mexicans in the vicinity and Several bad White Men that assist them in their depredations. I think that Captain Jones body lay in the Sun Nearly all day & was in a bad condition—his wife was not allowed to look at it. My address for the Ensuing month will be at Alpine."[6]

What Baz Outlaw failed to mention, presumably because he was wholly unawares, it would seem that Frank B. Simmons, since elected to Sheriff of El Paso County, had been in some form or fashion forced to bend to the well known and well accepted borderland practice colloquially known as the bite—*la mordida*—the bribe. Reading between the lines of Sheriff Simmons message to Governor Hogg is necessary, but not complicated:

> I have been to quite an expense in getting the body of Capt. Frank Jones, Company D State Rangers from Mexico. Will the state help me pay these expenses. . . .[7]

Once more the untimely and murderous death of a Company D supervisor had created a vacuum. Suitably replacing Captain Frank Jones in the eyes of not just a few would be next to impossible. Figuratively, the captain's going under fostered a feeding frenzy before he even met Neptune. The sharks of ambition were circling. Sergeant John Reynolds Hughes was hungering for the job. Deputy U.S. Marshal Baz Outlaw was salivating, too. And both had friends and supporters throwing chum into the decision making sea, frantically clouding the governor's and the adjutant general's options, as if an octopus had inked its murkiness.

Though there would be no argument that it might border on an oversimplification, by and large the split between cliques clamoring and chumming for Baz Outlaw or John Hughes was somewhat dependent on where one dipped his oars—geographically. Both candidates for the Company D captaincy had groundswells of political and personal support, Hughes seemingly having a lock on the much more heavily populated El Paso County, while Outlaw had garnered no little backing from the Big Bend section. Naturally there were exceptions, as nothing in political doings is ever tied hard and fast. But certainly an overtaxed intellectual effort need not be expended to see the obvious orchestration of letters and telegrams touting one man or the other. Rather shamelessly it seems, most were addressed to Governor Hogg or Adjutant General Mabry but three days after Captain Frank Jones was foully murdered.[8] And perhaps somewhat surprisingly, being that there really were but two main contenders vying to lead Company D, voices from the partisan camps were not derogatory regarding the competitor, but only laudatory and ringing endorsements for their individual nominees.

Still, the Texas Ranger front office had heard naught—officially—from either aspirant. Although certainly fortuitously, the figurative light bulb came on in their heads simultaneously, each uneasily sensing the urgency of making known hopes of landing the prime leadership spot. The fact that Captain Jones had been buried less than a week was an untidiness best set aside. The man who tarried might miss the boat. From Ysleta on the fifth day of July 1893 Sergeant John Reynolds Hughes formally made application to be named as Captain Jones' replacement, due to the sad death of the company's "Brave and Beloved" captain. Not desirous of losing a flattering opportunity, Hughes pointed out that perhaps AG Mabry would want to consider his "record as a ranger," as well as peruse the telegrams and letters of his many pals and admirers which were, indeed, "all men of high standing in the country where they live and where I have worked as a ranger."[9]

From Alpine, on that very same day, U.S. Deputy Marshal/Special Ranger Baz Outlaw made his written pitch to AG Mabry, promising that should he receive such an appointment he would absolutely do all in his power "to imitate the Example set by my [his] old—and honored Co-Commander—in temperate habits" and that he would also pledge to "faithfully discharge all duties incumbent upon me—as an officer, hoping that this will receive your consideration."[10] Apparently—at this point in his life—the vow not to tip the bottle for five years was still holding the course: The whiskey river had run dry.

John Hughes and Baz Outlaw thought rather well of themselves, but plainly others did too. Citing but one example from each faction is—in a sense of fair play—right fitting and functional. For one petition claiming eighty signatories, including Brewster County's county judge, the tax assessor, and others numbering on the top side of eighty, the West Texas folks had this to say about their candidate, Bazzell Lamar Outlaw:

> Your petitioners, citizens of Brewster County having faith & confidence in B.L. Outlaw & believing him to be a man of undaunted courage and fine generalship, and from his long service in the frontier Battalion of the state & valuable services rendered to his country & his fit qualifications gained from his experience of many years upon the frontier, most respectfully ask you to appoint him Captain of Co. D front Batt to fill the place of the late hero & much lamented Capt Frank Jones so recently murdered by Mexican Bandits.[11]

Offsetting pleas favoring the candidacy of Baz Outlaw was the not insignificant number of missives imploring the state's executive officers to elevate Sergeant John Reynolds Hughes to the top line on Company D's Muster & Payroll:

> We the undersigned Citizens of Ysleta, El Paso County, Texas believing in the integrity, honesty, and capacity of Sgt. Jon. R. Hughes of Company D Frontier Battalion do most respectfully recommend him to succeed the late worthy Frank Jones as Captain of said Company.[12]

There, too, in truth and fact, were some things Baz Outlaw did not own and, speculatively, they were showstoppers. Former Ranger captain and political powerhouse George Wythe Baylor penned a letter to the adjutant general regarding the hearsay wishes of the deceased captain, his son-in-law: "In this connection I wish to say that Sergt Jno. R. Hughes had the entire confidence of Capt Jones and my daughter heard him say in case he resigned [to accept the U.S.

Marshal's position] he would use all of his influence in the Sergt's behalf & I believe in regular line of promotions he should have the position & trust you will give it to him."[13] And, whether or not Sergeant Hughes solicited the letter from his old boss, Ira Aten, then sheriff of Castro County in the Texas Panhandle, is immaterial. Aten wrote the adjutant general concerning Captain Jones' death: "I have just written to Gov Hogg in behalf of Sergt John R. Hughes of same Co for the Captaincy & I appeal to your Hon [title] to look over the record of John R. Hughes as an officer & judge whether he is entitled to a promotion or not. I have known them both for years & no better officers or men can be found in the State of Texas than they."[14]

There was more. Though little could he have realized at the time, Baz Outlaw had been hamstrung. The Company D Texas Rangers, many of whom he had worked with and supervised, were hawking the promotion of Sergeant Hughes. With Corporal Carl Kirchner as spokesman they were upfront with their high regard for 1st Sergeant Hughes and astutely sly with wording their petition to AG Mabry—reminding him of a lot, but saying a little: "Enclosed herewith please find petition signed by boys in camp asking the appointment of Sergt John R. Hughes to fill the vacancy caused by the death of our beloved Captain. Mr. Hughes has been in this Co. six years & from the first been considered honest brave & efficient officer with sober & industrious habits. He has for the last 5 years commanded detachments at every place Capt Jones has been stationed & has given the utmost satisfaction & has been on the Rio Grande border long enough to speak spanish [*sic*] sufficient to be of great help along the border And has worked in every County as a ranger from El Paso to Brownsville."[15]

Explicitly the Company D Rangers were making their preference known. Collectively they were not disparaging the competency or courage of their former Ranger colleague, but the remark about Sergeant Hughes' sober habits was no ill-aimed shot across Baz Outlaw's bow. From their viewpoint—even allowing for all else—the adjutant general should not forget facts: Despite his good qualities, Baz Outlaw was subject to shipwrecks.

Adjutant General Mabry was actively working hard to professionalize the Frontier Battalion, institutionally sculpting the outfit into a corps of first-rate crime busters and peace keepers. Selecting the right personnel for the right job was one of the crucial keys to that professionalism. He would not be bulldozed by political or factional or provincial preferences. Promotions from within—especially with rank and file approval—were but one method of maintaining unit cohesion and building *esprit de corps*. Arbitrarily shattering Company D privates' and noncoms' expressed desire and capriciously disregarding their input would not be sound or effective policy. Handing Baz Outlaw the captaincy would be a gamble. Promoting Sergeant John R. Hughes to capably command Company D may not have been a surefire bet, but for the mulling adjutant general—with the governor's blessing—the odds were better.

Pursuant to Special Order No. 105, the commander of Company D was Captain Hughes.[16] Corporal Kirchner was promoted to top-sergeant. Baz Outlaw, though he may have been disappointed at being passed over, could yet console himself with two—weighty—hard facts: He was yet a Deputy U.S. Marshal and had not been asked to, nor had he forfeited his commission as a Special Texas Ranger. Though it's suggested—in twentieth-century pulps—that Baz's losing out to Hughes sent him into a tailspin of disillusionment and depression and drinking, such may not be borne out by paying attention to archived paperwork. Hughes' promotion had come through at the end of the first week of July 1893. Baz Outlaw wasn't moping around crying the blues or too drunk to function as a Special Ranger. No, he had been busy.

Working in conjunction with the Brewster County Sheriff, Doc Gourley, Baz had nabbed Bill Dunman at Alpine on July 15, 1893. To the very best of Baz's knowledge the arrestee, his man, had earlier been convicted and sentenced to the state penitentiary for a murder committed in Kimble County. Now, here he was at Alpine? Special Texas Ranger Outlaw and the sheriff had criminal charges lodged against Bill Dunman, a misdemeanor $20 theft case (perhaps with the elements for upgrading to a robbery), but after pocketing confidential information from a snitch Baz was suspicious that he might have jailed an escaped convict.[17] The day following the arrest Baz Outlaw messaged the adjutant general via an urgent telegram: "Has Bill Dunman served his term out for Killing man in Kimble County—answer immediately."[18] Baz Outlaw, seemingly still on the wagon of sobriety, assured the concerned legal authorities that even though Bill Dunman was "a hard case" and his being drunk and trying to "take in the town" of Alpine had caused Baz to notice him in the first place, until he heard otherwise, Baz would hold on to his prisoner on grounds of the local charges.[19]

U.S. Deputy Marshal/Special Ranger Baz Outlaw hadn't precisely scored a bull's-eye, but he'd come damn close. There is not room for too much speculation that while a resident of Kimble County some years earlier he was a least somewhat familiar with the ongoing buzz about the calculated murder of cowboy John Condy by Bill Dunman, also a free-spirited cowboy then working at Creed Taylor's ranch on the James River's headwaters in eastern Kimble County. When it happened the crime was a real newsmaker, sustaining residual curiosity statewide. Though later arrested for the ambush, Bill Dunman had made good his escape—with the help of local lawmen—while he and another prisoner, the notorious John Potter, were handcuffed and being hauled in a horse-drawn hack back to Junction City from their temporary steel-barred hotel at San Antonio, the cold and dank Bexar County Jail. John Potter was unceremoniously and fatally lynched at the roadside—with buckshot—by savagely minded revenge seekers and the then-unshackled Bill Dunman was purposefully cut loose, allowed to strike the Owl Hoot Trail. Bill Dunman was a high-flying and wide-ranging fugitive from justice for the next dozen or so years.[20] Baz Outlaw and/or his spy may have been somewhat confused about whether or not Dunman was an escaped convict or an escaped prisoner on the road to being a convict, but clip the wings of Mr. Bill, the sheriff and Baz Outlaw had done. And now, those elated lawmen in Bexar County wanting him for horse theft and burglary, or the prosecutorial authorities in Kimble County—if they chose to bring an indictment for killing Condy—well, they knew where to find him, right there in jail at Alpine.[21] Encouragingly, not content to dawdle too long with police business, a week later U.S. Deputy Marshal/Special Ranger Outlaw—again at the seldom dull little village of Alpine—arrested Dickey Baker for theft.[22]

Returning to his headquarters base at Alpine from a sojourn into Reeves County hunting for a band of horse thieves, Special Ranger Outlaw once more took pen in hand, particularly messaging the adjutant general about the ongoing "feud existing between the Sheriff of that County & the city marshal of Pecos City & some citizens which is liable to terminate in trouble at any time, in fact I don't think it will be Settled So long as the present Sheriff holds office—if I have been correctly informed by some of the citizens!"[23] Of course, he was right, dead right, but that makes for another story. Shortly thereafter, at the end of September 1893, putting on his Deputy U.S. Marshal's hat, Baz informed the Frontier Battalion's headquarters at Austin that for the foreseeable future he would be tied up at El Paso attending federal court, but for November expected to be again working out of Alpine.[24] Presupposing that at this point in his law-enforcing life Baz Outlaw was suffering some sort of banishment from contributing his two cents' worth with the upper-echelon brass would be wrongheaded. Like pimps and prostitutes, who have to nap once and a while, the ogres and trolls of an alcoholic's subconscious periodically doze, too. While they were snoozing Special Ranger Outlaw offered a suggestion. To his way of sober reflection the Ranger detachment then stationed at Pecos City—which was to be deployed somewhere else anyway—be assigned to Alpine so that they might work along the Rio Grande, which was becoming unsafe for any officer working by himself.[25] Understandably, in the sometimes comedic and sometimes tragic turf wars, the Brewster County Sheriff, Doc Gourley, this time took exception with Baz's thinking, stating that "I would feel as safe at the River as I do here in Alpine. . . ."[26] Thoroughly committed to his beliefs, Special Ranger Outlaw once again penned his recommendation:

> I have just returned from a trip down on the Rio Grande River [and] found that there is a bad State of affairs down there.

> Especially—about—what—is called the big bend. Just oposite [*sic*] the old Train Robber's Camp there is a regular organized gang of horse and cow thieves operating thorough that vicinity. I accidently found one of their notes left in a vacated Camp to one of their confederates. The Mexican Soldiers had fired on them from the other Side & they ran off & left their Saddles. Sergt [Daniel Lynch] Musgrave of Co. F. was with me on this trip. [27]

How much stock Captain Hughes was putting into Sheriff Gourley's assessment might be up for debate, but whether he agreed with Baz Outlaw's evaluation on the face of it, or was respectfully showing deference to his old boss—the former 1st Sergeant of Company D—is in an abstract sense unknowable. Practically speaking, however, he bent to Baz Outlaw's proposal, advising the adjutant general: "I think I will move the Pecos Detachment to Alpine. . . ."[28] Then he wavered, changing course in midstream after consulting with Sheriff Gourley and, more notably, Texas State Senator J.M. Dean, one of his strongest political backers and one of the ardent voices championing him for the captaincy of Company D.[29] Although characterized as a bulldozing fellow that "forced his way," Senator Dean was undeniably successful at and accustomed to winning, regardless.[30] Knowing which side of the bread is buttered and who buttered it is astute. John Hughes was no dummy.

Enumerating with specificity all of Baz Outlaw's arrests is not necessary for taking a measure of the man as 1893 began giving way for what a new year would have in store for that gusty—and sometimes guzzling—transplanted Georgian. Baz had arrested Tom Patten for Smuggling, Vicente Lujan for Assault to Murder, Mariano Ortiz for Assault to Murder, and A. Collison and James Wilson for Receiving Stolen Horses, turning the latter two prisoners over to Doc Anderson, U.S. Mounted Customs Inspector.[31] While making these arrests was there a whiff of liquor escaping each time law enforcer Outlaw exhaled? Had he really been true to his word? Or, had he, despite his best try, slipped the track of sobriety? The answer to that question—for 1893—is unknown and uncertain. History will duly record he should have made and stuck with a New Year's resolution.

Once again with unparalleled style Donald M. Yena captures the essence of then and now's perennial borderland evildoing: Smugglers. Baz Outlaw was specifically asked to assume an undercover identity and stop an epidemic of Big Bend area liquor smuggling. Yena's *Mescal & Muddy Water* spotlights the challenge U.S. Deputy Marshal/Special Ranger Baz Outlaw faced. *COURTESY THE ARTIST, DON YENA.*

Marfa the shiretown of gargantuan Presidio County. Sharing an international line with Mexico, Presidio County's secluded stretches of the snaking Rio Grande, was/is perfectly designed geography for folks with smuggling on their agenda. Marfa could boast of mountainous beauty and manmade badness, obliging the presence of Texas Rangers, and at times because of the Texas Rangers: Akin to the time Company D's Sergeant Baz Outlaw jumped the track, running amok with a magic show manager. *Courtesy Archives of the Big Bend, Bryan Wildenthal Memorial Library, Sul Ross University.*

Carl Kirchner, a veteran Ranger and a survivor of the horrific gunfight on Pirate Island which claimed the life of Company D Captain Frank Jones. *From Texas Ranger Sketches by Robert W. Stephens.*

Although snapped at a later time during a railroad strike, Edwin Dunlap "Eddie" Aten, standing fourth from left Winchester in hand, was the youngest of the fighting Aten brothers. He, too, was a surviving veteran of the frightful shoot-out with Pirate Island gangsters that claimed Captain Frank Jones' life. *Courtesy Tobin and Anne Armstrong Ranger Research Center, Texas Ranger Hall of Fame & Museum.*

As an El Paso County deputy Peyton J. Edwards responded with other lawmen to the Rio Grande subsequent to Captain Frank Jones being murdered on Pirate Island. Later (1910–1916), Edwards would serve as the elected sheriff of El Paso County. *Courtesy Tobin and Anne Armstrong Ranger Research Center, Texas Ranger Hall of Fame & Museum.*

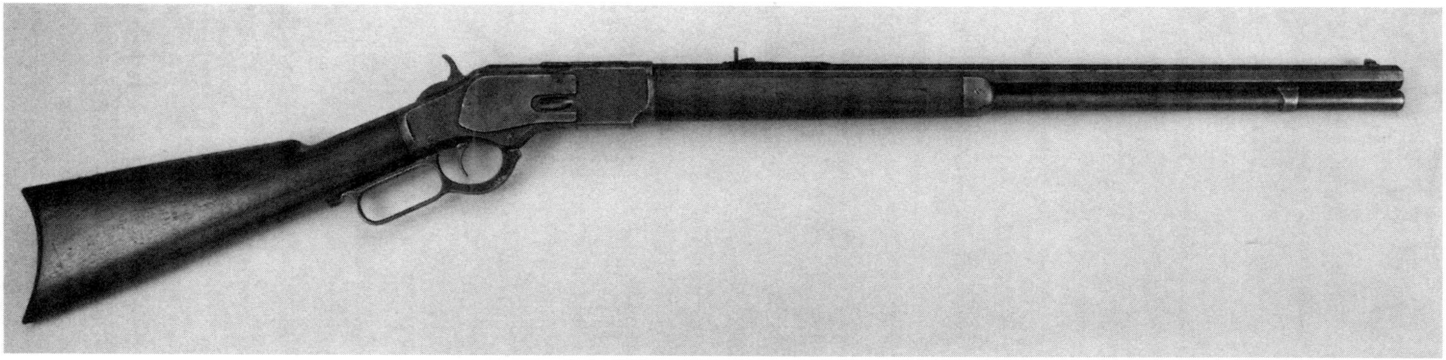

Captain Frank Jones' 1873 Winchester. Subsequent to negotiations and perhaps the greasing of greedy palms with a few greenbacks, this weapon was returned, along with the captain's badge, to the Texas side of the Rio Grande. However, Captain Jones' Colt's six-shooter and handcuffs were never returned. *Courtesy Kurt House Collection ©Paul Goodwin Creative Services.*

CHAPTER 11

In Arrest When He Died

THE PREVIOUS YEAR MAY HAVE BEEN PUT TO BED, but 1894 El Paso was wide awake, one of those emblematic towns of the popularized Wild West era that never slept. And if she did need to nap for a minute or two—or readjust unmentionables—well, Ciudad Juárez was across the river. Though there were many nice folks residing there, industriously earning wholesome livelihoods and occasionally attending performances at the opera house or variety theaters, or churchy socials, or even lacing up roller-skates at one of several rinks, other amusements were tolerable. Far and wide throughout the nineteenth-century Southwest—the lively city was not necessarily known by her proper name, but as already cited, Hell Paso, the Monte Carlo of the West. One scribe said the place was wide-open, "tough as an old boot, mean as a sore-headed bear."[1]

Aside from laying down a bet, were one so inclined laying down a whore was effortless, too. A business transaction—nothing more, nothing less—it was. Good for the patron, the prostitute, and the madam and the city who was taking her cut by winking and turning her head, all the time collecting fines—de facto licensing fees—from the daughters of joy.[2] Even the city's attorney would lament that the practice was "radically wrong in principle and right has been sacrificed to profit."[3] And one of those ladies of the night with a plunging neckline and plunging her indomitable spirit into America's dreamscape model of capitalism was Mathilde Weiler, aka Miss Tillie Howard, a Wisconsin native—maybe—who had scrimped and saved, investing her $2,200 in cash for a fancily appointed parlor house at 307 South Utah Street, in the very heart of El Paso's Tenderloin District—or the Reservation—as whore house row had then been euphemistically christened.[4]

Tillie was a looker! One Company D Ranger was anxious to pay her "a visit." He did, perhaps not dreaming his diary would someday be made public. Private Lon Oden was dazzled, then understood why immodest sporting lady Miss Tillie Howard was deliciously deserving of being "the talk of the border." In the obviously beguiled Texas Ranger's estimation Tillie, with her statuesque tallness and coal black hair was, really, one of the most gorgeous girls he'd ever seen. Good lawmen—Texas Rangers, too—are expected to be observant. Not bashfully Lon Oden also noticed and mentioned: "I imagine she doesn't need those artificial bosoms the ladies are using now; hers look natural enough. . . . I'll be seeing more of Tillie—as an experiment."[5] Madam Tillie Howard was apparently amply endowed and inside that peeking cleavage, besides a hidden and teasing promise of eroticism, also was nuzzling place for her tiny but loud whistle, the one given her by police should summoning security be necessary. Whoring and drinking were okay. Abusing women, fighting, or puking all over garish fixtures and costly carpet wasn't. Tillie ran a tight ship.[6]

Though it might be painstakingly possible and tediously accomplished, precisely tracking lawman Baz Outlaw's every footprint or horseshoe's dint is not essential for moving his story. There are two hard truths, however. Either by demands of acting as a Deputy U.S. Marshal or a simple personal preference for the sin town's gratifications, Baz was spending more and more time at El Paso—and visiting Tillie Howard's bordello. There, one of his favorites, Ruby, was turning tricks for a set salary, Tillie not believing in her girls blowing and going for commissions in an assembly line of decadence. Cash paying customers were treated with dignity and empathy; repeat business was necessary and highly valued, else lusting men might sample sin at another of El Paso's palaces of pleasure.[7]

The lure of the city's red lights and nightlife was corrupting competition when weighted against any treaty of abstinence made in a foreign land—say, like the faraway Big Bend Country. When at El Paso, at least sometimes Baz Outlaw buckled to booze—the tempting and tantalizing trips to euphoria were irresistible, overpowering and, as unreformed drunks know, one can really always quit—tomorrow. Purportedly and, there's scant reason for skepticism, one time while in attendance for federal court at El Paso, U.S. Deputy Marshal Baz Outlaw "made himself very offensive by frequent gun plays." And during one of those sprees, he vociferously threatened to shoot and "kill whoever opposed him." C.B. Dowd, one of the city's special policemen did what many were absolutely afraid to do, disarm the drunken Baz and read the riot act to him, to wit: "Mr. Outlaw I advise you to keep sober, for if you make any more gun plays in El Paso somebody will kill you."[8]At times, bending to hardcore reality that on occasions Baz Outlaw "became such a terror to this town," the El Paso Police Department appointed an officer to follow Baz's bar hopping outings. The surveillance was taken "with the understood purpose of quieting" any of Outlaw's sour-mash shenanigans.[9]

By another account—and there's not reason to doubt it—while in El Paso for one reason or another U.S. Deputy Marshal/Special Ranger Baz Outlaw tanked up on tarantula-juice and took off on an unmitigated and rip-roaring foot trip to McLane's Saloon. While there, staggering and stumbling in the drinking emporium's backyard Baz—as some wasted Texans were often prone to do—unleashed his six-shooter and let it bark at the moon. Outlaw may have even howled, too. So it seems, legendary town tamers and lawdogs were safely kenneled elsewhere for the night. Supposing what might have happened isn't good history, but there's a certain rationale to suggesting had Baz Outlaw been broached about quieting down or harnessing the madness, his caustic retort would have been for that idiotic person to just go ahead and cut the wolf loose![10] Baz Outlaw was that way—when he was drunk.

Sanctimoniously suggesting Deputy U.S. Marshal/Special Ranger Baz Outlaw was, now, always inebriated and always at El Paso would be wrong, a subterfuge drowning truthfulness with mythos and misinformation. In fact, as required of Special Rangers, Baz Outlaw was reporting his address for the first part of 1894 as Alpine, Brewster County.[11]

During February a criminal enforcement action—hoped-for action—was underway, one to some degree forestalling premature—not necessarily wrong—but premature judgments about the reliability and trustworthiness of lawman Baz Outlaw. Captain John Hughes, according to his written report to the adjutant general, had received intelligence from W.R. Martin, Division Superintendent of the Galveston, Harrisburg, & San Antonio Railroad, that plans were afoot by five unnamed crooks to highjack that train or one operated by the Texas & Pacific Railway somewhere east of Alpine. In response, Captain Hughes "sent Segt. Kirchner and three men down to guard the trains a few days until we [he] can find out the particulars. I have six men in camp and have all the horses and pack mules ready to put on the car in a few minutes notice if there should be a robbery. I have also ordered Corpl. Tucker to make a few trips on the T. & P. road. I may leave one of my men in charge of the camp here with instructions to have every thing ready at any moment, and go down about Devils River myself tomorrow."[12]

Baz Outlaw's involvement in Captain Hughes' interdiction, investigative, or apprehension plans is revealing. Had Captain Hughes sought counsel from his old boss? Had he given Outlaw a special and unwritten assignment? There are no hints that John Hughes and Baz Outlaw were on the outs, for any reason, personal or professional. One of two scenarios is applicable: Captain Hughes had either cut Outlaw in on the know or quite coincidently Baz had, on his own, developed like criminal intelligence. Dutifully Special Ranger Outlaw made his report to the adjutant general for the month of February 1894:

> I have no arrests to report for the past month. I am watching the movements of some hard characters in this vicinity—I think it likely from the information I can get that S.P. Train will be held up Shortly. I have Some of the parties Spotted, and am Watching their Movements. [signed, "B.L. Outlaw, Special Ranger"][13]

So it would seem, at this point and place in time, the irrefutably disturbed Baz Outlaw was not staggering and slobbering in a continual mindless state of drunkenness and denial. His acts of deviltry were not everyday occurrences—but sporadic. At this stage in his life, when Baz Outlaw did take a drink, it led to another, and then another, awakening the lurking fiends of wickedness. The mind altering power of hard liquor is deceptive. Some drunks are funny. Some drunks are amorous. Baz Outlaw, following the hilarity and the lustfulness was predictably mean, maniacal. Too, it's but logically and historically germane to note, neither U.S. Marshal Ware or Adjutant General Mabry—or Captain Hughes—had yanked the law enforcing authority of Baz Outlaw, he was still on their books. Washing one's hands after-the-fact is widespread and not infrequent. Hindsight is flawless and faultless. Was Baz foolishly thinking he could leave an inkling his word about abstaining from alcohol was yet good in the Big Bend Country, but for frequent train trips into El Paso County attending the federal court's business, that a little binge drinking was or would go unnoticed—undetectable? Many good drunks and many bad drunks feel invisible! Sadly, Baz Outlaw would prove to be a bad drunk—the worst of the worse.

For the Western Federal Judicial District of Texas, the first Mondays in April and October were designated as dates to initiate formally calling the court's docket for the El Paso Division, that geographically humongous chunk of West Texas real-estate but a subdivision not necessarily overpopulated.[14] During the nineteenth-century, especially in the wild and woolly west, court doings were big doings. Newspapermen could write good copy and turn the tabloids into profit. At El Paso the 1894 April term had been called into session and Deputy U.S. Marshal/Special Texas Ranger Baz

Outlaw was in town. His presence was demanded at the relatively recently constructed United States Customs House at the corner of Mills and Oregon Streets which also housed the U.S. Post Office and the U.S. District Court.[15]

Certainly one of the more notable—and controversial—federal lawmen working out of the Untied State Customs House was the former Sheriff of both Cochise and Yavapai Counties in Arizona Territory, John Harris Behan. A thoroughly committed Democrat, Behan had received his initial appointment as a U.S. Customs Inspector and assignment to El Paso on 3 June 1893. By quirk of fate, the very same month and year Ranger Captain Frank Jones had been murdered on Pirate Island and, for the story at hand, just before Deputy U.S. Marshal/Special Ranger Outlaw and Texas Ranger Sergeant Hughes were vying for and impatiently eyeing the chance to jump into the dead captain's supervisory boots.[16]

Rather industriously it seems, Behan was quite busy as El Paso/Ciudad Juárez was haven for smugglers and hotbed for their inventiveness. Even American housewives and otherwise honest businessmen could rationalize not paying duty—on selected items. Especially for ladies the silks in Juárez were attractive and highly prized. Enterprising gals could and did purchase the finery and slyly tuck items into their bustles before returning to Texas. Others, simply bought silk hose or expensive gloves, and wore them home—who would know the difference? Sometimes men who normally went hatless in the Lone Star State donned one for a trip to Juárez. There would be no amiable tip of the hat to the U.S. Customs man at the border on the return trip—lest those fancy and expensive cigars would be dislodged and seized.[17] But, as records clearly reveal, U.S. Customs Inspector Behan had more serious infractions to deal with, and he did.

During March 1894—just prior to the federal docket being called—Behan was conducting an investigation regarding a photographer at El Paso "making negatives of Chinamen" to be used with fraudulent immigration certificates. In another intriguing case he was covertly looking into allegations concerning the transshipment of more than half a ton of opium.[18] And though there's no actual paper record of Deputy U.S. Marshal/Special Ranger Baz Outlaw's or Texas Ranger Captain John Hughes' envy, it's not outlandish to suppose they also noticed Inspector Behan's promotion to Chinese Exclusion Agent at El Paso on 12 March 1894 and his subsequent raise in salary to $6.00 per day, plus expenses. Baz Outlaw's federal fee work, and John Hughes state pay warrants could hardly top that—and didn't.[19] Rhetorically, in light of upcoming events, would issues of pay disparity at the forefront of consciousness spark gunpowder?

During those first days of April 1894, when not providing security or testifying in federal court it seems lawman Baz Outlaw was incessantly visiting and philandering at Tillie Howard's rather plush brothel. And for part of that time, away from the district judge's and prosecutor's presence and notice, Baz Outlaw was blind drunk and belligerent, whiskey river washing him along Utah Street time and again, carrying the sludge of stupidity with him.

Tillie Howard was in no mood for any monkey business from Mr. Outlaw; she had had her fill and said so, later telling a reporter for the *El Paso Tribune* that Baz was at her house on Tuesday night, April 3, 1894, "drinking and we had some words about his behavior. He said he would kill me the next day. I thought he was joking and told him he had better kill me right there."[20] Baz stormed out of Tillie's in a huff and the madam breathed a sigh of relief.

It had all started—the big trouble—on the afternoon of April 5, 1894, when a few hours of downtime had presented itself for Baz Outlaw, a perfect opportunity—in his pickled psyche—to fornicate and further an infusion of alcohol into his bloodstream. He did both at Tillie Howard's place, having gained permission to enter with a promise of good—or better behavior. One purported witness, a Ranger who might have been there too, said that when Baz left Tillie's after his romp in the bed sheets he really wasn't three-sheets-to-the wind, but was "about half under, but not in an ugly mood."[21] After leaving the whorehouse, allowing time for his sexually spent internal batteries to recharge, the dually commissioned Baz Outlaw meandered up Utah Street, sampling the goods mixologists concocted and poured.[22]

As the drinks went down, not surprisingly to anyone, his ire went up—Baz Outlaw was, well just that way. While sober his grit was true: He'd stay hitched and stand by a friend regardless. The progression of alcoholism had taken its wretched toll. When Baz was drunk he was always spoiling for a fight, first with a foe, and if such wasn't handy, then with a friend. Blackouts are scary, knowing something had happened, but not just what? Clear-headed regret is insanity; morning after apologies—for whatever misbehavior—worthless! In this case Baz Outlaw was more than mad at his federal boss, U.S. Marshal Dick Ware, threatening to shoot him on sight for favoritism. Some federal fee work had been parceled out to another deputy marshal. A diligent fellow could earn easy money serving subpoenas and summons. It was an alleged affront Baz Outlaw could not live with when drunk. Dick Ware must die. Baz Outlaw, if left to his own devices would gladly and shamelessly pull the murder weapon's trigger. And therein lay lawmen's genuine predicament: He just might do it!

One of those El Paso gendarmes, a genuine hard-case with an unsavory gunfighter standing was the duly elected El Paso County Constable for Precinct No. 1, John H. Selman.[23] Sometimes Selman had been unwillingly caged as a hapless and chatterless jailbird; at least one time he'd been a thoroughly dishonest deputy sheriff in Shackelford County (seat Albany), and sometimes he worked as a legitimate lawman, but at all times he was intrepidly tuned into the need for earning credit as the last man standing when smoke cleared and six-shooter serenades quieted. Speaking directly to his firearms firing technique, a fellow who knew John Selman noted: "I saw him shoot a gun or pistol several times. He never closed an eye, just looked straight down the barrel, both eyes open. His eyes were unusual. They were such a light blue that it was hard to see where the blue began and the white stopped."[24] By any man's measure Constable Selman was the real deal, cueing one riveted El Paso newsman to remark: "He has the reputation for courage as well as promptness and effectiveness in the use of a pistol."[25]

Too, it seems Selman had other uses for a pistol than just shooting. Indicative of unchecked quarrelsomeness—if his past history wasn't amply illustrative—would come several months later when Jeff Davis Milton was named the city's chief of police. Clearly and not lovingly trying to foster the idea that at El Paso he was yet standing as the big-dog with the brass collar, Constable Selman had a message for Jeff Milton—and it wasn't polite and nicely worded: When the time was right John would take Milton's Colt's six-shooter and stick the barrel in a spot where the sun didn't shine and then, well, he would just proceed to kick the handles off.[26] Though it sidetracks Baz Outlaw's story for a moment, ex-Texas Ranger Milton wasn't too thrilled with Selman's big talk, or too timid to discuss the proposed rectal placement of his six-shooter. During a latter day interview Jeff Milton elaborated:

> When I first come in as chief of police I think somebody come and told me Selman made quite a talk about me—what he was going to do with me, about a six-shooter. He was standing at a bar when I went in. I walked in and slapped him on the shoulder and told him. "I am Milton, I am the new chief of police here, and would like to have that thing fixed." He said, "What is the matter! I am glad to meet you." And we talked a while. I said, "If you want to do that thing we had better find out about it." He just roared, and said he never thought of such a thing, and I said, I didn't think so. I expect the old boy meant it—a new chief there, and he was pretty drunk, and wanted to make a pretty wild speech.[27]

Later, another journalist would spin his characterization of John Henry Selman: "He was rather a large man, big-boned, rough-hewn and shaggy. He moved slowly, did not talk much, and drank plenty of whisky. Fearless, he was deadly with a pistol."[28] Shortly, John Wesley Hardin could verify Selman's deadliness—were he not face down and dead in the Acme Saloon, Selman's bullet in his head.

The nomadic Englishman, Frank Collinson, adventuring throughout the American West, sought out Baz, questioning him about Tom Patten, the fellow Baz had arrested for Smuggling on 14 November of the previous year, inquiring of him as to the probalities of pending legalities on El Paso's morning horizon: Was there any likelihood that the federal grand jury would return an indictment? Baz told Frank, yes, Patten would suffer an indictment, and then Outlaw began badly ranting and raving about wanting to off Dick Ware "before sundown."[29] Frank Collinson also said, right after that, Baz rather vehemently invited him for a quick drink—or two—at Ernest Bridger's Bank Saloon:

> I took a beer. He called for whisky, threw the empty glass on the floor, and called for more. He kept drinking and talking about killing Ware, and I suggested we go to his hotel, the Lindel, and talk the matter over. I could see that he was in an angry mood, and I wanted to get away from him.[30]

About this time, in walks Constable Selman. Collinson winks and gives Selman the all knowing nod, suggesting that everyone retire to Baz's hotel room for a drink, a ploy to get him out of the barrooms, off the street, and keep him out of serious and irrevocable trouble. The tactical theory was sound, most drunks sooner or later pass out, but Baz would hear none of it. While swimming in alcohol's abyss of blackness, U.S. Deputy Marshal/Special Ranger Baz Outlaw, hormonally revitalized, was up for another visit at Tillie's—at least he thought he could be up. Rather insistently he prescribed the path to peacefulness, Collinson, Bridges, and Selman should, must, accompany him back down to 307 South Utah—and he would then introduce the guys to "his girl." The easiest, though not necessarily the best course, is to placate a drunk—then outlast him. The figurative boat to Tillie's launched.

What happened next at Miss Tillie's whorehouse is pretty well known and even after allowing for the submerged discrepancies and undertows of storytelling debris, the bottom line washes out the same, the end result unpolluted. The weird spiders in Baz Outlaw's mind had collaborated, spinning and twisting their webs tight; forevermore choking to death any semblance of good sense or level-headedness. Baz Outlaw was, now, over the edge. Constable John Selman was rattlesnake mean and lawman Baz Outlaw was damnably drunk and deadly poisonous.

Selman, Bridges, and Collinson entered through Tillie Howard's front door, while Baz went around back to ingress through the back-door or down into the basement. The plan was simple: Allow the mindlessly drunken Baz Outlaw time to enjoyably cavort with Ruby and either pass out or sober up. Meanwhile Constable John Selman and wanderer Frank Collinson and saloon man Ernest Bridges would civilly pass time innocuously visiting in the downstairs parlor. Vicariously and mentally picturing the carousing and partying taking place inside and behind drawn curtains of the somewhat posh establishment might tend to satisfy voyeuristic inclinations—but it was a surprising gunshot that moved fantasy to fright.

In Tillie's backyard (water closest in other accounts)—and surely not out of character—Baz Outlaw had wildly cut loose with his Colt's six-shooter, a chopped down slip gun, not at any one thing or at any one somebody—just thoughtlessly popped a cap. Tillie Howard knew why Baz Outlaw was mad: "because he could not see a certain girl in the house."[31] Had he slipped into idiocy's blind rage—again? Madness it was, but as earlier highlighted, not just a few thoroughly drunk Texans—then or now—customarily like to shoot and showoff with their guns. For this particularly sad scenario, the a wildly frolicsome and fun-filled tradition or a burning anger vis-à-vis a perceived insult to his masculinity, had conspicuously transferred to the transplanted Texan from Lee County, Georgia.

Tillie Howard was not amused—not one little bit. Constable John Selman was not too concerned. However, both Tillie and John let their fingers touch for security. Subsequent to gingerly fingering his six-shooter, confirming it had not somehow slipped from its scabbard, John Selman told Miss Tillie not to worry—Baz had probably just dropped his pistol, no big deal. He would step outside, see, and quickly report back. Tillie was young, pretty, and due to trying obligations imposed by a hard life, wholly her own woman—and utterly independent. Tillie could and would sometimes suffer fools, but never loud-mouthed disorderly six-shootin' nitwits, not even Baz. Not even for one second. While Constable Selman had reassuringly toyed with his Colt's revolver, Tillie had hurriedly and dexterously reached for the little police whistle nestled between twin peaks of voluptuousness. Mr. Selman and Mr. Outlaw could be damned. Tillie sounded the alarm![32]

Hearing the echoing gunshot and then a shrill blast from Tillie's police whistle, Texas Ranger Joe McKidrict aka Buckskin Joe McKidrict, in El Paso and on standby, scheduled to offer additional testimony before the federal grand jury, began hustling toward the scene of whatever hubbub was taking place at the notoriously well-patronized bed and booze bordello.[33] Joe McKidrict wasn't rushing to the scene of trouble all alone—one riot, one Ranger—he was accompanied by "Leon Chavez, a deputy constable from the Smelter."[34] Something was assuredly amiss? Even though it was after normal quitting time—about five o'clock—and the grand jury and court would not take up until the next morning, 6 April 1894, young Joe McKidrict knew Texas Rangers were never really, unconditionally, off duty, an annoying and niggling inconvenience in the past often overlooked and disregarded by Baz Outlaw.

Though some might argue it was wholly self-serving, nonetheless eyewitness and player Constable John Selman picks up the story: ". . . I heard a pistol shot in the back yard or on the back porch. I went out as quick as I could go and found Outlaw and Joe McKidrict, a ranger, in the back yard. Joe had beat me out there without knowing what the matter was. Joe was saying there must be no more shooting as that would call the police down there."[35] Ranger McKidrict no doubt thought he was making sense, warning a fellow officer to straighten-up and wise-up before harmless fun challenged city policemen to handcuff him and haul him before El Paso's municipal judge. If he parked his disorderliness he probably wouldn't even have to pay a fine. Baz was too far gone.

Constable Selman, though a six-shooting dynamo in his own right, tried to defuse the dustup, telling Ranger McKidrict that Baz had "shot his pistol off by accident and that there would be no more." Selman continued with his spine-chilling replay: "Joe repeated that it would not do, when Outlaw threw his gun almost against Joe's temple and fired, saying 'You want that, don't you?'

He fired another shot into the boy's body and let fly at me without my ever thinking that he would do such a thing. The first shot was so close to my face that my eyes were powder burnt till I was blind, but I pulled on him at random, and I think I got him. I know that if I could have seen his bulk I would have got him, for I can't miss a man with that gun of mine."[36]

Constable Selman was not speciously bragging. Although his eyebrows were singed, his already pockmarked face stippled with hot granules of unspent gunpowder, and momentarily blinded, he accurately—or luckily—had not missed the mark with that gun of his; a bullet from his speedily drawn and fired six-shooter had punched through Baz Outlaw's upper torso, just atop his excitedly thumping heart, tearing through his left lung and exiting beneath his right shoulder blade.[37] But the Deputy U.S. Marshal/Special Ranger was a pretty handy shootist too! With six beans in the wheel (six cartridges in the cylinder, a decidedly unsafe mode for carrying a Colt's six-shooter—one under the hammer) Baz's first hot round had missed the moon or whatever, but the next two were at close range straight into the dumfounded Joe McKidrict, one bullet "in the head just over the left ear and shot him once in the back" while the near lifeless Ranger was falling to the ground.[38] Ranger Joe McKidrict, his six-shooter unfired, was dead within two minutes. Baz Outlaw's next three rounds had been not politely reserved for Constable John Selman, the first burning his face and blinding him, followed by two more plowing painful furrows into his right leg and thigh. A shot to the gut, the lung, or sometimes even the heart, does not by default at all times drop someone in their tracks. Gushing blood and crazily fueled by adrenaline's rush, Baz staggered away from Tillie's backyard, the scorching nightmare spitting out the barrel of another mean guy's gun compelling his getaway. He didn't get far.

Constable John Selman's bullet smashing into Outlaw's upper left chest causing him to copiously leak blood and whiskey onto South Utah Street while desperately fleeing the tragedy he had just triggered, also brought Baz Outlaw back into real world reality: He was the outlaw! Baz had cold-bloodedly murdered an esteemed

Ranger, senselessly and stupidly and undeniably. The Blind Mistress of Justice would be vigilant with her imposition of justice in an El Paso courtroom or vigilantes would set things right in the street, underneath a shade tree's stout limb. One way or the other—quite soon—Baz would pay, that much he knew. Luckily for a fleeing felon, Deputy U.S. Marshal/Special Ranger Outlaw stumbled into the arms of Ranger Francis Marion "Frank" McMahan, who was also carrying dual credentials as a federal and state lawman. Facing the Texas Ranger's cocked Colt's six-shooter, Baz Outlaw meekly surrendered his empty pistol, butt first. Captain John Hughes reported, officially: "Outlaw then walked up Utah street very near one block, where Private McMahan of Co 'D' met him and ordered him to surrender. Outlaw surrendered to McMahan[,] gave up his pistol and begged McMahan to protect him from a mob. McMahan and a Mexican [Leon Chavez] led Outlaw to a saloon, that being the nearest house where they found a bed for him."[39] Dutifully Frank McMahan had arrested the seriously wounded killer, but now was legally and morally obligated to see to his immediate medical wellbeing and protection from lynch rope injustice.

Rather quickly Private McMahan and Deputy Constable Chavez had ushered their charge into the Barnaum Show Saloon where they lay the sinking Baz Outlaw on a table (a prostitute's bed in some accounts), and ordered someone to fetch a doctor—fast. In but short order Doctor S.T. Turner made his appearance, conducted physical examination of the patient stretched before him, and rendered his thoughtful prognosis: Death was imminent—hands on the clock behind the bar would make the call—a matter of minutes or a few hours but the unstoppable final chime would strike—sounding eternal stillness.[40]

Meanwhile at Tillie Howard's things were understandably astir. Within two minutes after the sound of gunfire, "there was a rushing of the idle and excitable in that direction." The crowd of rubbernecking onlookers swelled to one hundred or so. Justifiably so, Tillie's whores were upset. One of the girls, Edna Hoyt, from an upstairs window had seen it all, scary and stressful stuff.[41] A newspaperman writing for the *El Paso Times* elaborated: "The inmates were also excited. There were cries and exclamations and explanations by the women boarders, but nobody seemed to know more than that there was a dead man in the backyard."[42] Ever so slowly the excitement dwindled to curiosity, then soon dissipated, after all it was Hell Paso, and Texas Ranger McKidrict was only the second unlucky fellow murdered that day. Julian Mendoza had been fatally stabbed at two o'clock "just west of the Santa Fe railroad track."[43]

At the Barnaum Show Saloon the Death Watch had begun. Delirious, feverish, and seemingly unrepentant—though nobody knows for sure—Baz Outlaw drifted back and forth between awareness and unconsciousness. He was alone and afraid, implications Baz Outlaw was himself communicating through sometimes rational and sometimes befuddled ramblings. Purportedly, between gasping for the saloon's stale air and with shallow breaths he faintly hummed a tune, murmuring and mouthing words to the mournful refrain about playing the fife slowly and beating the drum lowly, the "Streets of Laredo."[44] Angels, if there are any—were looking the other way. Powerhouse El Paso lawyer Will Burges who had made a trip to the dying man's bedside—or else was repeating hearsay strong as dynamite—was reported to have said that Baz Outlaw was in "mortal terror" of dying.[45] Passing into and out of responsiveness, Baz Outlaw—if the reports be true—persistently was asking: "Where are my friends?" Truthfully, at the time, his real friends were at Alpine, more than a hundred miles southeast of El Paso—but had they known what he'd just done, such friendships likely would have fractured.

For four torturous hours in the darkened recesses of a frontier era saloon, the hardwood floors spattered with spit and bloodstains, Deputy U.S. Marshal/Special Ranger Baz Outlaw lingered and suffered, cried and complained, the Grim Reaper patiently waiting, one foot on the bar's polished brass rail. There would be no glory for Baz Outlaw. For El Paso, all addresses were not too terribly far removed north of Lucifer's Line—the Rio Grande/Río Bravo—but it would be the whiskey river staking her claim at 9:15 after setting of the fifth of April's sun.[46] Booze and a bullet had taken its toll, everlastingly.

Captain Hughes particularly noted for the adjutant general and posterity: "Outlaw was in arrest when he died."[47] Literally Baz Outlaw was respectfully interred in El Paso's Evergreen/Alameda Cemetery.[48] Figuratively as his very best and trusted Ranger pal Alonzo Van Oden might have lamentably charged, Baz Outlaw had "gone under," drowned in an ever proliferating waterway of whiskey, washing his bones out into the timeless seas of dissipation and debauchery.

Wild West peace officer Jeff Milton, a legendary Southwest lawman with a no nonsense reputation, would be—and was—far less charitable and compassionate, even after declaring he personally knew Baz Outlaw "quite well." The ever salty brother of the badge commented that the guy he knew really "wasn't bad," and "the trouble with him was he just howled too much."[49] The Lone Wolf would howl no more.

Baz's onetime nemesis Professor Zamloch of California's Congress of Wonders fame had imparted words of wisdom: "Enjoy yourself while you live, for you will be a long time dead." Bazzell Lamar Outlaw did and is!

For a time possibly the best known and best liked El Paso, Texas, bordello proprietor was Tillie Howard. U.S Deputy Marshal/Special Ranger Outlaw and other Rangers would know Tillie well—perhaps quite well. Of particular interest in this remarkable collection of her artifacts, aside from a business card and the pearl-handled English Bulldog revolver, would be her ornately engraved cane, with the inscription "*Tillie, From Charlie.*" Though absoluteness is elusive, there is likelihood that Tillie was given the cane by the notorious Charles "Colorado Charlie" Utter, a sporting man known for flashy clothes, lavish jewelry, and pasteboards usually turning as Aces, rather than Deuces. He gambled and caroused at El Paso often. *Courtesy the Donald M. and Louise Yena Collection.*

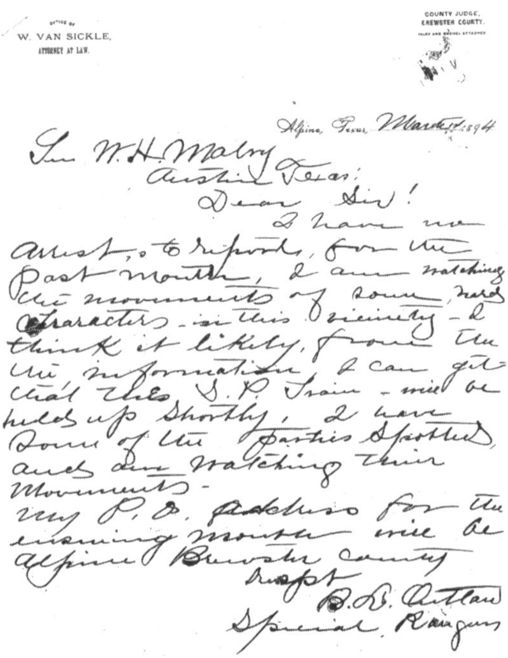
Office of W. Van Sickle, Attorney at Law.
County Judge, Brewster County

Alpine, Texas, March 1st 1894

Gen W. H. Mabry
Austin Texas:
Dear Sir!
I have no arrest, to report, for the past month, I am watching the movements of some hard characters in this vicinity – I think it likely, from the information I can get that the S.P. Train will be held up shortly, I have some of the parties spotted, and am watching their movements –
my P.O. address for the ensuing month will be Alpine Brewster county
Respt
B.L. Outlaw
Special Ranger

As a Special Texas Ranger, Baz Outlaw was obligated to submit activity reports to the adjutant general's office. This was one, updating AG Mabry with regards to his not making arrests the preceding month, but also that he had some "hard characters" under surveillance. *Courtesy Tobin and Anne Armstrong Ranger Research Center, Texas Ranger Hall of Fame & Museum.*

Constable John H. Selman, one of the Wild West's most noted gunmen. Selman was adept at working both sides of legality's line, sometimes a law officer, sometimes an offender, but at all times poisonous. On April 5, 1894, he cashed Baz Outlaw's ticket to eternity in the backyard of Tillie Howard's upscale bordello at El Paso. *Courtesy Nita Stewart Haley Memorial Library and J. Evetts Haley History Center.*

Jeff Milton [L] and George A. Scarborough, both Southwest lawmen of hard repute. Milton during the course of his duties as El Paso chief of police faced down Selman regarding his incautious remark regarding where he would stick the barrel of Milton's six-shooter. Later, Selman would kill the psychotic John Wesley Hardin, but soon meet his Maker and a mortician at the business end of Scarborough's smokin' six-gun. *Courtesy Nita Stewart Haley Memorial Library and J. Evetts Haley History Center.*

This Colt's six-shooter may or may not have been the weapon pictured in Selman's scabbard. However, it was a revolver belonging to John, and could have been the pistol issuing U.S. Deputy Marshal/Special Ranger B.L. Outlaw's death wound. *Author's photo courtesy the James H. Earle Firearms Collection.*

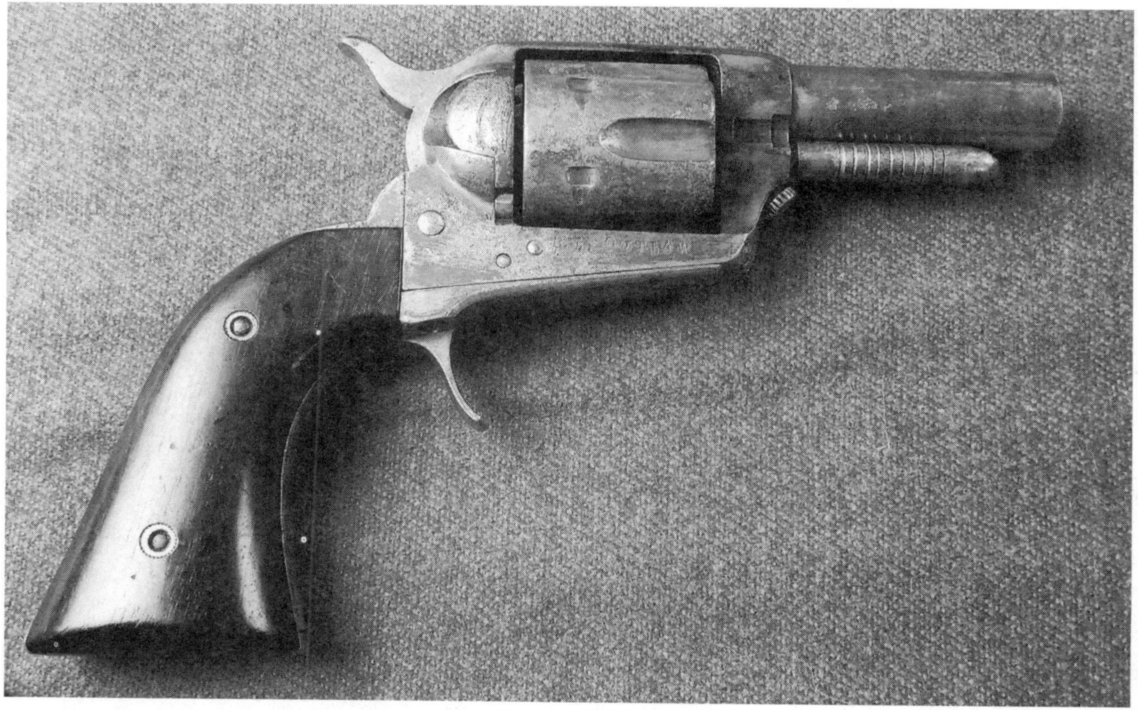

At the time U.S. Deputy Marshal/Special Ranger Baz Outlaw mercilessly killed young Ranger McKidrict and severely wounded the ever dangerous John Selman behind Tillie Howard's whorehouse he was armed with this radically modified Colt's revolver. Sometimes, due to the significantly shortened barrel these weapons are referred to as "belly guns." More precisely in this instance, the common terminology would be a "slip gun." For slip guns the trigger is either tied back or completely removed, and the weapon fired solely by slipping the hammer back and instantly slipping the thumb off, letting it fall on its own mainspring's momentum, no split-second trigger engagement delay: The technique is exceptionally fast for close action, but the handy and simple mutation is wildly inaccurate at more than just a few feet. *Courtesy Frank Jardim/Frazier History Museum Collection.*

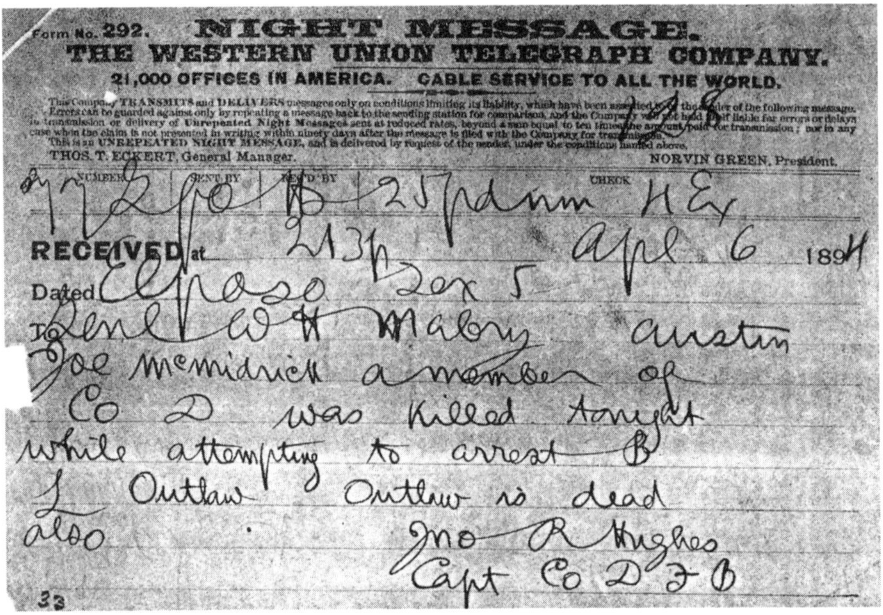
Form No. 292. NIGHT MESSAGE.
THE WESTERN UNION TELEGRAPH COMPANY.
21,000 OFFICES IN AMERICA. CABLE SERVICE TO ALL THE WORLD.
THOS. T. ECKERT, General Manager. NORVIN GREEN, President.
RECEIVED at 213p Apl 6 1894
Dated El Paso Tex 5
To Genl W H Mabry Austin
Joe McKidrict a member of Co D was killed tonight while attempting to arrest B L Outlaw Outlaw is dead also
Jno R Hughes
Capt Co D F B

Captain John R. Hughes' telegram to Adjutant General Mabry, informing him of the death of Ranger Joe McKidrict and U.S. Deputy Marshal/Special Ranger Baz Outlaw. *COURTESY TOBIN AND ANNE ARMSTRONG RANGER RESEARCH CENTER, TEXAS RANGER HALL OF FAME & MUSEUM.*

Texas Ranger Joe McKidrict's headstone in the Oakwood Cemetery at Austin, Texas. Unfortunately the DOD inscription should read 1894, rather than the incorrect 1893. *COURTESY DOUG DUKES.*

Baz Outlaw's headstone at El Paso's Evergreen Cemetery: His unmanageable Whiskey River calm at last. *Courtesy Ron Hyatt.*

Notes

Chapter 1 A Magnetic Lone Star

1. U.S. Census, 1850, Lee County Georgia, District 15; Arthur T. Outlaw, Lieutenant Colonel U.S. Army, Ret. to Bill O'Neal, June 5, 1982. In this letter, Mr. Outlaw is emphatic: "My Grand Father's First name was MESCHAK." Most contemporary sources do not use the ancient version "Meschak" but almost universally accept and use "Meshack." The series of letters are courtesy of Bill O'Neal, the State Historian of Texas, and a well-known nonfiction author.
2. U.S. Census, 1850, Bibb County Georgia; John Bennett Boddie, editor, *Historical Southern Families*, vol. 16, 67; Dorothy H. Price, ed., *Chinkypin: 1, 2, 3, and Addendum*, 504; U.S. Census, 1860, Seguin, Guadalupe County, Texas: "Y.P. Outlaw, Stock raiser."
3. U.S. Census, 1850, Lee County Georgia, District 15; Arthur Outlaw to Bill O'Neal, January 6, 1981.
4. Robert W. Stephens, *Bullets and Buckshot in Texas*, 33, 46, n. 1; Census records as cited.
5. Ibid. "By all indications it seems that Baz Outlaw was born in 1854 in Lee County, Georgia," 34–35. Surveys of several U.S. Census enumerations are in alignment with Robert Stephens' findings. The birth year of 1854 is inscribed on Baz Outlaw's headstone at the Evergreen Cemetery in El Paso, photograph within text.
6. James M. Browning, *Violence Was No Stranger*, vol. 2, Janice B. McCravy, ed., 91-A. Assuredly this treatment of Baz Outlaw, *Whiskey River Ranger,* is not centered on contradicting or challenging several Outlaw family members' longstanding beliefs or genealogical postings, but a touch of circumspection might be relevant before this author commits to naming Baz Outlaw's birth mother. For the U.S. Census, 1860, Lowndes County, Georgia, six-year-old Baz is enumerated in the household of his father Dr. Meshack N.B. Outlaw, age 39, and his second wife, Mary Ann E. Outlaw,

age 21. This enumeration places Baz's birth year as 1854 which, if Mary Ann was, indeed his mother, puts her giving birth at age 15, and possibly conceiving at age 14. Certainly not impossible for the place and time, but was it likely? In the 1850 U.S. Census for Georgia, Mary Ann, age ten, is living with her parents in Lee County, Georgia, which taken at face value, would have her giving birth to Baz at age fourteen, most likely conceiving at age thirteen. Adding to the muddle and fanning the puzzlement would be Mary Ann's enumeration for the U.S. Census, 1900, Clay County, Arkansas, where her husband was buried, as were more than one son and other kinfolks. At the time of the 1900 enumeration, Mary Ann is living with her son Morgan, a physician, and his wife Maud. Mary Ann's month and year of birth is unmistakably recorded as "May 1843" and she—or someone in her behalf—listed her age as 57 years. If all this be true, the mathematical computation is plain. Mary Ann would have been born during 1843 and would have—if she were Baz's mother—given birth at age eleven years, possibly conceiving at ten years of age. Further complicating the matter would be Mary Ann's obituary in the *Rector Vitascope*, listing her year of birth as 1840, as is the birth year of 1841 on her headstone in the family plot at Mary's Chapel Cemetery. No argument will be given any Outlaw descendant unwavering in their belief that Mary Ann was Baz Outlaw's birth mother, but that avow, based on the documentable record, would have the widely well respected Dr. Meshack Napoleon Bonaparte Outlaw bending to sexual congress with a pre-teen or early teenager. As it should be, the discerning reader is granted liberty and/or afforded discretion for furthering their own genealogical research and formulating their own conclusions. For this particular treatment, and in this writer's humble opinion from the perspective of the most reasonable logic, Mourning Temperance "Mona" (Smith) Outlaw might very well be Baz's natural mother, and her niece Mary Ann Elizabeth (Smith) Outlaw was Baz's adoring and loving stepmother. Rhetorically, could baby Baz Outlaw have been raised thinking and/or being told Mary Ann was his mother? Certainly she was standing in that role, and was the only mama Baz Outlaw would ever know. Mona Outlaw dying at age twenty-four in the fall of 1854, Baz's birth year, subsequent to giving birth to her first-born, Young M. Outlaw, four years earlier at age twenty, does somewhat bolster her as—*possibly*—the more judicious choice. Chuck Parsons, "An Lawman Named Outlaw," *True West*, September 1995, names "Temperance" as Baz's mother, page 57. Affably and courteously lending his expertise at helping—or trying to—untangle this morass of confusion was the award-winning writer and researcher Rick Miller, a first-rate history detective and friend.

7. Stephens, *Bullets and Buckshot in Texas*, 33, 46, n. 1; Descriptive List (a Texas Ranger's official document of identification and law enforcing authority) for B.L. Outlaw, August 11, 1885, and Application to the Texas Adjutant General for the position Special Texas Ranger as submitted by B. L. Outlaw, February 6, 1893. Both records enumerate his place of birth as the state of "Georgia, Lee, Co." Courtesy Texas State Library & Archives Commission (TSA), Austin, Texas, and the Texas Ranger Hall of Fame & Museum (TRHF&M) Research Center, Waco, Texas. There is and has been a great deal of confusion concerning the correct given name for the subject of this treatment, as there are variances in spelling—probably phonetic misunderstandings and/or misinterpretations between several U.S. Census reports and their reporters. Bazzell Lamar Outlaw is most likely correct. In the above cited letter of January 6, 1981, Arthur T. Outlaw, a nephew of our subject, is emphatic: "It was of particular personal interest to me in that Bass (real name BAZ) was my uncle." Federal census records, in the main, comport with the numerous secondary sources, of which many—if not most—will be later cited herein.
8. Assuredly readers desirous of expanding knowledge about this Indian raid must access the commendably researched and enjoyably readable account by Donaly E. Brice, *The Great Comanche Raid: Boldest Indian Attack of the Texas Republic*.
9. Gregory F. Michno, *Encyclopedia of Indian Wars: Western Battles and Skirmishes, 1850–1890*, 25–26; Luke Gournay, *Texas Boundaries: Evolution of the State's Counties*, 52, 117; Fred Tarpley, *1001 Texas Place Names*, 23. Another U.S. Army/Lipan Apache engagement—a direct aftermath of the clash cited in the body of this text—may be accessed in Gregory F. Michno's and Susan J. Michno's *Forgotten Fights: Little Known Raids and Skirmishes on the Frontier, 1823–1890*. 125–126.
10. Ibid., 27.
11. Ibid., 29; Lieutenant Eugene Asa Carr, popularly known as "War Eagle" for his aggressiveness, would be a future Congressional Medal of Honor recipient for action during the Civil War and later during the Indian Wars a U.S. Army Brigadier General. See, Dan L. Thrapp, *Encyclopedia of Frontier Biography*, vol. I, 230. Also, Robert Wooster in "A Difficult and Forlorn

Country: The Military Looks at the American Southwest, 1850–1890," *Arizona and the West*, Winter 1986, 350. For Rodriguez, see Frankie Davis Glenn, *Capt'N John: Story of a Texas Ranger*, 113: "Polly became famous as a scout for the United States Army, an Indian fighter, hunter and guide for Texas Rangers." Also, Polly Rodriguez, Clara Watkins, ed., "The Long, Hard Road to El Paso With Polly Rodriguez," *Wild West*, February 2005, 38–45.

12. Ibid. For additional information on Fort Inge, "the only four company post on the Texas frontier" during 1854, Baz Outlaw's birth year, the reader is referred to the excellent treatment by Thomas Tyree Smith, *Fort Inge: Sharps, Spurs, and Sabers On the Texas Frontier, 1849–1869*. Quotation, 66.
13. U.S. Census, 1860, Lowndes County, Georgia; Parsons, "A Lawman Named Outlaw," rather strangely reports: "The 1860 Georgia census does not list the Outlaw family, which suggests they may have moved on, possibly due to the impending war. Nor have I found any of this family on an 1870 census," see pages 57–58. The Outlaw family was enumerated in both the 1860 and 1870 Georgia census records for Lowndes and Echols Counties, respectively.
14. Browning, *Violence Was No Stranger*, vol. 2, 91-A.
15. Telephonic interview with Patty Martin, Administrative Coordinator, Valdosta-Lowndes County Chamber of Commerce, Valdosta, GA, May 29, 2014 and related Chamber of Commerce literature.
16. Texas Muster Roll Index Cards, 1838–1900, Y.P. Outlaw, January 20, 1861. Guadalupe Rangers Cavalry Company, Captain John P. White, commanding. Courtesy Rick Miller.
17. Janet B. Hewett, ed., *The Roster of Confederate Soldiers, 1861–1865*, vol. 12, 75. Also see, Texas Muster Roll Index Cards, 1838–1900, Y.P. Outlaw, April 18, 1862, Texas Mounted Rifles Company, William L. Foster, commanding. Courtesy Rick Miller.
18. A.J. Sowell, *Early Settlers and Indian Fighters in Southwest Texas*, 458–459; Ron Tyler, ed., *The New Handbook of Texas*, vol. 3, 316–317: "A few days later, on April 12, 1864, [Tom] Green died while leading an attack on federal gunboats patrolling the Red River at Blair's Landing."
19. Gary L. Roberts, *Doc Holliday: The Life and Legend*, 16–17.
20. Sylvia D. Lynch, *Aristocracy's Outlaw: The Doc Holliday Story*, 31:"The army did continue to occupy Valdosta, just as it did other areas in the South

during Reconstruction, and there were many reported incidents of violence and disagreement between the military and the citizens."

21. Roberts, *Doc Holliday: The Life and Legend*, 45; Janet B. Hewett, ed., *Georgia Confederate Soldiers, 1861–1865*, vol. 2, "Outlaw, N.M.B. 11th Cav. (St. Guards) Smith's Co.," 627. The initials listed for this roster are "N.M.B." rather than M.N.B. and therefore either a slight mix-up occurred or there is a possibility that Dr. Meshack Napoleon Bonaparte Outlaw did not stand at the ready for a call out of the Georgia State Guards.
22. Ibid.; Karen Holliday Tanner, *Doc Holliday: A Family Portrait*, postulates on page 62 that there was no explosion: "A number of Valdosta's prominent citizens discouraged the conspirators by announcing that they were going to be in the courthouse on the designated night to hear a political speaker. The kegs of powder that had been secretly placed beneath the courthouse were then quietly removed."
23. Ibid., quoting the *South Georgia Times* of April 8, 1868, page 45.
24. Ibid., 46.
25. David Johnson, *John Ringo, King of the Cowboys: His Life and Times From the Hoo Doo War to Tombstone,* 152: "On April 4, 1868, he [Holliday] was linked to a terrorist act when an explosion that rocked the Valdosta, Georgia, courthouse was detonated by Reconstruction resistance." Thrapp, *Encyclopedia of Frontier Biography*, vol. 2, page 670: "took part in a plot to blow up the courthouse at Valdosta. . . ."; Roberts, *Doc Holliday: The Life and Legend*, 46: "John Henry was said to have been one of them."
26. Roberts, *Doc Holliday: The Life and Legend*, 46.
27. Alonzo Van Oden, *Texas Ranger Diary and Scrapbook*, Ann Jensen, ed., page 10: "Bass Outlaw was a true Southern gentleman, soft spoken, well educated and courteous." Lest there be a degree of understandable confusion, the subject of this biographic profile, Baz Outlaw, was also referred to in both primary and secondary source writings as "Bass" Outlaw. In one example he is listed as "Baz" Outlaw in a federal census and in a family letter from a brother he is referred to as "Bass." As frequently the case, Bazzell Lamar Outlaw, himself, simply utilized his initials, his signature registering as "B.L. Outlaw." Mary'n Rosson, "The Day Bass Outlaw Tried to Drink Up The Town," *Frontier West*, December 1974, 18: "Bass Outlaw was a true Southern gentleman, soft spoken, courteous. . . . Bass Outlaw was apparently well-educated with good family background and some social graces."

28. C.L. Sonnichsen, *I'll Die Before I'll Run: The Story of the Great Feuds of Texas*, 254.
29. Roberts, *Doc Holliday: The Life and Legend*, 42.
30. First quotation is from Eugene Cunningham, "Bass Outlaw," *Frontier Times*, January 1928, 145. Second quotation is from W.T. Wayne, "The Fast Guns of Bass Outlaw," *Great West*, June 1972, 12. Certainly the time Baz Outlaw reached maturity and mastered the revolver was subsequent to the introduction of self-contained cartridges and the interested reader may wish to access K.D. Kirkland's *Colt: America's Premier Gunmaker*, "Metallic Cartridges," 38–41.
31. Price, *Chinkypin, 1, 2, 3 and Addendum*, 8, 13.
32. U.S. Census, 1870, Statenville, Echols County, Georgia; Browning, *Violence Was No Stranger*, Vol. II, 91-A.
33. Interview, Jackie Culpepper, Director, Allen Statenville Public Library, Statenville, Georgia, June 23, 2014.
34. Browning, *Violence Was No Stranger*. Vol. II. 91-A; Wayne and Judy Dasher, *Cemeteries of Echols County, Georgia*, 99. There are, as would be expected, minor variances relating to enumerations in the census data for the respective years covered in this narrative. Baz had several brothers and sisters, several uncles, and many, many cousins. Understandably it is hoped, painstakingly resolving those discrepancies unless they significantly impact Baz Outlaw's story will not be undertaken: That will remain the purview of Outlaw family and/or other likeminded genealogists.
35. Stephens, *Bullets and Buckshot in Texas*, 35.
36. Gregory and Susan Michno, *A Fate Worse Than Death: Indian Captivities in the West, 1830–1885*, 438–431.
37. Clayton W. Williams, *Texas' Last Frontier: Fort Stockton and the Trans-Pecos, 1861–1895*, Ernest Wallace, ed., 155; Gournay, *Texas Boundaries.*, 93.
38. Michno, *A Fate Worse Than Death*, 438–441.
39. Williams, *Texas' Last Frontier*, 156.
40. Michno, *A Fate Worse Than Death*, 439.
41. Ibid., 440–441; Gary Clayton Anderson, *The Conquest of Texas: Ethnic Cleansing in the Promised Land, 1820–1875*. Even Anderson, at least in this particular instance, was obligated to characterize the raid. Skirting around specifics of brutality, he does register the deaths of Mr. and Mrs. Able and their daughter as a "slaughter" (355).

42. Williams, *Texas' Last Frontier*, 160; Michno, *Encyclopedia of Indian Wars*, 255–256.
43. Robert M. Utley, *Lone Star Justice: The First Century of the Texas Rangers*, 137.
44. Certainly the seminal research resulting in a published analysis of the Texas State Police is Donaly E. Brice's (and the late Barry Crouch), *The Governor's Hounds: The Texas State Police, 1870–1873*; William T. Field, Jr., "The Texas State Police, 1870–1873," *Texas Military History*, Fall 1965, 131–141. Also see, Ann Patton Baenziger, "The Texas State Police During Reconstruction: A Reexamination," *Southwestern Historical Quarterly*, April 1969. For an abbreviated introduction to the organization, Bob Alexander, *Winchester Warriors: Texas Rangers of Company D, 1874–1901*, Chapter 1, "A carnival of crime and corruption," 1–17. For a sharp analytical breakdown of the incident wherein Texas State Police and the Horrell brothers and their compatriots engaged in a vicious and deadly shootout, the interested reader is referred to *The Horrell Wars: Feuding in Texas and New Mexico* by noted researcher and author David Johnson, the foremost authority on Texas feuds and related aftermaths.
45. Alexander, *Winchester Warriors*, 6.
46. *Dallas Daily Herald*, April 22, 1873.
47. H.P.N. Gammel, comp., *The Laws of Texas, 1822–1897*, Vol. VIII, 86–91.
48. *U.S. Register of Civil, Military and Naval Service, 1863–1959*, 1873 Post-Office Department, Contractors—Georgia-Idaho-Illinois, "Y.M. Outlaw, $150." 465. Like entry for the year 1875. Courtesy Rick Miller.
49. *U.S. School Catalogs, 1765–1935*, Eastman National Business College, Directory of College Graduates, 1876. Courtesy Rick Miller.
50. U.S. Census, 1880, Mifflin, Henderson County, Tennessee; Miscellaneous biographical file correspondence, notes, newspaper clips, and interviews relating to the Outlaw family courtesy Deana Mills, Director, Rector City Library, Rector, AR; E.B. Outlaw to Texas Adjutant General W.H. Mabry, April 16, 1894,TSA. Also, Browning, *Violence Was No Stranger*, Vol. II, 91-A.
51. Jack Martin, *Border Boss: Captain John R. Hughes—Texas Ranger*, 102; Phillip J. Rasch, "Bass Outlaw: Myth and Man," *Real West*, July 1979, 13: "It is usually stated that Outlaw came to Texas after killing a man in Georgia, but the who, when, and where of this alleged crime are never specified." Within context it is also key to note that one person may kill another, and it may not measure a criminal act, such as an unintentional

and/or unavoidable accident or an instance of justifiable self-defense. The person may carry a moral feeling of guilt, but would not be legally culpable. The unexplained deaths of Baz's younger sisters or half-sisters and his subsequent alcoholism gives rise to an intriguing and yet unanswered rhetorical question.

Chapter 2 Great Prudence and Good Judgment

1. Captain James T. "J.T." Gillespie to Adjutant General Wilburn Hill King, December 15, 1885, TSA: "have enlisted in his stead B.L. Outlaw from Siguine [*sic*]."
2. Ibid.
3. Betty Dooley Awbrey and Claude Dooley, *Why Stop? A Guide to Texas Historical Roadside Markers*, 457. Also see *Spanish Texas, Yesterday and Today* by Gerald Ashford with specific mentions of Alonzo De León throughout, and of particular interest may be Chapter 7, "Texas Established and Abandoned." Captivatingly, it may be noted that such Spanish *entradas* were or would have been logistical nightmares: "with 110 soldiers, 150 loads of flour, two hundred cows, four hundred horses, fifty long firelocks, twelve hundredweight of powder, and three hundredweight of shot, as well as the usual gifts for the Indians." See page 81.
4. Ed Blackburn, Jr., *Wanted: Historic County Jails of Texas,* 145. For another glimpse at early day confinement of local prisoners, see Bill Moore, "The Texas Calaboose," in the June 2015 edition of *Texas Co-op Power*, 29.
5. U. S. Census, 1870, Guadalupe County, Texas. Y.P Outlaw would later, 1882, relocate to Moore City, then simply Moore, Frio County, southwest of San Antonio, where among other public spirited endeavors he served as a trustee for the School District. For interesting mentions of Y.P. Outlaw and other members of his family throughout, see *Historical Sketch of Moore, Texas*, Mrs. T.E. Terry, ed.
6. Sowell, *Early Settlers and Indian Fighters in Southwest Texas,* 458.
7. Gournay, *Texas Boundaries*, 79.
8. Ranger H.B. Waddill to Frontier Battalion Major John B. Jones, February 27, 1877, TSA. Also see the award-winning biography of Jones, *Texas Ranger John B. Jones and the Frontier Battalion, 1874–1881* by Rick Miller, page 144.

9. David Johnson, *The Mason County "Hoo Doo" War, 1874–1902*. This, the definitive treatment of the seemingly never-ending feud, deftly explores and provides thoughtful, sometimes critical and sometimes laudatory but always impartial, analysis of Texas Rangers' participation and behavior throughout the conflict. For quick synopsis of Major John B. Jones' affiliation with the Masons, see Joseph E. Bennett, *Sixguns and Masons: Profiles of Selected Texas Rangers and Prominent Westerners*, 4.
10. Gammel, *The Laws of Texas,* vol. 8, 86–91; Frederick Wilkins, *The Law Comes to Texas: The Texas Rangers, 1870–1901*, 28.
11. Lieutenant Dan Roberts to Major Jones, February 16, 1876, TSA.
12. Mike Cox, *The Texas Rangers: Wearing the Cinco Peso, 1821–1900*, 276.
13. Peter R. Rose, *The Reckoning: The Triumph of Order on the Texas Outlaw Frontier*, 66–72.
14. Major John B. Jones to Adjutant General William Steele, May 6, 1877, TSA.
15. Ibid. Also, for a parallel look at the early day criminality and resultant Ranger raid, see O.C. Fisher, *It Occurred in Kimble*, 207–213.
16. Testimony Taken by the Committee on Military Affairs in relation to the Texas Border Troubles, 45th Congress, 2nd Session, House of Representatives, misc. Doc. No. 64. January 1878, page 249.
17. Ibid.
18. U.S. Census, 1880, Kimble County, Texas. Baz L. Outlaw is enumerated as living with freighter William Estes, giving his occupation as a farmer, and his age as twenty-three. The seeming age discrepancy with previous census reports, 1860 (age 6), 1870 (age 16), is inexplicable. Though puzzling, the inconsistency will not significantly impact Baz Outlaw's spine-tingling Wild West-era narrative.
19. Ibid.
20. Captain E.B. Outlaw (Baz's brother), Arkansas National Guard to AG Mabry, April 16, 1894, TSA: "I had not seen my brother for nearly (20) years . . ."
21. Descriptive List, Frontier Battalion, B.L. Outlaw, August 11, 1885, TSA.
22. Alton Hughes, *Pecos: A History of the Pioneer West*. 20; Muster & Pay Roll, Company E, Frontier Battalion, June 1, 1885 to August 31, 1885, TSA.
23. Gournay, *Texas Boundaries*, 107; Sammy Tise, *Texas County Sheriffs*. 436; Blackburn, *Wanted: Historic County Jails of Texas,* 279.

24. Awbrey and Dooley, *Why Stop?* 498; June Rayfield Welch, *The Texas Courthouse Revisited,* 195: "Toyah had seven saloons. Gaming tables operated 24 hours a day a Pecos City, which had more saloons per capita than any town in Texas."
25. Telegram, Captain George A. Baylor to AG King, July 8, 1883, TSA.
26. Captain Baylor to AG King, July 21, 1883, TSA.
27. Captain Baylor to AG King, December 30, 1883, TSA; George Baylor, *Into the Far, Wild Country: True Tales of the Old Southwest*, Jerry D. Thompson, ed., 27.
28. Muster & Pay Roll, Company E, Frontier Battalion, September 1885, TSA; Descriptive List, B.L. Outlaw, August 11, 1885, TSA; Application as Special Ranger, B.L. Outlaw, February 6, 1893, TRHF&M Research Center; State of Texas, Certification of Payment, B.L. Outlaw, TSA. Although it's generally penned from the secondary perspective, there seems to be a fixation with Baz Outlaw's height. Not just a few popular type magazine articles suggest Outlaw was a runt of sorts among physical stalwarts. Characteristically trying to weed fact from folklore, Rash, in the 1979 *Real West* article seems to tackle and debunk the notion. Certainly, Baz Outlaw was not of imposing physical stature as his photographs—which there are quite a few displayed herein—amply reveal, but certainly the images do not indicate an abnormality regarding height, or, on the other hand, nearly every Texas Ranger in the photos was grossly stunted. Perhaps, relying on the primary source documents where he lists his height at 5'10 during 1885 and 5'9 when applying for a Special Ranger commission in February of 1893 would border closer to reality. Regarding height, so it seems, he wasn't too big and he wasn't too little. Too, and keeping in line with how many writers have characterized Outlaw, would be Glenn Shirley's article appearing in the November 1968 edition of *True Frontier: Actual Stories of the Old West*, "A Ranger Named Outlaw," page 9, in which the author charges: "He [Outlaw] drank heavily when he joined the Rangers in 1885." Primary source records do not reveal this to be the case, at least not at this point in time. That Baz Outlaw and Mr. Barleycorn had a relationship is true and will be herein addressed as becomes chronologically relevant.
29. Monthly Return, Company E, Frontier Battalion, August 1885, TSA.
30. Captain Gillespie to AG King, August 18, 1885, TSA.
31. Clifford R. Caldwell and Ron DeLord, *Texas Lawmen: The Good and the Bad, 1835–1899*, 192.

32. Captain Gillespie to AG King, August 19, 1885, TSA.
33. Petition to AG King, August 25, 1885, signed, "Charles M. Fields," *et al.*, TSA.
34. Captain Gillespie to AG King, August 19, 1885, TSA.
35. Ibid.; Report of Operations of State Troops, From January 1, 1882 to November 30, 1885, TSA.
36. Ibid.; Monthly Return, Company E, Frontier Battalion, August 1885, TSA; Mike Cox, *Texas Ranger Tales: Stories That Need Telling*, 188: ". . . [Rangers] found Morris in The Favorite Saloon, six-shooter in hand and mean drunk."
37. Telegram, Captain Gillespie to AG King, August 19, 1885, TSA.
38. Petition to AG King, August 25, 1885, as cited; Caldwell and DeLord, *Texas Lawmen*, 345.
39. AG King to Captain Gillespie, August 22, 1885, TSA.
40. Captain Gillespie to Captain John O. Johnson, Quartermaster, Frontier Battalion, August 28, 1885, TSA; Hughes, *Pecos: A History of the Pioneer West*, 76; Tise, *Texas County Sheriffs*, 436; Program for Memorial Service Honoring Lycurgus S. "Kirk" Turnbo, 1856–1935, Elmwood Cemetery, Wagoner, Oklahoma, April 21, 2012.
41. Captain Gillespie to AG King, August 27, 1885, TSA.
42. Sam Lane, Proprietor, Favorite Saloon, Toyah, Texas to AG King, August 25, 1885, TSA; Captain Gillespie to Captain Johnson, August 22, 1885, TSA: "I have given to Mr. W.F. Youngblood a Voucher for the Burial and expenses of the funeral of T.P. Nigh deceased member of my co. The citizens of Toyah have proven very generous in raising some money for the Two little children of Nigh. The company has the entire sympathy of the good People of Toyah and say all that was done on night of 18th was right and should have been done with the exception of the Killing of Nigh." That the prohibition about Texas Ranger privates and noncommissioned officers being married was now somewhat overlooked and left to the judgment of individual company commanders was given credence by award-winning nonfiction writer Jan Devereaux during a working session of Texas Ranger laureates at the TRHF&M Research Center, July 18–19, 2014. Devereaux quoted the wife of Texas Ranger J.T. Bird, who was serving during the Frontier Battalion era: "He hated to leave the company, but we could have only stayed four months longer, as married men were not allowed in the

company. They were allowed to stay six months only after marriage." Devereaux sourced the quotation as being extracted from *Ella Elgar Bird Dumont: An Autobiography of a West Texas Pioneer*, Tommy J. Boley, ed.

43. Captain Gillespie to AG King, September 15, 1885, TSA.
44. For the death of Ranger Warren, see Caldwell and DeLord, *Texas Lawmen*, 34. Regarding the death of Ranger Sieker, see Bob Alexander, *Riding Lucifer's Line: Ranger Deaths along the Texas-Mexico Border*, 91–100.
45. Captain Gillespie to AG King, September 26, 1885, TSA.
46. Robert W. Stephens, *Texas Ranger Sketches*, 137.
47. J. Evetts Haley, *Jeff Milton: A Good Man with a Gun*, 49.
48. Alexander, *Winchester Warriors*, 166–170; Telegram, Captain Dan Roberts to Adjutant General John B. Jones, May 31, 1881, TSA; Captain Roberts to AG Jones, June 1, 1881, TSA; Lieutenant L.P. Sieker to AG King, March 20, 1882, TSA.
49. Captain Gillespie to AG King, April 26, 1885, TSA.
50. Lieutenant J.M. Sedberry to AG King, October 2, 1885, TSA.
51. Frontier Battalion, General Order No. 27, to take effect October 5, 1885, TSA.
52. AG King to Captain Gillespie, October 1, 1885, TSA.
53. Monthly Return, Company E, Frontier Battalion, October 1885, TSA.
54. Captain Gillespie to Captain Sieker, November 24, 1885, TSA.
55. Monthly Return, Company E, Frontier Battalion, December 1885, TSA; Captain Gillespie to AG King, December 15, 1885, TSA: "I have the honor to report that on 13th I discharged Pvt. J.L. Adair who I did not think an efficient Ranger, have enlisted in his stead B.L. Outlaw from Siguine [*sic*]."
56. Monthly Return, Company E, Frontier Battalion, January 1886, TSA.
57. Muster & Pay Roll, Company E, Frontier Battalion, March 1, 1886 to May 31, 1886, TSA.
58. Alexander, *Winchester Warriors*, 200–201. Any blanket indictment of Special Rangers, lumping the good with the bad, quite honestly is misguided and not factually sustainable. Also see, Utley, *Lone Star Justice*, 228–229.
59. Operations of Frontier Battalion and Report of Special Rangers: From December 1, 1885 to November 30, 1892, Company E, May 1886, 112, TSA: Monthly Return, Company E, Frontier Battalion, May 1886, TSA.

60. Monthly Return, Company E, Frontier Battalion, June 1886, TSA.
61. *Fort Worth Daily Gazette*, August 8, 1886, TSA; Cecilia Thompson, *History of Marfa and Presidio County, Texas, 1535–1900*, 200; Lucy Miller Jacobson and Mildred Bloys Nored, *Jeff Davis County, Texas*, 130. Also, Elton Miles, *Stray Tales of the Big Bend*, 16–17.
62. Captain Gillespie to Captain Sieker, August 8, 1886, TSA.
63. Monthly Return, Company E, Frontier Battalion, August 1886, TSA. Joe Mize had enlisted June 30, 1886, see, Monthly Return, Company E, Frontier Battalion, June 1886, TSA.
64. J.H. Bowles, "A Fight in the Big Bend" from the June edition of *Range and Field*, and reprinted in *Frontier Times*, August 1926, 34–35. Writing from memory four decades post the incident, author Bowles understandably misidentifies Joe Mize as Joe Meyers. Primary source Texas Ranger records are not indistinct: Joe Mize was the Ranger partnered with Baz Outlaw; Ron C. Tyler, *The Big Bend: A History of the Last Texas Frontier*, 155: "He [Gillett] left his marshal's post to become foreman of the G4 Ranch. . . ." For the killing of Roselle Pulliam, see C. A. Hawley, "Life Along the Border," *Sul Ross State College Bulletin*, September 1964, 82–83.
65. Rasch, "Bass Outlaw: Myth and Man," 13.
66. Monthly Return, Company E, Frontier Battalion, August 1886, TSA.
67. Ibid.; Stephens, *Bullets and Buckshot in Texas*, 36.
68. Bowles, "A Fight in the Big Bend," 34.
69. Operations of Frontier Battalion and Report of Special Rangers: From December 1, 1885 to November 30, 1892, Company E, Frontier Battalion, August 1886, page 114, in TSA: "Outlaw wounded over eye & in hip & Mize wounded in Shoulder." Miles, *Stray Tales of the Big Bend*, 16–17.
70. Monthly Return, Company E, Frontier Battalion, August 1886, TSA.
71. Bowles, "A Fight in the Big Bend," 35; Clifford B. Casey, *Mirages, Mysteries and Reality: Brewster County Texas, The Big Bend of the Rio Grande*, 332.
72. Monthly Return, Company E, Frontier Battalion, August 1886, TSA.
73. Captain Gillespie to Captain Sieker, September 19, 1886, TSA.
74. Muster & Pay Roll, Company E, Frontier Battalion, September 1, 1886 to November 30, 1886, TSA; Monthly Return, Company E, Frontier Battalion, September 1886, TSA.

75. AG King to Captain Gillespie, October 13, 1886, TSA.
76. Monthly Return, Company E, Frontier Battalion, October 1886, TSA.
77. Monthly Return, Company E, Frontier Battalion, November 1886, TSA.
78. Captain Gillespie to Captain Sieker, November 6, 1886, TSA.
79. C.M. Fields to L.L. Keller, December 29, 1886, TSA.
80. C.M. Fields to George W. Baylor, January 18, 1887, TSA.
81. Fields to Keller, December 29, 1886, TSA.
82. John C. Brown to AG King, January 4, 1887, TSA.
83. AG King to Captain Gillespie, January 7, 1887, TSA; AG King to J.C. Brown, January 7, 1887, TSA.
84. Monthly Returns, Company E, Frontier Battalion, January and February 1887, TSA; Monthly Return, Company E, Frontier Battalion, November 1886, TSA; Captain Gillespie to AG King, December 27, 1886: "W.L. Cartwright left 'without leave of absence' about the 20th and as he has not reported I mark Him a Deserter with loss of Pay. . . ." TSA.
85. Captain Gillespie to Captain Sieker, January 31, 1887, TSA.
86. Captain Gillespie to AG King, February 5, 1887, TSA.
87. AG King to Captain Gillespie, February 9, 1887, TSA.
88. Gourney, *Texas Boundaries,* 108. Gourney places Brewster County's land mass at 5,935 square miles, while the *Texas Almanac* sets the figure at 6,169 square miles. By any measure Brewster County was/is a whopper, a geographical subdivision larger than the state of Connecticut, plus Rhode Island.
89. Captain Gillespie to Captain Sieker, February 25, 1887, TSA.
90. Captain Gillespie to Captain Sieker, February 19, 1887, TSA.
91. L.F. Cartwright to AG King, February 10, 1887, TSA.
92. Sergeant W.F. Sheffield to Genl. H.E. McCulloch, February 14, 1887, TSA; Petition supporting Sergeant Sheffield's promotion, forwarded to AG King, February 14, 1887, signed by B.L. Outlaw, *et al.*, TSA.
93. Christina Stopka, Director, Texas Ranger Research Center (TRHF&M), *Partial List of Texas Ranger Company and Unit Commanders*, "Frontier Battalion, 1874–1901." The notations for service dates for Company E include "Capt. J.T. Gillespie (December 1883–April 1887) Company E mustered out of service April 15, 1887." Texas Ranger Co. E would be brought

back to life during June 1891. Also see, Operations of Frontier Battalion, Company E, From December 1, 1885 To November 30, 1892, TSA.

94. Captain Sieker to AG King, April 15, 1887, TSA.

Chapter 3 A Fighting Business—Robbing a Train

1. For a more-or-less comprehensive look at Frank Jones the reader might wish to peruse Bob Alexander's biography, *Six-Shooters and Shifting Sands: The Wild West Life of Texas Ranger Captain Frank Jones*.
2. Monthly Return, Company D, Frontier Battalion, April 1887, TSA.
3. Gournay, *Texas Boundaries*, 78, 121; Tise, *Texas County Sheriffs*, 169; Blackburn, *Wanted*, 109–110.
4. Ira Aten interview with Earl Vandale, Evetts Haley, and Hervey Chesley, July 1941, El Centro, CA. Hereafter Aten-1941. Courtesy Haley Memorial Library & History Center (HML&HC), Midland, TX.
5. Monthly Return, Company D, Frontier Battalion, April 1887, TSA; *Galveston Daily News*, April 20, 1887: "Will Odle, Alvin Odle, and Henry Corence [*sic*], wanted in Burnet county upon charge of horse stealing were lodged in Uvalde jail yesterday by Company D rangers. . . . They are also thought to be wanted in Williamson county. All are young men, from twenty-two to twenty-six. Telegrams from Burnet state that officers are en route to Uvalde to take charge of the prisoners."
6. Ibid.; Stephens, *Texas Ranger Sketches*, 123.
7. Captain Frank Jones to Captain Sieker, May 2, 1887, TSA.
8. Alexander, *Riding Lucifer's Line*, 91–100.
9. A womb to tomb biography of Austin Ira Aten is the award-winning *Rawhide Ranger, Ira Aten: Enforcing Law on the Texas Frontier* by Bob Alexander; For a comparative analysis regarding the speciously puffed reputation of an alleged Wild West gunman, Wyatt Earp, against the very real and demonstrable gunfighting and law enforcing exploits of Ira Aten, the reader is referred to "Square Deals and Real McCoys," by Bob Alexander as published in the June 2011 edition of the *Wild West History Association Journal*; Adding substantiation to the fact—and perceptible fact it was—touting the positive characterizations of the near legendary Ira Aten may be, among other primary and secondary source cited pieces, underscored in

a laudatory article in the September 1945 edition of *Reader's Digest*, "The Ranch That Changed the West," a condensed rendering of Lewis Nordyke's commentary about the XIT Ranch first appearing in *The American Mercury*: "By then the fires and depredation had grown so bad that he sent for Ira Aten, famed Texas Ranger and sheriff, asking him to take over the constantly raided western part of the range. Aten investigated, then doubled his life insurance. As assistants he hired two of the boldest straightest-shooting Texas Rangers, Wood Saunders and Ed Connell, and organized an armed patrol. Day and night Aten and his men rode the New Mexico border of the ranch. They shot first and investigated later." 110.

10. Certificate of Commission as U.S. Deputy Marshal for Ira Aten by John T. Rankin, U.S. Marshal, Western Judicial District of Texas, 4 March 1887. Courtesy Gary Boyce Radder, Ira Aten's one and only grandchild.
11. For a reader interested in this aspect of Old West law enforcement Larry Ball's companion volumes, *The United States Marshals of New Mexico & Arizona Territories 1846–1912* and *Desert Lawmen: The High Sheriffs of New Mexico and Arizona, 1846–1912* would be recommended.
    Although specifically highlighting federal and local enforcement activities in the territories of New Mexico and Arizona, much of the data is also applicable to policing procedures and protocols within Texas—and elsewhere. The reader might also wish to consult *The Western Peace Officer: A Legacy of Law and Order* by Frank Richard Prassel.
12. Jeff Burton, "'A Great Man Hunt'—Correspondence From 'W.B.S.': Some Scenes of Outlawry and Gunplay in Texas," *English-Westerner's Brand Book* No. 18, 1975–1976. 11–34; R. Michael Wilson, *Great Train Robberies of the Old West*, 64–65; Bill S. Price, *Bill Whitely: Outlaw*, 39–41; Jeff Burton, "The Most Surprised Man In Texas," *Frontier Times*, March 1975. 18–21, 50–53, and 69.
13. Rick Miller, *Rube Burrow, Desperado*. Quotations are from this excellently researched and written treatment of an Old West train robber, one who cut a wider swath and held up more trains than did the James-Younger gang, the Dalton gang, Sam Bass and his gang, or Butch Cassidy and the Sundance Kid of the so-called Wild Bunch.
14. Stephens, *Bullets and Buckshot in Texas*, 60–69; Alexander, *Rawhide Ranger, Ira Aten*, 133.
15. Amendment to Monthly Return, Company D, Frontier Battalion, June 1887, TSA: "May 7—Private Piper and detachment reached Del Rio and

located camp near town." Captain Frank Jones to AG King, May 4, 1887, TSA.

16. Candice DuCoin, *Lawmen on the Texas Frontier: Rangers and Sheriffs*, 86–87.
17. Gourney, *Texas Boundaries*, 107.
18. Awbrey and Dooley, *Why Stop?* 139.
19. Tise, *Texas County Sheriffs*, 505; Blackburn, *Wanted*, 199, 228, 334, and 336.
20. The late Professor John D. Tanner, Jr. writing in the Introduction for *Lynch Ropes and Long Shots: The Story of An Old West Train Robbery* by Bob Alexander, page 2.
21. Alexander, *Rawhide Ranger, Ira Aten*, 132.
22. Richard Dillion, *Wells, Fargo Detective: A Biography of James B. Hume*, 235–236; Stephens, *Bullets and Buckshot in Texas*, 62.
23. Jeffrey Burton, *Western Story*, European Edition, 91, n. 17.
24. Dillon, *Wells, Fargo Detective*, 236.
25. *Galveston Daily News*, June 12, 1887; Blackburn, *Wanted*, 54.
26. Monthly Return, Company D, Frontier Battalion, June 1887, TSA; AG King to Captain Jones, June 20, 1887, TSA.
27. Captain Jones to AG King, July 1, 1887, TSA.
28. Captain Jones to Captain Sieker, July 1, 1887, TSA.
29. Monthly Return, Company D, Frontier Battalion, June 1887, TSA.
30. Monthly Return, Company D, Frontier Battalion, July 1887, TSA.
31. AG King to Captain Jones, August 12, 1887, TSA.
32. AG King to Captain Jones, August 21, 1887, TSA; Also see, Captain Jones to AG King, August 17, 1887, TSA.
33. Monthly Return, Company D, Frontier Battalion, August 1887, TSA.
34. Ibid.
35. Monthly Return, Company D, Frontier Battalion, September 1887, TSA; For more on the life, career, and crimes of Bill Mitchell, see, C.L. Sonnichsen, *Outlaw on the Dodge With Baldy Russell.*
36. Sergeant Ira Aten to Captain Sieker, August 6 and 7, 1887, TSA. Interestingly, the letter of August 6th makes mention of modern and advancing technology. Ira Aten wrote: "We have just rec'd. a telephone [call] from Wm. Stanley. . . ." a deputy sheriff from Williamson County.

37. Monthly Return, Company D, Frontier Battalion, October 1887: "16—Private John Hughes reached camp." TSA.
38. Ibid.; *Galveston Daily News*, August 24, 1887.
39. Captain Jones to AG King, October 31, 1887. "Your letter of the 25th inst. was rece'd only yesterday morning and I at once broke camp. . . ." TSA; Monthly Return, Company D, Frontier Battalion, October 1887, TSA.
40. AG King to Starr County Judge James Livingston, October 26, 1887, TSA.
41. AG King to Captain Jones, October 25, 1887, TSA.
42. AG King to Captain William Scott, Company F, Frontier Battalion, October 25, 1887, TSA.
43. Monthly Return, Company D, Frontier Battalion, November 1887, TSA; Awbrey and Dooley, *Why Stop?* 535; Gournay, *Texas Boundaries*, 83.
44. Captain Jones to AG King, November 21, 1887, TSA; Captain Jones to Captain Sieker, November 25, 1887, TSA.
45. The biography of this fascinating fellow is Robert W. Stephens' *Captain George H. Schmitt: Texas Ranger*; Stopka, *Partial List of Texas Ranger Company and Unit Commanders*. "Frontier Battalion (1874–1901), Company C, Captain George H. Schmitt (September 1883–November 1887) Company C mustered out of service November 30, 1887." Utley, *Lone Star Justice*, 290: "Certainly there were outstanding Rangers. Jack Hays, Matt Caldwell, Ben McCulloch, Sam McMurray, Lam Sieker, Frank Jones, Ira Aten, and the four captains come to mind. On the other hand, William Tobin, Warren Wallace, George Schmitt, Joe Shely, J.S. McNeel, and Toms Ross hardly measured up to the stereotype." Cox, *The Texas Rangers: Wearing the Cinco Peso*, 330: "Unlike some captains, he [Schmitt] also had a habit of criticizing his colleagues in letters to Austin. He even once boasted that he could run the Frontier Battalion better than King." Paul N. Spellman, *Captain John H. Rogers, Texas Ranger*, 42: "Meanwhile, Captain George Schmitt of Ranger Company C officially criticized Captain Scott for his hasty actions that resulted in the death of two fence-cutters and the dismissal of other charges. Although Schmitt had not been present, he wrote into the official records his opinion that Scott could have spared those two lives and put the others in prison if he had acted more responsibly: Irascible and from the 'old school' of discipline, George Heinrich Schmitt expended a great deal of vitriolic energy over several years on Scott and what Schmitt considered questionable leadership abilities." Captain George Schmitt to Captain

Sieker, March 31 and April 4, 1887, TSA. See, Alexander, *Winchester Warriors* for rank and file membership of Company D being more than disgruntled with the political motivated appointment of George Schmitt as their new lieutenant, especially 183–185. Wilkins, *The Law Comes to Texas*, page 278, takes a different approach: "Despite King's strict financial controls and the disbanding of two companies, it again became necessary to reduce the Rangers as the end of 1888 [*sic* 1887] approached. In a rather ironic turn of events, Captain W. Schmitt's Company C was the unlucky unit to be selected; like other reductions, the choice was based on which company could be spared with the least loss of protection, an indirect tribute to Schmitt for cleaning up his territory."

46. Captain Jones to Captain Sieker, November 28, 1887, TSA.
47. Captain Jones to AG King, November 25, 1887, TSA.
48. Captain Jones to Captain Sieker, November 25, 1887, TSA.
49. Captain Jones to Captain Sieker, December 5, 1887, TSA; Monthly Return, Company D, Frontier Battalion, December 1887, TSA.
50. Captain Jones to AG King, December 2, 1887, TSA; Monthly Return, Company D, Frontier Battalion, December 1887, TSA.
51. J. Walter Durbin Manuscript. During 1914 Durbin prepared a rather detailed and certainly fascinating account of his life—with considerable emphasis on the time he served as a Texas Ranger. Of particular interest for this narrative is the fact that Durbin knew and supervised Baz Outlaw, as well as John Reynolds Hughes, when they were in the Frontier Battalion, and the trio worked together later as equals during a dangerous private enterprise venture in Mexico. Durbin's first-hand knowledge regarding Baz Outlaw is exceptionally perceptive. The copy herein cited as "Durbin Manuscript" was graciously provided to this author by long-time researcher and prolific writer Robert W. Stephens, the preeminent authority on J. Walter Durbin and many other frontier-era Rangers, lawmen, and outlaws and their spine-tingling shootouts. Also see Robert W. Stephens, "Ambush in the Chaparral," *Frontier Times*, May 1967, p. 30: "In 1914, two years preceding his [J. Walter Durbin's] death in San Antonio, he wrote an account of his experiences from 1880 to 1894. . . ."
52. Bob Alexander, *Bad Company and Burnt Powder: Justice and Injustice in the Old Southwest*, 5; Andrés Sáenz, *Early Tejano Ranching: Daily Life at Ranchos San José and El Fresnillo*, Andrés Tijerina, ed., xiv.

53. AG King to Sheriff A.J. Lewis, Milam County, January 21, 1888, TSA; Tise, *Texas County Sheriffs,* 374.
54. Dudley G. Wooten, ed., *A Comprehensive History of Texas, 1685–1897*, 349.
55. Captain Jones to Captain Sieker, March 1, 1888, TSA.
56. Monthly Return, Company D, Frontier Battalion, February 1888, TSA.
57. The pocket watch presented to Captain Jones from the Company D Rangers, has been until relatively recently on display at TRHF&M through courtesy of the Donald and Louise Yena Collection. However, on March 1, 2014, well-known collector Kurt House was the winning bidder at a sale conducted by and at the Burley Auction Gallery, New Braunfels, Texas. Mr. House also acquired Frank Jones' especially hand-crafted badge and 1873 Winchester.

Chapter 4 Making the Shoe Pinch Too Close

1. Durbin Manuscript.
2. Robert W. Stephens, *Walter Durbin: Texas Ranger and Sheriff*, 62–61.
3. AG King to Captain Jones, March 10, 1888, TSA.
4. Captain Jones to AG King, March 15, 1888, TSA.
5. Ibid.
6. Shirley, "A Ranger Named Outlaw," asserts that Baz Outlaw was troublesome, quarrelsome, and was ". . . highly irascible and grudge-holding, shot at the least interference, and often ended up rowing with those he was sent to protect." 9; Eugene Cunningham's "Bass Outlaw—The Little Wolf" for the Summer 1971 edition of *Badman* follows suit, particularly well: "But he [Outlaw} was a bad-tempered, grudge-holding little man, always quarreling with those around him." 44. These characterizations of Baz Outlaw, in due time, will earn varying degrees of credit, but at this point in the Texas Ranger's life there is not a sound basis for the premature award. To the contrary, it seems that he was particularly well liked and recognized as a competent frontier era lawman.
7. Stephens, *Texas Ranger Sketches,* 86–90.
8. Stephens, *Walter Durbin.* 62; Rather oddly, Chuck Parsons, *Captain John R. Hughes: Lone Star Ranger,* chooses to wholly omit—for one reason or another—the subject of his biography's deployment to Wharton, though the primary source citation—as will bee seen—is distinct.

9. Adjutant General's Office, State of Texas: To Agents and Conductors of Mexican National Railway—Texas Division, Pass for "Corporal Durbin, Company 'D' Frontier Battalion and 3 men, with 1 mule and 4 horses from Realitos to Corpus Christi, March 15, 1888." TSA; Captain Jones to Captain Sieker, March 23, 1888, TSA.
10. Stephens, *Walter Durbin*. 62; Durbin Manuscript: ". . . Capt Jones sent me in charge of a Scout to Wharton. I taken John R. Hughes now Capt Hughes and Ed Lindsey and Bass Outwaw [*sic*]. . . . Shipped Horses and pack mule to Eagle Lake[.] Hughes went from Corpus with Stock rest of us went on Passinger [*sic*] freight train. . . . reck [wreck] near Cuero and Hughes a bout a day late. . . ."
11. Corporal J.W. Durbin to Captain Sieker, March 23, 1888, TSA; Tise, *Texas County Sheriffs*, 528; Durbin's letter to Captain Sieker was written on letterhead stationery: "Office of Sheriff and Tax Collector, J.W. Jones, Sheriff and Tax Collector, Wharton, Texas.
12. "Record of Scouts and Arrests of Corporal Durbin's detachment from Mch 15th 1888 to Sept 30th 1888." TSA; Blackburn, *Wanted*. 348.
13. Corporal Durbin to Captain Sieker, March 23, 1888, TSA.
14. Durbin Manuscript.
15. Corporal Durbin to Captain Sieker, March 23, 1888, TSA.
16. Record of Scouts and Arrests—Wharton Detachment, TSA.
17. Ibid.
18. Monthly Return, Company D, Frontier Battalion, April 1888, TSA; For a biographical sketch of Calvin Grant "Cal" Aten, see, Alexander's *Bad Company and Burnt Powder*, Chapter 1, "Battle at Bullhead Mountain." 1–34.
19. Record of Scouts and Arrests—Wharton Detachment, TSA.
20. Corporal Durbin to Captain Sieker, April 10, 1888, on C.H. Waterhouse & Co. letterhead stationery, TSA.
21. Corporal Durbin to Captain Sieker, April 15, 1888, TSA.
22. Ibid.
23. Stephens, *Walter Durbin*. 63.
24. Record of Scouts and Arrests—Wharton Detachment, TSA; Corporal Durbin to AG King, May 14, 1888: "I started J.R. Hughes to day as ordered in your letter to Navarro County." TSA.

25. Barbara Uzzell, cont., *A History of Waller County, Texas,* 373: "A few items from the Hempstead Golden Anniversary Edition, concerning the early 1820s–1830s are appropriate here; Quote: 'Stage Coach robbed near Six Shooter Junction, March 11, 1834. Money and valuables taken, but mail got through to Washington and Austin.' . . . This is the first place in research where we found mention of the name 'Six-Shooter Junction' as an alias for Hempstead, but it seems from later quotes from Hempstead and Houston papers that this name was widely known and much feared by some."
26. Blackburn, *Wanted*, 342–343.
27. Record of Scouts and Arrests—Wharton Detachment: "[May] 25th—Corpl Durbin and 2 men left Wharton for Hempstead by order from Genl King. . . ."; Stephens, *Walter Durbin*, 64; Bruce A. Glasrud and Harold J. Weiss, Jr., eds., *Tracking the Texas Rangers: The Nineteenth Century*.
Here the editors cite the work of James M. Day in a chapter titled "Rangers of the Last Frontier of Texas." Day asserts that when Ranger Baz Outlaw traveled from Wharton to Hempstead on the train he was suffering from a "rising on his thigh and could not ride [a horse]," 273.
28. Stephens, *Walter Durbin*, 64; Durbin Manuscript; Jack Taylor, cont., *A History of Waller County, Texas,* 163.
29. Durbin Manuscript.
30. Utley, *Lone Star Justice*, 227.
31. Durbin Manuscript.
32. Ibid.
33. Ibid.; Monthly Return, Company D, Frontier Battalion, May 1888, TSA; Stephens, *Texas Ranger Sketches*, 12 and 29–32. For additional information regarding Ranger Britton, with citations throughout, see *Yours to Command: The Life and Legend of Texas Ranger Captain Bill McDonald* by Harold J. Weiss, Jr.
34. Ibid.; Tise, *Texas County Sheriffs*, 524.
35. Ibid.; Blackburn, *Wanted*, 131; AG King to Captain Jones, March 15, 1888, TSA; Tise, *Texas County Sheriffs*, 202.
36. Special Sheriff's Account Against the State for Conveying Prisoners, from Galveston, Galveston County, to Hempstead, Waller County, Assigned and approved, "Wm H. Burkhart, Judge 23rd Judicial District," TSA.
37. Durbin Manuscript; Record of Scouts and Arrest—Wharton Detachment, TSA.

38. Ibid.; Special Sheriff's Account Against the State For Conveying Prisoners from Hempstead, Waller County, to Houston, Harris County. Assigned and approved, "Wm H. Burkhart, Judge 23rd Judicial District." TSA.
39. Ibid.; Stephens, *Walter Durbin*, 66.
40. Ibid.
41. Captain Jones to AG King, May 31, 1888, TSA.
42. Private John R. Hughes to Captain Sieker, June 13, 1888, TSA; Parsons, *Captain John R. Hughes,* charitably rescues his protagonist. "The fault lay not with Hughes, but a careless cattleman. The official ledger relates: 'In Navarro County Hughes was unsuccessful in locating fence cutters by the indiscretion of one of the stock men, who gave the case away.'" 42. Regarding Hughes statement to Sieker that the Navarro County fence cutters were "the best organized band that I ever worked after," is curious in light of his service with the Texas Rangers, at the time, registering as less than a year. Certainly taking into account his status as a more-or-less inexperienced lawman the Navarro County fence-cutters may have very well been his toughest investigative challenge to date. Thus far Ranger records do seem silent in that regard. For the case at hand the question of relevance, though unasked, is whose injudiciousness spotlighted the undercover operation in the first place, so that the "careless cattleman" was even in a position to be indiscreet?
43. Monthly Return, Company D, Frontier Battalion, June 1888, TSA.
44. For a reasonably complete treatment of Ira Aten's undercover operations in Navarro County, with reference to primary source citations, see Alexander's *Rawhide Ranger, Ira Aten*, 148–163. Unfortunately, Parsons, *Captain John R. Hughes*, in a jumbling of chronology has Private Hughes being assigned to undercover operations in Navarro County subsequent to Sergeant Aten and Private King being there, when adherence to archived Ranger records clearly reveals the opposite. Though it somewhat skews worshipful chronicles, Aten and King were sent to Navarro County because Hughes' cover—for one reason or the other—had been blown, not vice versa, as clearly demonstrated by AG King's message to Captain Jones of July 7, 1888 in TSA: "The Governor directs that you detail Sergt Ira Aten for Special duty in Navarro County in connection with fence cutting cases occurring there lately. Aten, before leaving his post might ascertain from Hughes, what he knows about the matter in that Section. Instruct Aten to report here, before proceeding to Corsicana." Those

same records will also reveal that Rangers Ira Aten and Jim King did not arrest any fence cutters either.

45. During an August 11, 2014, interview with the preeminent authority on the conflict over the introduction of and gunfights and murderers associated with barbed-wire in Texas, Harold D. Jobes advised that Ira Aten may not have been the first to think of placing bombs along fence lines. This subject will be discussed and dissected at length in his forthcoming book about the life and death struggles associated with stringing barbed-wire throughout Texas.
46. Sergeant Aten to Captain Sieker, August 31, 1888 and October 8, 1888, TSA.
47. Walter Prescott Webb, *The Story of the Texas Rangers*. "There is no record that his invention was ever used but for years the rumor persisted that certain pasture fences were dangerous to monkey with." 126; Utley, *Lone Star Justice* backs Webb's play: "No dynamite bomb ever blew up a nipper, but the fear of one produced a marked decline in fence cutting in Navarro County." 237.
48. Stephens, *Walter Durbin*. 67; Tise, *Texas County Sheriffs,* 520.
49. Corporal Durbin to AG King, September 15, 1888, TSA.
50. Record of Scouts and Arrests—Wharton Detachment, TSA; Tise, *Texas County Sheriffs*. "R.M. Thornton was appointed on September 7, 1888. . . ." 520.
51. Ibid. "25th—Corpl Durbin and detachment left Hempstead for Rio Grande City by order of Genl King via Austin & Laredo." TSA.
52. AG King to Captain Jones, September 22, 1888, TSA; TSA; Captain Jones replied to AG King by telegram the next day: "Men are all out[,] will try and call them in but it may take several days." TSA; Captain Jones to AG King, September 24, 1888, TSA; Monthly Return, Company D, Frontier Battalion, September 1888, TSA.
53. Stephens, *Walter Durbin*. Waller County Sheriff Tom McDade's slayer ". . . was tried for the killing and acquitted." 65.
54. Alexander, *Six-Shooters & Shifting Sands*; Captain Jones to AG King, September 30, 1888, TSA.
55. AG King to J.W. Saunders, August 17, 1886, TSA; AG King to Captain Jones, August 17, 1886, TSA: "I would not under the circumstances reenlist him [Saunders] & assign him to any other Company & will not put him

back in your Company unless by your endorsement you can show your willingness to try him once more."

56. Captain Jones to AG King, October 17, 1888, TSA; Monthly Return, Company D, Frontier Battalion, October 1888, TSA: "J.W. Saunders discharged Oct 16th 1888 by Capt Frank Jones."
57. Alexander, *Six-Shooters and Shifting Sand.* Though speaking of Catarino Garza's misguided operation a few years later, Alicia M. Dewey in her compelling treatment, *Pesos and Dollars: Entrepreneurs in the Texas-Mexico Borderlands, 1880–1940,* page 66, is historically correct and journalistically candid in measuring the actual financial breadth of support attributed to Garza.
58. Ibid.; Spellman, *Captain J.A. Brooks,* 67–69; Spellman, *Captain John H. Rogers,* 62. Aside from the chain-of-command structure, Brooks a lieutenant and Rogers a sergeant, the fact that Captain Frank Jones was the commander in charge is further buttressed by AG King's letter to Captain Jones of October 18, 1888, TSA: "As you have been Some time in your present locality & have probably formed an opinion as to existing troubles in your section, I would request that you make to this office a complete & detailed report of recent occurrences, the status of affairs at present & any Suggestions & recommendations looking to the preservation of the peace in future."
59. Stephens, *Walter Durbin.* 69.
60. Monthly Return, Company D, Frontier Battalion, October 1888, TSA: Durbin Manuscript: "I arrived with Hempstead Detachment & Capt Brooks [Here Durbin is referencing the rank Brooks eventually attained, not the one he held at the time] come in with his co every thing was ready to start in on the leaders of this mob and in one day wee arrested an put behind the bars in the co Jail 40 of them. . . ." Also see, Corporal Durbin to AG King, October 29, 1888, TSA: "I made a Scout to Roma last week Arrested 5 men on Warrants. . . ."
61. Monthly Return, Company D, Frontier Battalion, November 1888, TSA: Blackburn, *Wanted.* 163–164.
62. AG King to Captain Jones, November 23, 1888, TSA; Captain Jones to AG King, November 29, 1888, TSA.
63. Durbin Manuscript.
64. Ibid. Regarding the unauthorized layover at Laredo, Corporal Durbin goes on to say: ". . . every thing went off O K and Cap never asked me afterward if I stopped over night[.]"

Chapter 5 One of the Worst and Most Dangerous

1. Monthly Return, Company D, Frontier Battalion, December 1888, TSA.
2. Ibid.
3. Monthly Return, Company D, Frontier Battalion, January 1889, TSA.
4. Durbin Manuscript.
5. Captain Jones to AG King, January 31, 1889, TSA.
6. Monthly Return, Company D, Frontier Battalion, March 1889, TSA.
7. B.D. Lindsey, to Captain Jones, March 5, 1889, TSA.
8. *San Antonio Daily Express*, September 19, 1891.
9. Readers interested in exploration of this quadruple homicide, with an emphasis on examination of primary source materials, may wish to access Alexander's *Rawhide Ranger, Ira Aten*, Chapter 10, "Would as soon go to a fight as a frolic," pages 170–188. From the nonfiction perspective the reader should review with caution and circumspection Eugene Cunningham's "Frontier Justice: How Old-Time Texas Rangers Solved a Baffling Murder Mystery" as carried in the September 1935 edition of *Startling Detective Magazine*. In a similar vein, Parsons, *Captain John R. Hughes*, rather deftly elevates the status of his subject: "When authorities requested assistance from Captain Jones he immediately assigned Hughes and Aten to 'ferret out the murderer of these four people,'" page 48. Noting that at the time Sergeant Aten, in the lead, was tasked with solving the crime, while assisted by Private Hughes is not inappropriate—but may be troubling in an arena for perpetuating legends. At no point in time did Sergeant Aten ever serve in the Frontier Battalion as a subordinate of Private John R. Hughes. Aten—a life long friend and staunch admirer of John R. Hughes, would also—seemingly unconsciously and nonchalantly—write: "Whenever I had a bad case I always took Hughes with me," in Aten-1941, HML&HC. Also see, Aten-1928, HML&HC: "[John] Hughes helped me in this case a great deal. . . . It was a very noted case."
10. AG King to Captain Jones, April 15, 1889, TSA.
11. Monthly Return, Company D, Frontier Battalion, April 1889, TSA; Stephens, *Walter Durbin*, 73–74,
12. AG King to Captain Jones, April 18, 1889, TSA.
13. Monthly Return, Company D, Frontier Battalion, May 1889, TSA.
14. Corporal Durbin to Captain Sieker, May 9, 1889, TSA.

15. Monthly Return, Company D, Frontier Battalion, May 1889, TSA; Private Baz Outlaw was discharged on May 16, 1889, followed the next day by Corporal Durbin and Private Hughes. Shirley, "A Ranger Named Outlaw," 9. Quite typically, but somewhat disappointedly, Texas Ranger John Reynolds Hughes' biographers seldom refrain from glossing their treatments with idealism and romanticism, hardly acknowledging their worshipful hero was but a mere mortal. Stephens, *Walter Durbin*, 77. Author Stephens taking his cue straight from the Durbin Manuscript cites Bill O'Grady as the mining person recruiting the three Rangers, while Parsons, *Captain John R. Hughes,* opts for John O'Grady. Census records do indicate that William O'Grady was one of Grace O'Grady's siblings, and therefore a brother-in-law to Captain Frank Jones. Since Durbin is a primary source, for this text Bill O'Grady seems the most likely—although no absoluteness attaches.
16. Shirley, "A Ranger Named Outlaw," 9.
17. Captain Jones to Captain Sieker, May 21, 1889, TSA; Corporal C. H. Fusselman to Captain Sieker, May 23, 1889, TSA: "As J.W. Durbin has quit I take his place."
18. Eugene Cunningham, "Bass Outlaw," *Frontier Times*, January 1928, 145.
19. Durbin Manuscript: "made arrangements with Capt Jones to dispose of our horses to new men who take our places. Carl Kirchner got mine. . . ." Phraseology of putting saddles "in a sack" was/is of both a figurative and literal meaning. Figuratively it implied one no longer owned or had ready access to a horse, such as when a cowboy changed ranches, "I put my saddle in a sack and quit." Or, when involuntarily discharged, "I was sacked." Literally, without the horse, when traveling the saddle was actually put in a burlap or canvas sack to prevent the riggings and stirrups from dragging and becoming entangled in first one thing then another.
20. Ibid. For an as of yet unexplained reason, J. Walter Durbin also included the physical address of McCracken in San Antonio, 415 Camden Street.
21. Ibid.
22. Ibid.
23. Stephens, *Walter Durbin*, 79.
24. Durbin Manuscript.
25. Ibid. Although certainly less than wholly reliable, biographer Jack Martin in *Border Boss,* asserts the shipments of silver were transported on pack

animals rather than wagons, see page 77. Durbin's memoirs are explicit: He and his ex-Ranger buddies were escorting and guarding wagons loaded with treasure.

26. Ibid. The fact that the ex-Rangers slept in their clothes, boots on, six-shooters belted around their waists, was also confirmed during writer Robert W. Stephens' 1965 interview with J. Walter Durbin's son, Marshall, at Uvalde, Texas. Marshall Durbin advised Stephens that the work in Mexico was so very dangerous that his father told him the three ex-Rangers slept wearing boots and clothes and never took their six-shooters off and their Winchesters were always within reach.
27. Martin, *Border Boss*. 79; Shirley in his *True Frontier* story picks up on Martin's tale about viperous reptiles and "mountain cats." 11.
28. Leon C. Metz, *Border: The U.S.-Mexico Line*, 364.
29. Bob Alexander, *Fearless Dave Allison: Border Lawman*, 117.
30. Stephens, *Walter Durbin*. 79.
31. Durbin Manuscript. Durbin also says that many of the American mill-house employees were armed with their personal six-shooters as well as the Winchesters furnished by the mining superintendant; Rather oddly it seems, writer Parsons for his biography *Captain John R. Hughes*, opts to wholly omit John R. Hughes' participation during the miners' strike, although his protagonist stood tall.
32. Ibid.
33. The suggestion that Baz Outlaw, on occasion, was a two gun man is somewhat bolstered in "The Latest on 'Bass' Outlaw" from the August 1982 edition of *Real West* by Bill O'Neal, Texas State Historian: "He became known as a good man with a gun, sometimes carrying two revolvers." 41.
34. Martin, *Border Boss*. 80.
35. Ibid. 81.
36. Durbin Manuscript. Here, J. Walter Durbin is clearly referring to Baz Outlaw as being a "bad man" in the context that he was dangerous and—drunk or sober—would always fight rather than retreat. Although as will later be plain in this text, Outlaw would commit acts that could and would be classed as criminal, there is, however, not any record that he was considered a cow or horse thief, train or stagecoach or bank robber, embezzler, child molester, or sly con artist, etc.

37. Captain Jones to AG King, June 5, 1889, TSA: Corporal Fusselman to AG King, June 5, 1889, TSA; Monthly Return, Company D, Frontier Battalion, September 1889, TSA.
38. AG King to Captain Jones, September 3, 1889, TSA.
39. Captain Jones to AG King, August 29, 1889, TSA.
40. Monthly Return, Company D, Frontier Battalion, September 1889, TSA; State of Texas, Certification of Pay, B.L. Outlaw, November 30, 1889, reflecting payment as a private in the Frontier Battalion's Company D, for three months, beginning on September 1, 1889, TSA.
41. Captain Jones to AG King, September 4, 1889, TSA. A brief biographical sketch of Ranger Jim King is found in Stephens' *Bullets and Buckshot in Texas*, 117–121.
42. Ibid.
43. *Galveston Daily News*, April 12, 1888.
44. Durbin Manuscript: "A Short time after Outlaw left the mines I quit[.] Hughes remained until in the winter. . . ."; Somewhat strangely in the apparent absence of corroborative archived Frontier Battalion records, Parsons asserts absent citation in *Captain John R. Hughes*, that subsequent to Baz Outlaw vacating Mexico, "Then it was Durbin's turn to return to Company D, leaving Hughes alone." 51; Durbin clearly states in his memoirs that when he resigned from the battalion to accept employment at the mines in Mexico, "this was my last days Service in Ranger force. . . ."; Stephens, Durbin's astute biographer in *Walter Durbin*, is not indistinct, following his subject's trail from Mexico to San Antonio, then to Laredo, Webb County, and finally to Pearsall, Frio County, where Durbin purchased during December 1889 a saloon "from Cap Tumlinson." 85. There is not then, or later, any mention of Durbin reenlisting with the Texas Rangers, though he would become the Frio County Sheriff, and even later a policeman at San Antonio and yet after that a Special Officer with the Southern Pacific Railroad.
45. Monthly Return, Company D, Frontier Battalion, October 1889, TSA.
46. Monthly Return, Company D, Frontier Battalion, November 1889, TSA; W. W. Jones, Mart, McLennan County, to Captain Sieker, November 28, 1889, TSA.
47. Captain Jones to AG King, December 4, 1889, TSA.

Chapter 6 Worth Two or Three Ordinary Men

1. Monthly Return, Company D, Frontier Battalion, December 1889, TSA.
2. Captain Jones to AG King, December 16, 1889, TSA.
3. Paul Frickie, United States Marshal for the Western District of Texas, to AG King, December 12, 1889, TSA; Parsons, *Captain John R. Hughes*, apparently misread the U.S. Marshal's letter to AG King, for he cites the document but writes: "A Ranger holding another office was technically against policy, but Jones chose to let it pass, as 'the two positions dovetail.'" See page 58. True, according to the U.S. Marshal's letter the two positions did "dovetail" but Captain Jones had done anything but let it "pass," ordering Charley Fusselman to resign. Had Fusselman ignored a direct order he was subjecting himself to a possible dishonorable discharge for insubordination.
4. AG King to Captain Jones, December 14, 1889, TSA.
5. Captain Jones to AG King, October 11, 1889, TSA.
6. Author Stovall in his regional histories, as cited herein, somewhat tempers his characterizations of Will and Alvin Odle suggesting—perhaps rightly so—that they were pretty good fellows, until they turned bad. At this late date and this far removed there is no merit in challenging such depictions. The criminal records, indictments, and jailbreaks will speak to those issues.
7. Alexander, *Bad Company and Burnt Powder*, 13–14; *Austin Daily Statesman*, December 1, 1885: "Bryant McCarty, an old and respected citizen was interred at cemetery yesterday. The procession was the longest ever witnessed in this county. One Odle, his son-in-law, shot him last Wednesday. Odle made his escape. One of the jury of inquest informed us it was a heartless cold-blooded murder." During an informative June 24, 2015, conversation with Derek Carlon, a straight-line descendant of John B. Odle, the following oral history was ascertained: John B. Odle, during an earlier agreement, had been promised transfer of ownership of a certain number of livestock—or a calf—by his father-in-law Bryant McCarty. When John Odle attempted to take possession of the animals, according to the Odle family version, McCarty went back on his word, reneging in whole, and during the dispute John B. Odle resorted to a six-shooter settlement, killing McCarty at the corral.
8. Alexander, *Rawhide Ranger, Ira Aten*, 220.

9. Allan A. Stovall, *Breaks of the Balcones: A Regional History*. "In the presence of the sheriff, the district attorney, and the district judge, he made a solemn agreement to betray Alvin and Will Odle." 243; Tise, *Texas County Sheriffs*, 169.
10. Stephens, *Bullets and Buckshot in Texas*, 53; Allan A. Stovall, *Nueces Headwater Country: A Regional History,* 109: "there was a party going on at the Taylor home above Vance, and a large crowd of people had gathered for a dance in Vance."
11. Ibid.
12. Alexander, *Bad Company and Burnt Powder*, 16 and Alexander, *Winchester Warriors*, 227–228; Parsons, *Captain John R. Hughes*, somewhat oddly, but certainly consistently, chooses to place the confrontation with Will and Alvin Odle hours ahead of when it actually took place, despite the retrievable primary source clarity in official Ranger correspondence, which will shortly be cited in this text: Parsons says, "It was a little after midnight, the beginning of Christmas Day 1889," 55. And see, Chuck Parsons, "The Lost Guns of Bass Outlaw," *True West*, May 1997, 56: "Shortly after midnight on Christmas Eve the brothers rode into the Ranger ambush." Commendably in transitioning from the article to the book, author Parsons does recalibrate and change the inaccurate 1890 to the correct 1889, and does properly replace Sergeant Ira Aten, who was not there, with Aten's brother Cal, who was there.
13. Stovall, *Nueces Headwater Country*, 110; Stephens, *Bullets and Buckshot in Texas*, 54.
14. Handwritten memoir of Calvin Grant Aten, author's copy courtesy Robert W. Stephens, hereafter cited as Aten Memoir.
15. Frederick Majors, "Bass Outlaw Was a Texas Riddle," *The West*, October 1965, 20.
16. Tarpley, *1001 Texas Place Names,* 61–62: "On a divide near Rocksprings, a sunken cavern was discovered in 1875 by Amon Billings. It is the home of millions of bats, and an underground river passes through it. The forbidding nature of the cavern suggested its name."
17. Ibid. Interestingly, Stovall, *Breaks of the Balcones*, based on hearsay comments repeated by Walter Lockhart, "who moved to the Nueces Canyon shortly after the two boys were killed," does assert specific behavior to Ranger Baz Outlaw: "As they drew nearer, Outlaw sprang to his feet

and shouted 'Halt there!' Instantly both sides began firing. . . . Outlaw snatched his [Alvin Odle's] pistol from his hand. . . . Outlaw had one ear burned, several others had felt the hiss of lead, but there were no casualties," from pages 242–249. Unfortunately author Stovall also—though quite innocently—puts Sergeant Ira Aten at the scene of the gunplay, rather than his brother, Ranger Private Cal Aten. At the time Will and Alvin Odle were killed Ira Aten was sheriff of Fort Bend County and no longer a Texas Ranger.

18. Aten Memoir.
19. Private Hughes to AG King, December 25, 1889, TSA.
20. Captain Jones to Captain Sieker, December 29, 1889, TSA. Rather unfortunately, when this letter is cited by Parsons, *Captain John R. Hughes*, the actual wording of Captain Frank Jones seems to have undergone a sanctimonious readjustment, from "Xmas" to "Christmas." 55.
21. Captain Jones to Captain Sieker. December 31, 1889, TSA.
22. Monthly Return, Company D, Frontier Battalion, December 1889, TSA.
23 Supplement to the Monthly Return, Company D, Frontier Battalion, December 1889, TSA.
24. Sheriff Ira Aten to C.G. Aten, April 20, 1890, copy courtesy Robert W. Stephens. This particular legal matter is also covered in Alexander's *Rawhide Ranger, Ira Aten*. 222
25. Captain Jones to AG King, January 3, 1890, TSA. Quite interestingly and, this seems about the place to note it, Frederick Majors for his piece in the October 1965 edition of *The West* melodramatically credits Baz Outlaw with mortally gunning down two Hispanic brothers at an Edwards County whiskey still; see page 21. Aside from the fact the article is encumbered with numerous factual inaccuracies, at least thus far, for this author, this purported event seems to have escaped primary source mention. Such, however, would not make the episode unequivocally bogus. Though unsupported by historical evidence, some Outlaw family oral history suggests Baz and several more Rangers rode into the camp of Mexican rustlers and killed them all during a horrific gunfight. ¿Quién sabe? That Baz Outlaw would be the subject of much misinformation is plainly driven home in William's *Texas' Last Frontier,* 386: "an oldtimer told him that the shot had been fired by a Ranger named Outlaw, who had been paid $500 to do the [murder] job. The only Ranger by that name on record, however, is Bass Outlaw, who had been killed in El Paso by John Selman over seven

months before the death of A.J. Royal." Award-winning authors Charles H. Harris III and Louis R. Sadler in *The Texas Rangers and the Mexican Revolution: The Bloodiest Decade, 1910–1920* in speaking of another Texas Ranger, Frank Hamer, not inappropriately challenge: "However, as often happens, his reputation was inflated. It would be interesting to see documentation for the fifty-three men his biographers claimed he killed." See page 222. Yes, it would! For *Whiskey River Ranger*, hopefully an accurate assessment, journalistic hoopla will be shortstopped with the application of what in a courtroom would be admissible evidence.

26. AG King to Captain Jones, March 22, 1890, TSA.
27. Captain Jones to AG King, March 24, 1890: "I will start Private Outlaw and 2 men to Junction City in the morning. . . ."; Monthly Return, Company D, Frontier Battalion, March 1890, TSA.
28. Captain Jones to AG King, April 20, 1890, TSA; Monthly Return, Company D, Frontier Battalion, March 1890, TSA.
29. The seminal work recording the low life and high crimes of Sam Bass is Rick Miller's outstandingly researched and compelling biography, *Sam Bass and Gang*. A short sketch of Herold may also be accessed in Robert W. Stephens' *Texas Ranger Indian War Pensions*, 44–45.
30. A biographical profile of Sergeant Fusselman may be reviewed in Alexander's *Riding Lucifer's Line,* Chapter 6, 101–110. Also see, Antonio Croc's piece "In the Line of Duty" as published in the Fall 1996 edition of the *Texas Gun Collector*; For the capture and execution of at least one of Fusselman's murderers an interested reader may wish to access Douglas V. Meed's piece "Daggers on the Gallows: The Revenge of Texas Ranger Captain 'Boss' Hughes," as published in the May 1999 edition of *True West*; Parsons, *Captain John R. Hughes*, somewhat oddly for a historian, conjures up speculation regarding the presence of Hughes at the El Paso County hanging of Geronimo Para for killing Fusselman: "Although the extensive newspaper coverage of the double hanging failed to mention him by name as being present, as a witness or as one of the officials, John R. Hughes was certainly there. . . . Certainly he was there among the witnesses to see justice carried out." 166; Certainly?
31. Ibid.; Captain Jones to AG King, May 2, 1890, TSA: "When Sergeant Fusselman was killed he was riding a horse owned by Sheriff White and had a gun belonging to a man named Ross. The gun and horse were both carried off. White wants $40.00 for the horse and Ross $15.00 for the gun."

At the time, although there would be later debate and tweaking of legalese, Texas Rangers were considered peace officers and Texas peace officers were dutifully sworn to uphold the laws of Texas and arrest violators. Stealing livestock was a criminal offense within the Texas Penal Code—and Rangers were expected to chase, capture, and cuff thieving offenders. The statutory jurisdiction of the U.S. Marshal and his fulltime and part-time deputies was to concern themselves with violations of federal statutes.

32. Captain Jones to AG King, February 22, 1890, TSA.
33. Ibid.; AG King to Captain Jones, March 25, 1890, TSA; Tise *Texas County Sheriffs*, 561.
34. Monthly Return, Company D, Frontier Battalion, April 1890, TSA; Captain Jones to AG King, March 21, 1890, TSA: "Akers of Zavalla [*sic*] County will need help shortly in making some important arrests in the King murder case. . . ." Engaged readers may also want to review Robert W. Stephen's piece, "A Ranger's Grave: The Murder of Jim King" as published in the October–December 2005 edition of the *National Outlaw/Lawman History Association Quarterly*.
35. State of Texas: Certificate of Pay, May 31, 1890, B.L. Outlaw, 1st Sergt. Company D, TSA; Monthly Return, Company D, Frontier Battalion, May 1890: "Sergt Outlaw and one man. . . ."; Stephens, *Bullets and Buckshot in Texas*, 37; Alexander, *Six-Shooters and Shifting Sands*.
36. Captain Jones to Adjutant General Woodford Haywood Mabry, June 21, 1892, TSA. Quite interestingly and astutely, Utley, *Lone Star Justice*, page 290, grades Baz Outlaw as Captain Frank Jones saw him at the time of the promotion: "an incomparable sergeant. . . ." Certainly Utley in the same assessment mentions Sergeant Outlaw's addiction to alcohol, but he, and we, are advantaged with hindsight unavailable to Captain Jones living and making his decisions in real time.
37. Rasch, "Bass Outlaw: Myth and Man," 13.
38. Of course, as it should be, the reader may stand as judge, but it does seem writer Parsons, *Captain John R. Hughes*, fails to even mention Baz Outlaw when writing of filling the Company D vacancy created due to Sergeant Fusselman's demise: "With the death of Fusselman on April 17, Adjutant General King had to determine who would take his place. On the following day, John Reynolds Hughes became 1st Corporal of Company D, Frontier Battalion of the Texas Rangers." Certainly employing the device

of implication by omission opens the doorway for not just a few rhetorical questions. For sure, after 1st Sergeant Fusselman was killed, Corporal Baz Outlaw was promoted, becoming Company D's 1st Sergeant. That Hughes, subsequent to the death of Fusselman was nominally placed in charge of the Company D detachment in far West Texas, first as a private, then as a corporal is not disputed. However, though it may somewhat shatter previously held perceptions, at no time during their service with the Frontier Battalion did Sergeants Ira Aten or Baz Outlaw ever answer to John R. Hughes in the chain-of-command structure and, in fact, it was he who was subordinate to them until each discharged from the Texas Rangers.

39. Monthly Return, Company D, Frontier Battalion, May 1890, TSA.
40. AG King to Captain Jones, May 3, 1890, TSA.
41. Monthly Return, Company D, Frontier Battalion, May 1890, TSA.
42. Parson, *Captain John R. Hughes*. 63.
43. AG King to Captain Jones, May 3 and 7, 1890; Spellman, *Captain J.A. Brooks*. 66; Captain J.A. Brooks to AG King, May 15, 1890, TSA.
44. Captain Jones to AG King, April 21, 1890, TSA.
45. AG King to Captain Jones, May 7, 1890, TSA.
46. Captain Jones to AG King, May 25, 1890, TSA.
47. A quick comment regarding Ranger travel is not out of place. The Monthly Return for a Texas Ranger company, among other things, enumerated a brief commentary about individual unit's Scouts—patrols or law enforcement actions—then concludes with a recap of time expended and distance covered. As an example: "Out 3 days, marched 75 miles." The time expenditure is not confusing, and is self-explanatory. On the other hand the term "marched" begs clarification. In the earlier days "marched" meant just that, not on foot but on horseback. Later, taking advantage of technology and expansion of the railroad system Texas Rangers, when they could, traveled by train—but the term "marched" was not dropped from the Monthly Return when summarizing their trek. It was, however, not to be literally interpreted. Therefore when a particular Ranger or a detachment or an entire company of Texas Rangers were "Out 3 days, marched 400 miles" clearly the indication is travel by railroad. Quite often, somewhat adding to the perplexities of accurate reporting, Texas Rangers frequently navigated getting from point A to point Z by a combination of railroad and horseback travel.

48. Monthly Return, Company D, Frontier Battalion, June 1890, TSA.
49. Petition from residents of Presidio County Texas to Governor L.S. Ross, May 3, 1890, signed by County Judge B.F. Adams, *et al.*, TSA.

Chapter 7 Couldn't Leave Liquor Alone

1. Corporal Hughes to Captain Sieker, May 6, 1890, TSA.
2. Captain Jones to AG King, June 30, 1890, TSA; Monthly Return, Company D, Frontier Battalion, June 1890, TSA: "Corpl Hughes did not scout any this Month." Clearly, based on the primary source documents—some already cited in this text—Corporal Hughes was sticking close to the town of Presidio keeping the peace and trying to effect a workable strategy for enticing fugitives wanted in Texas to return to his side of the Rio Grande. Subsequent to noting that Hughes "did not scout any this month," Parsons, his biographer in *Captain John R. Hughes*, seemingly feels compelled to rescue his subject from any implied suggestion that the corporal might have been malingering, by reeling out his piece of guesswork: "Perhaps Hughes was ill during June," se page 63. Perhaps he was!
3. An interesting and compelling overview of Shafter, Texas, may be accessed in Glenn Justice's *Little Known History of the Texas Big Bend: Documented Chronicles From Cabeza de Vaca to the Era of Pancho Villa*, 45–60.
4. T. Lindsay Baker, *Ghost Towns of Texas,* 134–136; Alexander, *Riding Lucifer's Line*, 111.
5. Ibid. Author Baker states that at one time as many as four thousand residents called Shafter home.
6. Henry B. McCulloch to Governor L.S. Ross, October 27, 1889, TSA.
7. Private C.G. Aten to Captain Sieker, April 22, 1890, TSA.
8. Report of the Adjutant General: State of Texas, 1889–1890, TSA.
9. Sergeant C.H. Fusselman to AG King and/or Captain Sieker, November 16, 1889, TSA; Sergeant Fusselman to Captain Sieker, February 2, 1890, TSA.
10. Stephens, *Bullets and Buckshot in Texas*, 37, is clear: "While serving at Shafter he [Baz Outlaw] met the postmistress, a widow named Laura Hay, and was often invited to her home for meals." During a September 9, 2014, conversation, Robert Stephens related that he had received this information directly from Ann Jensen, who was Laura Carr Hay Oden's

daughter. Ann Jensen was the editor of the 1936 publication *Texas Ranger's Diary & Scrapbook* by Alonzo Van Oden. Stephens personally interviewed Jensen at Dallas, Texas, during the late 1960s. On page 107 in his earlier work, *Texas Ranger Sketches*, author Stephens reports that during 1897 Laura Carr Hay was then serving as postmistress at Ysleta, El Paso County. Likewise, George L. (Jack) Richardson, a grandson of Lon Oden, in his historically significant—and admittedly rare—treatment of his grandfather, *The Rest of the Story and Scrapbook of Alonzo Van Oden*, also places his grandmother as an El Paso County postmistress, at Fabens. Author's copy of Richardson's revealing tome is courtesy of the late John D. Tanner, Jr., one of the leading authorities on crime and criminality in the American Southwest, with an especial emphasis on train robbers and their misdeeds. Also, in their most informative piece regarding relative Alonzo Van Oden, Karen Holliday Tanner and John D. Tanner, Jr., "Lon Oden: The Rhymin' Ranger" as published in the Summer 1998 edition of *Old West*, unequivocally enlighten: "In 1894, he [Lon Oden] met another Laura, Laura Carr Hay, Ysleta's postmistress and a young widow with three children," page 14. Admittedly this is Baz Outlaw's narrative and delving with precision into divorce or death dates of Laura's past or subsequent husbands was not and will not be considered beyond the scope of this treatment. From the information at hand, through oral history as provided by Laura's daughter there could be a distinct possibility that Laura Carr Hay Oden was both married and/or single when or/if living at Shafter. That she knew Baz Outlaw quite well, wherever, is indisputable. Reconciling those dates and places remains the realm of family historians or raring-to-go genealogists.

11. Monthly Return, Company D, Frontier Battalion, July 1890, TSA.
12. Ibid. This Monthly Return indicates Sergeant Outlaw returned to the Company D camp near Marfa on or about July 16, 1890, and is silent regarding his making any additional scouts during the month. Whether he was on peace-keeping duty in town or tied down by administrative tasks—or a combination of both—stands unrecorded.
13. Caldwell and DeLord, *Texas Lawmen*, 348; Darren L. Ivey, *The Texas Rangers: A Registry and History*, 243.
14. Captain Jones to Captain Sieker, August 9, 1890, TSA.
15. A chapter-length biographical profile of John F. Gravis is found in Alexander's *Riding Lucifer's Line*, Chapter 7, 111–118.

16. Ibid.; Tise, *Texas County Sheriffs*, 424. Regarding Sheriff Russell, also see Glenn P. Willeford and Gerald G. Raun, *Cemeteries and Funerary Practices in the Big Bend of Texas, 1850 to the Present*, 208–209.
17. Wilkins, *The Law Comes to Texas*, 294.
18. Alexander, *Riding Lucifer's Line*, 114–115; Monthly Return, Company D, Frontier Battalion, August 1890, TSA: "J.F. Gravis Killed in action Aug 4th 1890." Caldwell and DeLord, *Texas Lawmen*, 348; Ronald G. DeLord, ed., *The Ultimate Sacrifice: Trials and Triumphs of the Texas Peace Officer, 1823–2000*, 62.
19. *Luling Signal*, August 7, 1890, TSA.
20. *Brooklyn Daily Eagle*, August 5, 1890, for quote. The story was also carried in the *Galveston Daily News* of August 5, 1890, and the *El Paso Times* of August 6, 1890. Also see, Carlysle Graham Raht, *The Romance of Davis Mountains and Big Bend Country*, 305: "As the Americans approached they were suddenly fired upon, evidently by ten or twelve men hidden in a clump of trees and behind a pile of adobe huts. Gravis was instantly killed and Lee was badly shot in the wrist."
21. Monthly Return, Company D, Frontier Battalion, August 1890, TSA.
22. Report of Adjutant General: State of Texas, 1889–1890, TSA.
23. AG King to Captain Jones, August 22, 1890, TSA.
24. Monthly Return, Company D, Frontier Battalion, September 1890, TSA; Wilkins, *The Law Comes to Texas*, pens that the sheriff was "arrested" but such legal formality is not reflected in the Monthly Return—his source—which simply makes note that the intoxicated Sheriff was "disarmed." See page 294.
25. Ibid.; Tise, *Texas Count Sheriffs*, 65.
26. Monthly Return, Company D, Frontier Battalion, October 1890, TSA; Captain Jones to AG King, September 25, 1890, TSA.
27. Ibid.
28. Captain Jones to Captain Sieker, October 14, 1890, TSA: "Sergt. Outlaw is in Shafter with four men. . . ."
29. Ibid.; Monthly Return, Company D, Frontier Battalion, October 1890, TSA.
30. Alexander, *Winchester Warriors*, 239.
31. Captain Jones to Captain Sieker, October 28, 1890, TSA.

32. Monthly Return, Company D, Frontier Battalion, October 1890, TSA. Rather interestingly it may also be registered that on January 27, 1891, Corporal John R. Hughes arrested a J.B. Humphreys for Assault to Murder and escorted him to the Presidio County Jail. Certainly this particular subject could not have been—if the October 1890 Monthly Return for Company D is correct—the same Jim Humphrey killed by prostitute Maria at Shafter, leaving open the highly likely probability that the two Humphreys arrested by Texas Rangers were related.
33. Captain Jones to AG King, October 14, 1890, TSA.
34. AG King to Captain Jones October 20, 1890, TSA.
35. Glasrud, *Tracking the Texas Rangers*, 274.
36. Stephens, *Bullets and Buckshot in Texas*, 37. As previously cited, Stephens acquired this account from Ann Jensen. That the actual incident occurred and took place at Laura Carr Hay's residence is believable, even allowing for a touch of oral history confusion as to whether she was living at Shafter, Ysleta, or Fabens at the time.
37. Oden, *Texas Ranger's Diary and Scrapbook*, 10.
38. Stephens, *Bullets and Buckshot in Texas*, 37. Typically, and it's easy to make the jump, there is an assumption that when Baz and Laura were first acquainted, that she was married to Alonzo Van Oden and, correspondingly, Baz's visits to Laura's home were also visits to Lon's home. Such was not the case. Certainly Baz Outlaw and Lon Oden would be friends and Texas Ranger colleagues, but the marriage of Lon and Laura would not take place until January 17, 1897, three years after Baz Outlaw's death. In fact, according to the Tanners' research appearing in *Old West*, it is clearly stated that Lon Oden and the widow Laura Hay did not even meet until 1894, the year Baz died (see page 14). Also see Richards, *The Rest of the Diary and Scrapbook of Alonzo Van Oden*. Lon Oden was not a Ranger when he married Laura Hay, having already discharged from Company D the month after Baz Outlaw's death.
39. Oden, *Texas Ranger's Diary and Scrapbook*, 40.
40. Tise, *Texas County Sheriffs*, 65. Gillett spelled his name sans the "e" as clearly revealed on the Brewster County Sheriff's letterhead stationery and, more importantly, by his own signature, "J.B. Gillett."
41. Monthly Return, Company D, Frontier Battalion, November 1890, TSA.
42. Glasrud, *Tracking the Texas Rangers*, 274.

43. M.R. Daniels (depending on the source, there are various spellings for Daniels' last name) to Adjutant General Woodford Heywood Mabry, May [?] 1892, TSA.
44. Ibid.
45. Monthly Return, Company D, Frontier Battalion, December 1890, TSA.
46. Captain Jones to AG Mabry, June 21, 1892, TSA. This report, made a year and a half after the episode, was in response to a litany of complaints registered against Baz Outlaw by a bitter personal enemy, ex-Texas Ranger M.R. Daniels, but that in and of itself does not make the charges specious.
47. Ibid.
48. Monthly Return, Company D, Frontier Battalion, December 1890, TSA.
49. Ibid.
50. Captain Jones to AG Mabry, January 31, 1891, TSA.
51. Jacobson and Nored, *Jeff Davis County, Texas,* 131–132.
52. Monthly Return, Company D, Frontier Battalion, January 1891, TSA.
53. Ibid.
54. Monthly Return, Company D, Frontier Battalion, February 1891, TSA; Captain Jones to AG Mabry, February 1, 1891, TSA; Captain Jones to Captain Sieker, February 12, 1891, TSA; Ron C. Tyler, *The Big Bend: A History of the Last Texas Frontier*, 134; Virginia Madison, *The Big Bend Country of Texas*, discusses the killing of Powe and the legend of the steer branded M U R D E R, 143–146. For a brief profile of Ranger Thalis Cook, see Stephens' *Texas Ranger Sketches*, 43–47; Parsons in *Captain John R. Hughes*, somewhat bizarrely it seems, cannot resist putting John Hughes into the story even though he was miles away at the time. Though the statement may be measured as ludicrous, author Parsons postulates: "Hughes certainly became aware of this notable fight, and no doubt would have preferred to be a participant," page 67. Really?
55. Captain Jones to AG Mabry, January 6, 1891, TSA.
56. Captain Jones to AG Mabry, March 9, 1891, TSA; AG Mabry to Captain Jones, March 12, 1891, TSA: "you are hereby authorized to discharge Private Homer Nix of your Company to enable him to accept employment as a clerk in Shafter, Tx."
57. Captain Jones to AG Mabry, May 21, 1891, TSA.

58. Captain Jones to AG Mabry, May 26, 1891, TSA; AG Mabry to Captain Jones, May 29, 1891: "Authority is hereby granted you to discharge J.W. Saunders as requested. . . ." TSA.
59. AG Mabry to Captain Jones May 29, 1891, TSA.
60. Captain Jones to AG Mabry, May 31, 1891, TSA.
61. Monthly Return, Company D, Frontier Battalion, January 1891, TSA; Captain Jones to AG King (before W.H. Mabry took office), January 22, 1891, TSA.
62. Alexander, *Riding Lucifer's Line*, 148–149.
63. Captain Jones to AG Mabry, February 21, 1891, TSA.
64. Sergeant Outlaw to Charles Murphy, January 28, 1891, HML&HC.
65. Captain Jones to AG Mabry, March 17, 1891, TSA; Glasrud, *Tracking the Texas Rangers,* includes James M. Day's assessment: "Money continued to nag him [Baz Outlaw]. In a series of letters in 1891 and 1892 between Outlaw and Charley Murphy of Marfa, written on letterhead from the Buckhorn Saloon in Alpine, he told the merchant clearly not to pry into his financial affairs. He did the same to Humphrey and Company." See page 274.
66. AG Mabry to Captain Jones, March 19, 1891, TSA.
67. Captain Jones to AG Mabry, March 1, 1891, TSA.
68. Captain Jones to AG Mabry, March 14, 1891, TSA.
69. AG Mabry to Captain Jones, March 17, 1891, TSA.
70. Oden, *Texas Ranger's Diary and Scrapbook*, 40.

Chapter 8 Insulted in the Presence of Ladies

1. Gournay, *Texas Boundaries,* 117. Subsequent to this episode, during 1908, Terrell County was created and organized, real-estate carved from Pecos County, which now borders Val Verde County's western edge.
2. Jeff Burton, *Dynamite and Six-Shooter*, 195–196; Alexander, *Lawmen, Outlaws, and S.O.Bs.*, 10–11. There was an assertion at the time that perhaps the robbers numbered five; however, such was never proven. During a plea agreement with federal prosecutors one of the cooperative defendants failed to make mention of a fifth co-conspirator. At this stage in

the legal proceedings, knowingly lying to the U.S. Attorney would have been figuratively suicidal. The best evidence places the number of train robbers at four. W.T. Wayne, "The Fast Guns of Bass Outlaw," for his article in *Great West* of June 1972 puts the number of train robbers at six. He, too, from somewhere, seems privy to inside information, as his piece is jam-packed with dialogue which, sorry to say, is not source cited—and in certain instances, does not comport with documentable and demonstrable truths.

3. *El Paso Daily Times*, September 3, 1891.
4. *San Antonio Daily Express*, September 3, 1891. Certainly the most compelling article-length treatment of this fascinating crime and its aftermath is Franklin W. Daughtery's "Las Vegas de los Ladrones and the Flynt Gang," which appeared in the 1991 edition of the *Journal of Big Bend Studies*, 1–28.
5. *San Antonio Daily Express*, October 24, 1891.
6. *El Paso Daily Times*, September 3, 1891. Understandably, other newspapers cabbaged onto the good story, particularly a series of articles in the *San Antonio Daily Express* as appropriately cited herein.
7. *San Antonio Daily Express*, October 24, 1891.
8. Jeffrey Burton, *The Deadliest Outlaws: The Ketchum Gang and the Wild Bunch*, 71.
9. *San Antonio Daily Express*, September 5, 1891.
10. *El Paso Daily Times*, September 3, 1891.
11. Daughtery, "Las Vegas de los Ladrones and the Flynt Gang," 6–7.
12. Alexander, *Lawmen, Outlaws, and S.O.Bs.*, 12; *San Antonio Daily Express*, September 7, 1891: "Roy Bean followed three hours later and stopped at the river, as did the sheriff's posse, to await the Rangers' arrival."
13. AG Mabry to Captain Jones, August 17, 1891, TSA.
14. Captain Jones to AG Mabry, September 11, 1891, TSA.
15. *San Antonio Daily Express*, October 24, 1891: "The money will be paid over to the captors upon conviction of the accused or proof of the guilt of the dead." For *Lawmen, Outlaws, and S.O.Bs.*, this author inadvertently reversed the rewards paid by Wells, Fargo & Company and the Southern Pacific Railroad. Hopefully, future researchers and writers will note this correction.

16. Daughtery, "Las Vegas de los Ladrones and the Flynt Gang," 22.
17. Ibid. The author's geographical description, herein quoted in part, is masterful and based on a thorough knowledge of geology, one of his particular fields of professional expertise. That Sergeant Outlaw commanded this scout after the train robbers is reflected in Company D's Monthly Return for September 1891, found in TSA: "Sergt Outlaw and seven men went to the Rio Grande river after train robbers. Not returned."
18. Captain Jones to AG Mabry, September 22, 1891, TSA.
19. Monthly Return, Company D, Frontier Battalion, October 1891, TSA; Daughtery, "Las Vegas de los Ladrones and the Flynt Gang," 9.
20. *San Antonio Daily Express*, November 3, 1891, TSA; Daughtery, "Las Vegas de los Ladrones and the Flynt Gang." 19; Captain Jones later would write, regarding Flynt, that "gambling and drinking ruined him."
21. AG Mabry to Captain Jones, September 28, 1891, TSA.
22. Daughtery, "Las Vegas de los Ladrones and the Flynt Gang," 19.
23. Certainly there are other versions as to how writers credit Joe Sitter with locating the train robbers' trail and campsite, however, for this narrative, going straight to the horse's mouth—so to speak—seems the most fitting. There is a reasonably lengthy handwritten document at the Archives of the Big Bend (ABB), Bryan Wildenthal Memorial Library, Sul Ross University, Alpine, Texas, titled "Joe Sitter's Account of the Trailing and Capture of the Train Robbers." This is a first-person statement of Joe Sitter as recorded by Harry Warren during an interview. Though extensively cited in *Lawmen, Outlaws, and S.O.Bs.*, this fascinating primary source commentary from an authentic on-the-ground participant in a bona fide Wild West saga has been seldom—if ever—cited elsewhere. Fellow researchers and writers are alerted to its accessibility. Hereafter cited as Sitter to Warren. Certainly based on Joe Sitter's first-person account, Wayne T. Walker, "Joe Sitters: The Best Damn Tracker in Texas," as published in the December 1978 edition of *Oldtimers Wild West* and Kevin Michaels' "Tracker" as written for the September 1974 issue of *Great West*, interject Joe Sitter into the story too early. However, Dane Coolidge, *Fighting Men of the West*, page 157, aptly does recognize Joe Sitter's manhunting talents: "Joe could hardly spell his name, but he could read a cold trail like a book." And, as a point of interest, during the October 26, 2002, interview with Joe Sitter's grandson, Jake Sitters, confusion concerning the proper spelling of the

family name was rectified. The "s" at the end of the last name was added by subsequent generations. Our subject—the career lawman—came into this world January 13, 1863 and was baptized in the St. Louis Catholic Church at Castroville, Medina County, Texas, on the twenty-second of January as Joseph Russell Sitter. Also refer to Alexander's *Lawmen, Outlaws and S.O.Bs.*, 25, n. 24 for this clarification and see, 169–201, for a dedicated chapter covering Joe Sitter's biographical profile and exciting law enforcing career, aside from the train robbery narrative.

24. Sitter to Warren, ABB.
25. Monthly Return, Company D, Frontier Battalion, October 1891, TSA: "Jones was absent from Camp from Sept. 20th to Oct. 29. The men out from Oct. 11 to 23rd. Three men were in attendance in Federal Court in El Paso." Daughtery, "Las Vegas de los Ladrones and the Flynt Gang," page 22, reports that Sergeant Outlaw was "involved in the pursuit of the robbers from beginning to end." And that very well may be the truth: Sergeant Outlaw, in one way or the other, might have been tending to the business of testifying or working on the criminal case from the evidentiary standpoint, not necessarily in the field chasing *mal hombres*. That he was not with Captain Jones during this phase of the narrative is made perfectly clear by his own hand in a letter to the adjutant general. See Sergeant B.L. Outlaw to AG Mabry, October 20, 1891, TSA: "Captain Jones has been away for about ten days & is down near the country of Devils River after those Train Robbers—There is no one in Camp but myself, I just got in this Evening from El Paso—Was up there attending Court. . . ." In a May 1, 1892, letter to AG Mabry, Captain Jones' remarks support Outlaw's physical positioning at the time of the Crockett County shoot-out: "Sergt Outlaw was on all the scouts after these men except the time of the capture and could not leave on account of being a witness in Court." Letter in TSA. Quite unfortunately from an honestly honed historic perspective, Parsons, *Captain John R. Hughes*, once again, cannot bring himself to acknowledge that the subject of his biography had absolutely no involvement with this case, at this time. That he wants naive readers to be taken in with a journalistic sleight of hand is patently clear: "Corporal Hughes was with a detachment down at Shafter, or else he would have been in charge of the scout after the train robbers," he writes on page 70. For military and law enforcement staffing models there is a chain-of-command pecking order, and corporals are one notch from the bottom, not the top; and certainly

corporals are subordinate to sergeants, in this case Sergeant Baz Outlaw, and captains, in this case Captain Frank Jones. History will bear witness Texas Ranger John R. Hughes will make a name for himself—a good name—absent any twenty-first-century armchair boost.

26. Sitter to Warren, ABB.
27. Gournay, *Texas Boundaries*, 93; Tise, *Texas County Sheriffs*, 136; Blackburn, *Wanted*, 88–89.
28. Alexander, *Lawmen, Outlaws, and S.O.Bs.*, 16–17.
29. Sitter to Warren, ABB; *San Antonio Daily Express*, October 22, 1891, refers to the ranching headquarters as the "7 D" ranch, rather than Joe Sitter's assertion that it was the "77" Ranch.
30. Ibid. For the January 1929 edition of *Frontier Times*, J. Marvin Hunter published an article titled "The Killing of Captain Frank Jones." Within the piece Hunter reprints a letter from Captain Jones to Pauline Baker, Uvalde, Texas, wherein he describes the chase and ensuing gunfight with the train robbers. As a primary source record of events it is quite revealing and interesting and valuable. Excerpts and information from this letter will be cited hereafter as "Jones to Baker, *Frontier Times*."
31. Ibid. Sitter refers to the lady as Mrs. Roy, Captain Jones identifies her only as a Northern lady.
32. Ibid.; Alexander, *Lawmen, Outlaws, and S.O.Bs.*, 18.
33. Ibid. Using terminology such as "saddle up" was/is widespread, but often saddles themselves were/are referred to by other names, most commonly "hulls" or "caques." See, Ramon F. Adams, *Western Words: A Dictionary of the Old West*, 81, and Thomas H. Rynning's *Gun Notches: A Saga of Frontier Lawman Thomas H. Rynning. . . .* 144. Or, visit with a legit cowboy.
34. Alexander, *Lawmen, Outlaws, and S.O.Bs.*, 18–19.
35. Sitter to Warren, ABB.
36. Jones to Baker, *Frontier Times*.
37. Ibid. For Jones' remark about Wellington's gun shooting cartridges as long as one's finger, the reader may wish to access R.D. Kirkland's *Winchester: America's Premier Gunmaker*, "Winchester and the Age of Smokeless Powder," 14–29.
38. Sitter to Warren, ABB; Alexander, *Lawmen, Outlaws, and S.O.Bs.*, 20; Captain Jones to AG Mabry, October 24, 1891, TSA: "The other [Flynt]

ran about 8 miles and after being wounded blew his brains out. We buried him as well as we could and then came back. . . ."

39. Jones to Baker, *Frontier Times*; Telegram, Sheriff Kieffer to AG Mabry, 10, 23, 1891, TSA: I have this day demanded of Captain F. Jones Co. D Ranger three train robbers which I had capiases & were indicted here. . . ." Daughtery, "Las Vegas de los Ladrones and the Flynt Gang," 13: "On arriving at Comstock Captain Jones found Sheriff Kieffer awaiting him with a demand that the robbers be placed in his custody. Jones refused on the grounds that the federal offense of robbing the U.S. Mails took precedence over any crime for which local authorities had jurisdiction."
40. *San Antonio Daily Express*, October 23, 1891: "Sheriff Kieffer went up today with warrants for the men, but Captain Jones refused to deliver them to him."
41. *San Antonio Daily Light*, October 24, 1891.
42. *San Antonio Daily Express*, October 29, 1891. That Sergeant Baz Outlaw would be a witness in the case is reflected in Captain Jones to AG Mabry, March 31, 1892: "Early in April Sergt Outlaw, private Kirchner and myself will have to attend Court in El Paso as witnesses in the S.P. [Southern Pacific] train robbery case." Also see, Monthly Return, Company D, Frontier Battalion for April 1892, in TSA: "Capt. Jones and 2 men went to El Paso to attend Federal Court. Private Kirchner returned on the 22nd. Sergt Outlaw on the 26th and Capt Jones on the 29th." And see, Daughtery, "Las Vegas de los Ladrones and the Flynt Gang." "Captain Frank Jones, Sergeant Outlaw, and other Rangers gave testimony as to the pursuit and capture of Wellington, Fields [Stouts] and Lansford, and the death of Flynt," 15.
43. Sergeant Outlaw to AG Mabry, October 20, 1891, TSA.
44. *Albuquerque Morning Democrat*, September 5, 1891.
45. *San Antonio Daily Light*, October 14, 1891. An article in the *Oakland Tribune* of April 3, 1927, highlights the fifty-year magic career of Zamloch and his retirement to Oakland, California.
46. C.E. Van Horn, Zamloch's Congress of Wonders, to Governor Hogg, November 4, 1891, TSA.
47. Ibid.
48. Ibid. Occasionally, an "e" is tagged onto C.E. Van Horn's last name (Van Horne) in secondary writings, but primary source documents are clearly sans the "e." See documents in TSA. On the return trip to California the

show made a scheduled performance at Tombstone, and the newspaperman's critique is delightfully penned: "Tombstone has been humbugged so often by snide tricksters that the house was not as full last night as it would have been had people known what was in store for them. . . ." See, *Tombstone Daily Prospector*, November 20, 1891.

49. Captain Jones to AG Mabry, November 6, 1891, TSA: "This morning I reced a letter fro C.E. Van Horn manager of the Zamloch show complain [*sic*] of the bad conduct on the part of Sergt. Outlaw at Alpine and Marfa."
50. Ibid.
51. Captain Jones to AG Mabry, November 12, 1891, TSA.
52. Captain Jones to AG Mabry, November 7, 1891, TSA.
53. Ibid.
54. Captain Jones to AG Mabry, November 12, 1891, TSA.
55. AG Mabry to Captain Jones, November 30, 1891, TSA.
56. Ibid.
57. Monthly Return, Company D, Frontier Battalion, November 1891, TSA; Captain Jones to AG Mabry, November 27, 1891, TSA.
58. Jacobson and Nored, *Jeff Davis County, Texas,* 161–162.
59. Ibid.; Tise, *Texas County Sheriffs*, 285.
60. Captain Jones to AG Mabry, November 30, 1891, TSA.
61. Ibid.; Monthly Return Company D, Frontier Battalion, November 1891, TSA: "Sergt Outlaw went to Fort Davis to investigate the reported lynching of 2 Mexicans by a mob. Learned the Mexicans were killed but got no clue as to who did it."
62. Jacobson and Nored, *Jeff Davis County, Texas,* 162.
63. Copies of checks drawn on Humphries & Co. and signed by B.L. Outlaw, dated, June 6, 7, and 24, 1891; August 31, 1891; September 1, 1891; December 2 and 5, 1891, HML&HC.
64. Sergeant Outlaw to [John] Humphries and Co., HML&HC.

Chapter 9 Simply Cannot Control Himself

1. Alexander, *Riding Lucifer's Line*, 149; *Chicago Daily Tribune*, July 3, 1892; Leon Claire Metz, *Encyclopedia of Lawmen, Outlaws, and Gunfighters*,

233–234; *Los Angeles Times*, August 31, 1898; *El Paso Daily Times*, September 1, 1898; Coolidge, *Fighting Men of the West*, 147; John L. Davis, *The Texas Rangers: Their First 150 Years*, 74–76. Interestingly, sometimes writers owning an accumulation of Hollywood's versions of how life in the Old West was supposed to be, not how it was, and absolutely no platform of practical experience, suggest that because Ernest St. Leon was not named in any official reports, his actual presence at this Shafter shoot-out is doubtful. Even Virgil E. Baugh, *A Pair of Texas Rangers: Bill McDonald and John Hughes*, in his totally worshipful and less than reliable mini-biographical sketches credits Ernest St. Leon with infiltrating the gang of ore thieves and participating in the gunfight that marked their demise (17). Only three days after the encounter, January 15, 1892, Captain Jones updated AG Mabry (emphasis added): "Corporal Hughes reports that on the night of the 12th inst in attempting the arrest of *four* Mexicans caught in the act of stealing ore from the Shafter miles [sic] he and his party were fired on by the Mexicans they returned the fire Killing three" (in TSA). The dead ore thieves' cohorts and families were possibly well aware of just who and how many were up to nefariousness that particular night. Not being able to account for the one that got away, Ernest St. Leon would have been brainless on the part of competent investigators and lawmen, which by this point in time, Company D Rangers were well on the rocky pathway to professionalism. On that very same day and, perhaps not at all coincidently, Corporal John R. Hughes penned this: "The bearer, Ernest St. Leon wishes an appointment as Special Ranger. He has assisted me in detecting a lot of Mexican ore thieves and is in danger of being killed at any time in this country and wishes to carry his pistol for self defence [*sic*]," TSA. As well, though there is never any dispute that Private Oden was with Corporal Hughes when the shooting commenced, he, too, is not mentioned in the official correspondence. Though admittedly troubling for both grass-roots historians as well as credentialed scholars, simply because it is not written on paper doesn't unequivocally mean that it didn't happen. Sometimes, in the real world, especially in the mysterious Texas/Mexico borderland country some things are best left unsaid. Perhaps somewhat helpful in putting the matter to bed would be Captain Jones to AG Mabry, March 9, 1892, and although he personally did not have a high regard for Ernest St. Leon, the captain did acknowledge that "he had been very useful" at Shafter (TSA). Also, AG Mabry's, March 21, 1892, letter to Captain Jones, in the TSA: "You will take up on your rolls the name of Ernest St. Leon as a special ranger attached to your Company under provisions of Special Order No. 6. . . ." Though in reality Texas Ranger John R. Hughes' law-enforcing record is admirable in its own right, it seems as demonstrated in these endnotes and elsewhere that some writers are hopelessly afflicted with making a superman out of a mere mortal. Raht, *The Romance of Davis Mountains,* in his writing of *Ranger John Hughes vs. Ore Thieves at Shafter*, reports: "In 1892, he apprehended a band of fifty robbers who were stealing ore from the Shafter mine," 320. Corporal John Hughes, or his supervisor Sergeant Baz Outlaw, or his company commander Captain Frank Jones, wholly failed to enumerate these specific arrests in the Monthly Returns or other Company D correspondence.

2. Monthly Return, Company D, Frontier Battalion, January 1892, TSA.
3. Captain Jones to AG Mabry, January 31, 1892, TSA.
4. Captain Jones to AG Mabry, June 21, 1892, TSA.
5. Ibid. Sometimes, though inaccurately, Baz Outlaw's confrontation with Mr. Watts has been transplanted to El Paso. A review of primary source documents reveals quite the contrary, though such innocent geographical mix-ups are completely understandable within the broad scope of untangling Baz Outlaw's unique story. The dustup occurred at or near Alpine, Texas.
6. Glasrud, *Tracking the Texas Rangers*, 274: "Then he [Baz Outlaw] went to the house of Watts' prostitute and spent the night with her."
7. Monthly Returns, Company D, Frontier Battalion, December 1891 and January 1892, TSA.
8. Captain Jones to AG Mabry, March 19, 1892, TSA.
9. Ibid.; Monthly Return, Company D, Frontier Battalion, March 1892, TSA.
10. AG Mabry to Captain Jones, March 22, 1892, TSA.
11. Captain Jones to AG Mabry, May 31, 1892, TSA; Monthly Return, Company D, Frontier Battalion, May 1892, TSA: "May 31—Sergt Outlaw and 3 men left for Pecos County, on urgent call from the Sheriff to assist in making some arrests. . . ."
12. Williams, *Texas' Last Frontier*, 343–347.
13. Monthly Return, Company D, Frontier Battalion, June 1892, TSA.
14. Ibid.; Alexander, *Winchester Warriors*, 253; Tanner and Tanner, "Lon Oden: The Rhymin' Ranger," 13; Cox, *Texas Ranger Tales*, 97–98; Captain Jones to AG Mabry, July 1, 1892, TSA.

15. M.R. Danniel to AG Mabry, May ?, 1892, TSA; multi-page list of charges against B.L. Outlaw, May ?, 1892, TSA. The exact date these documents were written is close but imprecise; however, a handwritten notation by the adjutant general indicates his office was reviewing them for possible administrative action on June 9, 1892.
16. Ibid.
17. Monthly Returns, Company D, Frontier Battalion, July and August 1892, TSA. The reader desirous of learning more about the aforementioned Stillwell Ranch in the Big Bend Country, would quite naturally be referred to the classic little tome, *I'll Gather My Geese* by Hallie Crawford Stillwell. For the fascinating biographical profile of and narrative about the tragic death of Texas Ranger William P. Stillwell, the reader is referred to Alexander's *Riding Lucifer's Line*, Chapter 18, 254–266.
18. Monthly Return, Company D, Frontier Battalion, September 1892, TSA.
19. James M. Day, "El Paso's Texas Rangers," *Password*, Winter 1979, 167.
20. Ibid.
21. Captain Jones to AG Mabry, September 30, 1892, TSA: ". . . I will be married on the 3rd proximo at Ysleta to a daughter of Col Baylor, and want to run down to San Antonio after my little girl." AG Mabry to Captain Jones, October 3, 1892, TSA: "Replying to the interesting part of Said letter I heartily congratulate you on the approaching nuptials & wish you and Mrs. Jones all the happiness & long life deservedly."
22. Captain Jones to AG Mabry, June 21, 1892, TSA.
23. Captain Jones to AG Mabry, September 18, 1892, TSA.
24. Undoubtedly the Company D commander was somewhat growing weary of Rangers opting for less than professional off-duty conduct. See Captain Jones to AG Mabry, December 1, 1892, TSA: "I discharged private [E.H.] Hart on account of general unfitness. He drinks considerably and did not pay his debts." Also, Monthly Return, Company D, Frontier Battalion, December 1892, TSA.
25. Oden, *Texas Ranger's Diary and Scrapbook*, 40.
26. AG Mabry to Captain Jones, September 27, 1892, TSA.
27. Monthly Return, Company D, Frontier Battalion, September 1892, TSA. For a thumbnail biographical sketch of Carl Kirchner, see Stephens, *Texas Ranger Sketches*, 77–80.

28. Captain Jones to AG Mabry, August 3, 1892, TSA; AG Mabry to Captain Jones, August 5, 1892, TSA; Monthly Return, Company D, Frontier Battalion, September 1892, TSA.
29. El Paso County Criminal Case 1485, *State of Texas vs. Bass Outlaw*. Copy of the legal document (which appears to be a receipt for property confiscated) is courtesy of knowledgeable researcher and writer Frank Jardim, an author specializing in particular firearms and/or corollary issues. For the text in hand, this writer not being an Old West artifact or photo collector, defers regarding ownership and/or provenance matters to those who are masters of their craft. The noted—and ever gracious—Old West firearms collector James H. Earle now owns the particularized Merwin and Hulbert revolver, see photos accompanying this text.
30. For the most part it appears that Baz's career as a lonesome Big Bend County treasure hunter may be traced to the reprint of Cunningham's story about Baz Outlaw in the January 28, 1928, edition of *Frontier Times*, followed up quite naturally in his oft-cited *Triggernometry: A Gallery of Gunfighters*. From that well, so it seems, the windlass has turned and buckets of misinformation have been splashed across pages of melodramatic Old West narratives, pieces undoubtedly not immune to creative writing, invented dialogue, and myth maintenance; Wayne, "The Fast Guns of Bass Outlaw," 38: "The little man [Baz Outlaw] took many mysterious rides out of Alpine after this, returning to sit and brood over his whiskey glass." Walker, "Bass Outlaw, Renegade Ranger," 52: "The little man [Baz Outlaw] took many mysterious rides out of Alpine after this, returning to sit and brood over his whiskey glass." Identicalness of the quotations, the first appearing in a June 1972 edition of *Great West* and the latter in the August 1979 edition of *Oldtimers Wild West* as quoted herein, would be troubling were it not amusing. Whether the like articles were written by the same person with application of a pseudonym, or the later piece plagiarized from the former is—in the final analysis of legit history—meaningless. The preeminent authority on Old West magazines, Larry J. Walker, Proprietor, The Magazine House, La Pine, Oregon, was also somewhat puzzled—though not surprised—by this, apparently purposeful, contradiction, relating as much to author during a pleasant and productive September 30, 2014, telephone interview. Primary source documents clearly reveal that Sergeant Outlaw was very much a part of the investigation, chase, and prosecution of the train robbers.

Therefore, it would seem highly unlikely—especially after the debriefing and plea agreement with defendant Lansford and sworn testimony of trainmen and express messengers—that there would be much credence to be given ideas or gossip of supposed buried loot in the lonesome Big Bend Country or elsewhere along the Rio Grande's twists and tangles. However, Cunningham was accurate with regards to specifically identifying Jim Gillett's 1873 Winchester by Serial Number 13401 in his piece "Bass Outlaw: The Little Wolf" for the Summer 1971 edition of *Badman*. Such specificity makes for an engaging sidebar, but that tidbit in and of itself is wholly devoid of propping up the treasure hunting scenario with unbending legs. Interestingly, this particular Winchester is a part of the remarkable Jim Gillett exhibit at the Texas Legislature's officially designated repository for the Texas Rangers, the TRHF&M. The ever gracious and always accommodating Shelly Crittendon, Collections Manager and her equally conscientious assistant, Kate McCarthy, advised the author that this particular Winchester has been a part of the museum's remarkable collection since 1968.

31. Monthly Return, Company D, Frontier Battalion, December 1892, TSA: "Dec 20—Prvt Fulgham accompanied by Dpty U.S. Marshal Outlaw to the Rio Grande in search of smuggled horses. . . ." September 30, 2014, interview with David S. Turk, Historian, United States Marshals Service, Washington, D.C. by author. Though it's generally written that Baz Outlaw received his initial appointment as a Deputy U.S. Marshal from Richard Clayton "Dick" Ware, such is not borne out by careful attention to chronology. Ware would not become U.S. Marshal for the Western District of Texas—a recess appointment—until April 25, 1893, subsequent to Baz Outlaw's commissioning as a federal deputy. Upon Ware's taking office he continued Outlaw's appointment as a part-time Deputy U.S. Marshal. Also refer to below citation.
32. Deputy U.S. Marshal B.L. Outlaw to AG Mabry, December 31, 1892, TSA.
33. Petition submitted to AG Mabry on Brewster County Sheriff letterhead stationery, December 31, 1892, signed J.B. Gillett *et al.*: "The undersigned Citizens & County officials respectfully request that you appoint B.L. Outlaw a Special of Capt. Jones Company," in TSA. A brief biographical sketch of Caruthers is found in Stephens' *Texas Ranger Indian War Pensions*, 19.
34. Captain Jones to AG Mabry, December 30, 1892, TSA.

35. AG Mabry to Captain Jones, January 2, 1893, TSA.
36. Bill O'Neal, *Best of the West*, 54–55.
37. U.S. Deputy Marshal Outlaw to AG Mabry, January 26, 1893, TSA.
38. Oath of Office, B.L. Outlaw, Special Ranger, TSA; For more regarding William Ward Turney the interested reader is referred to J. Morgan Broaddus, *The Legal Heritage of El Paso*, 169–180.
39. Special Ranger Baz Outlaw to AG Mabry, April 3, 1893, TSA; Monthly Return, Company D, Frontier Battalion, May 1893, TSA.
40. Special Ranger Outlaw to AG Mabry April 30, 1893, TSA.
41. Interview with U.S. Marshal Service's Historian Dave Turk, as cited.
42. In the main, nearly all works mentioning Baz Outlaw make reference to his appointment as a Deputy U.S. Marshal by the then U.S. Marshal Dick Ware.
43. Special Ranger Outlaw to AG Mabry, May 30, 1893, TSA; Monthly Return, Company D, Frontier Battalion, May 1893, TSA.
44. Robert M. Utley, *High Noon in Lincoln: Violence on the Western Frontier*, 176.

Chapter 10 Undaunted Courage and Fine Generalship

1. John Humphries to Baz Outlaw, June 22, 1893, in HML&HC.
2. Ibid.
3. Readers interested in a more inclusive examination of the political maneuverings and analysis of criminal intelligence that fostered Company D's deployment to El Paso County and a cursory genealogical peek at the Olguin crime family may wish to consult Alexander's *Six-Shooters and Shifting Sands*, particularly Chapter 15, "Boys, I'm Killed."
4. The actual events of this particular incident—a truly horrific gunfight between bandits and Rangers—are also covered in detail, based on primary source documents, in Alexander's *Riding Lucifer's Line*, Chapter 9, 127–138.
5. Telegram, Special Ranger Outlaw to AG Mabry, June 30, 1893, TSA.
6. Special Ranger Outlaw to AG Mabry, July 2, 1893, TSA.
7. Sheriff Frank B. Simmons, El Paso County, to Governor Hogg, July 7, 1893, TSA; Parsons, *Captain John R. Hughes*, puzzlingly proffers: "Sheriff Simmons did not realize that Kirchner had recovered the body, and anticipated trouble in attempting to do so." 87; In real time Corporal Carl

Kirchner certainly wasn't confused: "We [an editorial 'we'] then made a demand on the chief officer at Juarez, Mex. Who acted very nicely (I am told by Sheriff Simmons who made the demands) & ordered the body delivered to us at the State line." See, Corporal Carl Kirchner to AG Mabry, July 2, 1893, TSA; Nor were newspapermen at faraway Dallas, Texas, baffled: The *Dallas Morning News* of July 1, 1893, picking up the story from El Paso, reported: "The sheriff's posse and rangers returned to Ysleta and El Paso this evening with the body of Capt. Frank Jones of the rangers, who was killed across the Mexican line yesterday morning at sunrise, while in pursuit of a gang of smugglers and murderers in the bosque, twelve miles below San Elizario in this county." And the edition of July 2, 1893: "The murder of Capt. Frank Jones by Mexicans yesterday morning is still causing much excitement on the border. The sheriff's posse, which made a demand on the Mexicans for Capt. Jones' body, met with refusal, backed by 100 armed Mexicans. Sheriff Simmons was taken by a special train to Juarez, Mexico, where he made a request on the Mexican war department for the necessary aid and the lieutenant commanding at once repaired to the scene of trouble with a troop of cavalry and gave the sheriff the necessary help, which secured the body at 11 a.m." Additionally, the *Dallas Morning News* of December 19, 1893: ". . . Sheriff F.B. Simmons of El Paso county was in the city yesterday. It was he who on the 30th of last June recovered the body of Capt Frank Jones, who was killed at Tres Jacales, in the state of Chihuahua, Mexico. " Also, C. L. Sonnichsen, *Pass of the North: Four Centuries on the Rio Grande*: "Next day Sheriff Simmons and a posse demanded the body of the dead Captain, but got nowhere until the Mexican authorities were asked to help. Lieutenant Rafael García Martínez, the Juárez *jefe politico*, rode with Simmons down the Mexican side of the border with a Mexican police escort. They had better luck than they expected, for not only did they bring home the body of Captain Jones—they met three members of the gang making their way out of the brush and rounded them up without a fight." 315.

8. Numerous are the archived telegrams supporting the candidacy of Sergeant John Hughes to replace Captain Jones as commander of Company D. That most carry exactly the same date of submission would clearly suggest that they were not spontaneously inspired, but were part of a politically coordinated and orchestrated movement. That said, however, does not and should not distract from the fact John Hughes was well

thought of and owned considerable support. That his backers were willing to put their name on the dotted line in his behalf is revealing.

9. Sergeant Hughes to AG Mabry, July 5, 1893, TSA.
10. Special Ranger Outlaw to AG Mabry, July 5, 1893, TSA.
11. Petition to AG Mabry from citizens of Brewster County in support of Baz Outlaw being named captain of Company D, Frontier Battalion, July 3, 1893, signed, W. Van Sickle, County Judge, *et al., TSA.*
12. Petition from citizens of Ysleta, El Paso County in support of Sergeant John R. Hughes being named captain of Company D, Frontier Battalion, July [?] 1893, signed, Tom smith, *et al.*, TSA.
13. George W. Baylor to AG Mabry, July 5, 1893. Interestingly, in this same letter George W. Baylor bemoans the fact that several years before his company of Rangers had been disbanded: "but having had my own feelings deeply wounded by the action of Genl King in disbanding my Co. without even having made any charge against me or giving me any chance to refute one (and I don't know to this day why it was done). . . ." in TSA.
14. Sheriff Ira Aten, Castro County, to AG Mabry, July 10, 1893, TSA.
15. Corporal Carl Kirchner, Company D, Frontier Battalion to AG Mabry, July 5, 1893, TSA; Petition to AG Mabry, July 5, 1893: "We the undersigned members of Co 'D' Frontier Battalion heartily recommend & endorse our 1st Sergt John R. Hughes for the appointment as Captain to fill the vacancy caused by the death of our Gallant Capt. Frank Jones. We know Mr. Hughes to be of sober & industrious habits & a good officer." Signed, Corporal Carl Kirchner, and Ranger Privates J.V. Latham, E.D. Aten, J.W. Fulgham, Robt. Speaks, T.F. Tucker, Ike Herrin, J.W. Saunders, and R.E. Bryant, TSA.
16. Captain John R. Hughes to AG Mabry, July 8, 1893, TSA.
17. Special Ranger Outlaw to AG Mabry, July 15, 1893, TSA.
18. Telegram, Special Ranger Outlaw to AG Mabry, July 16, 1893, TSA.
19. Ibid.; Special Ranger Outlaw to AG Mabry July 15, 1893, TSA.
20. A recounting of this extraordinarily interesting story, which offers an unvarnished look at the application of criminal justice—or lack of justice—in early day Kimble County may be accessed in Rose's exhaustively researched *The Reckoning,* 144–163.
21. Ibid.; Monthly Return, Company D, Frontier Battalion, August 1893, TSA.
22. Special Ranger Outlaw to AG Mabry, July 31, 1893, TSA; Monthly Return, Company D, Frontier Battalion, August 1893. Though Special Ranger

Outlaw's arrest of Dunman and Baker had taken place on July 15 and 21, 1893, respectively, they were officially recorded in this, the Monthly Return for August 1893, TSA.

23. Special Ranger Outlaw to AG Mabry, September 6, 1893, TSA.
24. Special Ranger Outlaw to AG Mabry, September 30, 1893 and October 30, 1893, TSA.
25. Special Ranger Outlaw to AG Mabry, November 1, 1893, TSA.
26. Sheriff D.W. Gourley, Brewster County, to Captain John R. Hughes, November 7, 1893, TSA.
27. Special Ranger Outlaw to AG Mabry, November 29, 1893, TSA.
28. Captain Hughes to Captain G.A. Wheatley, Frontier Battalion Quartermaster, November 25, 1893, TSA.
29. Captain Hughes to AG Mabry, November 30, 1893, TSA.
30. John Ernest Gregg, "The History of Presidio County," *Voice of the Mexican Border*, Centennial Edition, 1936. This particular edition reprints—absent endnotes—Gregg's 1933 Master of Arts Thesis for the University of Texas, under the direction of Walter Prescott Webb. Ernest Gregg's characterization of J.M. Dean, in part, reveals: "J.M. Dean had acquired the land around the [railroad] station of Marfa. . . . The man who owned the section of land whereon Marfa is now located wanted a county seat on his section, and he proceeded to move the county seat of Presidio County from Fort Davis to Marfa. It is not our desire to condemn or criticize this departed individual; we are merely stating the facts in the case. He was accused by some for ruthless, selfish acts. This we know, he forced his way, but he was always witty and amusing, and his sins, public and private, are easily forgotten," see pages 55, 77.
31. Monthly Returns, Company D, Frontier Battalion, November and December 1893, TSA; Special Ranger Outlaw to AG Mabry, December 27, 1893, TSA.

Chapter 11 In Arrest When He Died

1. *El Paso Times*, June 25, 1916: "At the time it was called 'Hell Paso'. . . ."; Richard Selcer, ed., *Legendary Watering Holes: The Saloons That Made Texas Famous*, Contributor for Chapter 3, "Ben Dowell's Saloon and the 'Monte Carlo of the West' (El Paso)," Nancy Hamilton, 123–168; Haley, *Jeff Milton*, 209.

2. Leon C. Metz, *Turning Points in El Paso Texas,* 76: "Prostitution flourished for approximately fifty years, and the city controlled it with $5 fines per girl each month, a form of licensing." John Selman, Jr. penned a manuscript titled, *John Selman of El Paso* (in the El Paso Public Library), in which he specifically elaborates though he doubles author Metz's dollar amount: "All of these women [prostitutes] were checked upon. For this purpose we had a policeman, an old fellow by the name of Johnson. He looked like the picture you see of Saint Peter with his snow-white beard, but the girls could not fool him. Johnson collected a ten dollar fine once a month and in return he protected them from the Juarez girls who were inclined to come over the river on Saturday nights and muscle in on the profits. The money Johnson collected in this way payed [*sic*] the police and firemen of El Paso," 61.
3. H. Gordon Frost, *The Gentlemen's Club: The Story of Prostitution In El Paso*, 97.
4. Sonnichsen, *Pass of the North*, 283–295. Utah Street is now South Mesa. See Harriot Howze Jones, ed., *El Paso A Centennial Portrait*, contributor Levin L. Lee, "The Names of El Paso Streets," page 147. For *Jeff Milton,* author Haley writes that Tillie Howard opened up her Utah Street brothel by dipping into her monetary reserves of "$65,000 in cash, an impressive adornment of jewels, and a beautiful tiger skin that she sentimentally cherished all her days," see page 215. Apparently in offering comments regarding these treasures author Haley is referencing Tillie Howard's return to El Paso, subsequent to her extensive worldwide travels. Frost, *The Gentlemen's Club*, pages 72–79, also offers numerical figures for Tillie Howard's financial investments in whorehouse property and accoutrements.
5. Oden, *Texas Ranger's Diary and Scrapbook*, 21–22.
6. John Selman, Jr., manuscript, *John Selman of El Paso*: "I will speak a word here about Tillie Howard. As a police officer I had occasion to know her quite well. . . . I passed her 'house' on Utah Street one evening as she was sitting on her front steps. She said: 'Hello, Kid. Are you on this beat?' Then she told me that any time I heard a loud noise or disturbance in her house all I had to do was call it to her attention and she would see to it that it did not occur again. She ran a square place, and all she asked was a square deal . . . ," 61–62.
7. Oden, *Texas Ranger's Diary and Scrapbook*, 21–22: "They are paid a straight salary. Tillie thinks this is more protection for the girls, and she

thinks it also keeps them honest; on commission they are sometimes inclined to cheat." Leon Metz, in a classic and refreshingly readable treatment of one of Texas' most notorious frontier era murderers, *John Wesley Hardin: Dark Angel of Texas*, particularly identifies Baz Outlaw's favorite *nymph du pave* as Ruby, then turning tricks at Tillie Howard's brothel, see page 226. Attentive readers are cautioned to review works about John Wesley Hardin with fitting circumspection, as much written about him is questionable from a factual platform and, even in the twenty-first century, unsupported melodrama and worshipful speculation seems to be no stranger in recreating somewhat stilted portraits of the implacable killer.

8. J. Marvin Hunter, ed., "The Killing of Bass Outlaw." Here Hunter is quoting in full an article he asserts appeared in the April 5, 1894, edition of the *El Paso Tribune*. Clearly the meat of the article and quotations from the Inquest testimony are solid, but there seems to be a discrepancy with the article's date as presented by Hunter, it being a day or two premature of the events described, perhaps result of an innocent typo.
9. *El Paso Daily Times*, April 6, 1894.
10. Rasch, "Bass Outlaw: Myth and Man," 15.
11. Special Ranger Outlaw to AG Mabry, February 4, 1894, TSA.
12. Captain Hughes to AG Mabry, February 22, 1894, TSA.
13. Special Ranger Outlaw to AG Mabry, March 1, 1894, TSA.
14. For the Western Federal Judicial District, there were four Divisions: San Antonio, meeting in May and November; Austin meeting in February and August; Brownsville, meeting in January and July; and as mentioned in this text, El Paso meeting in April and October.
15. J.E. Hulse, *Texas Lawyer: The Life of William H. Burges*, 25.
16. For more than a cursory look at Behan the reader may choose to access Bob Alexander's *John H. Behan: Sacrificed Sheriff* a womb to tomb treatment with rather extensive endnotes.
17. *El Paso Herald*, November 1, 1922.
18. National Archives RG 36, Customs Agents Division, John H. Behan, El Paso, Texas, official activity report to Washington, D.C. headquarters, March 2, 1894. The investigation into the alleged opium smuggling case is found in Behan's report of January 2, 1894.
19. Alexander, *John H. Behan*, 240.

20. Hunter, "The Killing of Bass Outlaw," 84.
21. Oden, *Texas Ranger's Diary and Scrapbook*. 40.
22. Ibid. For not only a delightful but informative look at the professionalization of frontier-era bartenders, readers would be advised to access the fascinating contribution of Byron Johnson and Sharon Peregrine Johnson, "The Fine Art of Mixology," Chapter 1, in the previously cited *Legendary Watering Holes*, 43–51.
23. Allen G. Hatley, *Texas Constables: A Frontier Heritage*. John Selman was popularly elected constable, and began such service on November 23, 1892. See pages 72–73.
24. Frank Collinson, *Life in the Saddle*, Mary Whatley Clarke, ed., 93.
25. *El Paso Daily Times*, April 6, 1894; Richard C. Marohn, in his thoroughly researched and insightful biography free of speculative melodrama, *The Last Gunfighter: John Wesley Hardin*, also confirms Selman's official law enforcing status: "He was elected El Paso Constable in November 1892," see page 260.
26. Haley, *Jeff Milton*, 217.
27. Typescript, Jeff Davis Milton interviews, by historians J. Evetts Haley, Harold Bugbee, and Hervey Chesley, December 8–22, 1938, HML&HC.
28. Leon Claire Metz, *John Selman: Texas Gunfighter*, 131. Mentions of John Selman are numerous within the body of literary work focused on the Old West's outlaws and lawmen. Metz's treatment, however, is a full-fledged biography. Interested readers may also wish to access the exceptional work of noted author Robert K. DeArment, in *George Scarborough: The Life and Death of a Lawman on the Closing Frontier* and *Bravo of the Brazos: John Larn of Fort Griffin*. Both of DeArment's volumes include important biographical and thoughtful analytical material regarding John Selman's numerous adventures and misadventures in the Southwest.
29. Collinson, *Life in the Saddle*, 97–98.
30. Ibid. Quite wittily, Frank J. Mangan in his delightful little tome, *Bordertown: The Life and Times of El Paso del Norte*, page 99, caps off the characterization of many frontier era shootists: "Even though some of them were criminals, they had a different code from the men on today's wanted list. They didn't use dynamite or bullet-proof vests or push old ladies down stairs. They carried the fight to the enemy in person. And they weren't afraid to die."

31. Hunter, "The Killing of Bass Outlaw," 84.
32. Bob Boze Bell, "Cathouse Melee: Bass Outlaw vs. John Selman," *True West*, Travel Annual, 2003, page 74; Bill O'Neal, "Bass Outlaw vs. John Selman and Joe McKidrict," *True West*, October 1988, 68–69. Tillie Howard would tell a reporter for the *El Paso Tribune*: "When I heard him shoot I thought he was after me and I called the police [blew the whistle]."
33. A biographical sketch of Ranger Joe McKidrict may be accessed in Alexander's *Riding Lucifer's Line*, 139–145. Also, Stephens' *Texas Ranger Sketches*, 91–92. Joe McKidrict's father had been killed by Indians, and his mother remarried to prominent Austin attorney and state legislator Albert O. "Alby" Cooley. Though not formally adopted, in and around Austin young Joe McKidrict was known by his stepfather's surname, which has led to no little biographical confusion. His correct name is McKidrict, and in adulthood and as a Texas Ranger that is the name he reverted to. Also see, Stephens' *Bullets and Buckshot in Texas*, 43; *Dallas Morning News*, April 6, 1894: "Joseph McKidrict was a ranger of Company D, now stationed at Ysleta, and was known as 'Buckskin Joe.'" Perhaps it should also be noted that occasionally Texas Ranger devotees wish to disregard Baz Outlaw's official standing with the Frontier Battalion at this point—for this episode—making especial note that he was, indeed, at the time it happened a Deputy U.S. Marshal. Likewise, sometimes aficionados of the U.S. Marshals Service choose to emphasize Baz Outlaw was yet commissioned by the State of Texas as a Special Ranger. Captain Hughes, who would know, succinctly offers clarification in his April 6, 1894, message to the adjutant general: "B.L. Outlaw who held a commission as Deputy U.S. Marshal of the western District of Texas and was also a special Ranger attached to Co. 'D' Frontier Batt," in the TSA.
34. Hunter, "The Killing of Bass Outlaw," 83.
35. *El Paso Daily Times*, April 6, 1894.
36. Ibid. As would be expected, the newsy story was also carried in other Texas newspapers, such as the *Austin Daily Statesman*, also on April 6, 1894; Collinson, *Life in the Saddle*, 97: "While there [Fort Davis, Texas] he [John Selman] nearly died with smallpox, but was nursed back to life by a Mexican woman. He was deeply pitted for the rest of his days." DeArment, *George Scarborough*, 66: "His [Selman] face badly pitted and his body wasted by the smallpox ordeal. . . ."
37. Ibid.; *The McKinney Democrat*, April 12, 1894.

38. Captain Hughes to AG Mabry, April 6, 1894, TSA; Monthly Return, Company D, Frontier Battalion, April 1894, TSA; also, Telegram from Hughes to Mabry, same date, TSA. The telegram was repeated verbatim in the April 7, 1894, edition of the *Austin Daily News*:

> Joe McMidrick [*sic*] a member of Co D was killed tonight while attempting to arrest B L Outlaw Outlaw is dead also

For an insightful look at the extraordinarily altered Colt's six-shooter Outlaw was using in this instance an interested reader is referred to the fascinating piece by Frank Jardim, "Bass Outlaw's Arsenal," *Guns of the Old West*, Summer 2015, 18–23. Also see, Robert E. McNellis, "Bass Outlaw: Lawless Lawman," *Guns Magazine*, December 1976, 46–47. For additional information on what were referred to as "slip guns" the engrossed reader may also wish to review John Tappin's article, "The Croft/Keith Slip Gun" as published in the April 2015 edition of *Guns Magazine*, 89–90.

39. Captain Hughes to AG Mabry, April 6, 1894, TSA. For an informative article length piece about the law-enforcing life of Frank McMahan, an interested reader is referred to researcher and writer Doug Dukes' exceptionally helpful "Frank McMahan: In Custody," as published in the August 2009 edition of the *Wild West History Association Journal*, 36–39.

40. *El Paso Daily Times*, April 6, 1894; Alexander, *Riding Lucifer's Line*, 144. For his manuscript treatment, *John Selman of El Paso*, John Selman, Jr.—who was actually at his father's bedside—identifies the physician treating his wounded daddy as Doctor Alward White. That the seriously injured El Paso County constable was attended to by more than one medical practitioner is not and should not be surprising.

41. Hunter, "The Killing of Bass Outlaw," 84.

42. *El Paso Times*, April 6, 1894.

43. Ibid.

44. Bill O'Neal, "The Latest on 'Bass' Outlaw," *Real West*, August 1982, page 43. Author O'Neal offers insightful musical clarification, stating that the "Streets of Laredo" was originally "a chanty about an English soldier dying of the pox, which, like other British songs, had been adapted by American cowboys."

45. Frost, *The Gentlemen's Club*, 96.

46. *El Paso Times*, April 6, 1894. During an enlightening and pleasurable interview with Robert Ernst, author of *Deadly Affrays: The Violent Deaths of the*

U.S. Marshals, and also a Research Consultant for the U.S. Marshals Museum (ground broken, facility yet to be completed and opened for spectators) in Fort Smith, Arkansas, revealed the following: That he is also on the committee regarding the U.S. Marshals Wall of Honor and for that memorial as well as a particularized alphabetical biographical profile in *Deadly Affrays*, Baz Outlaw's name was/is purposefully omitted. The logic was forthright and uncomplicated: Admittedly Baz Outlaw was a part-time Deputy U.S. Marshal when killed at El Paso and, just as factually, when he murdered Texas Ranger Joe McKidrict at Tillie Howard's whorehouse he was not acting in accord with his responsibilities as a duly commissioned federal officer. The Wall of Honor and a specific profile within *Deadly Affrays* was/is reserved and designed to honorably and appreciatively memorialize the U.S. Marshals and their deputies killed in the line of duty.

47. Captain Hughes to AG Mabry, April 6, 1894, TSA. Not unexpectedly occasionally conspiracy theorists spin their webs, as weak as the conjecture may be. The unknown author writing the Foreword for *The Killing of Bass Outlaw* offers conformation: "Some say that 'the Rangers' killed Bass Outlaw to revenge the slaying of Joe McKidrict. It has also been said that John Selman killed both McKidrict and Outlaw. In the letter reproduced here, Captain John Hughes gives his version of the affair, and he wasn't one to file a false official report."
48. According to several sources, and there is a paper trail confirming same, Tom C. Powell, proprietor of the Star Stables and Undertaking Parlor, was awarded possession of Baz Outlaw's three recoverable firearms, the engraved Colt's six-shooter and Winchester (probably in his hotel room) and the Colt's slip gun he was carrying at the time of his death, in lieu of the undertaker's embalming and burial fees submitted to El Paso County for settlement. For photographic copy of the court ordered transfer of Baz Outlaw's firearms, see, McNellis, "Bass Outlaw: Lawless Lawman," 47. For additional information on Outlaw's weapons, also see Jardim, "Bass Outlaw's Arsenal," 19–23. Of the firearms that may be at one time or another conclusively placed in Baz Outlaw's hands, all are accounted for: Two handguns in private collections and two (a Winchester and handgun) at The Frazier History Museum. Another Winchester, one that may or may not have actually been borrowed by Baz Outlaw from Ranger/Sheriff James B. Gillett, is on display at the Texas Ranger Hall of Fame & Museum.
49. Milton to Haley, Bugbee, and Chesley, as cited during December 1938, HML&HC.

Bibliography

Non-published sources—manuscripts, typescripts, theses, dissertations, tape recordings, official documents, courthouse records, tax rolls, petitions, correspondence, prison records, census records, licensing records, interviews, etc—are cited with specificity in chapter endnotes.

Books:

Adams, Ramon F. *Western Words: A Dictionary of the Old West.* New York: Hippocrene Books, 1998.

Alexander, Bob. *Six-Shooters and Shifting Sands: The Wild West Life of Ranger Captain Frank Jones.* Denton: University of North Texas Press, 2015.

________. *Bad Company and Burnt Powder: Justice and Injustice in the Old Southwest.* Denton: University of North Texas Press, 2014.

________. *Riding Lucifer's Line: Ranger Deaths along the Texas-Mexico Border.* Denton: University of North Texas Press, 2013.

________. *Rawhide Ranger, Ira Aten: Enforcing Law on the Texas Frontier.* Denton: University of North Texas Press, 2011.

________. *Winchester Warriors: Texas Rangers of Company D, 1874–1901.* Denton: University of North Texas Press, 2009.

________. *Lynch Ropes and Long Shots: The Story of an Old West Train Robbery.* Silver City, NM: High-Lonesome Books, 2006.

________. *Fearless Dave Allison: Border Lawman.* Silver City, NM: High-Lonesome Books, 2003.

________. *Lawmen, Outlaws, and S.O.Bs.* Silver City, NM: High-Lonesome Books, 2004.

________. *Lawmen, Outlaws, and S.O.Bs.* Vol. II. Silver City, NM: High-Lonesome Books, 2007.

________. *John H. Behan: Sacrificed Sheriff.* Silver City, NM: High-Lonesome Books, 2002.

Anderson, Gary Clayton.*The Conquest of Texas: Ethnic Cleansing in the Promised Land,1820–1875*. Norman: University of Oklahoma Press, 2005.

Ashford, Gerald. *Spanish Texas, Yesterday and Today*. Austin, TX: Jenkins Publishing Company, 1971.

Awbrey, Betty Dooley, and Claude Dooley. *Why Stop? A Guide to Texas Historical Roadside Markers*. Houston, TX: Lone Star Books, 1978.

Ball, Larry D. *The United States Marshals of New Mexico & Arizona Territories, 1846–1912*. Albuquerque: University of New Mexico Press, 1978.

________. *Desert Lawmen: The High Sheriffs of New Mexico and Arizona, 1846–1912*. Albuquerque: University of New Mexico Press, 1992.

Baugh, Virgil E. *A Pair of Texas Rangers: Bill McDonald and John Hughes*. Washington, DC: Potomac Corral, The Westerners, 1970.

Baylor George W. *Into the Far, Wild Country: True Tales of the Old Southwest*. Jerry D. Thompson, ed. El Paso: Texas Western Press, University of Texas at El Paso, 1996.

Baker, T. Lindsay. *Ghost Towns of Texas*. Norman: University of Oklahoma Press, 1986.

Bennett, Joseph E. *Sixguns and Masons: Profiles of Selected Rangers and Prominent Westerners*. Highland Springs, VA: Anchor Communications, 1991.

Blackburn Jr., ed. *Wanted: Historic County Jails of Texas*. College Station: Texas A&M University Press, 2006.

Boddie, John B., ed. *Historical Southern Families*. Baltimore, MD: Genealogical Publishing Company, 1994.

Brice, Donaly E., and Barry Crouch. *The Governor's Hounds: The Texas State Police, 1870–1873*. Austin: University of Texas Press, 2011.

________. *The Great Comanche Raid: Boldest Indian Attack of the Texas Republic*. Austin, TX: Eakin Press, 1987.

________, and Chuck Parsons. *Texas Ranger N.O. Reynolds: The Intrepid*. Denton: University of North Texas Press, 2014.

Broaddus, J. Morgan. *The Legal Heritage of El Paso*. El Paso, TX: Texas Western Press, University of Texas at El Paso, 1963.

Browning, James M. *Violence Was No Stranger: A Guide to the Grave Sites of Famous Westerners*. Stillwater, OK: Barbed Wire Press, 1993.

________. *Violence Was No Stranger*. Vol. II. Janice B. McCravy, ed. Douglasville, GA: Self published, n.d.

Burton, Jeffrey. *The Deadliest Outlaws: The Ketchum Gang and the Wild Bunch.* Denton: University of North Texas Press, 2009.

_________. *Dynamite and Six-Shooter*. Santa Fe, NM: Palomino Press, 1970.

_________. *Western Story*. European Edition. England: Palamino Books, 2008.

Caldwell, Clifford R., and Ron DeLord. *Texas Lawmen: The Good and the Bad, 1835–1899*. Charleston, SC: The History Press, 2011.

Casey, Clifford B. *Mirages, Mysteries and Reality: Brewster County Texas, The Big Bend of the Rio Grande*. Hereford, TX: Pioneer Books Publishers, 1973.

Casey, Robert J. *The Texas Border: And Some Borderliners*. Indianapolis, IN: The Bobbs-Merrill Company, 1950.

Collinson, Frank. *Life in the Saddle*. Mary Whatley Clarke, ed. Norman: University of Oklahoma Press, 1963.

Coolidge, Dane. *Fighting Men of the West*. New York: E.P. Dutton and Company, 1932.

Cox, Mike. *The Texas Rangers: Wearing the Cinco Peso, 1821–1900*. New York: Forge Books, 2008.

_________. *Texas Ranger Tales: Stories That Need Telling*. Plano, TX: Republic of Texas Press, 1997.

Cunningham, Eugene. *Triggernometry: A Gallery of Gunfighters*. Caldwell, ID: The Caxton Press, 1956.

Dasher, Wayne, and Judy Dasher. *Cemeteries of Echols County, Georgia*. Statenville, GA: Echols County Historical Society, 2004.

Davis, John L. *The Texas Rangers: Their First 150 Years*. San Antonio, TX: Institute of Texan Cultures, University of Texas at San Antonio, 1975.

DeArment, Robert K. *Bravo of the Brazos: John Larn of Fort Griffin, Texas*. Norman: University of Oklahoma Press, 2002.

________. *George Scarborough: The Life and Death of a Lawman on the Closing Frontier*. Norman: University of Oklahoma Press, 1992.

DeLord, Ronald G., ed. *The Ultimate Sacrifice: Trials and Triumphs of the Texas Peace Officer*. Austin, TX: Police Officers Memorial Fund, 2000.

Devereaux, Jan. *Pistols, Petticoats, and Poker: The Real Lottie Deno, No Lies or Alibis*. Silver City, NM: High-Lonesome Books, 2008.

Dewey, Alicia M. *Pesos and Dollars: Entrepreneurs In The Texas-Mexico Borderlands, 1880–1940*. College Station: Texas A&M University Press, 2014.

Dillon, Richard. *Wells, Fargo Detective: A Biography of James B. Hume*. Reno: University of Nevada Press, 1986.

Douglas, C.L. *The Gentlemen in the White Hats: Dramatic Episodes in the History of the Texas Rangers*. Dallas, TX: South-West Press, 1934.

DuCoin, Candice. *Lawmen on the Texas Frontier: Rangers and Sheriffs*. Round Rock, TX: Riata Books, 2007.

Dumont, Ella Elgar Bird. *Ella Elgar Bird Dumont: An Autobiography of a West Texas Pioneer*. Tommy J. Boley, ed. Austin: University of Texas Press, 1988.

Ernst, Robert, and Stumph, George R. *Deadly Affrays: The Violent Deaths of the U.S. Marshals*. n.p: Scarlet Mask, 2006.

Fisher, O.C. *It Occurred in Kimble*. Houston, TX: The Anson Jones Press, 1937.

Frost, H. Gordon. *The Gentlemen's Club: The Story of Prostitution in El Paso*. El Paso, TX: Mangan Books, 1983.

Gammel, Hans Peter. *The Laws of Texas, 1822–1897*. 10 vols. Austin, TX: Gammel Books, 1898.

Gillett, James B. *Six Years with the Texas Rangers, 1875 to 1881*. New Haven, CT: Yale University Press, 1925.

Glasrud, Bruce A., and Harold J. Weiss, Jr., eds. *Tracking the Texas Rangers: The Nineteenth Century*. Denton: University of North Texas Press, 2012.

Glenn, Frankie Davis. *Capt'n John: Story of a Texas Ranger*. Austin, TX: Nortex Press, 1991.

Gournay, Luke. *Texas Boundaries: Evolution of the State's Counties*. College Station: Texas A&M University Press, 1995.

Haley, J. Evetts. *Jeff Milton: A Good Man with a Gun*. Norman: University of Oklahoma Press, 1948.

Harris III, Charles H., and Louis R. Sadler. *The Texas Rangers and the Mexican Revolution: The Bloodiest Decade, 1910–1920*. Albuquerque: University of New Mexico Press, 2004.

Hatley, Allen G. *Texas Constables: A Frontier Heritage*. Lubbock: Texas Tech University Press, 1999.

Hughes, Alton. *Pecos: A History of the Pioneer West*. Seagraves, TX: Pioneer Book Publishers, 1978.

Hewett, Janet B., ed. *The Roster of Confederate Soldiers, 1861–1865*. Vol. XII. Wilmington, NC: Broadfoot Publishing Company, 1996.

__________. *Georgia Confederate Soldiers, 1861–1865*. Vol. II. Wilmingon, NC: Broadfoot Publishing Company, 1998.

Hulse, J.E. *Texas Lawyer: The Life of William H. Burges*. El Paso, TX: Mangan Books, 1982.

Ivey, Darren L. *The Texas Rangers: A Registry and History*. Jefferson, NC: McFarland & Co., 2010.

Jacobson, Lucy Miller, and Mildred Bloys Nored. *Jeff Davis County, Texas*. Fort Davis, TX: Fort Davis Historical Society, 1993.

Johnson, David. *John Ringo, King of the Cowboys: His Life and Times from the Hoo Doo War to Tombstone*. Denton: University of North Texas Press, 2008.

__________. *The Horrell Wars: Feuding in Texas and New Mexico*. Denton: University of North Texas Press, 2014.

__________. *The Mason County "Hoo Doo" War, 1874–1902*. Denton: University of North Texas Press, 2006.

Jones, Harriot H., ed. *El Paso: A Centennial Portrait*. El Paso, TX; El Paso County Historical Society, 1973.

Justice, Glenn. *Little Known History of the Texas Big Bend: Documented Chronicles from Cabeza de Vaca to the Era of Pancho Villa*. Odessa, TX: Rimrock Press, 2001.

Kirkland, K.D. *Colt: America's Premier Gunmakers*. East Bridgewater, MA: World Publications Group, Inc., 2014.

________. *Winchester: America's Premier Gunmakers*. East Bridgewater, MA: World Publications Group, Inc., 2014.

Lynch, Sylvia D. *Aristocracy's Outlaw: The Doc Holliday Story*. New Tazewell, TN: Iris Press, 1994.

Madison, Virginia. *The Big Bend Country of Texas*. New York: October House, 1968.

Mangan, Frank J. *Bordertown: The Life and Times of El Paso del Norte*. El Paso, TX: Carl Hertzog, 1964.

Marohn, Richard C. *The Last Gunfighter: John Wesley Hardin*. College Station, TX: The Early West, Creative Publishing, 1995.

Martin, Jack. *Border Boss: Captain John R. Hughes—Texas Ranger*. Austin, TX: State House Press, 1990.

Metz, Leon C. *John Selman: Texas Gunfighter*. New York: Hasting House, 1966.

_________. *John Wesley Hardin: Dark Angel of Texas*. El Paso: Mangan Books, 1996.

_________. *Border: The U.S.-Mexico Line*. El Paso, TX: Mangan Books, 1990.

_________. *Encyclopedia of Lawmen, Outlaws, and Gunfighters*. New York: Checkmark Books, 2003.

_________. *Turning Points In El Paso, Texas*. El Paso, TX: Mangan Books, 1985.

_________. *The Shooters*. El Paso, TX: Mangan Books, 1976.

Michno, Gregory F. *Encyclopedia of Indian Wars: Western Battles and Skirmishes, 1850–1890*. Missoula, MT: Mountain Press Publishing, 2003.

_________. and Susan J. Michno. *Forgotten Fights: Little Known Raids and Skirmishes on the Frontier, 1823–1890*. Missoula, MT: Mountain Press Publishing, 2008.

_________. and Susan J. Michno. *A Fate Worse Than Death: Indian Captivities in the West, 1830–1885*. Caldwell, ID: Caxton Press, 2007.

Miles, Elton. *Stray Tales of the Big Bend*. College Station: Texas A&M University Press, 1993.

Miller, Rick.*Texas Ranger John B. Jones and the Frontier Battalion, 1873–1881*. Denton: University of North Texas Press, 2012.

_________. *Rube Burrow, Desperado*. Bloomington, IN: iUniverse LLC, 2014.

_________. *Sam Bass and Gang*. Austin, TX: State House Press, 1999.

Oden, Alonzo Van. *Texas Ranger's Diary and Scrapbook*. Ann Jensen, ed. Dallas, TX: The Kaleidograph Press, 1936.

O'Neal, Bill. *Encyclopedia of Western Gunfighters*. Norman: University of Oklahoma Press, 1979.

_________. *Best of the West*. Lincolnwood, IL: Publications International, Ltd., 2006.

Parsons, Chuck. *Captain John R. Hughes: Lone Star Ranger*. Denton: University of North Texas Press, 2011.

Prassel, Frank R. *The Western Peace Officer: A Legacy of Law and Order*. Norman: University of Oklahoma Press, 1972.

Preece, Harold. *Lone Star Man, Ira Aten: Last of the Old Texas Rangers*. New York: Hastings House, 1960.

Price, Bill S. *Bill Whitley:Outlaw*. Austin, TX: Nortex Press, 1995.

Price, Dorthy H., ed. *Chinkypin: 1, 2, 3 and Addendum*. Knoxville, TN: Echols County Historical Society, 2003.

Raht, Carlysle Graham. *The Romance of Davis Mountains and Big Bend Country*. Odessa, TX: The Rahtbooks Company, 1963.

Richardson, G.L. (Jack). *The Rest of the Story and Scrapbook of Alonzo Van Oden*. n.p: Self published, 1995.

Roberts, Gary L. *Doc Holliday: The Life and Legend*. Hoboken, NJ: John Wiley & Sons, 2006.

Rose, Peter R. *The Reckoning: The Triumph of Order on the Texas Outlaw Frontier*. Lubbock: Texas Tech University Press, 2012.

Rynning, Thomas. *Gun Notches: A Saga of a Frontier Lawman Captain Thomas H. Rynning as Told to Al Cohn and Joe Chisholm*. San Diego, CA: Frontier Heritage Press, 1971.

Sáenz, Andrés. *Early Tejano Ranching: Daily Life at Ranchos San José and El Fresnillo*. Andrés Tijerina, ed. College Station: Texas A&M University, 1999.

Selcer, Richard, ed. *Legendary Watering Holes: The Saloons That Made Texas Famous*. College Station: Texas A&M University Press, 2004.

Smith, Thomas Tyree. *Fort Inge: Sharps, Spurs, and Sabers on the Texas Frontier, 1849–1869*. Austin, TX: Eakin Press, 1993.

Sonnichsen, C.L. *Pass of the North: Four Centuries on the Rio Grande*. El Paso: Texas Western Press, University of Texas at El Paso, 1968.

__________. *I'll Die Before I'll Run: The Story of the Great Feuds of Texas*. Lincoln: University of Nebraska Press, 1964.

__________. *Outlaw on the Dodge With Baldy Russell*. Athens, OH: Swallow Press, 1965.

Sowell, A.J. *Early Settlers and Indian Fighters in Southwest Texas*. Austin, TX: State House Press, 1986.

Spellman, Paul N. *Captain J.A. Brooks: Texas Ranger*. Denton: University of North Texas Press, 2007.

__________. *Captain John H. Rogers, Texas Ranger*. Denton: University of North Texas Press, 2003.

Stephens, Robert W. *Texas Ranger Sketches*. Dallas, TX: Self published, 1972.

__________. *Bullets and Buckshot in Texas*. Dallas, TX: Self published. 2002.

__________. *Walter Durbin: Texas Ranger and Sheriff*. Dallas, TX: Self published, 1970.

__________. *Captain George H. Schmitt: Texas Ranger*. Dallas, TX: Self published, 2006.

_________. *Texas Ranger Indian War Pensions*. Quanah, TX: Nortex Press, 1975.

Stillwell, Hallie C. *I'll Gather My Geese*. College Station: Texas A&M University Press, 1991.

Stovall, Allan A. *Breaks of the Balcones: A Regional History*. Barksdale, TX: Self published, 1967.

_________. *Nueces Headwater Country: A Regional History*. San Antonio, TX: The Naylor Company, 1959.

Tanner, Karen Holliday. *Doc Holliday: A Family Portrait*. Norman: University of Oklahoma Press, 1998.

Tarpley, Fred. *1001 Texas Place Names*. Austin: University of Texas Press, 1980.

Taylor, Jack, and Barbara Uzzell, conts. *A History of Waller County, Texas*. Waco, TX: Texian Press, for The Waller County Historical Survey Committee, 1973.

Terry, T.E. (Mrs.). *Historical Sketch of Moore, Texas*. Moore, TX: Moore Historical Commission, 1971.

Thompson, Cecilia. *History of Marfa and Presidio County, Texas, 1535–1946*. Austin, TX: Nortex Press, 1985.

Thrapp, Dan L. *Encyclopedia of Frontier Biography*. 3 vols. Lincoln: University of Nebraska Press, 1988.

Tise, Sammy. *Texas County Sheriffs*. Hallettsville, TX: Tise Genealogical Research, 1989.

Tyler, Ron, ed. *The New Handbook of Texas*. Austin: Texas State Historical Association, 1996.

_________. *The Big Bend: A History of the Last Texas Frontier*. College Station: Texas A&M University Press, 1996.

Unknown Editor *The Killing of Bass Outlaw*. Austin, TX: The Brick Row Book Shop, 1963.

Utley, Robert M. *Lone Star Justice: The First Century of the Texas Rangers*. New York: Oxford University Press, 2002.

_________. *High Noon in Lincoln: Violence on the Western Frontier*. Albuquerque: University of New Mexico Press, 1987.

Webb, Walter Prescott. *The Story of the Texas Rangers*. Austin, TX: Encino Press, 1957.

Weiss Jr., Harold J. *Yours to Command: The Life and Legend of Texas Ranger Captain Bill McDonald*. Denton: The University of North Texas Press, 2009.

Wilkins, Frederick. *The Law Comes to Texas: The Texas Rangers, 1870–1901.* Austin, TX: State House Press, 1999.

Welch, June Rayfield. *The Texas Courthouse Revisited.* Waco, TX: Yellow Rose Press, 1984.

Willeford, Glenn P., and Gerald G. Raun. *Cemeteries and Funerary Practices in the Big Bend of Texas, 1850 to the Present.* Alpine, TX: Johnson's Ranch & Trading Post Press, 2004.

Williams, Clayton W. *Texas' Last Frontier: Fort Stockton and the Trans Pecos, 1861–1895.* Ernest Wallace, ed. College Station: Texas A&M University Press, 1982.

Wilson, R. L. *Colt—An American Legend.* New York: Abbeville Publishing Group, 1985.

Wilson, R. Michael. *Great Train Robberies of the Old West.* Helena, MT: Twodot-Globe Pequot, 2007.

Wooten, Dudley G., ed. *A Comprehensive History of Texas, 1685–1897.* Dallas, TX: William Scharff, 1898.

Periodicals:

Alexander, Bob. "Square Deals and Real McCoys." *Wild West History Association Journal.* June 2011.

Baenziger, Ann Patton. "The Texas State Police During Reconstruction: A Reexamination." *Southwestern Historical Quarterly.* April 1969.

Bailey, Tom, and Ralph J. Weaver. "The Nine Lives of Captain Frank Jones." *Frontier Times.* Spring 1960.

Bell, Bob Boze. "Cathouse Melee: Bass Outlaw vs. John Selman." *True West.* Renegade Roads, Travel Annual 2003.

Bowles, J.H. "A Fight in the Big Bend." *Frontier Times.* August 1926.

Burton, Jeffrey. "A Great Manhunt—Correspondence From 'W.B.S': Some Scenes of Outlawry and Gunplay in Texas." *English-Westerners Brand Book* No. 8. 1975–1976.

__________. "The Most Surprised Man in Texas." *Frontier Times.* March 1975.

Croc, Antonio. "In the Line of Duty." *Texas Gun Collector.* Fall 1996.

Cunningham, Eugene. "Bass Outlaw." *Frontier Times.* January 1928.

__________. "Bass Outlaw—The Little Wolf." *Badman.* Summer 1971.

__________. "Frontier Justice: How Old-Time Rangers Solved a Baffling Murder Mystery." *Startling Detective Magazine*. September 1935.

Daughtery, Franklin W. "Las Vegas de los Ladrones and the Flynt Gang." *The Journal of Big Bend Studies*. 1991.

Day, James M. "El Paso's Texas Rangers." *Password*. Winter. 1979.

Dukes, Doug. "Frank McMahan: In Custody." *Wild West History Association Journal.* August 2009.

Field, Jr., William T. "The Texas State Police, 1870–1873." *Texas Military History*. Fall. 1965.

Gregg, John Ernest. "The History of Presidio County." *Voice of the Mexican Border*. Centennial Edition. 1936.

Hawley, C.A. "Life Along the Border." *Sul Ross State College Bulletin*. September 1964.

Hunter, J. Marvin. "The Killing of Captain Frank Jones." *Frontier Times*. January 1929.

__________. "The Killing of Bass Outlaw." *Frontier Times*. December 1944.

Jardim, Frank. "Bass Outlaw's Arsenal." *Guns of the Old West*. Summer 2015.

McNellis, Robert E. "Bass Outlaw: Lawless Lawman." *Guns*. December 1976.

Majors, Frederick. "Bass Outlaw Was a Texas Riddle." *The West*. October 1965.

Meed, Douglas V. "Daggers on the Gallows: The Revenge of Texas Ranger Captain 'Boss' Hughes." *True West*. May 1999.

Michaels, Kevin. "Tracker." *Great West*. September 1974.

Moore, Bill. "The Texas Calaboose." *Texas Co-op Power*. June 2015.

Nordyke, Lewis. "The Ranch That Changed the West." *Reader's Digest*. September 1945.

O'Neal, Bill. "The Latest on 'Bass' Outlaw." *Real West*. August 1982.

__________. "Baz Outlaw vs. John Selman and Joe McKidrict." *True West*. October 1988.

__________. "100 Years Ago: April 5, 1894: El Paso, Texas." *True West*. April 1994.

Parsons, Chuck. "A Lawman Named Outlaw." *True West*. September 1995.

__________. "The Lost Guns of Bass Outlaw." *True West*. May 1997.

Rasch, Phillip J. "Bass Outlaw: Myth And Man." *Real West*. July 1979.

Rodriguez, Polly. "The Long, Hard Road to El Paso with Polly Rodriguez." Clara Watkins, ed. *Wild West*. February 2005.

Rosson Mary'n. "The Day Bass Outlaw Tried to Drink Up the Town." *Frontier West*. December 1974.

Shirley, Glenn. "A Ranger Named Outlaw." *True Frontier: Actual Stories of the Old West*. November 1968.

Stephens, Robert W. "A Ranger's Grave: The Murder of Jim King." *National Outlaw/Lawman History Association Quarterly*. October–December 2005.

__________. "Ambush in the Chaparral." *Frontier Times*. May 1967.

Taffin, John. "The Croft/Keith Slip Gun." *Guns Magazine*. April 2015.

Tanner, Karen Holliday, and John D. Tanner, Jr.. "Lon Oden: The Rhymin' Ranger." *Old West*. Summer 1998.

Walker, Wayne T. "Joe Sitters: The Best Damn Tracker in Texas." *Oldtimers Wild West*. December 1978.

__________. "Bass Outlaw, Renegade Ranger." *Oldtimers Wild West*. August 1979.

Watkins, Clara, ed. "The Long Hard Road to El Paso with Polly Rodriguez." *Wild West*. February 2005.

Wayne, W.T. "The Fast Guns of Bass Outlaw." *Great West*. June 1972.

Wooster, Robert. "A Difficult and Forlorn Country: The Military Looks at the American Southwest, 1850–1890." *Arizona and the West*. Winter 1868.

Newspapers:

Dallas Morning News
Dallas Daily Herald
Fort Worth Daily Gazette
Galveston Daily News
San Antonio Daily Express
San Antonio Daily Light
Austin Daily Statesman
Austin Daily News
El Paso Daily Times
The McKinney Democrat
Luling Signal
Brooklyn Daily Eagle
South Georgia Times
Clay County Democrat

Rector Vitascope
Chicago Daily Tribune
Los Angles Times
San Francisco Chronicle
Oakland Tribune
Albuquerque Morning Democrat
Tombstone Daily Prospector

Index

P

R

S